A Rhetoric for Writing Program Administrators

- Comppile
- Rhetmap

Read Bitzer -
Rhet. Situatn
disting. scholar ot
rhetori (

WRITING PROGRAM ADMINISTRATION
Series Editors: Susan H. McLeod and Margot Soven

The Writing Program Administration series provides a venue for scholarly monographs and projects that are research- or theory-based and that provide insights into important issues in the field. We encourage submissions that examine the work of writing program administration, broadly defined (e.g., not just administration of first-year composition programs). Possible topics include but are not limited to 1) historical studies of writing program administration or administrators (archival work is particularly encouraged); 2) studies evaluating the relevance of theories developed in other fields (e.g., management, sustainability, organizational theory); 3) studies of particular personnel issues (e.g., unionization, use of adjunct faculty); 4) research on developing and articulating curricula; 5) studies of assessment and accountability issues for WPAs; and 6) examinations of the politics of writing program administration work at the community college.

Books in the Series

A RHETORIC FOR WRITING PROGRAM ADMINISTRATORS

Edited by Rita Malenczyk

Parlor Press
Anderson, South Carolina
www.parlorpress.com

Parlor Press LLC, Anderson, South Carolina, USA

S A N: 2 5 4 - 8 8 7 9

Library of Congress Cataloging-in-Publication

A rhetoric for writing program administrators / Edited by Rita Malenczyk.
    pages cm. -- (Writing Program Administration)
   Includes bibliographical references and index.
   ISBN 978-1-60235-433-3 (pbk. : alk. paper) -- ISBN 978-1-60235-434-0 (hardcover : alk. paper) -- ISBN 978-1-60235-435-7 (adobe ebook : alk. paper) -- ISBN 978-1-60235-436-4 (epub : alk. paper) -- ISBN 978-1-60235-437-1 (ibook : alk. paper) -- ISBN 978-1-60235-458-6 (kindle : alk. paper)
   1. Writing centers--Administration. 2. English language--Rhetoric--Study and teaching (Higher)--United States. 3. Report writing--Study and teaching (Higher)--United States. 4. Interdisciplinary approach in education. 5. Academic writing--Study and teaching. I. Malenczyk, Rita, 1959- editor of compilation.
   PE1405.U6R493 2013
   808'.042071173--dc23
                                            2013025810

2 3 4 5

Cover photo, "Giovanina's Garden" by Greg Glau. See gglau.zenfolio.com
    for more of Greg's photography.
Cover design by David Blakesley
Printed on acid-free paper.

Parlor Press, LLC is an independent publisher of scholarly and trade titles in print and multimedia formats. This book is available in paper, cloth and eBook formats from Parlor Press on the World Wide Web at http://www.parlorpress.com or through online and brick-and-mortar bookstores. For submission information or to find out about Parlor Press publications, write to Parlor Press, 3015 Brackenberry Drive, Anderson, South Carolina, 29621, or email editor@parlorpress.com.

Contents

A RHETORIC FOR WRITING PROGRAM ADMINISTRATORS

Introduction, with Some Rhetorical Terms

Rita Malenczyk

Exigence

From Holly M. Wells of Texas Lutheran, writing on WPA-L, a listserv for writing program administrators:

> I'm a brand-new writing program director at a SLAC [small liberal arts college] with a very small writing program (thank God). Was wondering if some folks may have some info stored somewhere that would be helpful to new faculty who have no idea what they are doing—a "WPA for Dummies," if you will. A cursory search of the archives netted me a whole lot of stuff, but nothing that seemed relevant at first glance. Any advice you care to send my way off-list is gratefully accepted. . . . Nothing in my ten years of adjuncting/TFing prepared me for this!

Writing program administration has grown as a discipline within rhetoric and composition over the last three decades, with a variety of books and courses as well as a refereed journal, *WPA: Writing Program Administration*, dedicated to scholarly and political issues within that discipline. While it does draw on other fields within rhetoric and composition—a writing program administrator (WPA) developing a new first-year composition program will, for example, take into account work on writing process, genre theory, and other fields—writing program administration nevertheless grounds itself, perhaps more than any other discipline, on the rhetoric and politics of departmental and university life and structure, as well as on the lived experiences of its practitioners. There is, therefore, a need for those practitioners to be not only knowledgeable about the discipline of composition and rhetoric but savvy about workplace politics and day-to-day maneuvers. What are the major issues confronted by writing program administrators? How do most WPAs deal with said issues?

This collection is designed to fill that need, to provide a *WPA For Dummies* for readers like Holly M. Wells while providing experienced WPAs with new perspectives on what may be, for them, old concerns. It is called *A Rhetoric for Writing Program Administrators* because, like Erika Lindemann's *A Rhetoric for Writing Teachers*—to which it owes its title—it provides background on issues just about every WPA will, at some point or another, confront and ask questions about; it exists under the assumption that said background will help readers construct and put into practice informed answers to those questions. Like Edward P.J. Corbett and Robert J. Connors's *Classical Rhetoric for the Modern Student*, it also attempts to classify those questions in a way that comments on the nature of the questions themselves. It is *not* primarily a guide to effective persuasion—though some chapters (see, for example, Ianetta) do address the issue of how WPAs might reenvision themselves in relation to other faculty or administrators in their departments and institutions. It *is* a look at how experienced WPAs, all of whom have expertise in the issues they describe in their chapters, conceptualize and frame the essence of those issues, thereby providing the reader with a basis for reflection and action.

AUDIENCE

But what *is* a WPA anyway? Is it somebody with a PhD in rhetoric and composition, with graduate coursework in writing program administration, now directing the first-year composition (FYC) program at a large research institution? Sometimes; but not always, and maybe even not that often—though the data is only suggestive, not conclusive. Take, for instance, the membership of the Council of Writing Program Administrators (CWPA), the national professional organization that advocates for those who direct writing programs. In March 2011, I conducted some research (I am, at this writing, CWPA's president-elect) to determine whom, exactly, the organization represented. While CWPA does not keep personal demographic information in its membership files, it does keep institutional information. I found that CWPA members were scattered among all types of insti-tutions—bachelor's- and master's-granting universities, small liberal arts colleges, historically black colleges and universities (HBCUs), and community colleges—with a variety of missions, student bodies, and therefore writing programs. Writing program administrators are *not*, then, all the same, with the same needs.

Furthermore, if cocktail parties at conferences are any kind of mea-sure, a degree in rhetoric and composition is not, at this writing, a necessary credential for administering a writing program—and even if it were, there would still be variety in the training of the folks who come to the job(s). I speak here not of what should be but of what is. WPAs might—and I stress *might*—have written dissertations in writing program administration. Many, however, are scholars in the history and theory of rhetoric, in the theory and practice of teaching writing, in multimedia composing, in community literacy (see Gold-blatt, this volume), in any number of the fields that comprise rhetoric and composition. And some may have terminal degrees in other fields: creative writing (at least one of the contributors to this volume, for ex-ample), literature (at least two of the contributors to this volume), lin-guistics, education. Furthermore, as Colin Charlton et al. successfully claim in their recent book *GenAdmin: Theorizing WPA Identities in the Twenty-First Century*, time is of the essence. Those of us who began administering writing programs in the middle to late 1990s might view our work through a more theoretical lens than those who began twenty years earlier, when they may have been appointed WPAs sim-ply because they were the only faculty members on campus with even a remote interest in the teaching of writing. In contrast, WPAs begin-ning their work now may be markedly more invested in that work to the point of its being an essential part of their careers and identities (Charlton et al.).

Then there is the question of what a writing *program* is. Some-times it is an FYC program (see Downs, this volume) with teaching assistants (see Reid, this volume) or a mixture of part- and full-timers (see Schell, this volume); sometimes it is a series of first-year writing-intensive seminars; sometimes it is a set of courses that does not call itself a program at all. Sometimes it is a designated writing across the curriculum program (see Townsend, this volume); sometimes it is the teaching of writing in all disciplines grounded in faculty develop-ment (see Rutz and Wilhoit, this volume) with no official program designation. Writing centers (see Lerner, this volume) might also be considered programs, perhaps programs-within-programs. Whoever coordinates/guides/administers/is in charge of/helps with any of these is, in my book, a WPA.

This book's for you, then.

ARRANGEMENT

No collection of this nature can be exhaustive, unless it aspires to the heft of the *Oxford English Dictionary*. Even as the chapter drafts were rolling in, friends and colleagues were telling me, "There should be a chapter on [insert your particular concern or research area here]!" And, really, there probably should. However, with space considerations looming and with some help from the contributors, I narrowed the field of potential topics based on my experiences attending CWPA conferences, reading the WPA-L listserv, and reading and reviewing for the *WPA* journal.

The book addresses, then, the questions that seem to arise over and over again most frequently within and across those venues. There are, for example, chapters discussing the nature of the courses (e.g., Ashley; Downs) and other elements (e.g., Royer and Gilles; Harrington) commonly found in writing programs. Some, if not all, of the authors provide histories (e.g., Fitzgerald) and definitions (e.g., Wardle) of their subjects; most take their chapters as occasions to reflect not only upon what their topic means but upon what it *could* mean for writing program administrators. On the vexed issue of class size, for example, Gregory Glau writes, "While 'class size' of course refers to the number of students in any particular class [. . .] the issue itself needs to be complicated [. . .] in two ways: the *practical* and the *administrative/political* aspects of what 'class size' is and what it means to a WPA." Glau goes on to ask:

> What will a college writing class in the year 2020 or 2025 look like? Do you think your writing teachers will still teach small classes with perhaps twenty to twenty-five students to work with? How many and what kinds of papers will students be asked to construct? Will some (many? most?) writing classes be scheduled on the traditional quarter or semester basis? Will some (many? most?) writing classes be self-paced, based on a set of measurable learning outcomes, and if so, what might those be? Will some (many? most?) writing classes be completely online, perhaps self-paced, with "instructional modules" students can watch at their convenience [. . .]?

With these questions, Glau encourages readers to think about "class size" not only through a numerical lens but also through a conceptual one. Similarly, Joseph Janangelo, writing on the intellectual work of the WPA, considers that work through the metaphor of "gleaning" in order "to discern useful ideas for conceptualizing, presenting, and explaining WPA work in ways that are professionally rewarding, intellectually intriguing, and personally sustaining." Gail Shuck, asked to answer the question "What Is *ESL*?" responds:

> When answering the question "What Is ESL?" [. . .] we must ask not just who ESL students are but also what the *consequences* are of naming, identifying, dividing students by language background. And then we must also ask this: what are the consequences of *not* naming, identifying, dividing students by language background? Why not take the common stance of focusing only on differences at an individual level? Why do we need to label anyone? Can't we create programs that work for all students without worrying about whether they're multilingual or monolingual?

The book also contains chapters prompted by WPAs' frequently-expressed worries about their status in their academic departments (Ianetta) and institutions (e.g., Fox and Malenczyk, Kahn, Weiser); the educational experiences and expectations their students are bringing with them to college (e.g., Hansen, Ritter); the need to compromise either their personal lives (Hesse) or their values (Adler-Kassner); and, not coincidentally related to values, increasing outside control of higher education (e.g., Gallagher, O'Neill, Paine et al., Schwalm). Not all of these chapters are reassuring; they are, however, realistic, and prompt the reader to move beyond simplistic thinking and into the complicated realms of thought that, for better or for worse, we must be comfortable with in order to negotiate our current educational landscape.

So while you should and will get some practical advice from this volume, I hope that it will be for you not only a helpful guide but also a point of departure, a prompt (as it were) for reflection that can help you understand your work—and, at the risk of sounding highfalutin, your life—more deeply, no matter where in your career you find yourself. Because you are, in Mary Boland's only-slightly-kidding words in her chapter on academic freedom, the steward—cultivator, promoter, and protector—of the study of language use at your institution, a subject intrinsically linked to the conscious making (and questioning) of meaning, to self-expression and reflection, and to academic and civic empowerment.

Really, you know. You are.

ENCOMIA

First, thanks are due to all the contributors, who shared my enthusiasm for this project—but particularly to Seth Kahn, for being Steward of the Google Docs. In his capacity as publisher at Parlor Press, Dave Blakesley gave me a contract for this book, and I thank him and the rest of the staff at Parlor for their interest and support. Melissa Ianetta gave me the organizing principle of the book ("A rhetoric!") and she, along with Kelly Ritter and Lauren Fitzgerald, has been the source of much intellectual and personal camaraderie over the years—so, ladies, here's to a hundred more. The Council of Writing Program Administrators has been my professional home for the last seventeen years, and most of the good questions I've learned to ask as a WPA have come from continued interactions, both professional and personal, with its members. My three teenage sons—Sam, Pete, and Nick, aka The Fabulous Mayer Boys—ask different kinds of questions, such as "When are you going to be off the computer?" "Where's my hockey jersey?" and "Can you take me to the mall?" (Answers, in order: "Never," "In the basement," and "Sure.") And finally, to my husband, Bruce Mayer: I think I owe you gas money.

WORKS CITED

Charlton, Colin, Jonikka Charlton, Tarez Samra Graban, Kathleen J. Ryan, and Amy Ferdinand Stolley. *GenAdmin: Theorizing WPA Identities in the Twenty-First Century.* West Lafayette, IN: Parlor Press, 2011. Print.

Corbett, Edward P.J., and Robert J. Connors. *Classical Rhetoric for the Modern Student.* 4th ed. New York: Oxford UP, 1998. Print.

Lindemann, Erika. *A Rhetoric for Writing Teachers.* 4th ed. New York: Oxford UP, 2001. Print.

Wells, Holly M. "Newbie WPA." WPA-L. 25 August 2011. Online posting. 10 February 2013.

Part One: Initial Questions

1 What Are Students? ✓

Kelly Ritter

Glossing all of the terms this book will help new writing program administrators (WPAs) navigate on their campuses and in their professional lives, I think it's safe to say that *students* is the one most readers feel they can already define, at least in terms of what students, definitionally speaking, are and are not. Students are learners, working under the tutelage of a variety of teachers and mentors in classrooms and out. That much is clear. The rest is a bit murkier. Students are not teachers (unless they are graduate students). They are not parents (unless they are). They are not administrators (unless they are adult students who work in administrative offices on campus).

Students are the reason you have a campus in the first place, and the reason teachers, and administrators, have jobs, and why, in general, universities and colleges exist. (Though lately—with the kinds of moves made by upper administration or governing boards at various institutions—it may not seem campuses need, or want, or value students at all.) Our lives, as teachers and as WPAs, revolve around students, or at least the *idea* of a student, the student-function that drives our program curricula, populates our classes, and brings life to our campuses. Indeed, 7,731 articles, books, or chapters in rhetoric and composition studies have the word *student* or *students* in their titles, according to a quick Comppile search. Additionally, we have all been students, and some of us have children or family who are students right now. So why bother to spend a whole chapter defining them? I mean, what's more elemental a concept than *student*?

Well, let's go ahead and parse this out a little further, and from the position of not just a regular faculty member but also a WPA. Clearly, students can't be defined by any one thing—as is briefly illustrated above. But students also do not occupy fixed definitions, or roles, if you will, in relation to the other actors and agents with whom they interact. Faculty who take up administrative positions—and here, I'm going to talk specifically about first-year composition (FYC) program administrators, though some of what I'll discuss could also apply to writing center administrators, as well as writing across the curriculum (WAC) directors—find themselves in what is a multifaceted, and sometimes multifarious, identity position in relation to students.

First, faculty who become WPAs are no longer "just" teachers to the mass of students before them (whether at a small college or a giant university). They are now faculty and something more, wherein the "more" moves and shifts across the job description: A permission slip. A site of arbitration. A devil's advocate. A sounding board. A mentor. A supervisor. A ticket to graduation. Some of these roles are specific to undergraduate students—i.e., the first-year writers who populate the classes that a WPA oversees. Some of these are specific to graduate students—or the teaching assistants who work in some writing programs. Some of these roles apply to the care and development of both undergraduates and graduates. Thus, what I want to think about over the next few pages is not what students *are*, in a philosophical or philological sense, by pulling apart and reassembling a dictionary definition of the term. Instead, I want to think about how being a WPA necessarily changes *who* students are, *why* they come into our orbit, and *how* they work and function differently, specifically as undergraduates in the system that is a writing program. This chapter is thus less about defining students *per se*, and more about redefining the general positionality and agency of students as they interact in specific and repeated ways with you, the WPA. I will organize this discussion through a series of declarations, many of which will have echoes, I think, across other chapters and other terms that follow in this book.

1. The student is one of many; you are one of one.

It's fairly obvious to state that WPAs are responsible for interacting with hundreds, if not thousands, of first-year students on a given college campus. Sometimes the students can feel like a swarm of bees. They are faceless, needy beings who want your full attention and often want it in ignorance of the rules of decorum or general university policy. They have transcripts and add slips and faculty notes in hand, and they are loud and squawking and crying and on the phone and in your doorway and talking VERY VERY loudly. Or they appear as carefully chosen *Candid Camera* cases, lining up patiently and diligently outside your door (or following you on the way back from lunch, or peppering your e-mail inbox with persistent messages, all the while employing reasonably earnest manners) with surprisingly outlandish requests. You may wonder when handling these calm but determined students, in Ashton Kutcher-MTV terms, am I being punk'd? Did this young woman *really* just make the case that since she won her middle school spelling bee and her mother is a high school English teacher, she should be exempted from first-year composition? And she's graduating next month? What???

Here is the first way in which I will define students, for the purposes of your new life as a WPA: They are many and you are one. When you are a regular faculty member (whether you teach one course a semester or five—though if you teach five, you have a pretty good leg up on that whole "one versus many" thing), you are responsible for *your students only* (and maybe departmental/major advisees). You can reasonably expect that these students will ask you certain types of questions at certain times, and that when you are done teaching them, they will only come back to (a) chat in a friendly way because they really like you; (b) ask you for a letter of recommendation (see "chat" of previous); or (c) ask to borrow your stapler.

When you are a WPA, however, all first-year students are your responsibility all the time. This fundamentally changes your relationship to the entity known as *student*. In fact, it forever changes *student* singular to *students* plural. You are no longer able to predict which, or how many, students will come to your door, and for what reasons. You are beholden to students who are no longer in the first-year course but who have lingering problems with their experience(s) in it (whether this be a grade appeal, a teacher complaint, a credit question—all of which are daily administrative situations that you will need to learn how to address, with the help of your fellow faculty and probably staff in many offices across your campus). You are also beholden to all the students who might be in your first-year classes in the future: The area high school students who tour your campus and stop in with their parents to ask if they need to take this "high school" course (because they all took AP, naturally). The students from area community colleges who could eventually transfer to your four-year institution after or before taking their AA degrees. The students from area four-year institutions who might transfer to your college (or your community college, as "backwards" transfer is becoming increasingly common in this difficult national economy) and who have complex questions about articulation agreements (see Schwalm, this volume) and common course numbering—other terms that identify with students, and that you will need to learn as WPA. The international students who are on your campus for a semester or a year or longer and who may or may not understand or have experience with American standards of and expectations for writing, and who may have complex credit situations and transcripts that may need, quite literally, a translator. The students who wait in the shadows on your own campus, completing their sophomore, junior, or senior years of college without having taken the first-year course, hoping they will be waived from it—like magic, with you as the sorcerer.

Therefore, you must remember, as you transition from being a faculty member to being a faculty member who is also a WPA, that you are one in relation to many. The concept of "student" has just increased ten- or twenty- or thirty-fold in relation to your job description, even if you have an assistant WPA or a staff member(s) to help you with your work. As you walk to the campus cafeteria for a sandwich, or to the library, or to your car, everyone you see is, potentially, *your* student, and you—in a manner of speaking—are *theirs.*

2. The students are the system and the system is the students.

I don't mean to get all existential as you seek practical and ideally right-now applicable advice for being a WPA, but there is a very fine (and often imperceptible) line between the system that guides—and controls—the ways in which students move through the college or university and the students who occupy that system. Nowhere is this overlap more clear than from the perspective of the WPA. Students will come to you with myriad problems, and these are problems both caused by and solved by the system. You, as a WPA, have now become the actor that understands and responds to the system, and also has the power to enforce its rules and, occasionally, override them. Let's take a specific example for illustrative purposes.

That young woman I mentioned a little while back—the one who won her spelling bee in seventh grade and who has the high school teacher for a mom and who thinks she is graduating in a month—she's sitting in your office, quiet and calm, because she knows a little bit about the system and her place in it. She's gone this far—she's ready to graduate except for *your first-year course* (as WPA, you now are also *the course*, in terms of how students see your own embodiment[s]). She's done her part, jumped through the hoops, met the requirements. She's taken all those classes she didn't want, plus some she did, and she's navigated the university website and your department office staff and the advice of her friends in order to find herself sitting across from you now. This one course—this first-year composition course—she has resisted, and purposely so. She tells you, *I know I should have taken this course. But I didn't need it. I don't need it. Look at my transcript. I have a B+ average. And look at the grades in my writing-intensive courses. All that's stopping me is this course. I don't understand. Can't you do something?*

And she is right, even as she is wrong: She has been absorbed by the system and she has subsumed it as well. She knows that the first-year composition requirement is a ruse, of sorts; she was able to do "just fine" without it, in GPA and course completion terms. She knows that you can deny her the ability to graduate, but she also knows that you are human, and that you may (or may not; this is where she gambles) be able to give her a pass and let her go on her merry way. She represents the flaws in the system, in a variety of ways (letting a student get past her first year without completing the requirement; letting her writing-intensive courses happen without clear dialogue back to the course she is "missing." But also: did she "need" this course—could it be that it would have offered her little to no added value to her education? Has this deliberate resistance of one piece of the system made her an independent human being?). In any case, she's in front of you and now you have to decide: Will I uphold the system, which is embodied by this student sitting in my office, or will I reject the system, and thereby send this particular cog in it (happily) on her way, breaking the system apart just a little in the process?

There are other WPA collections out there that can help you solve a scenario like this one (see, for example, Myers-Breslin), so I'm not going to parse out what you should or should not do. Instead I provide this extended example of this student to emphasize this: The interconnectedness between your university's system—of general education, of writing education, of larger graduation requirements—is going to be now embodied by real students taking up real space in your real office. And you, who may have had limited interaction with that system outside your own classes, now will find yourself intimately aware of that system's ins and outs, courtesy of real, live students with requests for waivers—like this young woman presented—as well as those with transfer credit amendments, AP, CLEP, and ACT/SAT cut score questions and challenges, placement issues (covered elsewhere in this book), teacher complaints (because teachers are the system as well), and grade challenges (because there is no system, one might argue, without hierarchies of evaluation to move it forward and motivate its actors). And your awareness of all of this will fundamentally change how you define *students.*

3. The students are (sometimes) wise, and they are feeling beings. And they have rights.

Not everything you do in relation to or on behalf of students will be about signing papers, enforcing rules, or challenging or modifying policies. Not every student is interchangeable or faceless. Sometimes, students will simply be people with problems that you may not be able to solve, but whom you want to try to help. Remembering that theoretically, all students of your college or university are "yours," these students have a lot of problems. This is because, particularly in the twenty-first century, they are busy. They work a lot—some figures say as much as thirty hours per week on a commuter-heavy campus. They play a lot—spending twenty or more hours a week on social media, experts say, and more hours beyond that socializing face to face in clubs, sports, community gatherings, and the like. They study some— as much as they can, given what's left in that 168-hour week that time management specialists try to make them understand at orientation (or in learning community or other "university seminar" courses), but rarely succeed in doing so. They have families—spouses or partners or children or other dependents.

All of these things that they do intersect in positive and negative ways. You, as the WPA and as the person who supervises their first-year composition teacher (who herself may or may not want to listen to or address non-course-based problems—and for that I blame thee not a bit), and who has probably more office hours and greater reliability than the college academic advising office, and who is less stigmatizing to visit than the college counseling office, will hear about some of these intersections, particularly the negative ones. You will listen, because the student is not always wrong. You will have at your disposal the names and numbers of all the relevant campus offices that can better help the student than you can. And you will help as much as you can, within the boundaries of your position and of your own personal comfort, because you know that your responsibilities are to all the students and the whole system, but that these responsibilities do not preclude common, professional sense. What is important to remember from this declaration of mine is that students embody systems, and systems represent students, but students also cry real tears, tears that may or may not be meant for you. Don't forget that as you become increasingly aware of your growing world of responsibilities.

Moreover, don't forget that students have rights as well as feelings. You may come to think of students as they are defined by something called FERPA—or the Family Educational Rights and Privacy Act, a.k.a. the Buckley Amendment of 1973. In sum (and I encourage you to read the actual legislation at http://www2.ed.gov/policy/gen/guid/fpco/ferpa/index.html), FERPA says that once a student reaches eighteen years of age *or enrolls on a college campus* (this caveat will be very important in a minute; stick with me), he or she can control who has access to her personal and educational information, both (to an extent) inside the institution and outside of it.

FERPA is your friend, because it is one of those rare pieces of federal legislation that keeps students from being harmed by persons, including their own families, based on their academic progress (or lack thereof). Most institutions have a clear FERPA policy—particularly public colleges and universities, I've found—and many have very strict rules about when it can and cannot be overridden. For example, at my previous institution, students could "sign away" their FERPA rights, but only in the presence of a witness and only if the witness and the university representative (from student or legal affairs) concluded that the student was not under any duress. Why would a student be under duress? Well, just as you will come to identify "student" as "students" in your WPA work, you will also come to understand "parent" as a plural as well. You will learn the term "helicopter parent," which is a mother or father (and the two genders are pretty equal in representation here, in my experience) who monitors his or her child's every single action, feeling, and decision. These parents call the child numerous times a day. They are accustomed to fastidious checking of grades and other reports from secondary school times. And they will call you, or e-mail you, to ask a variety of questions. *How can my son change his class section? He doesn't like his teacher. How did my daughter get a C in this composition class? She's so smart. Why was my son told he cannot take section 71 of English composition? I thought you could make exceptions to full courses. We pay a lot to attend this school, after all.* And so on.

The vast majority of the time, parents are annoying, but harmless and well-meaning. But sometimes they are not. I've been in the presence of more than one parent who, upon learning of a poor grade his or her child has earned (from the report card, which comes in the mail and is beyond your control), looks ready to blow, and not in a get-over-it kind of way. We want to protect students from those parents insofar as we can, but we also want to protect ourselves from entanglement in family situations of any kind—from mildly annoying to dangerous. FERPA says that we cannot—and will not, without the student's express written permission—give out any academic information on that student to third parties without a clear institutional role in that student's education, including parents. So, when a parent calls and asks for one or more pieces of information about a student in your writing program, you just say, "I'm sorry, but federal law prohibits me from sharing that information with you. I would, however, be happy to speak directly with your son/daughter about this matter."

We also want to help students grow from students—in the tutelage sense, under mentors and as part of systems—to Real People who control their own academic pasts and futures and take responsibility for their own mistakes (and triumphs). FERPA helps this along a little, by forcing the student—not her mother—to come see you about a grade dispute, whereupon you can help her understand why Professor Z gave her that failing grade. FERPA forces the student to e-mail you—not have her mother e-mail you, and copy her (or not)—to get information about the placement exam, or the credit transfer policy, or just the general description of the required first-year course. FERPA, as the legislation explicitly states, is about *trust.* The student trusts you (and other university officials) to keep her information safe, and you trust the student to use FERPA's rules to develop her own independent academic identity. FERPA does not keep you from finding out more information about the student: As a WPA, you are an "eligible" party with rights of access to the records of a student in your program. But it does keep people who don't need to know—or whose points of view are not necessary—from having that information.

4. Students, in some cases, are yours *and* someone else's.

Because I've talked about FERPA, and trust, and feelings, and independence, when continuing to parse out the term "students," I had better talk about the newest breed of students: high school students, or those who take your first-year courses but who are still in high school. Sometimes they can be as young as *fourteen years old*. They are still in high school (whether a traditional high school or a charter high school or even home school)—they are not Doogie Howser types who will become doctors at twenty-two. They are dual credit or concurrent enrollment students, and you, as WPA, need to learn about these students right now. Because they are coming to your campus, if they are not already there, and they are your students *and* someone else's.

An excellent primer and commentary on dual credit and concurrent enrollment is Kristine Hansen and Christine R. Farris's *The Taking Care of Business: College Credit for Writing in High School* (which, coincidentally, won the 2012 CWPA best book award, so you should read it anyway). Hansen has a chapter later in this collection that discusses dual credit more extensively, in fact, so I'll just say here that your campus may not have an early college program, but chances are that in less than ten years, it will. It is a money-saver without much thought to other issues—like developmental differences between fourteen- and eighteen-year-old students, for example—and parents universally love it because to their mind, saving money is a great thing.

Dual credit means you will have students, potentially, in your program who are *yours* but not "yours." They are covered by FERPA, which is good, because they are a lot younger than the students you thought you (or your TAs) would be teaching. They are also not eighteen years old, or high school graduates, so this may affect how you and your instructional staff for first-year composition design assignments. After-hours field trips or ethnographic studies? R-rated films as course texts? Small group work that involves partnering with the nontraditional adult students and working out writing projects over the weekend? Maybe not. Dual credit students change what "student" means, as they blow open any gates that we could previously use to define—productively or otherwise—who and what our first-year composition students are.

5. Students are free agents, but the educational market is not free.

For this last definition, I'm going to dip back a bit into my previous work to talk about what students do when they are not in your presence. In my 2010 book *Who Owns School? Authority, Students, and Online Discourse*, I spent considerable time discussing the ways in which students use extra-institutional online resources (RateMyProfessor.com, Pink Monkey, various online paper mill web sites) to exchange ideas about and evaluate the components, process, and outcomes of higher education. I argued that students are interested in being a greater part of the system of education, but feel fairly powerless to be heard. One example of this is course evaluations. Students know we have to give them out (in most cases), but they also assume we really don't read them, or if we do, nothing comes of it. So, a whole class might have a truly (and verifiable, and tangible) horrible experience with a particular professor. They fill out the course evaluations and make all kinds of specific comments about this professor and this course. Then they wait. And nothing happens. Or they rally 'round a professor who is going up for tenure. They fill her evaluation forms with specific and concrete praise, not just laudatory remarks. Then they wait. And nothing happens (or something happens—she doesn't get tenure).

We know the system rarely is this cut-and-dried. No system is perfect, let alone higher education.

My larger point in *Who Owns School?* was, however, mostly about power and authority. We folks in rhetoric and composition studies talk a lot about empowering students, and many of us try very hard to do so; still more succeed, in their own local and institutionally-specific ways. However, my book's argument pointed to the tangible, visible presence of students online who state their own feelings of powerlessness in the system of higher education. I asked: If we are empowering students (specifically through critical pedagogy, or later versions of it in a post-process type of program), and more specifically in computer-mediated classroom settings, then why are they seeking power *outside* the classroom, in extra-institutional digital spaces? Why are they going online to talk with each other and help each other out with academic or school-related problems and issues—from positive help, like reading one another's work and sharing professor evaluation stories, to negative help, like writing one another's term papers and selling "A" papers to fellow students with the capital to buy them? Where have we gone wrong—especially given how technologically-driven we are in our pedagogies in the twenty-first century?

That's the question I'd like to address just a bit here before I close this chapter. WPAs get a pretty bad rap for being those people who hold all the power (see the work of Bousquet, Harris, Sledd, Strickland, White, and others for views on both sides of this issue). We run programs, we control curricula (to an extent, depending upon the campus), and concomitantly, we have a great deal of power over students, particularly first-year students. Whether or not this "managerial" image of the WPA is real and true for all of us right now, or whether it was ever true for some of us, I'll leave aside. We do, however, often see ourselves as empowering students, specifically through the first-year composition course—which has morphed over and over through the past thirty to forty years partially in response to this very field-specific anxiety about power, control, correctness, and agency in writing instruction and in student writing.

I thus challenge you, the new WPA, to therefore think about your own assumptions about students and power, but maybe not in the ways that WPA scholarship has done previously. Yes, students have more access to technology than ever before; but no, they do not all have equal access—and so providing a tech-heavy classroom may work only insofar as it supports or replaces the kind of writing work they do outside your classroom. Yes, students are savvy about investigating systems and their actors (or agents); but no, they do not feel empowered simply because you give them information and step back from the podium (or sit in circles, or declare the class "student-centered," or let them use their phones and their iPads and their laptops and their social media and . . . in class). They are seeking out communities to give them agency *outside* your classroom, and are doing so in droves. Yes, you run a progressive writing program and you give your TAs or other instructional staff a good deal of leeway in designing and implementing course syllabi; but no, you cannot be in every classroom at once, and no, you cannot guarantee that every student will come out of his or her writing experience feeling more powerful than he or she did sixteen weeks prior. In short, you think you are giving students more than you really can. And this will never change.

Your influence—as a faculty member, and now as a WPA—is not really as much as you think it is. This is both a freeing and a limiting concept, in ways I'm sure I don't have to explain. What I would emphasize, however, is that students are other people when they are not with you. They are *consumers*, in the sense that they rate, evaluate, and reflect on their educational experiences in product-based terms (the educational market is far from free—hence the appeal of dual-credit programs). They are *community members*, in the sense that they talk with one another and form opinions and values based on how many of their friends liked or did not like this course, that book, those professors, that institution. They are *multiple persons*, really, in that they operate within home and school identities, and in that they spend a great deal of time online, where they may "be" someone you don't recognize.

But you are still, in every place students go or occupy, the same WPA. Your definition does not change. So, as you consider what students are, or are not, I ask, what are *you*? I'm afraid no one in this book can answer that one. But if you keep reading, you might get the information you'll need to eventually answer it yourself.

Works Cited

Bousquet, Marc. "Composition as Management Science: Toward a University Without a WPA." *JAC* 22.3 (2002): 494–26. Print.

Hansen, Kristine, and Christine R. Farris. *College Credit for Writing in High School: The "Taking Care of" Business.* Urbana, IL: National Council of Teachers of English, 2010. Print.

Harris, Joseph. "Meet the New Boss, Same as the Old Boss: Class Consciousness in Composition." *College Composition and Communication* 52.1 (2000): 43-68. Print.

Myers-Breslin, Linda. *Administrative Problem Solving for Writing Programs and Writing Centers: Scenarios in Effective Program Management.* Urbana, IL: National Council of Teachers of English, 1988. Print.

Ritter, Kelly. *Who Owns School? Authority, Students, and Online Discourse.* Cresskill, NJ: Hampton Press, 2010. Print.

Sledd, James. "Return to Service." *Composition Studies* 28.2 (2000): 11–32. Print.

Strickland, Donna. *The Managerial Unconscious in the History of Composition Studies.* Carbondale: Southern Illinois UP, 2011. Print.

White, Edward. "Use it or Lose It: Power and the WPA." *WPA: Writing Program Administration* 15.1/2 (1991): 3–12. Print.

Th: No such thing as correct placement,
+ placement apparently
impossible
·stand tests
·essay
- student directed /portfolio

2 What Is Placement?

Dan Royer and Roger Gilles

Placement is the effort to get new students into the most appropriate beginning composition course. Like our colleagues in mathematics and modern languages, we don't want students in over their heads, but we don't want them bored either. We want them to thrive, learn new things, build on what they have learned in high school, and integrate new concepts and strategies that are important to the local college curriculum where they find themselves in their first semester.

In other words, through placement we are trying to set our students up for success in our program. However, placement is not only about helping the student. Faculty benefit from teaching to a student group that is reasonably homogeneous in its background and abilities. The texts we choose, the readings we ask our students to study, and the way we build our syllabi are contingent on some predictable range of writing competence.

Even student success and course management are not the only concerns. As an administrator, the WPA has to worry also about institutional issues such as course enrollments and staffing. Just how many sections of developmental (or basic) writing will be needed? How many teachers will that mean we need to hire this summer for next fall? What contracts are needed for which classes? Can we afford them? These questions need to be anticipated months in advance in order to secure classrooms, hire teachers, print a schedule, and find ourselves ready for summer student orientation. Institutions require some predictability.

All told, the ways we foster student success, help faculty manage their courses, and deal with the institutional pressures of staffing and enrollment say something important about our composition program. What are our primary program values? What are our philosophies of *indeed*

23

teaching and learning? What is good writing, and how do writers develop into good writers? How do we, as a program, juggle the needs and concerns of students, teachers, and the institution itself?

In this chapter, we'll not offer the right way to do placement (the placement program at our university reflects our program values and practical concerns), but something more like a framework for how to think about getting it right given the program values at whatever institution you might find yourself. Our argument is that placement is not merely an empirical matter, although there are empirical ways to look at it, but as much an educational, curricular, and rhetorical matter as a class syllabus—and good syllabi vary; different teachers and students thrive under widely differing methods of instruction. For the WPA, making decisions about placement is about making value choices that reflect the culture of the program and the culture of the institution—while at the same time, these decisions build that culture.

Placement as Rhetorical Triangle

In the discussion above, we highlight what can be viewed as three points on a rhetorical triangle: students, teachers, and the institution. The triangle looks like this:

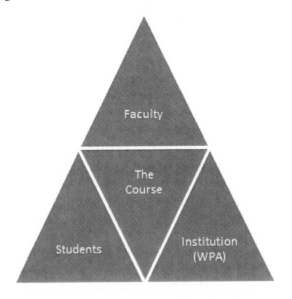

Figure 1

The classic rhetorical triangle comprises the writer, the subject, and the audience, all connected to the text itself, and different modes of discourse emphasize or privilege particular points of the triangle while de-emphasizing or even abstracting the others. We see this same kind of dynamic at work with various modes of placement. Each placement method concerns itself most intently with particular points of the triangle, and by doing so it tends to generalize or abstract the other elements, indicating what is gained or lost as we look at the dynamic from one point of view on the triangle or another. Like different modes of discourse, then, each placement method also sends a particular "message" about the placement act itself and about the importance of students, teachers, and administrators. So let's consider each of the four most common placement methods in relation to the rhetorical triangle.

Nationally normed standardized tests. These make primary the administrative interests of the institution. Designed by the College Board (the SAT Verbal, the SAT Writing, and ACCUPLACER) and ACT (the ACT English, the ACT Plus Writing, and Compass), these tests may be purely multiple choice (SAT-V and ACT-E), human-scored essays (SAT-W and ACT Plus), or computer-scored essays (ACCUPLACER and Compass). Such tests are efficient, predictable, and in many cases effective—all very appealing to administrators. The cost of the tests is very low, often free, for institutions that use them, and once you set a cut-off point, you can predict practically to the decimal point how many students will end up in each of your courses. So they are very reliable. Besides their efficiency and reliability, the main selling point of these tests has been their "predictive validity"—how well they predict future performance. In general, standardized tests correlate well with success in the freshman year, about as well as high school GPA. In other words, like a good high school GPA, good standardized test scores are a pretty good indicator of solid performance in college (see, for example, Zwick). As Emily Isaacs and Sean A. Molloy have most recently pointed out, however, the College Board itself has found only a medium correlation (.32) between the SAT-W, a writing-specific standardized test, and success in first-year composition (529). Still, given their ease, cost-effectiveness, and reliability, standardized tests continue to appeal to a great many institutions.

As appealing as standardized tests may be to the administrative mindset, they are less attentive to the other two points of the triangle: students and teachers. Standardized tests treat all students exactly the same, failing to account for a great many important factors—how long ago the student took the test, whether or not the student was at his or her best that day, how clear or mature-looking the student's handwriting might be, and so on. The tests are scored, at worst, by computers, and at best, by teams of unknown people in California or New Jersey. The individual student thus becomes "abstracted," just another number. The number—a 7, a 22, a 540—does claim a kind of certainty, but only those students with the high scores typically feel that the scores reflect their full ability.

Perhaps even more significantly, standardized tests blot out all particularities of your teachers and curriculum. They are, after all, standardized—meant to work in all contexts. They ignore the living, breathing, local contexts in which all writing programs and courses exist. Standardized tests don't know whether your program emphasizes research-based writing or narrative essays; they don't know if your developmental course is taught by veteran full-time faculty or first-time graduate students; they don't know anything about the rigor of your grading standards. In short, standardized tests do not say anything about how your incoming students relate to your particular courses and your particular faculty: They tell you how your incoming students relate to the national pool of first-year college students.

Placement essays. These represent a compromise between the administrative concerns of the institution and the curricular interests of the faculty. Typically, placement essays are brief essays written by hand or by computer in response to a locally-produced writing prompt. They may be written at home and sent in electronically, but most placement essays are written on campus during orientation and scored on the same day by teams of composition faculty. Historically, placement tests were hailed as "direct assessments" of writing—that is, they actually asked students to write something, and what the students wrote actually got read by teachers at the school the students were actually attending. This was a great advance over what at the time were entirely multiple-choice standardized tests. Locally-administered placement essays involve faculty in the placement process, and this has a number of residual benefits: It requires faculty to think about their program and how their courses differ from one another, and it empowers faculty to articulate, through their scoring decisions, what distinguishes a student who is well-prepared for the standard first-year course from one who is not.

However, one-shot placement essays may send an inaccurate message to students about college writing and, perhaps even worse, may encourage faculty to start thinking that such essays do represent college writing. In other words, they may encourage faculty to think that such essays necessarily and "directly" reveal the real writer behind the discourse—that is, they reveal his or her native abilities and near-term essential writing ability.

While such essays do put before us something much more thick and interesting than a numerical score, the very writing itself conceals the nature of the piece as abstraction: abstraction from context, mood, purpose, desire, motivation, classroom, the influence of instruction, feedback from other writers, and the dozens of other real elements that we know influence good writing. We are not saying this mistaken identity cannot be avoided. It can, but mistaking the abstraction for the concrete thing is a danger with all models and abstraction, and we should be aware that such a fallacy becomes more sneaky as the abstraction more closely resembles the real thing.

For students, the rhetorical message here is that as writers they simply are what they write. The writing sample, drawn over the summer, reveals enough about them to send them for triage or perhaps to exempt them from first-year composition altogether. Of course in these matters we are looking for good enough, not absolute certainty, but while placement essays bring something tangible and important to the placement decision, the rhetorical message can reinforce the essentialist blood work that has been following them from grade school: "I'm a good writer" or "I'm a bad writer," and it's obvious to all, even at a glance.

Directed self-placement (DSP). DSP represents a primary emphasis on the students' informed sense of their own readiness for the demands of college writing. Thus, while it emphasizes student agency on the triangle, it abstracts the institution and gives faculty the role of guides or directors, but not deciders, in the placement process. Directed self-placement begins with faculty clarifying for themselves the practical differences in the first-year composition courses and then communicating those differences to the students before they place themselves into a course. Typically, information about the course differences or student readiness is presented to students in short descriptions, lists, choice cards, letters, orientation talks, small group discussion, or even small writing groups. Students are then asked to reflect on their own readiness to succeed in one course option or the other. Whereas a German teacher using DSP might say, "In GER 101 we spend the first five weeks with a review of very basic grammar and vocabulary, much like you did in high school, but in GER 102 we begin on the first day writing short essays in German," the writing program and teachers are asked to help guide and direct students into the course most suitable for their level of confidence and familiarity with the curriculum as advertised.

Standardized tests are quick and efficient, and placement essays are reader-intensive. Norming readers and scoring essays is the work involved with using placement essays, while the work of DSP is in the discussion with students, student self-awareness, and the materials that constitute the "guidance" or "placement" that prevents the process from becoming mere self-placement—a world where, as Kelly Ritter points out in this volume, students lose their engagement with our programs simply because we neglect to engage their concerns. What fade to abstraction in this dynamic are the administrative concerns of the institution and the course one is placing into. Abstraction does not mean absent, but for students involved in DSP, the course is merely a set of descriptions, promises, and outlines about what to expect. Institutional concerns with staffing, section numbers, percentages of basic writers to regular writers are of no concern to the student. The teacher is the stubborn fact in this triangle, expected to deliver the course as described to the students. In this sense, the teacher is also abstracted from the placement decision, a presence vaguely anticipated rather than directly involved as students are guided by trained advisers, faculty, and student advisers during summer orientation through the placement process. The message DSP sends to students is that if given enough information about the aims, demands, and expectations of our various courses, they are, with guidance from those who know the program, in a better and more appropriate position than we are to determine which course is best suited to their situation.

Each of these placement approaches instigates a unique dynamic within the rhetorical triangle. Standardized tests are quick and neat, originating in the need for institutional efficiency. Placement essays are slow and laborious, emerging from the teachers' sense of authority and expertise in the placement decision. Directed self-placement is rhetorical and uncertain, an exigency of student agency dominating the placement process.

Authentic assessment. Authentic assessment includes approaches to placement that use assessment practices as close as possible to what the course itself uses. In other words, they aim for "construct validity," an effort to mimic or even replicate ordinary classroom practices such as peer review and revision so that the assessment authentically measures what it purports to measure—namely, the very kind of work that students are expected to perform during the semester. In this way, authentic assessment involves faculty most directly, but also asks students to behave as authentically as possible as students, so two points of the triangle are actively in play.

There's no one exemplar of this modality. Placement portfolios, pioneered at Miami University, the University of Michigan, and the State University of New York, were an early form of authentic assessment. Students submit a portfolio of their best high school writing, or perhaps writing done over the summer in response to assignments supplied by the WPA. The portfolios typically include reflective cover essays, multiple drafts, and final copies—whatever a teacher might expect in an actual course. The portfolios are then read by the same faculty, or "expert readers," who teach the various writing courses. Emily Isaacs and Catherine Keohane recently coined the acronym PTT ("Placement and Teaching Together") to refer to any placement method that both replicates features of the local curriculum and calls on expert faculty readers to make the placement decisions. Their own method combines a summer writing assignment with peer review, revision work, and faculty responses done during the first week of classes. Another recent move toward authentic assessment in placement is a hybrid approach (see Peckham) that combines standardized and student-centered approaches with an online writing assignment that replicates the culminating assignment in the entry-level course.

Like placement essays, authentic assessment involves teachers directly with the writing activity. The message is, "In our classes, you will follow a full writing process and receive regular feedback from faculty, so that is what we want you to do before we place you into a course." As we mentioned above, however, the closer we get to these authentic activities, the more quietly lurks the fallacy of misplaced identity. The very practices that mimic and replicate classroom practice conceal from us the way they abstract from context, mood, purpose, desire, motivation, classroom, the influence of instruction, feedback from other writers, computer skills, the use of writing centers and libraries, and the many other real activities that we know influence good writing over the course of a full semester. Indeed, the ultimate authentic assessment might be imagined as a full semester of the very same course that the student is considering placing into—an absurd but truly authentic approach that would require a time machine to implement with precision—but this ultimate ideal of authentic assessment also points out the inevitable inadequacy of lesser versions.

GETTING PLACEMENT RIGHT

Readers of the placement literature will find frequent references to claims and assertions about "correct placement" and "misplacement," "placement errors," "wrong placement," "better placement," and laments about students being in the "wrong class." After the publication of our 1998 article on directed self-placement, we had many discussions with faculty at other universities who wanted to judge the "accuracy" of DSP by comparing its placement consequences to what SAT or ACT scores would have determined for placement (and they judged their own placement essay accuracy by this same standardized test benchmark). We spoke with program directors who were convinced that a predetermined percentage of basic writers was required in order for placement to be "accurate," and we spoke with administrators and faculty who could not believe that placement could be configured in ways that would get students to make intelligent, informed, and self-serving decisions that might include taking a basic writing course as an elective. They found it difficult to imagine designing programs that appeal to student self-interests or simply felt it was their job to determine these interests. These beliefs about the essential nature of the writer and the essential correctness of placement are much more common among proponents of placement essays or authentic placement modes than from those using standardized tests because the standardized tests foreground their own mere predictive validity and make little or no pretense about construct or content validity.

The main point here is not about what should be considered the gold standard or benchmark for correct placement, but rather about the essentialist assumption about any placement. For example, Isaacs and Molloy—proponents of authentic assessment—make these observations about standardized tests:

> In effect, [the Academic Assessment Center] found that many GSU students were similar to almost half of the other SAT takers across the country: they were either better at writing prompted, 25-minute essays or better at answering multiple-choice questions about writing. But both sets of scores could not be right. On the other hand, both could be wrong. (523)

That is, they say that conflicting scores on multiple-choice tests and essay tests meant that at least one of those scores had to be "wrong" for placement. As you might guess, they end up arguing that both scores are wrong, but the point is that they assume a "right" and "wrong" placement in the first place.

Irvin Peckham, another proponent of authentic assessment in placement, uses similar language: "By giving students the choice of submitting an essay [to challenge their initial placement], we would both lower the reading cost and target the students most likely to be misplaced by their ACT/SAT/AP scores" (522). Over three years, only about 5% of the ACT-placed students challenged their initial placement, so the assumption appears to be that 95% of the students were placed "correctly" by ACT. But then, of the students who challenged, Peckham and his colleagues "recommended reassignment almost half the time. In other words, whether we would accept the placement on the basis of the ACT scores was close to a flip of a coin: heads, ACT got it right; tails, the student should be in a different course" (533). In the end, then, the standardized test score "got it right" almost 98% of the time.

Is there really an essentially correct placement decision? We believe there is not and cannot be because appropriate placement is relative to students' subjective aims, and writing abilities are difficult to generalize from a single, even "authentic," instance or moment in time. More to the point, the very meaning of "correct placement" is best understood by the consequences of the placement, not as a discoverable fact about the student. The meaning is tied up in the future, not buried in the past. This pragmatic meaning of "correct placement" gives us a perspective that holds whether placement is chosen by the student, the teacher, or determined by an SAT score. As we said in the beginning, good placement is about getting students into the most appropriate course. If a college offers options for basic or advanced coursework, correct placement means getting the student into the course where he or she can succeed, thrive, and learn in ways that match the student's own private purposes. As Ritter reminds us in this volume, students are academic free agents with purposes we may never imagine. For one student, "an easy A" is the appropriate course; for another student, "after much effort, I just need a C" is the appropriate course. These are personal matters that WPAs should not condescend to answer for the student. And this, just one simple example, is why determining appropriate placement is such a vexing assignment for a WPA, especially if the notion of an essentially correct placement creates a misunderstanding of the nature of the problem. From the teacher's point of view, the placement is correct if the placed students remain within a proximal range of a classroom competence. There is no essentially correct placement; there is only a placement that works out for students and teachers or doesn't work out for students and teachers. "Works out," as every teacher knows, often has very little to do with some alleged essential writing ability, whatever that notion might mean. That's why we view placement as more of a rhetorical matter than an empirical matter.

Our approach (in no way limited to DSP) is to view the most appropriate placement in terms of the future consequences of that placement, consequences that are not limited to grades earned (though that is an important consequence) but that also include student purposes, program expectations, teacher expectations, and the learning that goes on as a consequence of a placement decision. Students are famous for rising to expectations—and infamous for failing in spite of native ability.

What Is Placement?

There are several ways to understand the problems we face as WPAs regarding placement. The prevailing view is that we face an empirical problem that can be solved by investigating scores on standardized tests or taking a close look at writing samples—either one-shot essays, portfolios, or the outcome of some other authentic writing assessment. In this view the aim is to determine as precisely as possible the student's writing ability (as elusive as it may be) as close as possible to the beginning of the semester and create numerical or rubric-based cutoffs where students are sorted into one class or the other. With standardized tests, we all seem to accept that we are using very rough sorting criteria with decent enough predictive validity to distinguish those students most likely to succeed in our classes from those most likely to fail. For many WPAs, however, this sorting and predictive validity is just not enough. Our problem, we might say, is more complex than sorting. Standardized tests are too blunt an instrument. With placement essays, we introduce student writing into the placement decision, requiring that we project from a writing sample onto the outcome expectations of our course. Yet for others, even a writing sample is a paltry representation of the rich depths of student writing ability—not accurate enough and off message. The message we send when we use standardized test scores or one-shot writing samples is that successful college writing is a thin veneer. Students need to see what, to borrow Bob Broad's phrasing, we really value, and in an effort to discover the really real writer behind it all, we should mimic or replicate the classroom practices that we are placing students into. Rich, authentic, accurate assessment is for some the holy grail of placement.

We have suggested in the discussion above that the placement problem is at least as rhetorical as it is empirical. We entertain the idea that, when viewed as a rhetorical dynamic, placement is never a static, one-way street. It necessarily involves the mutual influence of institution, teacher, and student. Seen this way, it is a deliberative rhetoric, not a forensic rhetoric. The appeals of deliberative rhetoric focus on the consequences and the possibilities of success. DSP, for example, asks students to join advisers in making judgments and taking action with regard to the future. Other placement approaches can also take on a deliberative posture. In his defense of timed placement essays, for example, Edward M. White argues that "most American campuses find students ready for freshman composition if they can read pretty well and write complete sentences" (33), so a few paragraphs in response to a reading can be enough to predict the "readiness" of a student to succeed in a program.

A deliberative placement process sets its sights on the student of the entire semester, or more precisely, the student at the end of the semester. The goal of placement is to set students up for success—and from the perspective of the student, the teacher, and the institution alike, success is perhaps best measured at the end of the term. From this rhetorical point of view, rather than discovering in forensic manner things about the past, we are deliberating about future action—which class the student should begin with in order to most likely reach a particular level of success in the future. Although one placement method may seem more akin to this kind of rhetoric than another, any placement method can take its orientation from this rhetorical posture.

WORKS CITED

Broad, Bob. *What We Really Value: Beyond Rubrics in Teaching and Assessing Writing*. Logan: Utah State UP, 2003. Print.

Isaacs, Emily, and Catherine Keohane. "Writing Placement that Supports Teaching and Learning." *WPA: Writing Program Administration* 35.2 (2012): 55–84. Print.

Isaacs, Emily, and Sean A. Molloy. "SATs for Writing Placement: A Critique and Counterproposal." *College English* 72.5 (2010): 518–38. Print.

Peckham, Irvin. "Online Placement in First-Year Writing." *College Composition and Communication* 60.3 (2009): 517–40. Print.

Royer, Daniel, and Roger Gilles. "Directed Self-Placement: An Attitude of Orientation." *College Composition and Communication* 50.1 (1998): 54-70. Print.

White, Edward M. "An Apologia for the Timed Impromptu Essay Test." *College Composition and Communication* 46.1 (1995): 30–45. Print.

Zwick, Rebecca. "College Admission Testing." Arlington, VA: National Association for College Admission Counseling, 2007. Web. 10 Nov. 2012.

3 What Is Basic Writing?

Hannah Ashley

INTRODUCTION AND HISTORY IN 456 WORDS

Attention-getter. *What is Basic Writing? Or, Venting the University—Snapshots of Catachresis. To voice, escape, expel, exhaust. An opening, outlet, gap.* Basic writing (or developmental, or remedial, "basic" being the term *de jure* at this punctuation mark) is the university's vent. My own university's current tag line is "Learn More," but a colleague at a conference recently cited another colleague (and so on, a note on citation later) who said, "Knowing the answer is a learning disability." (This chapter will not cover learning disabilities, a serious gap in this volume, but we can't cover everything, can we? Get to know your campus disabilities office and read a little Cindy Lewiecki-Wilson.) **Thesis:** In several significant ways, when a student gets basic writing done to them, they are being schooled to know less. This is sometimes, even, a good (all meanings implied) thing.

Universities in the United States have been doing basic writing "to" their students since before the invention of the electric light bulb (Ritter, Stanley). The "basic writer" was not invented through open admissions at The City University of New York (CUNY) by Mina P. Shaughnessy in the 1970s; Ivy League schools established their "Awkward Squads" and English A courses while American women were struggling for suffrage. Even then, there were pulls against the popular framing of "remediated writers" as lazy, incompetent, or unworthy of university education. A well-documented shift in the discipline did occur, however, in the 1960s and 1970s. Rather than students themselves being seen as flawed (deficit models), they were more often framed as marginalized; that is, the past and present systems at work on these students were flawed. In recent decades, some rhetoric and composition research and theory implicitly situates basic writers and/ or their writing as the salvation of the university, capable of critiquing and therefore changing the flawed institution by reflecting back to it- self its own limitations, and rhetoric and composition's own awkward role there (Gray-Rosendale). If you buy this archaeology, you can see there is an ideological payoff—for a discipline that at present sees itself on the cutting edge of critical pedagogy—in calling basic writers into the subject position of "knowing less." ← **Explicit tie of developed example to thesis**

Yet, on the other hand, basic writing has served an access function for at least a century and a half, and in particular, at times when elite universities opened to new populations and public universities expand- ed. During this time frame, the opportunities of university education expanded for veterans through the GI Bill, and for immigrants and working class and poor students through changes in recruitment and open admissions policies; basic writing supported success for many of these students—and still does. Some of these egalitarian moves have been reversed recently, with open admissions policies being eliminated and calls to purge basic writing from higher education altogether.

BIG THEORIES THAT YOU CAN'T DO WITHOUT, AND ONE YOU CAN: INITIATION, CONFLICT, LAUNDRY

Initiation. If basic writers are on the margins, then initiation theories examine why that marginalization is and what might help move them toward the center. The margin/center of what? The discourse com- munity that is academe. At the heart of this discourse community is the notion, often associated with the Enlightenment, that we must in- quire against every assumption and commonplace, and dig for what is True and Right. It is this very assumption that marginalized students, according initiation theories, simply don't get. David Bartholomae's "Inventing the University" (and a great deal of work that riffs off that seminal piece), suggests that knocking aside popular commonplaces is at the core of academe, and students deemed basic writers don't make that indispensable move.

Thus, the initiation solution is to help basic writers "know less." ← **Another example!** → That is, basic writers need to understand that the commonplaces of everyday discourse(s)—I like to use the example of "No one loves you like your mom" with my students—need to be brought under examination. Even if you are quite sure that a particular commonplace is true, you must be less sure; you mustn't know it so much. "Y'know what I mean?" is an even less acceptable move in academic discourse than citing the Bible. At least the Bible works in some disciplines under some circumstances (religion, philosophy, English, etc.). However, the move of rhetorically conjoining two minds (and therefore two Subjects) together under a discursive assumption is the big no-no. Initiation theories say that once students understand that move, they are golden.

Laundry. Before we get to the why and the how of initiation theories, this is a good place to say what basic writing is not. It is not a mechanics laundry. There is strong agreement in the discipline that basic writing is not a place to merely "clean up" error and usage problems. That is, even if your local context (and the local contexts within your local context, as in, "Well, that personal voice works over here in English, but I have to teach my students to write for _____ ... business/elementary education/psychology/that stodgy colleague down the hall") adheres strongly to formal surface conventions of Academic Written English (AWE), it is not enough to teach/mentor/drill those surface conventions. If you don't believe that, then please try this: In the preceding paragraphs, does my use of contractions, first and second person, informal word choice, or even fragments impair your understanding of my argument? And by contrast, if a student put together a mechanically pristine five-paragraph essay—or, go crazy here, a six-paragraph one—with the thesis, "No one loves you like your mom," would that be a stepping stone to academic discourse, even if somehow it got that student through your exit test (if you have to deal with one)?

That being said, mechanics can do *in* students, and so mechanics must be done *to* students to some extent. Expressivists since at least Peter Elbow have argued that we can let students write in whatever manner or dialect works for them to get ideas down on paper, and teach them to edit for surface conventions at the last stages of revision. Shaughnessy (and others) argue for error identification (looking with students only at outstanding patterns of error, not a single intrusion of an error/typo) as an effective strategy. In error identification, instead of drilling on everything in the grammar book (which has not seemed to work for students so far), teachers strive to uncover what each student's working theory of the grammar or usage issue is, and then help them understand the correct AWE rule. It might look like, "So, you use '—ed' for the past tense here, here, and here. But in this sentence, you don't. Can you tell me what's different in this one?" Students will often say, "I just messed up" or "I talk that way so I just didn't see it." A warning: Sometimes this "it's a typo" explanation is all the two of you can figure out together; the intention, however, is that there is more to recover about how the error pattern came to be (Lees, Lu).

Teachers of basic writing have utilized many other strategies, including generative grammar (Noguchi); close, recursive, in-context editing (Weaver); and utilizing the burgeoning technologies that not only "correct" spelling and grammar (though sometimes erroneously) but also attempt to teach the underlying "rules" (McAlexander). What is critical to understand is that: (1) these rules are actually conventions, a socially agreed-upon set of practices that change over time and by context; and (2) these conventions are not ideologically neutral (**a bunch of cites here**). Thus, "not all errors are equal." Some errors infuse student writing to a degree that they actually do impair understanding, but that is far rarer than faculty like to complain about, and those errors that mark a writer as "uneducated" (read, not white and middle-class) are penalized more heavily than other errors (Gray and Hauser, Williams). While I work to uncover and critique this situation with my students (their assumption is usually that grammar is the reason why they are "bad writers," so I want them to "unknow" that presupposition as well ← **there, another explicit tie of another developed example to thesis**), I also take a pragmatic approach to the top three: subject-verb agreement, sentence boundary problems (fragments and run-ons, with the former being evaluated in the academic and professional world far more severely than the latter), and spelling/homonym/apostrophe errors. With these errors, combinations of the above strategies, along with group grammar mini-lessons (students teach the class a lesson on errors with which they themselves struggle), often help with awareness and skill-building.

꙰

Now back to initiation theories. Why is it that the real underlying codes of academic discourse don't rise to the surface of basic writers' compositions, and how to work with that discursive difference? Like mechanical conventions, decades of cross-disciplinary research and theory—in linguistics, literacy, urban and rural anthropology, educa-tion, psychology, and rhetoric and composition—indicate that the un-derlying workings of academic discourse are not neutral. They are, in fact, hyper-white-middle-class and/or privilege white and middle- to upper-class learners. "Hyper" because everyone of all backgrounds has a range of discourse practices that occur in a range of settings; AWE is not anyone's "home" discourse. AWE demands an extraordinary level of explicitness and precision and the subsuming of the everyday by the academic (Giltrow); it demands an appearance of sacrificing all pathos in favor of logos, all relationality in favor of rationality. In reality, AWE does demand subtle markers of pathos and relational-ity, but we like to call them "significance" and "citation" (Ashley). Finally, AWE when produced by students (not by you and me) often demands deference, redundancy, and the signaling of a willingness to be a contingent member of a disciplinary/academic discourse commu-nity, many of which are signified through citation practices (Giltrow, Robillard, Sullivan).

Some research has suggested that closer-knit working-class com-munities are less likely to require the explicitness of AWE and are more likely to use discourse practices that value intimacy; they count on community members "knowing what I mean" more of the time, and also *wanting* to "know what [the other] means" (Bernstein, Heath, Kinloch, Rodriguez, Rose). There may be more value placed on con-nection, shared experience, and shared identity; like all values, those values are marked in the language of the community. Thus, while a great deal of research counters the damaging myth that inner-city urban, rural, poor, working-class, and non-white communities are "simply illiterate," the oral communication and literacies found in those communities may be more likely to build on discourse practices such as hybridity, metalinguistic awareness, spontaneity and flexibil-ity, ethos, critical thinking, metaphor, and word play. These discursive strengths may rarely see the light of day in public schools, since there is little opportunity for these more subtle, creative, and higher-level strategies to emerge in the formal writing of schools, especially low-er-middle-class to poor schools (Anyon). This lost opportunity may be particularly true in an era of "Back to Basics." Ironically, "basic" writing classes can be a chance to capitalize on these often-neglected strengths.

English Q20 Statement of Goals—
West Chester University

ENG 020 is a course about both **writers** and **writing**.

The course should focus on **the process of producing writing**. It should help writers to learn about and practice the *process* of writing and to gain *confidence* in themselves as individuals able to express significant ideas in their writing. They should feel more empowered to recognize the areas that they want and need to improve on, including but not limited to grammar and syntax conventions in Academic Written English (AWE).

Methods to arrive at such learning are likely to include: composing complete pieces of writing in a variety of genres (narratives, shorts essays, letters, web pages, etc.), the use of multiple drafts and revision as a central part of the course, peer review and editing of drafts, individualized work with professors and/or tutors on error identification, discussion and/or writing about the act of writing and its meanings.

The course should also focus on **writing as a received, "final" product which can have an impact on the world**. It should help writers to understand the rhetorical situation of the university and their potential contributions to the institution. Therefore, English 020 should emphasize that students' "home discourses" (including the habits, beliefs, and values that are part of discourses) do have value in the university but that students often need to enact a "critical bilingualism" in order to get those ideas across to the academic audiences in the new world they are entering. In turn, the course should help students consider the value of the habits, beliefs, values, and language of the university in relation to their goals and lives.

Methods to arrive at such learning are likely to include: the study of model texts through reading, analysis, and discussion; the teaching of rhetorical concepts (audience, purpose, style, etc.); practice in logic and reasoning; studying the "voice" of the university and comparisons to other voices, especially the most prominent conventions of academic discourse, as well as those conventions of other discourses that may earn students the label of "outsider" to the academy. In other words, the course should focus on the critical study of language.

The course should have **significant outcomes**. ENG 020 is not a course focused on decontextualized grammar rules nor dedicated to teaching "the five-paragraph theme," and final exams should do more than evaluate students' abilities to follow these conventions. Rather, the course should provide students opportunities to improve their abilities to:

- Identify specific conventions of academic discourse.
- Question what types of discourse conventions are effective to use in different circumstances.
- Apply these understandings by producing at least one written piece which critically examines an idea or topic and supports that examination with evidence.
- Describe their own process of composing.
- Articulate strengths as well as areas to work on in their own writing.

Instructors of ENG 020 should have students produce portfolios which demonstrate the five bullet points above and collect those portfolios as part of the final evaluation of the course. Portfolios may include all types of written work for the course: drafts, outlines, cover letters, peer reviews, reflection papers, critical readings of published texts, narratives, mixed and non-traditional genres, etc.

Resistance and Conflict. Which brings us to conflict theories. If it were just a matter of exposure to a *different* set of discourse and literacy practices, it would be simple. Certainly initiation—supported and developed exposure to conventions such as explicitness and the use of "expert" voices to speak back to common sense—is part of most basic writing curricula. However, initiation assumes the desire of the initiate to join; it does not account for resistance. Sure, some of us resist *different*, but almost all of us resist being framed as *deficient*. A great deal of theory and research highlights the central problem for at least some basic writers (did I mention basic writers are not a monolith?): They are being forced to grab a golden ring that may mean the betrayal of community and self, and a separation from identification with values and material realities of home, family, and people (Delpit, Gilyard, kynard, Villanueva). This painful split is exacerbated for individuals whose people are/were "involuntary minorities" (Fordham and Ogbu). That is, it is easier to be assimilated (and thus initiation pedagogies may work for these groups) if one's ancestors came voluntarily to the United States, as opposed to experiencing forced migration, slavery, or colonialization. International research has demonstrated that the same ethnic group (i.e., similar educational values and discourse practices) in different countries with different statuses (voluntary versus involuntary minorities) performs differently, as a group, in educational contexts (Finn).

Many teachers who subscribe to conflict theories of basic writing like to use Mary Louise Pratt's "Arts of the Contact Zone" as a touchstone; the essay reframes writing classrooms from a race-class-nationality-gender-politics-neutral endeavor to a "contact zone" where discourses "clash" and relations of power must be made explicit. Some of us talk about forming "writing communities" in our classrooms without complicating what a community is; the contact zone notion offers an alternative to that idealized version of our peer review groups and "unbiased" reading responses.

Best Practices in the Contact Zone

Best practices in the contact zone are a mash-up of traditional, process, post-process, and cross-disciplinary approaches. When constructing goals for a basic writing program as a whole (see the West Chester University sample in the box above), model syllabi, or professional development for faculty, one should bear in mind the history and theories described above and the suggested best practices below.

- *Academic discourse as genre(s), a writing studies approach*—This approach acknowledges that academic discourse is not neutral or natural, but that it is one of many valued/valuable genres in our culture. Its strength is a post-process recognition that academic discourse is far from the monolith that handbooks sometimes pretend it to be (with the exception of teaching different citation conventions, which is the most ubiquitous handbook nod to the diversity of writing contexts at the university). As a pedagogy, it places the emphasis on developing writers. A strong writer is one who has the "rhetorical dexterity" (Carter) to capitalize on previous strengths (if you figured out how to write a hilarious Facebook post or unforgettable hip hop lyrics, you are rhetorically savvy … but you probably need the supports and encouragement to apply that savvy to academic contexts and genres). That is, good writing is not good writing is not good writing, but a good writer is. And a good teacher is one who can help students with that meta-analysis and to internalize that self- and contextual knowledge. Some of this genre/writing studies approach is reflected in our ENG Q20 Goals statement—see the above box.

- *Academic discourse as critique, a critical pedagogy approach*—This approach places more emphasis on problematizing academic discourse, an approach that Ira Shor (among many others), building on the work of Paulo Freire, made prominent. Its strength is pushing back against the notion that basic writers are unintelligent or lazy, in particular for basic writers themselves, who have internalized these notions. As a pedagogy, it starts from students' strengths: readings and writings that are already engaging for them—emphasizing students "reading their own world" and/or their language practices, as in Critical Language Awareness approaches. A good teacher is one who is flexible enough to let students set the agenda rather than "pour knowledge into students' heads," but who also "animates" and guides (Freire). Again, one can see the influence of this critical approach in the WCU document.

- *Academic discourse as performance, a queer theory approach*—This is the "carnival" approach. Academic discourse(s) are sets of conventions to play with and against in order to both appropriate them and change them in the same moment. Its strength is in laughter, which many recognize as a tactic of the weak, not only to disrupt power but also so that those "involuntarily" in positions of marginality and otherness (our basic writing students) can defiantly occupy the power positions and reclaim control of the discourses at work on them, but with skepticism and contingency, thus (ideally) without giving up on home and community. Performance as an approach to basic writing is rarely an entire syllabus, but is more likely to be enacted in pedagogical practices that value parody, irony, irreverence, code meshing (as opposed to code switching, which would be more of the writing studies approach), or the production of "outsider genres" that blend aspects of say, personal with research writing or fiction with argument (as opposed to assigning yet another five-paragraph/ bulletproof essay) (Canagarajah, Gee, Wallace, Young). A good teacher is one who recognizes that he/she too is performing, calling on the available discursive resources in order to be read as "a professor" or "an academic."

The difference between a queer interpretation and the "straighter" practices is that a queer approach is explicitly meant to call an affected attention to assumed dichotomies, conventional rhetorical moves, and reified subject positions in order to critique them. It is a roguish, sidelong combining of writing studies (which requires precise knowledge of discursive conventions and the ability to talk about them) and critical pedagogy (which tends to critique the languages, concerns and practices of the academy head-on). In this chapter, my blithe identifications of the conventions of academic discourse in **Rockwell** font are meant to hold up a **queer** mirror to academic discourse by making fun of my own performance. I point out my use of these conventions in order to critique them. My own thesis, evidence, synthesis and lack of/adherence to mechanical conventions—I hope—look very different than the formulas that are sometimes "done to" basic writers; and these labels are employed ironically, since much of the rest of this piece cannot be easily boxed in with a textbook label.

Models for Program Design and Final Questions to Ask

Now, down from high theory to a few final key issues on the ground.

To credit or not to credit? The answer to this question varies widely. At my own university, many battles have been waged to gain the English Q20 course graduation credit, at this writing to no avail. Currently, students pay for three full credits, which count toward their GPA but not elsewhere, despite the rigor of the course and its positive effect on their future writing course grades and retention. Some basic writing "courses" are noncredit tutorials, some carry four credits, some are two semester, six-credit sequences. Students often resent a course that labels them as "not ready for college," but they resent it more when "it's a waste of money." Research and persistence help in fighting this battle with administrations (it certainly has been done successfully on other campuses, hopefully on ours soon).

Program design also varies widely. However, there are three common models, with variations by population, context, and resources (Lalicker). There is a great deal of theory and empirical research on these models, and WPAs should educate themselves further when they are faced with program design questions.

- *Stand-alone course.* Typically three credits, which count toward student standing (say, for financial aid purposes) and sometimes toward graduation. Without graduation credit, even in the best designed courses, many students and faculty regard this type of course as a "gatekeeping" model that is slowing their time to graduation down, whether or not this is true. (As noted above, at my own university, one research study showed that students placed into basic writing were more likely to be retained and with better grades than their peers placed straight into first-year composition; this success contributes to our administration's limited willingness to tinker with this conventional model.)
- *Stretch.* This model and "intensive" program designs (below) are often seen as "access-building" paradigms, which do not withhold the "real university" from basic writing students. Stretch places students whom the university labels as remedial straight into the typical first-year course, but allows the work of that course to stretch over two semesters instead of one. That is, three credits of work at a slower pace, with more opportunity for support, revision, and peer- and faculty-relationship building (Glau).
- *Intensive.* By contrast, intensive program designs can be thought of as deepening, rather than widening the work of the typical first-year course. Writing studios, for example, are often one credit, and tend to be structured like lab components, with smaller numbers of students (three to twelve is the common range) meeting with faculty, graduate assistants, or tutors, to work hands-on on the work of the first- year course, another writing course, or any writing across the curriculum. In some cases, intensive can mean a whole additional three-credit course, taken at the same time as the first-year composition (FYC) course. Sometimes these programs are called "accelerated," not because they move faster

than the regular FYC course, but because they mainstream basic writing students into university-level work right away (Adams et al., Grego and Thompson).

Final questions to ask with regard to program and curricular design, some of which are addressed in other chapters in this volume, include:

- What is the relationship between basic writing and other "remedial" coursework at your institution, especially "pre-college" reading courses? Or is your course an integrated reading-writing course? If not, is there a possibility for co-teaching or curricular integration?
- How are students currently placed into basic writing and what is the relationship of the basic writing course to the rest of the writing program, in terms of philosophy, pedagogy, outcomes, and assessment?
- Is there an exit test, portfolio, or another external or internal hoop to jump for your students (and faculty)? At some institutions, students have to pass a mandatory, standardized, and timed exit test to "get out" of basic writing. WPAs should help faculty to assess the effect of such tests on their teaching and their students' actual learning and success in college, and then to work both with and against those constraints on the ground. At other institutions, there are more organic "quality control" measures, such as final portfolios, which are labor intensive, but can often be used to improve teaching as well as, for example, audience awareness for students. At other institutions, it remains the discretion of individual instructors whether a student is "ready" for the next course.

Conclusion: In several significant ways, when a student gets basic writing *done to* them, they are being schooled to know less. This is sometimes, even, a good (all meanings implied) thing. **Agree or disagree?**

WORKS CITED

Adams, Peter, Sarah Gearhart, Robert Miller, and Anne Roberts. "The Accelerated Learning Program: Throwing Open the Gates." *The Journal of Basic Writing* 28.2 (2009): 50–69. Print.

Anyon, Jean. "Social Class and the Hidden Curriculum of Work." *Journal of Education* 162 (1980): 67–92. Print.

Ashley, Hannah. "The Art of Queering Voices: A Fugue." *The Journal of Basic Writing* 26.1 (2007): 4–19. Print.

Bartholomae, David. "Inventing the University." *When a Writer Can't Write: Studies in Writer's Block and Other Composing-Process Problems.* Ed. Mike Rose. New York: Guilford, 1985. 134–65. Print.

Bernstein, Basil. *Class, Codes and Control.* London: Routledge & Kegan Paul, 1973. Print.

Canagarajah, Suresh A. "The Place of World Englishes in Composition: Pluralization Continued." *College Composition and Communication* 53.4 (2002): 594–630. Print.

Carter, Shannon. *The Way Literacy Lives: Rhetorical Dexterity and Basic Writing Instruction.* Albany: SUNY P, 2008. Print.

Delpit, Lisa. *Other People's Children: Cultural Conflict in the Classroom.* New York: The New Press, 1995. Print.

Elbow, Peter. *Writing Without Teachers.* New York: Oxford UP, 1973. Print.

Finn, Patrick J. *Literacy with an Attitude: Educating Working-Class Children in Their Own Self-Interest.* Albany: SUNY P, 1999. Print.

Fordham, Signithia, and John Ogbu. "Black Students' School Success: Coping with the Burden of 'Acting White'." *Urban Review* 18 (1986): 176–206. Print.

Freire, Paulo. *Pedagogy of the Oppressed.* New York: Continuum, 1995. Print.

Gee, James Paul. "Literacy, Discourse, and Linguistics: Introduction." *Journal of Education* 17.1 (1989): 5–17. Print.

Giltrow, Janet. *Academic Writing: Writing and Reading in the Disciplines.* Ontario: Broadview, 2002. Print.

Gilyard, Keith. *Voices of the Self: A Study of Language Competence.* Detroit, MI: Wayne State UP, 1991. Print.

Glau, Gregory R. "Stretch at 10: A Progress Report on Arizona State University's Stretch Program." *The Journal of Basic Writing* 26.2 (2007): 30–48. Print.

Gray, Loretta S., and Paula Heuser. "Nonacademic Professionals' Perception of Usage Errors." *JBW* 22.1 (2003): 50–70. Print.

Gray-Rosendale, Laura. "Back to the Future: Contextuality and the Construction of the Basic Writer's Identity in JBW, 1999–2005." *The Journal of Basic Writing* 25.2 (2006): 5–27. Print.

Grego, Rhonda, and Nancy Thompson. "Repositioning Remediation: Renegotiating Composition's Work in the Academy." *College Composition and Communication* 47.1 (1996): 62–84. Print.

Heath, Shirley Brice. *Ways With Words: Language, Life and Work in Communities and Classrooms.* Cambridge: Cambridge UP, 1983. Print.

Kinloch, Valerie, Arnetha Ball, and María Fránquiz. "Research on Literacy in Diverse Educational Contexts: An Introduction." *Research in the Teaching of English* 45.2 (2010): 93–96. Print.

kynard, carmen. "'New Life in This Dormant Creature': Notes on Social Consciousness, Language Learning in a College Classroom." *ALT DIS: Alternative Discourses and the Academy*. Ed. Helen Fox, Christopher Schroeder, and Patricia Bizzell. Portsmouth, NH: Boynton/Cook-Heinemann, 2002. 31–44. Print.

Lalicker, William B. "A Basic Introduction to Basic Writing Program Structures: A Baseline and Five Alternatives." *BWe: Basic Writing e-Journal* 1.2 (1999). Web. 7 January 2013.

Lees, Elaine O. "Proofreading as Reading, Errors as Embarrassments." *A Sourcebook for Basic Writing Teachers*. Ed. Theresa Enos. New York: Random House, 1987. 216–30. Print.

Lewiecki-Wilson, Cynthia, and Brenda Jo Brueggemann. *Disability and the Teaching of Writing: A Critical Sourcebook*. Boston: Bedford/St. Martin's, 2007. Print.

Lu, Min-Zhan. "Professing Multiculturalism: The Politics of Style in the Contact Zone." *College Composition and Communication* 45.4 (1994): 442–58. Print.

McAlexander, Patricia J. "Checking the Grammar-Checker: Integrating Grammar Instruction with Writing." *The Journal of Basic Writing* 19.2 (2000): 124–40. Print.

Noguchi, Rei R. *Grammar and the Teaching of Writing: Limits and Possibilities*. Urbana, IL: NCTE, 1991. Print.

Pratt, Mary Louise. "Arts of the Contact Zone." *Profession 91* (1991): 33–40. Print.

Ritter, Kelly. *Before Shaughnessy: Basic Writing at Yale and Harvard, 1920–1960*. Carbondale: Southern Illinois UP, 2009. Print.

Robillard, Amy E. "Young Scholars Affecting Composition: A Challenge to Disciplinary Citation Practices." *College English* 68.3 (2006): 253–70. Print.

Rodriguez, Richard. *Hunger of Memory: The Education of Richard Rodriguez*. New York: Random House, 1981. Print.

Rose, Mike. *Lives on the Boundary: The Struggles and Achievements of America's Underprepared*. New York: Free Press, 1989. Print.

Shaughnessy, Mina P. *Errors and Expectations: A Guide for the Teacher of Basic Writing*. New York: Oxford UP, 1977. Print.

Shor, Ira. *When Students Have Power: Negotiating Authority in a Critical Pedagogy*. Chicago, IL: U of Chicago P, 1996. Print.

Stanley, Jane. *The Rhetoric of Remediation: Negotiating Entitlement and Access to Higher Education*. Pittsburgh, PA: U of Pittsburgh P, 2010. Print.

Sullivan, Francis J. "Calling Writers' Bluffs: The Social Production of Writing Ability in University Placement Testing." *Assessing Writing* 4.1 (1997): 53–81. Print.

Villanueva, Victor, Jr. *Bootstraps: From an American Academic of Color.* Urbana, IL: NCTE, 1993. Print.

Wallace, David L. *Compelled to Write: Alternative Rhetoric in Theory and Practice.* Logan: Utah State UP, 2011. Print.

Weaver, Constance. *Teaching Grammar in Context.* Portsmouth, NH: Boynton, 1996. Print.

Williams, Joseph. "The Phenomenology of Error." *College Composition and Communication* 32.2 (1981): 152–68. Print.

Young, Vershawn Ashanti. *Your Average Nigga: Performing Race, Literacy, and Masculinity.* Detroit, MI: Wayne State UP, 2007. Print.

4 What Is First-Year Composition?

Doug Downs

It depends whom you ask.

The institution: *First-year composition (FYC) is a general education course designed to improve students' writing skills and prepare them for college and workplace writing.*

Parents, politicians, and the public: *A course to ensure that college graduates have the basic writing skills that employers seek, because so many students just can't write.*

Other professors: *An English course meant to ensure students can write when they get to us—but doesn't; our students can't complete a sentence, much less write well.*

Students: *A hoop to make me eligible for other classes; a place to polish my writing skills and refresh my grammar, which is what I really need help with.*

Graduate teaching assistants: *A hoop I would have had to jump through if I hadn't already been a good writer and AP'd out of it, so I've never actually taken the course I'm teaching.*

While all of these are conceptions of first-year composition that WPAs regularly encounter—so each is real and "true"—WPAs should understand it as something other than simply a required general education course to build or refresh writing skills that automatically transfer to other courses and jobs. First-year composition can and should be *a space, a moment, and an experience*—in which students might reconsider writing apart from previous schooling and work, within the context of inquiry-based higher education. A wide range of "best-practice" approaches to FYC create experiences that open new windows on writing for students. This sense of college composition as an exploratory moment for writers presents a marked split with popular stakeholder notions of FYC as a high-transfer how-to course centered on grammar instruction. We find the essence of composition in this divergence: FYC is what it is by virtue of being held in tension between these competing senses of its purpose.

To support this claim, I'll begin by exploring FYC's "public charter," which will build historical background on college composition and flesh out stakeholders' conceptions: what they expect from first-year composition, why they created and fund it. I then contrast these conceptions with expert accounts, based in empirical research and theory, which call the public charter into question. What should FYC be doing if satisfying stakeholder demands is impossible? I take up that question in the final part of the chapter by considering the "heart" of composition: what its expert practitioners have perennially tried to make it do for students. Therein lie foundational values of most rhetoric and composition specialists, including access to higher education and the power of a writer's voice. Such ideals will return us to the premised tension, FYC stretched between its public reasons and its expert desires, so that we find "what first-year composition is" in the many embodiments of that tension.

[handwritten: founda-tional values of RC]

STAKEHOLDER EXPECTATIONS: FYC'S PUBLIC CHARTER

This section draws on histories and critiques of FYC by Robert Connors, Sharon Crowley, Susan Miller, and David R. Russell. Their work suggests that FYC exists because of (1) the democratization of higher education, (2) the cultural equation of literacy with morality and of "writing" with grammatical correctness, and (3) the vocational role of higher education. These are the sources of FYC's public charter, but the charter is made without reference to whether its goal for FYC (building skills that transfer to college and workplace writing) can actually be met. The charter represents a felt need, but is itself an expert assessment of neither that need nor of the best means of meeting it.

The Democratization of Higher Education. We can find the roots of FYC in the radical redesign of American higher education between 1850 and 1900. Until the mid-1800s, American colleges followed British tradition, teaching medicine, law, and divinity to upper-class sons. The conversion to today's university model resulted from two central innovations. One was the German university model created in the early 1800s, organizing curricula not by professions but by newly developed disciplines (e.g., chemistry, botany, astronomy) whose faculty not only taught established knowledge but researched for new knowledge (see Russell, *Writing*). The resulting transformation of American colleges into engines of research and innovation engaged a national pragmatism that saw education improving everyday life and building new industries.

That pragmatic vision of the economic and cultural value of higher education led, by the end of the 1850s, to a second innovation consistent with America's democratic origins: college for the non-wealthy. The transformation of higher education from upper-class training in classical knowledge to research-based knowledge across a range of disciplines drew a wider range of students. The lever for this expansion of access was the Morrill Act of 1862, which deeded federal land to each state for agriculture and engineering colleges. Coed from their inception, by 1890 the "land grants" guaranteed access to people of color. These democratizing moves eventually brought student bodies to encompass all classes, genders, and races. However, they also challenged the monoculture upon which college curricula had been based.

Literacy, Morality, Writing, and Correctness. In the twentieth century, linguistics and literacy studies showed that language, dialects, literacies, accents, lexicons, and usage habits have no *inherent* value—one is no "better" than another intrinsically. What we call "better" and "worse" language, speech, or grammar is actually an external value (such as power, prestige, or morality) *imposed on* language. By this principle, the language habits of wealthy New England are no better than those of impoverished Appalachia, though most American English speakers think they are. So did faculty at Harvard in 1874 when instituting a written entrance exam, "a short English composition, correct in spelling, punctuation, grammar, and expression" (qtd. in Applebee 30). Susan Miller characterizes the results:

> The grotesqueries of handwriting and of paragraphing described in the Harvard Board of Overseers' report (one boy indented regularly, every five lines) were gleefully found and reported with the sympathy and understanding we might expect of young boys looking at a circus fat lady. These faults and others like them were snickered over, as they still are, so that they came to represent an "Other." [. . .] They took on

"dirty" associations that the nonelect, nonpredestined student could embody. (*Textual* 55)

In such ways, "proper" speech and writing associate with upright ("high") moral character. Speak "poorly," and be marked as an outsider of suspect morals, low education, and likely as lazy and shiftless. This perceived need for FYC to "scrub" the new, lower-class students, instilling "politeness" and "good breeding" (57)—an attempt to maintain the traditional college monoculture—is an important root of its public charter.

Another root lies in what matters to teach about writing, what makes writing "good." Consider the elements of writing the Harvard exam emphasized: grammar, punctuation, diction and organization ("expression"), and spelling. "Writing" is reduced to rules—unambiguous, basic, stable, and universal—for transcribing speech to print. Thus, writing becomes (as most Americans experience it today) about avoiding breaking rules, which students are to be adept with by the end of high school. And so, in 2013 as in 1896 when Harvard invented FYC, students who arrive at college not knowing "how to write"— how to follow grammar and usage rules—appear deficient, in need not of learning but of fixing. Thus composition can be exempted ("gotten out of the way") by good high school performance; in the public charter, it has little beyond high school to teach.

Writing for Jobs. The roots of FYC's public charter lie not just in the need to write correctly in order to demonstrate identity, belonging, and good breeding. A parallel purpose reflects in the National Commission on Writing (NCW)'s 2004 report, *Writing: A Ticket to Work . . . Or a Ticket Out: A Survey of Business Leaders*, with its judgment that "writing is a ticket to professional opportunity, while poorly written job applications are a figurative kiss of death" (3). Professional jobs require writing: "All employees must have writing ability [. . .] Manufacturing documentation, operating procedures, reporting problems, lab safety, waste-disposal operations—all have to be crystal clear," so "employers spend billions annually correcting writing deficiencies" (3). Applicants who write poorly will struggle for interviews, and employees who write poorly risk being denied promotions (3). To the extent college constitutes job training in the public imagination, FYC helps evade such risks.

What does *good writing* mean to stakeholders? In another report, *The Neglected "R": The Need for a Writing Revolution*, NCW states, "writing today is [. . .] an essential skill for the many" (11). A "skill"— not knowledge, activity, or performance. Vocational supporters of FYC tend to equate "good" with correct, clear, and concise (see chapters on style in Connors's *Composition-Rhetoric*). *The Neglected "R"* says writers must know "how to say things correctly, how to say them well, and how to make sure that what one has said makes sense" (9)—equating writing with accurately following rules for clarity. Thus, the 2003 report *Understanding University Success: A Report from Standards for Success*, which aimed to define what "college-ready" writers need to know, states that "Grammar is the basis for good writing. [. . .] Students in college are expected to know how to diagram a sentence and recognize how this process helps them understand words and their functions within a sentence. It is also important to understand the specific ways correct grammar makes writing clearer and helps communicate more effectively" (Conley 18). Here, a text's meaning is grammatically fixed, rather than arising from an interaction between itself and a situated reader. Clarity is grammatical and correctness is universal: Clear writing is clear writing, no matter the reader or the circumstances.

The public charter, then, is based on stakeholders' convictions that writing is the basic, transferable, grammatical skill of transcribing speech to print, a skill essential to both social standing and employment prospects, making an FYC course that teaches these skills a wise investment. And invest we do. Crowley estimated in 1995 that at least four million students enrolled in more than 160,000 sections of FYC (1). As a result, Crowley argues, FYC is "remarkably vulnerable to ideologies and practices that originate elsewhere than in its classrooms" (6). The public demand for writing instruction translates to public oversight of writing pedagogy. Understanding FYC starts with recognizing both this public charter and its conceptions of writing. Then, crucially, with testing their accuracy.

EXPERT RESEARCH: UNDERMINING FYC'S PUBLIC CHARTER

Even if writing were a basic, universal, grammatical skill of clearly transcribing speech to print, which naturally transfers to other writing situations from stand-alone essay-writing courses, writing instructors in the first half of the twentieth century still had to explore the best ways of teaching it—creating research on writing instruction. This in turn revealed a need to better understand writing itself, leading to research and the accumulation of expert knowledge on how writing works—which contrasts markedly with the public charter.

Research on the Nature of Writing. In 1963—generally counted as the birth of composition studies—Richard Braddock, Richard Lloyd-Jones, and Lowell Schoer published *Research in Written Composition*, a survey of more than one hundred studies on twenty-four questions central to FYC, such as effective instructional design and the influence of reading on writing. Their report, which proved composition a legitimate research subject, revealed cracks in the public narrative about what FYC should teach, and how.

Composition's public imagined "writing" as the transcription of existing ideas to print, but teachers knew that "writing ideas down" requires coming up with them to begin with. This observation inspired the Process movement in the late 1960s, which insisted, *contra* the public charter, that writing is a process, not a product. The notion that "writing" is not just *the saying of* ideas but *the invention of them* triggers a cascade of implications. Obviously, writing goes beyond transcription, and research is needed to observe writers at work. (See Daniel Perrin and Marc Wildi for a complex "phase" description of writing processes [380]. It models what Ann Berthoff calls "allatonce-ness," moments when a writer experiences several phases of the process simultaneously, such as invention via revision.)

Another implication: If FYC teaches only transcription of existing ideas into print, its focus can be on *form* (grammar); but with invention in play, FYC must also consider *content*. We can see the splitting of form from content, and treating the latter not as writing, in SAT and ACT writing exams, which purport to assess "writing" without judging its factuality or sense. Form and content can't be split, however: Changing one changes the other. Thus, another question: How does *writing quality* vary with *the writer's subject knowledge* (e.g., Ackerman)? The public charter imagines "writing" as varying little across subjects, so FYC proceeds heedless of subject. Voiding the form/content split also voids this assurance: Subject matters.

Once content and invention are on the table, so too is autonomy. While composition historically addressed an autonomous (inspired) writer and emphasized his "own" words, rhetorical theory, such as

Keith Grant-Davie's on rhetorical situations, shows the role of external influences: exigence, audience needs and values, historical context, and other constraints.

Rhetoric raises another challenge for traditional FYC: *Writing is situated, not universal.* FYC meant to teach universal rules for good writing, stable and immutable. Rhetoric predicts, and researchers find, otherwise: The "rules" vary by situation. Researchers see double standards, two wonderful take-downs of which are Joseph M. Williams's "Phenomenology of Error" and John Dawkins's "Teaching Punctuation as a Rhetorical Tool." They amass examples of errors and rules for which students are held accountable, but professionals aren't. The "rules" work more like situated rhetorical preferences, dependent on audience perception. Second, researchers find predictable preferences dependent on discipline, such as complex, semicoloned sentences valued in humanities, but not in engineering. So the limited set of stable, universal rules premised by FYC proves elusive.

Historically, the charter also assumed that those rules were stable across genre, and thus focused mostly on writing essays. Genre researchers again found otherwise—Carolyn R. Miller with "Genre as Social Action," then Charles Bazerman ("Speech Acts"), Anis Bawarshi, and David R. Russell. Russell links genre theory and activity theory, in which texts are analyzed as tools used by groups of people to accomplish an activity (like cancer research). A text's "rules" depend on its tool-use ("Writing"). If writing various genres were analogous to playing sports involving a ball, Russell argues, FYC would be teaching "general ball handling skills," imagining that teaching "catching a ball" (writing an essay) would prepare a player to catch footballs, basketballs, and baseballs ("Activity Theory"). The result, as Elizabeth Wardle has shown, is that FYC often teaches genres students will encounter *nowhere but* FYC—the very opposite of its mission.

Implications of Writing Research for Writing Instruction. In all these ways, expert knowledge built from writing research and theory suggest that public notions of writing are critically flawed. What fate, then, for instruction premised on them? Instruction, too, requires reconception. Given that writing is not universal but contingent on specific activities and rhetorical situations, its quality a function of community standards and subject knowledge, we can predict that writing will be learned best not in an isolated, universal course, but via actual genres written in the situations they're intended for, through apprenticeship. This is the lesson not only of situated-learning theory (see Artemeva) but also of composition's writing in the disciplines movement: Writing expertise develops with content expertise in situations where readers model *using* writing.

From this principle a number of predictions are possible. The "universal educated discourse" (Russell, "Activity Theory") FYC is predicated on doesn't exist, nor do "general writing skills" (Petraglia xi). So, teaching writing outside meaningful rhetorical situations won't work well; learning transfer from general instruction will be hit-or-miss. We even find what Anne Beaufort calls *negative* transfer, where FYC learning actively fails writers in later classes (104). Hopes of inoculating students against bad writing with a single course are also doomed. Like any performance activity, writing is practiced at point of need in many times and places, learning never perfected or completed.

By these predictions, FYC should have a poor record of achieving stakeholders' goals. And it does—its stakeholders ascribing blame to bad students and bad teaching. Traditional FYC has thus fragmented into a variety of approaches: Gary Tate, Amy Rupiper, and Kurt Schick's 2001 *Guide to Composition Pedagogies* offers twelve (e.g., process, rhetorical, critical), while commentators including James Berlin and Richard Fulkerson taxonomize broader ideologies. Fulkerson, most recently, categorized formalist, expressionist, mimetic, rhetorical/procedural, and critical/cultural studies focuses, each proceeding from a different sense of what matters most about writing. Major critical efforts, Stephen M. North's *The Making of Knowledge in Composition: Portrait of an Emerging Field* and Joseph Harris's *A Teaching Subject: Composition Since 1966*, have questioned even rhetoric and composition's most foundational research and principles. And as Bob Broad's *What We Really Value: Beyond Rubrics in Teaching and Assessing Writing* and Richard Haswell's *Gaining Ground in College Writing: Tales of Development and Interpretation* show, conceptions of writing-as-grammar run so deep that in their studies, writing instructors mistook textual flaws as grammatical even when they weren't.

It makes sense, then, to question the entire enterprise. Crowley advocates an end to mandatory composition instruction. Joseph Petraglia suggests shifting writing instruction to the disciplines, perhaps preserving FYC as preparatory. David W. Smit proposes that since FYC, the heart of composition studies, has an impossible mission, composition studies be eliminated altogether, its research and instruction blended into other disciplines.

The Heart of First-Year Composition

Yet the public charter for FYC remains. We don't get to wish it away. More importantly, good writing instructors see development happen in FYC that we should not discount, even if it's misnamed. Students may not learn transferable rules for writing, but they do learn. These two realities—continuing stakeholder investment in FYC, and our own itch that *something* worthwhile happens there—suggest that what first-year composition is can be of great value to students.

What We've Always Shared. What I think of as "the heart of composition" took root in the late 1960s and 1970s. I begin here with Mina P. Shaughnessy, because her book *Errors & Expectations: A Guide for the Teacher of Basic Writing* presents the most powerful early embodiment of one of our most central ideals: *access.* Compositionists want to invite students in rather than bounce them out, open rather than bar the doors. Shaughnessy spoke our enduring philosophy: Weak writers are teachable. Poor writing is not a moral failing. Writing problems are systematic and, with thoughtful reading, understandable: A good reader can identify problem patterns. We are people who take students seriously and use instruction to keep students in school rather than writing them off. We don't say, "You should already know that;" we say, "You're here to learn that, and we'll help."

A second ideal at the heart of composition is *interaction.* Here's Ken Macrorie in 1970's *Uptaught,* a scathing critique of FYC: "A professor lecturing to a class of three students [. . .] reading from a book or his notes. The students sat in the front row before him, looking up" (60). Again, "One of the most distinguished and published members of the department [. . .] slammed down his books and said with a sigh, 'Oh, my God! These kids don't know a thing. They haven't read anything. I really can't talk to them'" (66). Macrorie, Donald Graves, Peter Elbow, Janet Emig, Sondra Perl, Donald Murray—they turned writing instruction interactive, away from lecture to workshop and conference. Murray's "The Listening Eye: Reflections on the Writing Conference" describes teaching almost entirely via one-on-one office conversations. That spirit still imbues FYC.

Closely linked to an ethic of interaction is _voice_: Our heart is to care deeply about students being heard, learning to use and value their voices. One of our most anthologized articles, David Bartholomae's "Inventing the University," unites the ethos of access and voice with a call to valorize writing that tries hard ideas poorly over writing that safely offers easy ideas well.

Fourth, our heart lies in _textual production_, studying writing processes and technologies. Susan Miller points out that we study "_how texts got that way_"—what has made a text what it is. "Composition as a discipline first depended on our knowing more about composing than others do [. . .] taking up what, who, to what ends, and, especially, how people have written and do write" ("Writing" 52). How has a text emerged, processually and technologically, from its rhetorical situation? What are the material circumstances of its production? In every era and pedagogy, these are always our questions.

Finally, our heart is in _rhetoric_. We cannot well understand what we do apart from a rhetorical framework. Always, as we work with students to wield technology to voice ideas that give them access to and interaction with their college scenes, we consider exigence, audience, context, and motivation.

What Is First-Year Composition?

First-year composition _is_ these principles. Every one—access, interaction, voice, textual production, rhetoric—shows us something of what FYC, in its best moments, teaches. Rejecting a misguided and impossible mission, we do something else. We teach students that there's nothing "basic" about writing—that writing is _supposed_ to be difficult, and that to have difficulty writing is to be a _writer_, not a failure. That writers don't write alone. The power and importance of voice. We teach how texts are produced and how writing is technological. We teach rhetoric.

The world is full of ways to work the tension between what we're expected to teach and what we _ought_ to teach; that is a central source of diversity in composition pedagogy. Here are some principles for creating FYC in this tension.

Establish expertise. 2005 CCCC chair Douglas Hesse asked, "Who owns writing?" FYC lives in tension between public and expert ownership, because *everybody* owns writing. But writing teachers, Hesse asserted, "have the lens of research and reflective practice, polished carefully and long [. . .] Ours is the knowledge of what writing is and what it can be, the whole of it, in every sphere. Ours is the never-done knowledge of how writing develops, within a person or a populace" (354–55). Whatever else FYC is, it is a site where we explore and profess that knowledge.

Make writing the content of the writing course. Russell, in 1995, suggested that FYC should teach its own knowledge ("Activity Theory"). Elizabeth Wardle and I, in 2007 ("Teaching"), outlined a "writing-about-writing" pedagogy that does. Linda Adler-Kassner, in an address to the 2012 CWPA conference, asserted that FYC pedagogy *must* make writing the subject of the course if it is to be a "writing" course.

Write meaningful outcomes. When a program knows what it wants its students to learn, it can take many pedagogical paths. The challenge is in articulating what actually matters.

Work on misconceptions. Students largely accept FYC's public charter. Using the course to expose alternative conceptions of writing that better account for students' lived experiences is a terrifically productive use of the course.

Engage an activity system. Use service learning. Teach disciplinary writing. Require research on writing, or ethnographies of literacies and communities. Somehow, give students real texts to write for real readers. These tend not to exist in FYC unless we bring them in.

Emphasize rhetoric ceaselessly. Embed texts, both the ones students read and the ones they write, in rhetorical situations, in exigence and *mythos* and *kairos*, and have students articulate their details.

CONCLUSION

First-year composition is a space we have by happy misunderstanding. If its stakeholders understood writing as we do, writing instruction might be embedded in other courses, taught in concert with the subject-knowledge embodied in its texts, partaking of the activity systems it participated in. But we have *this* space, so long as we goodheartedly subscribe to the public charter of "teaching writing." We have this moment with students, to create with them experiences that might rework their sense of writing, changing their relationships with it for the better. In our best worlds, that is first-year composition.

WORKS CITED

Ackerman, John. "Reading, Writing, and Knowing: The Role of Disciplinary Knowledge in Comprehension and Composing." *Research in the Teaching of English* 25 (1991): 133–77. Print.

Adler-Kassner, Linda. "The Company(ies) We Keep: Tactics and Strategies in Challenging Times." 2012 Writing Program Administrators Conference. Council of Writing Program Administrators. Albuquerque, NM. 19 July 2012. Plenary Address.

Applebee, Arthur. *Tradition and Reform in the Teaching of English: A History.* Urbana, IL: NCTE, 1974. Print.

Artemeva, Natasha. "Toward a Unified Social Theory of Genre Learning." *Journal of Business and Technical Communication* 22 (2008): 160–85. Print.

Bartholomae, David. "Inventing the University." *When a Writer Can't Write: Studies in Writer's Block and Other Composing-Process Problems.* Ed. Mike Rose. New York: Guilford, 1985. 134–65. Print.

Bazerman, Charles. "Speech Acts, Genres, and Activity Systems: How Texts Organize Activity and People." *What Writing Does and How It Does It: An Introduction to Analyzing Texts and Textual Practices.* Ed. Charles Bazerman and Paul Prior. Mahwah, NJ: Erlbaum, 2004. 309–39. Print.

Bawarshi, Anis. *Genre and the Invention of the Writer.* Logan: Utah State UP, 2003. Print.

Beaufort, Anne. *College Writing and Beyond: A New Framework for University Writing Instruction.* Logan: Utah State UP, 2007. Print.

Berlin, James. "Contemporary Composition: The Major Pedagogical Theories." *College English* 44 (1982): 765–77. Print.

Berthoff, Ann. *The Sense of Learning.* Portsmouth, NH: Boynton/Cook, 1990. Print.

Braddock, Richard, Richard Lloyd-Jones, and Lowell Schoer. *Research in Written Composition.* Urbana, IL: NCTE, 1963. Print.

Broad, Bob. *What We Really Value: Beyond Rubrics in Teaching and Assessing Writing.* Logan: Utah State UP, 2003. Print.

Conley, David T. *Understanding University Success: A Report from Standards for Success.* Center for Educational Policy Research, University of Oregon. 2003. Web. 25 July 2012.

Connors, Robert. *Composition-Rhetoric*. Pittsburgh, PA: U of Pittsburgh P, 1997. Print.

Crowley, Sharon. *Composition in the University: Historical and Polemical Essays*. Pittsburgh, PA: U of Pittsburgh P, 1998. Print.

Dawkins, John. "Teaching Punctuation as a Rhetorical Tool." *College Composition and Communication* 46 (1995): 533–48. Print.

Downs, Doug, and Elizabeth Wardle. "Teaching about Writing, Righting Misconceptions: (Re)Envisioning FYC as Intro to Writing Studies." *College Composition and Communication* 58 (2007): 552-84. Print.

Fulkerson, Richard. "Composition at the Turn of the Twenty-first Century." *College Composition and Communication* 56 (2005): 654–87. Print.

Grant-Davie, Keith. "Rhetorical Situations and Their Constituents." *Rhetoric Review* 15 (1997): 264–79. Print.

Harris, Joseph. *A Teaching Subject: Composition Since 1966*. Logan: Utah State UP, 2012. Print.

Haswell, Richard. *Gaining Ground in College Writing: Tales of Development and Interpretation*. Dallas, TX: Southern Methodist UP, 1991. Print.

Hesse, Douglas. "CCCC Chair's Address: Who Owns Writing?" *College Composition and Communication* 57 (2005): 335–57. Print.

Macrorie, Ken. *Uptaught*. Rochelle Park, NJ: Hayden, 1970. Print.

Miller, Carolyn R. "Genre as Social Action." *Quarterly Journal of Speech* 70 (1984): 151–67. Print.

Miller, Susan. *Textual Carnivals*. Carbondale: Southern Illinois UP, 1991. Print.

—. "Writing Studies as a Mode of Inquiry." *Rhetoric and Composition as Intellectual Work*. Ed. Gary Olson. Carbondale: Southern Illinois UP, 2002. 41–54. Print.

Murray, Donald. "The Listening Eye: Reflections on the Writing Conference." *College English* 41.1 (1979): 13–18. Print.

National Commission on Writing. *The Neglected "R": The Need for a Writing Revolution*. New York: College Entrance Examination Board, 2003. Print.

—. *Writing: A Ticket to Work . . . Or a Ticket Out: A Survey of Business Leaders*. New York: College Entrance Examination Board, 2004. Print.

North, Stephen M. *The Making of Knowledge in Composition: Portrait of an Emerging Field*. Portsmouth, NH: Heinemann, 1987. Print.

Perrin, Daniel, and Marc Wildi. "Statistical Modeling of Writing Processes." *Traditions of Writing Research*. Ed. Charles Bazerman, Robert Krut, Karen Lunsford, Susan McLeod, Suzie Null, Paul Rogers, and Amanda Stansell. London: Routledge, 2010. 378–93. Print.

Petraglia, Joseph. "Introduction: General Writing Skills Instruction and its Discontents." *Reconceiving Writing, Rethinking Writing Instruction*. Mahwah, NJ: Erlbaum, 1996. xi–xvii. Print.

Russell, David R. "Activity Theory and its Implications for Writing Instruction." *Reconceiving Writing, Rethinking Writing Instruction*. Ed. Joseph Petraglia. Mahwah, NJ: Erlbaum, 1996. 51–78. Print.

—. *Writing in the Academic Disciplines: A Curricular History*. 2nd ed. Carbondale: Southern Illinois UP, 2002. Print.

—. "Writing in Multiple Contexts: Vygotskian CHAT Meets the Phenomenology of Genre." *Traditions of Writing Research*. Ed. Charles Bazerman, Robert Krut, Karen Lunsford, Susan McLeod, Suzie Null, Paul Rogers, and Amanda Stansell. London: Routledge, 2010. 353–64. Print.

Shaughnessy, Mina P. *Errors & Expectations: A Guide for the Teacher of Basic Writing*. New York: Oxford UP, 1977. Print.

Smit, David W. *The End of Composition Studies*. Carbondale: Southern Illinois UP, 2007. Print.

Tate, Gary, Amy Rupiper, and Kurt Schick. *A Guide to Composition Pedagogies*. New York: Oxford UP, 2001. Print.

Wardle, Elizabeth. "'Mutt Genres' and the Goal of FYC: How Can We Help Students Write the Genres of the University?" *College Composition and Communication* 60 (2009): 765– 88. Print.

Williams, Joseph M. "The Phenomenology of Error." *College Composition and Communication* 32.2 (1981): 152–68. Print.

5 What Is *ESL*?

Gail Shuck

INTRODUCTION: ONE POPULATION OR MANY?

Much has been said about the diversity in the population we often refer to as *ESL students*. Although the bulk of the research on second-language writing in the 1980s and 90s was concerned mostly with international students with visas to study in the US, significant attention in the last decade has been paid to an important distinction between international students and US-resident learners of English. Several books have been written about resident linguistic minority students (Harklau, Losey, and Siegal; Ferris; Kanno and Harklau; Roberge, Siegal, and Harklau) and the ways in which their needs as writers differ from the needs of international students (see also Reid; Matsuda and Matsuda). Several special issues of the *Journal of Second Language Writing* have been devoted to early childhood and adolescent second-language writing as well, and disciplinary links have been made in recent years with bilingual education (Edelsky and Shuck). In fact, the complexity that is the ESL population is so rich and intricate that I am tempted to use scare quotes every time I use the word *population*. After all, many multilingual learners of English have far more in common with native English speakers/writers than they do with other learners of English.[1] For now, however, I'll frame this paper with a summary of who multilingual students are. We're talking about:

- International students (holding visas to study in the US) who studied English but never used it for real communication.
- International students who studied in an intensive English program in the US or another English-dominant country.

- International students who spoke English at home or school or work in their native countries (one prominent example, Min-Zhan Lu, has written poignantly about her family's use of English at home before and during the Cultural Revolution in China; Suresh A. Canagarajah [*Resisting*] has painted a complex picture of the use of—and resistance to— English in Sri Lanka).
- Transnational students who spend significant educational time in two or more countries.
- US-born students who speak a language other than (more often, in addition to) English at home and might be English-dominant, L1-dominant, or fully bilingual.
- Immigrants who came to the US as children or teens (with varying degrees of proficiency in English and in their parents' languages, and varying degrees of literacy in any language).
- Adult immigrants (with similarly varying language and literacy expertise).
- Refugees—quite different in some critical ways from immigrants—who used or studied English in at least one other country before arriving in the US—for example:
    - ○ many of Boise State University's Nepali refugee students attended English-medium schools in Bhutan, Nepal, or India;
    - ○ some refugees from Iraq may have been interpreters for the US military before being displaced (but had little to no opportunity to develop advanced English literacy);
    - ○ some refugees from Sudan or Somalia fled to Kenya, where English is a primary public language;
    - ○ some refugees from Bosnia and Albania lived in Germany for some time and attained fairly high levels of English in public schools there.
- Refugees who had never used or studied English at all before coming to this country.
- Refugees whose first languages aren't written.
- Students who feel very strongly that they're English learners and are thankful for ESL programs.
- Students who feel they've "graduated" from ESL programs.
- Us (I'm not waxing metaphorical here—it's important to remember that many WPAs are also L2 users of English) .

No single label that has been used to describe this "population" can encompass all of the students we're talking about. We have *ELL*

(English language learner), *ESOL* (English for speakers of other languages, which is more appropriate for naming programs than naming students), *multilingual, bilingual, ESL, nonnative speaker, Generation 1.5, EAL* (English as an additional language), *second-language* (L2) *writer, English learner*, and even more. Students differ from each other along several dimensions with respect to English proficiency, none of them deterministic. Primary factors in students' acquisition of English include age upon arrival in the US, differential support for first-language literacy, differential access to educational opportunities, more or fewer opportunities to communicate with others in multiple languages in and out of school, previous experiences with English outside the US, and sociopolitical relations between learners and native speakers.

And that's only if we focus on *language* identities.

Add to that all of the ways monolingual native English-speaking students differ from each other—interests, political persuasions, personalities, social groups, current work situations, family obligations. What about students' identities *as* students? What kinds of educational and career aspirations do they have? All of this richness disappears when we conceive of multilingual students as primarily the sum of their troubles with English.

When answering the question "What Is ESL?" then, we must ask not just who ESL students are but also what the *consequences* are of naming, identifying, dividing students by language background. Then we must also ask this: What are the consequences of *not* naming, identifying, dividing students by language background? Why not take the common stance of focusing only on differences at an individual level? Why do we need to label anyone? Can't we create programs that work for all students without worrying about whether they're multilingual or monolingual?

While it's tempting to think that it doesn't matter what someone's native language is, doing so does not serve all students equally and effectively. There are still significant differences between native and nonnative English speakers in writing processes, appropriate placement options, instructional choices, and professional development issues that writing program faculty and administrators should take into account. Ignoring such differences almost always results in a privileging of native English writers—the unspoken norm—and an erasing of the needs of all multilingual writers but those who are perfectly or nearly fluent in English. We should, then, pay attention to all of the

ways in which composition has tacitly imagined itself as serving monolingual, English-speaking students (Horner and Trimbur; Matsuda,
"Myth") and replace this monolingual norm with a multilingual one
that accounts for such vast linguistic diversity from the start.

From this multilingual perspective, we can talk about what kinds
of strategies WPAs can use to make sure the needs of multilingual
and monolingual students alike are being met. The endless variation
in the population that we've historically called "ESL" was one of the
most important reasons why I named the programs that I developed at
Boise State "English Language Support Programs." Rather than label
students (inaccurately or at least in ways that students don't use to
describe themselves), I wanted the name of the program to describe
what we *do*.

That's really the crux of what "ESL" is. "ESL" is not a clearly identifiable group of students who have similar characteristics. Nor is it a list
of common grammar "troublespots" or exotic rhetorical conventions.
It's a lens through which we can see our work. It's a set of practices—
things we *do*—that increase educational opportunities and success for
all students, regardless of language background.

I urge WPAs, then, to think first from a multilingual perspective,
rather than imagining a monolingual population from the start and
only later realizing that they need to consider how their placement
procedures, curricula, faculty development avenues and topics, and
even scheduling decisions will have an impact on multilingual students. If we imagine multilingual classrooms as the norm, our whole
framework shifts.

In my 2006 WPA article, I described two primary directions for
providing English language support for multilingual writers, namely,
educating students (providing tutoring and cross-cultural course options) and *educating faculty* (workshops, cross-cultural teaching opportunities, and individual consulting). What I neglected to highlight
then was the need for partnerships across the institution (and indeed,
across institutions). As Coordinator of English Language Support Programs, I have an administrative role separate from that of our director
of first-year composition. That need for relationship-building between
academic and administrative units has become especially urgent as the
number of international students at our university has grown dramatically and has included more students with lower English proficiency
levels than we had seen before. You know the story: Administrators are

excited about the revenue that full-tuition-paying international students bring and are compensating for lower enrollments among domestic students by recruiting heavily abroad. To meet the challenges brought on by these increasing numbers, my colleagues in First-Year Writing, English Language Support, Admissions, and other campus units have worked more collaboratively than ever to develop creative solutions. Most transformative among them, although perhaps not terribly creative, has been a close structural relationship between our First-Year Writing Program office (Director, Associate Director, and Administrative Assistant) and the English Language Support Programs office (Coordinator and Assistant Coordinator). We work together to provide opportunities for faculty development, choose and schedule instructors for cross-cultural sections of first-year writing, strategize about other curricular structures that serve multilingual students most effectively, offer informed advice to multilingual students, and make sure that placement procedures account for those students' needs. We have also worked together with the registrar's office, Advising and Academic Enhancement, the (non-credit) Intensive English Program, and International Student Services to discuss how best to reach as many students in need of language support as we can. Although our particular challenges might have shifted, the lens through which I see these challenges remains the same.

DIVERSITY OF STUDENTS, DIVERSITY OF OPTIONS

What can language support look like? Writing programs come in lots of shapes and sizes, of course, and can address the needs of such an enormously diverse population in a variety of ways. Before I focus on two initiatives that I feel are particularly important, I would like to point out that the common curricular structure of offering parallel sequences of first-year composition (FYC)—one "mainstream" sequence and one sequence for multilingual students, which meets the English composition requirement—provides an important opportunity for students to self-identify, as long as the placement process is equitable (see below; see also Royer and Gilles, this volume) and students have the option to choose which sequence they want to be in.

I would like to highlight here a less common approach: cross-cultural classes (see also Shuck). Cross-cultural classes provide multilingual students with opportunities to be integrated into the regular curriculum while getting instructional support from an instructor who is prepared to work with multilingual students (Matsuda and Silva). At Boise State, we have set aside seats in several sections of FYC and closely monitored enrollments in an attempt to have at least a 50:50 ratio of nonnative to native English speakers. More and more instructors are now requesting these classes, hoping to encourage cross-cultural interactions and expand their pedagogical repertoires. Cross-cultural curricula are not limited to composition courses. Other departments on campus, including communication, foundational studies (an integrated general education program), literacy, theatre arts, and math have begun offering either multilingual-only or cross-cultural sections of their first-year courses as well.

No matter which departments offer cross-cultural sections, the academic landscape shifts significantly when such classes are available and when the pedagogies in those classes systematically consider the wide-ranging linguistic and cultural backgrounds of the students. No longer is the focus on English deficiency; suddenly, the cross-cultural courses are the cool ones. I now teach a first-year linguistics class, Language in Human Life, which in its current iteration has sixteen English learners and seven native English speakers in it (see discussion of learning community, below). On the first day, there were an additional five *native* English speakers sitting in, hoping for permission to enroll. All twenty-three enrolled in the class have the chance to reflect on the nature of language, drawing on knowledge right there in the room from seventeen languages besides English. They have internalized the value of language diversity, as Canagarajah (*Critical*) has advocated, embracing difference as a resource.

In addition to cross-cultural classes, Boise State has recently implemented a "fast-track" learning community for multilingual students, blending a linked-course model for supporting ESL students and a studio model for mainstreaming developmental writers (Adams, Miller and Roberts; Mlynarczyk and Babbit; Murie and Fitzpatrick; Rodby and Fox; Smoke). Mainstreaming students in such programs avoids stigmatization, decreases time to degree, fosters a sense of community, and offers extra support for the students who need it. Many of our new international students in the last year or two place into the lowest of three levels of ESL writing and do not have nearly the vocabulary or grammatical repertoire to handle the required FYC course (English 101). The reading and writing tasks even in the "regular" developmental writing course are simply overwhelming for them. That three-level ESL sequence still exists as an option, and students get credit for it (a key principle—see Silva, and the "CCCC Statement on Second Language Writing and Writers"), but many students want to speed up their entry into FYC. The pilot learning community links three credit-bearing courses as corequisites, with the three instructors meeting periodically and sharing assignments and readings:

- Academic English Writing for Speakers of Other Languages, Level III (after which students who pass will enroll in English 101);
- Language in Human Life (a cross-cultural, requirement-fulfilling course);
- and a Multilingual Writers' Studio—which assists students with the reading and writing they are doing in the other two courses.

The exception to our rule that students must co-enroll in all three is that Language in Human Life also has a few seats available to native English speakers.

This learning community model is not new, but it was the urgency of providing these newer, less proficient students with manageable courses that led me to partner with the multiple offices needed to make it happen: the Intensive English Program, the First-Year Writing Program, Advising and Academic Enhancement, the registrar's office, International Student Services, and the Testing Center. Such linkages require forging partnerships across campus, but don't require additional funding. Two of the courses already existed, and the studio simply replaced one section of the Level 1 ESL course, which students are trying to avoid, anyway. With the recent push to eliminate "remediation," I believe we will have support in funding this program in a sustainable way if we can demonstrate its success. I have no doubt that we can.

It is important to be aware that providing a variety of course options is not sufficient for supporting multilingual students. We offer one-on-one tutoring, which requires a knowledgeable faculty/staff member to coordinate the program, and a pool of knowledgeable, paid tutors (ours are undergraduates who have demonstrated patience, cultural sensitivity, and some education in applied linguistics). This support is in addition to the outstanding work that our writing center directors do to educate their consultants on second-language issues; they have built such preparation into their tutor training course. We have also partnered with several departments and units to place a peer tutor or teaching assistant in several courses, whose work can benefit both native and nonnative English speakers. This is an important reminder that what starts out as an ESL strategy might just become a regular form of support for all students.

LINGUISTICALLY INCLUSIVE PLACEMENT

Once multiple curricular options are in place for multilingual English learners, the procedures used for placement should have a mechanism for identifying English learners (including self-identification), primarily to avoid the too-common phenomenon of placing highly literate international students into developmental writing courses because of their performance on a native speaker-oriented test like Compass or ACCUPLACER or the SAT. This is tricky, though. International students are an identifiable population, and the majority of them are indeed second-language learners of English. The simplistic path is to rely on the office of international admissions to funnel all of the international students into an ESL track. However, the majority of the English learners we have on campus are not in fact international students (and not all international students are L2 learners of English). So a placement process whose primary means of identifying English learners is to divide the resident students from the international students is highly likely to be inaccurate at best and exclusionary at worst. Since we cannot and should not segregate multilingual learners, then, from the "mainstream" population, placement procedures have to take them into account.

If your institution has a directed self-placement process (see Royer and Gilles, this volume), advisors or online resources need to have enough information to guide students toward appropriate options such as the learning community, ESOL testing, and cross-cultural courses. Portfolio placement, for those institutions lucky enough to be able to offer it, is rarely feasible for multilingual students, some of whom came to the US as adults and do not have writing samples to submit, and some of whom are international students whose test-based educational systems did not ask them to produce sustained writing of any kind. For in-house or collaboratively developed direct writing assessments, writing prompts (this includes passages or articles students are asked to respond to) should account for a variety of cultural backgrounds.

That requires having faculty with experience working with second-language writers play a role in at least offering feedback on prompts. As for evaluating placement essays, it is quite possible to have readers learn how to evaluate the writing of English learners and to have scoring rubrics that recognize a wide range of ESOL proficiencies. This is one way to disrupt the practice of sending all papers with evidence of second-language errors off to an ESL Department, absolving WPAs of the responsibility for developing a linguistically sensitive set of placement practices.

Then there's mandated standardized testing—the use of ACC-UPLACER, Compass, SAT scores, and the like. As we all know, this is a persistent (and, in many places, intensifying) challenge. What does it mean for English learners? This is one time when some degree of "segregating" can actually be the more equitable option, allowing us to advocate at least for some kind of procedure that was designed for English learners. Few administrators would argue that second-language differences must be completely ignored and that ESL students must take exactly the same tests as native English speakers. However, because pressure still exists from administrators and state-level boards to use standardized tests, a lead faculty member or task force can arm themselves with research in second-language writing assessment practices (Crusan) and advocate for alternatives to those tests. Many of the same arguments apply when WPAs advocate for ethical placement practices for native English speakers, but for nonnative English speakers, it is particularly important to highlight the differences in language acquisition processes, literacy backgrounds, and test-taking experience, all of which can dramatically affect placement outcomes.

FACULTY DEVELOPMENT

In their chapter, "What Is Faculty Development?" in this volume, Carol Rutz and Stephen Wilhoit outline a number of forms of faculty development, which I won't repeat here. The question is: How do you guide faculty in working with multilingual writers if you don't feel like you have the knowledge to do so effectively? Does this mean that you, the WPA, have to be a second-language specialist? Well, yes and no. We should educate ourselves on as many aspects of second-language writing as we can, of course. Paul Kei Matsuda ("Let's Face It") urges WPAs to implement policies and pedagogies that "embrace the presence and needs of second-language writers" (159). One way to do that is to rely on such expertise that might be in your midst already. Writing faculty across the country are among the most creative, dedicated professionals that I personally have ever had the privilege to know. They know things. Even better, they're good at teaching and can share their wisdom with even the most inexperienced (or experienced) WPAs.

Let me give you an example of a recent all-day "TESOL Boot Camp" that Julie Geist Drew, my English Language Support partner, and I facilitated. The name was the brainchild of an adjunct faculty member who teaches developmental writing and, even after a four-part series of discussions of second-language writing, still lacked confidence about working with the ever-growing number of international students who are taking her classes. So we held an all-day workshop at the end of the semester. Eighteen faculty showed up, suggesting that their desire for TESOL-related education is urgent. We had asked workshop-goers to bring assignments that they wanted to revise for a multilingual classroom, and then, as participants talked about their own assignments, it became clear that they were teaching each other, and Julie and I didn't have to do much except type. The TESOL suggestions were actually developed by the "non-experts" in the room.

You can also avail yourself of resources for helping yourself as well as the faculty you work with develop L2 pedagogies. Bringing in outside specialists, if you have the resources, or developing TESOL inquiry groups can be great ways of providing opportunities for developing faculty knowledge about how to teach in multilingual classrooms without your having to be the expert. Build bridges with ESL departments or programs. Put together task forces with members of developmental studies departments, centers for teaching and learning, intensive English programs, and other units on campus. Yes, these things take time; but ultimately, this relationship-building can be one of the most important things you can do to change the landscape for multilingual writers.

CONCLUSION

In their article on the Accelerated Learning Program, Peter Adams, Sarah Gearhart, Robert Miller, and Anne Loomis Roberts describe their developmental courses as "more path than gate" (51). As we try to come up with more and better ways of supporting multilingual students, I often feel torn between wanting to widen and even out the path, on one hand, and building a better gate, on the other. Ideally, we could offer courses across the curriculum in multiple languages, allowing students to develop academic knowledge and literacy in languages other than English. Until then, we have to make sure we provide access to the curriculum for the students we have admitted. That's the question: Do we limit admission to students who have achieved higher levels of English? How high is high enough? How is high enough determined? Are we prepared to rely solely on a single test score for determining whether a student's English is ready for college work? What if we used a more multifaceted means of determining English proficiency—one that seemed fair and valid and reliable? Where would the line be between ready and not ready? We've heard many administrators' and even legislators' takes on "college readiness" as they urge us to keep "remedial" courses out of the university, but they're not usually talking about English language learners, especially because recruiting more international students is apparently so lucrative for the institution. Do the arguments change if we're no longer imagining native speakers of English? What if we're not talking about international students but rather immigrant and refugee English learners on financial aid? Do the arguments change further?

These questions are complex and difficult to answer. As Coordinator of English Language Support Programs, I'm asking them all the time. Fortunately, I'm no longer the "ESL person" (Shuck) charged with solving them all. Also fortunately, the pressure that many US institutions are feeling to provide support for much larger numbers of multilingual students has had some exciting outcomes. One of those is that it's not just ESL specialists thinking about these questions; WPAs are, too. Working together, we might be able to carve out smoother, wider paths, after all.

NOTE

1. My impulse is also to broaden our discussion to include writing program administration in any country and with languages other than English. If we see our work as translingual, an approach that Canagarajah and others (*Literacy*) have drawn attention to, then we should not limit ourselves to English. However, for simplicity's sake (keeping in mind whose interests such simplicity serves), I am after all going to use the United States as the setting and English as the language in question.

WORKS CITED

Adams, Peter, Sarah Gearhart, Robert Miller, and Anne Loomis Roberts. "The Accelerated Learning Program: Throwing Open the Gates." *The Journal of Basic Writing* 28.2 (2009): 50–69. Print.

Canagarajah, A. Suresh. *Critical Academic Writing and Multilingual Students*. Ann Arbor: U of Michigan P, 2002. Print.

—. *Resisting Linguistic Imperialism in English Teaching*. Oxford: Oxford UP, 1999. Print.

—, ed. *Literacy as Translingual Practice: Between Communities and Classrooms*. New York: Routledge, 2013. Print.

"CCCC Statement on Second Language Writing and Writers." Conference on College Composition and Communication: CCCC Position Statement. 2009. Web. 30 Aug 2012.

Crusan, Deborah. *Assessment in the Second Language Writing Classroom*. Ann Arbor: U of Michigan P, 2010. Print.

Edelsky, Carole, and Gail Shuck. "Second Language Writing Research across the Generations: It's All in the Family." Symposium on Second Language Writing. Arizona State University. Tempe, AZ. 7 Nov 2009. Plenary Address.

Ferris, Dana. *Teaching College Writing to Diverse Student Populations*. Ann Arbor: U of Michigan P, 2009. Print.

Harklau, Linda, Kay Losey, and Meryl Siegal, eds. *Generation 1.5 Meets College Composition: Issues in the Teaching of Writing to US-Educated Learners of ESL*. Mahwah, NJ: Erlbaum, 1999. Print.

Horner, Bruce, and John Trimbur. "English Only and US College Composition." *College Composition and Communication* 53 (2002): 594–629.

Kanno, Yasuko, and Linda Harklau, eds. *Linguistic Minority Students Go to College: Preparation, Access, and Persistence*. New York: Routledge, 2012. Print.

Lu, Min-Zhan. "From Silence to Words: Writing as Struggle." *College English* 49 (1987): 437–48. Print.

Matsuda, Aya, and Paul Kei Matsuda. "The Erasure of Resident ESL Writers." *Generation 1.5 in College Composition: Teaching Academic Writing to US-Educated Learners of ESL*. Ed. Linda Harklau, Kay Losey, and Meryl Siegal. New York: Routledge, 2009. Print.

Matsuda, Paul Kei. "Let's Face It: Language Issues and the Writing Program Administrator." *WPA: Writing Program Administration* 36.1 (2012): 141–63. Print.

—. "The Myth of Linguistic Homogeneity in U.S. College Composition." *College English* 68.6 (2006): 637–51. Print.

Matsuda, Paul Kei, and Tony Silva. "Cross-Cultural Composition: Mediated Integration of U.S. and International Students." *Composition Studies* 27 (1999): 15–30. Print.

Mlynarczyk, Rebecca, and Marcia Babbitt. "The Power of Academic Learning Communities." *–The Journal of Basic Writing* 21.1 (2002): 71–89. Print.

Murie, Robin, and Renata Fitzpatrick. "Situating Generation 1.5 in the Academy: Models for Building Academic Literacy and Acculturation." *Generation 1.5 in College Composition: Teaching Academic Writing to US-Educated Learners of ESL.* Ed. Mark Roberge, Meryl Siegal, and Linda Harklau. New York: Routledge, 2009. 153–69. Print.

Reid, Joy. "'Eye' Learners and 'Ear' Learners: Identifying the Language Needs of International Student and US Writers." *Grammar in the Composition Classroom: Essays on Teaching ESL for College-Bound Students.* Ed. Patricia Byrd and Joy Reid. New York: Heinle, 1998. 3–17. Print.

Roberge, Mark, Meryl Siegal, and Linda Harklau, eds. *Generation 1.5 in College Composition: Teaching Academic Writing to US-Educated Learners of ESL.* New York: Routledge, 2009. Print.

Rodby, Judith, and Tom Fox. "Basic Work and Material Acts: The Ironies, Discrepancies, and Disjunctures of Basic Writing and Mainstreaming." *The Journal of Basic Writing* 19.1 (2000): 84–99. Print.

Shuck, Gail. "Combating Monolingualism: A Novice Administrator's Challenge." *WPA: Writing Program Administration* 30.1–2 (2006): 59–82. Print.

Silva, Tony. "On the Ethical Treatment of ESL Writers." *TESOL Quarterly* 31 (1997): 359–63. Print.

Smoke, Trudy. "Mainstreaming Writing: What Does This Mean for ESL Students?" *Mainstreaming Basic Writers: Politics and Pedagogies of Access.* Ed. Gerri McNenny. Mahwah, NJ: Erlbaum, 2001. 197–217. Print.

6 What Are Writing Across the Curriculum and Writing in the Disciplines?

Martha A. Townsend

At their simplest, WAC (writing across the curriculum) and WID (writing in the disciplines) refer to the notion that writing cannot be taught and learned at one time, in one or two courses at one level of education, once and for all. In other words, students cannot be taught, or learn, to be "good writers" in high school, so that they arrive in college fully prepared for the demands of college-level writing. Likewise, college students cannot be taught, or learn, writing in one or two semesters of first-year composition such that they are prepared for all levels of college writing. Ideally, the teaching and learning of writing occurs across and throughout a student's entire educational career. Many would extend that to an individual's life, acknowledging that we all continue to "learn to write" throughout our personal and professional lives, even after our formal education is complete.

In its more complex terms, WAC/WID is one of the most intellectually fascinating, rewarding, and vibrant subdisciplines within rhetoric and composition—a universe of ideas, inquiries, actions, practices, and research wherein writing scholars could spend a happy lifetime working beyond the halls and walls of traditional English departments. (WAC/WID is often shortened for simplicity's sake to just WAC, thereby subsuming WID and its companion concepts CAC or CXC [communication across the curriculum], and ECAC [electronic communication across the curriculum]).

Initially I'd expected, as Kelly Ritter does in her opening chapter, to address this chapter primarily to first-year composition WPAs and secondarily to writing center WPAs. I wanted to assume that WAC

WPAs would already know most of what I'm going to say. Alas, I've encountered WAC WPAs over the years who were appointed or recruited without extensive background in this dynamic area, so if this applies to you, not to worry. Welcome aboard.

A BIT OF HISTORY

First and foremost, WAC is a pedagogical reform movement, with roots both in the United States and the United Kingdom. (I'll elaborate on WID in due course.) The phrase "writing across the curriculum" traces to research conducted on "language across the curriculum" by James Britton and colleagues from 1966 to 1971 at the University of London Institute of Education. Their report, *The Development of Writing Abilities (11–18)*, is one of WAC's founding documents. WAC's foremost US historian, David R. Russell, traces WAC's American origins to the 1960s as well (*Writing* 272). In addition to national forces operating at the time, Russell notes foreign influences, especially the 1966 Dartmouth Seminar, which brought together National Council of Teachers of English (NCTE) leaders and their UK counterparts, including James Britton.[1] Close attention to texts from that time shows that scholars on both sides of the pond were reading and citing one another's work. The UK scholars, for example, cite Janet Emig's *The Composing Process of Twelfth Graders*, while Emig cites Britton's *Language and Learning* in her essay "Writing as a Mode of Learning," which is seminal to WAC. Theorists that one or both sides were relying on include Jerome Bruner, Roman Jakobson, A. R. Luria, James Moffett, Jean Piaget, Michael Polanyi, and Lev Vygotsky.[2]

A big part of WAC's appeal in the US lies in our egalitarian approach to higher education and our "fix it" attitude when something is "broken." For example, higher education's open admission policies following the 1960s protests and political upheaval led to large numbers of "underprepared" students enrolling in the nation's colleges and universities (Shaughnessy). Likewise, declining test scores, increased workplace expectations, and the popular press—notably *Newsweek's* infamous "Why Johnny Can't Write" exposé—contributed to the perception of a national literacy "crisis." All of these helped WAC emerge as one solution to the "problem."

Early on, WAC enjoyed substantial philanthropic support from government agencies and corporate entities such as the Fund for the

Improvement of Postsecondary Education (FIPSE), the National Endowment for the Humanities (NEH), the Bush Foundation, the Ford Foundation, Exxon, General Motors, Lilly, and Mellon. These organizations offered seed money to help institutions start WAC programs that would address the country's supposed literacy crisis. By the mid-to-late 1980s, however, most donors had shifted their support to newer, more cutting edge initiatives, while WAC, by then no longer seen as new and sexy (if not yet firmly established), was left to carry forward on its own.

What Was WAC Supposed to Accomplish?

Today, with WAC some forty-plus years old and its ideas fairly well established, it's hard to remember that its concepts once seemed somewhat radical. As Russell describes it, WAC "originated as a grassroots effort to improve teaching and learning through writing, without any specific curricular or theoretical agenda" ("Introduction" 12). Britton's project, which Russell describes as providing WAC's intellectual roots, posited that school-based writing could be categorized by three main functions: expressive, or writing to discover; transactional, or writing to bring about an action; and poetic, or writing for creative purposes.

Longtime WAC proponents and practitioners Susan McLeod and Elaine Maimon describe WAC as

> a pedagogical reform movement that presents an alternative to the "delivery of information" model of teaching in higher education, to lecture classes and to multiple-choice, true/false testing. In place of this model, WAC presents two ways of using writing in the classroom and the curriculum: writing to learn and learning to write in the disciplines. (579)

A newer "consensus" definition appears in a report from Chris Thaiss and Tara Porter:

> Writing across the curriculum (WAC) is an initiative in an institution to assist teachers across the disciplines in using student writing as an instructional tool in their teaching. The program strives to improve student learning and critical thinking through writing and to help students learn the writing conventions of their disciplines. (562)

These references to writing in the disciplines give us WID, or writing in the disciplines, often construed as WAC's counterpart. The flip side of WAC's coin, WID has history majors learning the conventions of writing history; political science majors learning the methods of making arguments as political scientists do; engineering majors learning the presentation of text, graphs, charts, and data appropriate to engineering's expectations; and so on. An oversimplified schema, incorporating Britton's work and other descriptors, illustrates a continuum created by WAC and WID:

Table 1

Writing across the curriculum (WAC)	Writing in the disciplines (WID)
Writing-to-learn	Writing-to-communicate
Britton's expressive writing	Britton's transactional writing
Writing as exploratory	Writing as delivery of critical content
Writing as rehearsal	Writing as performance
Private audience	Public audience
Writer-centered	Reader-centered
Low stakes; writing often ungraded	High stakes; writing graded
Correctness relatively unimportant	Correctness extremely important

Genres toward WAC's end of the continuum include journals, learning logs, in-class writing, lab notebooks, and short, informal assignments, while WID examples include position papers, research reports, examinations, and longer formal papers. This admittedly simplistic schema obscures epistemological differences between WAC and WID, which this introductory essay does not delve into. It also belies what can be a rich blend of pedagogical practices and genres, all of which are dependent on the individual instructor's understanding, willingness to experiment, and teaching objectives.

Prior to the advent of WAC, many discipline-based faculty had conceived of writing primarily as a vehicle for students to demonstrate what they had learned via exams or end-of-semester one-draft papers. Writing was the means to an end: assessing what had been learned, so a grade could be assigned. With WAC funding provided by the philanthropic agencies listed above, front-runners like Maimon, McLeod, Toby Fulwiler, Barbara Walvoord, and Art Young offered faculty development workshops for instructors from all disciplines. The advantages of multiple drafts; revision; peer review; shorter, more frequent assignments; problem- or inquiry-based as opposed to topic-based assignments; the importance of explicit expectations for performance and for grading; and an array of other learner-centered ideas gradually became known (see Bean, for example). Instead of writing serving primarily as a way to evaluate what students know, writing became a way for students to learn the content of a field—any field—more meaningfully. It's fair to say that WAC matured in concert with process and post-process theories of writing.

THE "STAGES" OF WAC

WAC's maturation is described, in the first instance by McLeod, as having gone through several "stages." The first, mainly in the 1970s and 1980s, employed workshops, which became an essential feature of the movement. Proponents from within the ranks of composition became adept at presenting their ideas (diplomacy was key) to discipline-based faculty who became aware of ways to teach and use writing in ways they had not previously considered. However, institutional structures and rewards were needed to sustain those efforts. The second stage, then, mainly in the 1980s and 1990s—wherein WAC became "institutionalized" and thus no longer funded by external agencies—saw the implementation of "writing-intensive" course requirements along with programmatic initiatives to support faculty and students, such as enhanced writing centers, trained personnel appointed specifically to consult with faculty in the disciplines, and even (in some places) "rhetoricians in residence" housed in departments whose work focused just on those specific disciplines. This stage is also characterized by a proliferation of research by compositionists and discipline-based faculty, individually and collaboratively. Metaphors commonly applied to the movement and its proponents during various parts of WAC's history include "grassroots," "change agents," and "missionary zeal."

WAC's third stage is still unfolding. Donna LeCourt, taking a Marxist approach, notes that "any WAC work involves initiating both pedagogical and theoretical change" (403). She argues that a critical pedagogy approach informed by cultural studies and poststructural theory could help students "develop a meta-awareness of how disciplinary knowledge impacts them personally" (400). Jessica Yood suggests that present day WAC and composition operate "not as stages but as self-conscious layers of ideas and initiatives, attempting to be everything at once: progressive and progressing, expanding and reflective, locally relevant and globally important." Rather than continuing to think of stages, then, she invokes systems theory to provide "a way to understand the interconnections" that characterize many WAC programs around the country. Kate Ronald's "local" explanation of WAC's third stage for faculty at Miami University involves ongoing discussions between many constituents, longitudinal assessment of student writing, collaborative research on writing, and cross-disciplinary work with the composition program.

However WAC's current moment might be described, perhaps its most exciting development is its nascent move *away* from individually designated "writing-intensive" (or otherwise flagged) courses and *toward* writing that is deliberately embedded throughout a discipline, a degree program, or a department's whole curriculum. Instead of discipline-based writing instruction occurring in labeled, discrete courses, where one course and/or one faculty member in a discipline or a department carries the responsibility for teaching writing, larger units of faculty are now coming together to determine essential connections between programmatic, learning, and writing outcomes. Often tied in productive ways to assessment in the major, this development has been notably influenced by Michael Carter's work.[3]

WHAT'S HAPPENING AND WHERE?

WAC is always local. As an educational movement rather than a specific discipline, WAC's programs and principles are operationalized differently at virtually every institution, depending on resources, personnel, and degree of faculty and administrator acceptance. The WAC movement is also remarkably independent and its practitioners highly resourceful, as seen in the collection of related but separate support systems outlined below.

Although there's been talk of establishing one from time to time, there is no formal WAC organization to which proponents belong. The Conference on College Composition and Communication (CCCC) has remained the professional home for WAC advocates and practitioners, most of whom maintain fairly permeable boundaries between composition and WAC and many of whom are often known professionally for their work on both sides of the field. Chris M. Anson has recently shown the "almost certain influence" of composition scholars on the theory and practice over WAC's early history (17). Based on an analysis of 141 articles in fourteen teaching journals over a twenty-year period, his claim may be cautiously understated; it's difficult to imagine that WAC could have developed *without* the influence of composition scholars. Each CCCC annual gathering offers a number of WAC-related panels, sessions, and the occasional pre- or post-conference workshop.

Lack of an independent, formal organization hasn't kept WAC scholars from convening for regular professional conferences, however. The first three national WAC conferences were mounted by a consortium of schools and, except for one year, the event has continued biennially, each hosted on an *ad hoc* basis by a university with an active WAC program and a commitment to keeping the movement vital. The conference's brief history of dates and hosts shows WAC's persistence and scholarly presence:

> 1993: The Citadel, College of Charleston, Clemson
> 1995: The Citadel, College of Charleston, Clemson
> 1997: The Citadel, College of Charleston, Clemson
> 1999: Cornell
> 2001: Indiana University
> 2002: Rice University
> 2004: University of Missouri
> 2006: Clemson
> 2008: University of Texas at Austin
> 2010: Indiana University
> 2012: Georgia Southern University
> 2014: University of Minnesota (upcoming)

Missouri was the first to elect an overtly international conference theme, and henceforward the conference has billed itself as the International WAC Conference, or IWAC. Because no targeted funds exist to mount the event, each host assumes full responsibility for that year's bottom line. Traditionally, each host institution "pays forward" a portion of its proceeds to the next host to get that year's conference under way. Early in my WAC career, Toby Fulwiler pointed out to me that WAC is a collaborative, cooperative enterprise, with practitioners generously sharing knowledge and resources—generally in the pedagogical realm. In the case of these conferences, WAC conference hosts have lived up to that premise monetarily as well.

The Writing Research Across Borders conference (WRAB) isn't a WAC conference exclusively, but the scholars who attend often present WAC-related research. Begun in 2002 by preeminent WAC scholar Charles Bazerman as the Santa Barbara Conferences on Writing Research, these gatherings feature research on writing that is occurring around the globe. They have generated international collaborations among researchers around the world; two volumes of conference presentations, *Traditions of Writing Research* and *International Advances in Writing Research*, both edited by Bazerman et al.; and a new organization to carry on the conferences—The International Society for the Advancement of Writing Research (ISAWR)—which will host the next conference in Paris in 2014.

Much longer in tenure than the WAC and WRAB conferences is the WAC Network (now also International) founded by Thaiss in 1980. Initially the Network was a paper list of institutions that had WAC programs or wanted to begin them, maintained as a resource for others to know where to find like-minded colleagues. Schools could be added to list by contacting him, and interested parties could obtain a copy, with names and contact information, by forwarding the huge sum of three dollars, which increased to five dollars a whole decade later. In 1981, Thaiss convened a WAC Special Interest Group (SIG) at CCCC, which has been robustly attended for thirty-one consecutive years. Every year, newcomers arrive eager for advice. Attendees break into small discussion groups led by a board of thirteen consultants. Questions and answers fly for a quick hour, conversations ensue, and contacts are made. Not infrequently, campus visits by consultants result.

Thaiss is also the person behind the International WAC/WID Mapping Project, established to ascertain the status of WAC programs, which had been surveyed only once earlier, by McLeod in 1987. With several colleagues, Thaiss and Porter collected data from 2005 through 2008 from almost 1,300 institutions. In McLeod's survey, 38% of the 1,113 US colleges and universities responding had WAC programs. In 2008, 51% of 1,126 US responding institutions reported having WAC programs in place (Thaiss and Porter 563). International data are still to come.

Two refereed journals focus exclusively on WAC issues. *The WAC Journal* originated in 1989 at Plymouth State University as an in-house newsletter for its nascent WAC program. It rather quickly expanded to a refereed publication that serves the WAC population nationwide. Edited for many years by Roy Andrews, *The WAC Journal*, now housed at Clemson with the aid of Parlor Press, is available online at http://wac.colostate.edu/journal/. Another refereed print journal, *Language and Learning Across the Disciplines*, was published from 1994 to 2003. It has morphed into *Across the Disciplines*, which is devoted to language, learning, and academic writing and is now published exclusively online. Both journals have editorial boards comprised of scholars with breadth and depth in the field, and both now have prominent places within the WAC Clearinghouse.

The WAC Clearinghouse is an open-access, educational website supported by Colorado State University, which just celebrated its fifteenth anniversary. Clearinghouse lead editor Mike Palmquist saw the need to collect, organize, house, and make available the growing body of work being done across the country in the name of WAC. His efforts have led to a veritable cornucopia of articles, bibliographies, reference guides, citations, and other resources. Several out-of-print books related to WAC are available for download free of charge at the Clearinghouse. Other new work is being published in conjunction with Parlor Press, occasionally available for free or at minimal cost. The Clearinghouse is a "must check out" site for anyone interested in WAC: http://wac.colostate.edu.

The point is that all of these resources exist independently, without the imprimatur of an official disciplinary body or formal organization, whose participants nonetheless cooperate collegially with one another. WAC is grassroots indeed.

WHERE IS WAC NOW?

Despite concerns voiced by critics,[4] signs abound indicating WAC's vitality. The increase from 38% to 51% of institutions that report having, or wanting to start, WAC programs from 1987 to 2008 is one. The large number of writing-related QEPs (Quality Enhancement Plans) developed or being developed since 2004 in response to SACS

(Southern Association of Colleges and Schools) reaffirmation of accreditation is another. *U.S. News and World Report*'s annual publication *America's Best Colleges*, which since 2003 has included a writing in the disciplines category in the "Programs to Look For" section, is a third. A fourth is the sheer number of scholarly publications focused on writing by faculty in the disciplines: Chris M. Anson and Karla Lyles identify some 537 articles published in discipline-based pedagogical journals between 1986 and 2006 (9). Compared to 141 published in the twenty years immediately prior, WAC seems to have firmly captured the attention of discipline-based faculty—as further evidenced by the continued faculty presence at WAC workshops held around the country.

One final sign is the response I received in putting out a call for panelists for the 2012 IWAC conference in Georgia. Who, I wondered, had recently had an existing WAC program reaffirmed by their institution? Ten WAC directors quickly replied, from small and large institutions, both well-funded and minimally-funded. Together, we mounted what became a double session—"From Resistance to Reaffirmation: A New Trend in WAC/WID?"—in which we described our institutions' favorable responses to WAC and sought to determine whether a trend could be claimed. While I think we all would move cautiously toward any grand claims about WAC's future, especially given current economic constraints nationally, the panel clearly observed interest from many quarters and heard compelling examples of continued support for programs around the country.

Being a WAC WPA

If you're invited to head up a WAC initiative at your institution, should you do it? As one who is extremely satisfied with her WAC career, I enthusiastically recommend the enterprise—keeping these few points in mind:

- There's less resistance to WAC than existed in its early days, but you'll still find yourself explaining and campaigning, to multiple audiences. If interacting with faculty across disciplines, and with administrators at all levels of higher education, intrigues you, you'll have plenty of opportunities.

- There are some fundamental differences between FYC and WAC WPAs. *In general*, FYC WPAs focus on students and curriculum; report to department chairs; and may hold relatively high authority and autonomy with respect to their responsibilities. *In general*, WAC WPAs focus on faculty and faculty development (see Rutz and Wilhoit, this volume); report to a higher level institutional line (perhaps a provost or vice provost for undergraduate studies or academic affairs) as well as to a faculty oversight committee of some sort; and while they will hold authority and autonomy, they must be willing to downplay that authority in favor of maintaining diplomatic relationships with faculty—who are the disciplinary experts for knowledge in their respective fields.
- Assessment (see Harrington, this volume) has always been an issue for WAC WPAs, and although there have been many advances in this area, it's still tricky. Defining exactly what should be assessed is often the issue: the quality of faculty development conducted? Improvement in student writing? In critical thinking? Some combination of these? Or something else? Getting folks to agree on this can be problematic, especially if program goals aren't clearly shared by all. Additionally, because WAC programs vary from one institution to another, comparing programs for assessment purposes (or any other) is murky.
- Administrators may see WAC as an easy, cheap fix to student writing. Faculty are already teaching in their disciplines, so this is just one little thing to add to their jobs, right? Unfortunately, some administrators need constant reminders that support for faculty development, for consultants to work with faculty, for writing centers, and more is just as costly as running FYC. If solid fiscal commitment isn't in place, be very wary.
- Taking on a WAC WPA position pre-tenure can be hugely problematic. If you agree to do this, have clear expectations in place for how your work will be valued (and see Fox and Malenczyk, this volume). Read Debra Frank Dew and Alice Horning's *Untenured Faculty as Writing Program Administrators* and ask lots of questions of current WAC WPAs before you decide.

If after thinking through all this, you're still interested, attend a WAC conference or meet and talk with some WAC WPAs. Most will gladly talk with you; remember, it's part of WAC's ethos to share. If you're looking for writing program administration work that's out of the ordinary realm of FYC, WAC may just be the right home for you, for some time to come. WAC was born in the era of baby boomers, but frankly it's aging a lot better than many boomers are. While many boomers are retiring and looking into long term health care insurance, WAC is showing no signs of slowing down. It's a good time to get into the field; as long-time leaders step aside, there's plenty of room for new ones. The personal and professional rewards can be significant.

NOTES

1. Christiane Donahue at Dartmouth's Institute for Writing and Rhetoric hosted the "2012 Writing Summit" in October to commemorate the forty-fifth anniversary of the original 1966 Dartmouth Seminar.

2. Readers who wish to delve more deeply into WAC's history should consult Russell, *Writing in the Academic Disciplines 1870–1990*; Bazerman et al., "History of the WAC Movement;" and Susan H. McLeod and Margot Iris Soven, *Composing a Community*.

3. Anson's keynote for the 2012 International WAC Conference featured examples of this development. Pam Flash's work at the University of Minnesota is one of the more robust examples of this new model being implemented in a trial basis.

4. WAC has not been without its detractors, particularly with regard to the theory that writing about something helps students learn it. Notably, John M. Ackerman takes WAC/WID advocates to task for ignoring "complexities of cultures, classrooms, assignments, and other media that might equally facilitate learning" (334). His reading of thirty-five studies of writing and learning is that they do *not* provide empirical validation of writing as a mode of learning. Still, rather than "untrack or devalue" WAC advocates (362), he would instead reframe the question: "How, why, and with what consequences do you and your students carry on the work of daily classroom, disciplinary, or everyday practice?" (363). Noting three decades of overwhelming endorsement, Robert Ochsner and Judy Fowler examine more than eighty studies of WAC/WID published between the late 1960s and 2002, concluding that claims on its behalf have been uncritical and uninformed. While identifying WAC's "undeniable strengths," they also find a "general absence of internal debate" (120) and identify areas for dispute: poorly defined terms, lack of attention to modes of learning other than writing, over-reliance on testimonies of success, naïveté about program costs, and no clear indication of the expertise needed to teach writing. At the same time, however, Ochsner and Fowler acknowledge that their response is critical because "so little criticism has been expressed" (130). Both of these studies should be read by anyone entering into WAC work. My own personal

response to these criticisms has long been that WAC's importance to higher education lies more in its contributions to faculty development across the curriculum than in the improvement of student writing *per se*, but that notion warrants explication elsewhere—and careful consideration by any institution considering developing a new program.

WORKS CITED

Ackerman, John M. "The Promise of Writing To Learn." *Written Communication* 10 (1993): 334–70. Print.

Anson, Chris M. "The Intradisciplinary Influence of Composition and WAC, 1967–1986." *The WAC Journal* 21 (2010): 5–19. Print.

Anson, Chris M., and Karla Lyles. "The Intradisciplinary Influence of Composition and WAC, Part Two: 1986–2006." *The WAC Journal* 22 (2011): 7–19. Print.

Bazerman, Charles, Joseph Little, Lisa Bethel, Teri Chavkin, Danielle Fouquette, and Janet Garufis. "History of the WAC Movement." *A Reference Guide to Writing Across the Curriculum*. West Lafayette, IN: Parlor Press, 2005. 14–25. Print.

Bazerman, Charles, Chris Dean, Jessica Early, Karen Lunsford, Suzie Null, Paul Rogers, and Amanda Stansell. *International Advances in Writing Research: Cultures, Places, Measures*. West Lafayette, IN: Parlor Press, 2012. Print.

Bazerman, Charles, Robert Krut, Karen Lunsford, Susan McLeod, Suzie Null, Paul Rogers, and Amanda Stansell. *Traditions of Writing Research*. New York: Routledge, 2010. Print.

Bean, John C. *Engaging Ideas: The Professor's Guide to Integrating Writing, Critical Thinking, and Active Learning in the Classroom*. San Francisco, CA: Jossey-Bass, 2011. Print.

Britton, James. *Language and Learning*. New York: Penguin, 1971. Print.

Britton, James, Tony Burgess, Nancy Martin, Alex McLeod, and Harold Rosen. *The Development of Writing Abilities (11-18)*. London: Macmillan Education, 1975. Print.

Carter, Michael. "Ways of Knowing, Doing and Writing in the Disciplines." *College Composition and Communication* 58.3 (2007): 385–418. Print.

Dew, Debra Frank, and Alice Horning, eds. *Untenured Faculty as Writing Program Administrators: Institutional Practices and Politics*. West Lafayette, IN: Parlor Press, 2007. Print.

Emig, Janet. *The Composing Processes of Twelfth Graders*. Urbana, IL: NCTE, 1971. Print.

—. "Writing as a Mode of Learning." *College Composition and Communication* 28.2 (1977): 122–28. Print.

Fulwiler, Toby. Personal conversation. N.d.

LeCourt, Donna. "WAC as Critical Pedagogy: The Third Stage?" *Journal of Advanced Composition* 16.3 (1996): 389–405. Print.

McLeod, Susan H. "Writing Across the Curriculum: The Second Stage, and Beyond." *College Composition and Communication* 40 (1989): 337–43. Print. Rpt. in *Landmarks in Writing Across the Curriculum*. Ed. David R. Russell and Charles Bazerman. Davis, CA: Hermagoras Press, 1994. 79–86. Print.

McLeod, Susan, and Elaine Maimon. "Clearing the Air: WAC Myths and Realities." *College English* 62 (2000): 573–83. Print.

McLeod, Susan H., and Margot Iris Soven. *Composing a Community: A History of Writing Across the Curriculum*. West Lafayette, IN: Parlor Press, 2006. Print.

Ochsner, Robert, and Judy Fowler. "Playing Devil's Advocate: Evaluating the Literature of the WAC/WID Movement." *Review of Educational Research* 74:2 (2004): 117–40. Print.

Ronald, Kate. "The Howe Writing Initiative and the 'Third Stage' of WAC." n.d. Web. 31 August 2012.

Russell, David R. *Writing in the Academic Disciplines, 1870-1990: A Curricular History*. Carbondale: Southern Illinois UP, 1991. Print.

—. "Introduction: WAC's Beginnings: Developing a Community of Change Agents." *Composing a Community: A History of Writing Across the Curriculum*. Ed. Susan H. McLeod and Margot Iris Soven. West Lafayette, IN: Parlor Press, 2006. 3–15. Print.

Shaughnessy, Mina P. *Errors & Expectations: A Guide for the Teacher of Basic Writing*. New York: Oxford UP, 1977. Print.

Thaiss, Chris, and Tara Porter. "The State of WAC/WID in 2010: Methods and Results of the U.S. Survey of the International WAC/WID Mapping Project." *College Composition and Communication* 61:3 (2010): 534–70. Print.

Palmquist, Mike. *WAC Clearinghouse*. Colorado State University. 1997. Web. 29 March 2013.

Yood, Jessica. "The Next Stage Is a System: Writing Across the Curriculum and the New Knowledge Society." *Across the Disciplines* 2. 12 December 2004. Web. 1 September 2012.

Part 2: Complicating Questions

7 What Is General Education?

Lauren Fitzgerald

A hallmark of American undergraduate institutions, general education is, simply put, made up of requirements outside of the major. More expansively, the Association of American Colleges and Universities (AAC&U), a century-old organization increasingly involved with general education reform over the last thirty years, holds that this part of the curriculum provides "broad learning in multiple disciplines and ways of knowing" ("Liberal"). Whereas courses in the major aim to provide students with disciplinary skills and knowledge, general education courses, as Paul Hanstedt writes in his helpful *General Education Essentials: A Guide for College Faculty*, can have "a wide variety of purposes, ranging from exposing students to different fields, methodologies, or ways of understanding the world to creating opportunities for students to explore the connections and disconnections between different ways of understanding the world" (45).

WPAs should take special interest in general education for two reasons. First, writing is almost universally included in this broad learning at institutions across the country (Allen 34; Warner and Koeppel 246–52), especially in the form of first-year composition (FYC) but also writing across the curriculum (WAC) and writing centers. (See Gladstein and Regaignon for small college exceptions, 13–14, 96.) As a result, general education is one of college writing's many "owners," as Joyce Kinkead points out, with its director or committee often determining "what 'counts'" in this part of the curriculum (197) and influencing writing program budgets, scheduling, staffing, and overall vision. Second, writing is a key feature of the recommendations and policies of important external organizations in higher education, such as the AAC&U and regional accrediting agencies (AAC&U "Written"; Allen 23–26), the latter of which, Kinkead writes, "may specify experiences that students should receive and will also expect evaluation and assessment as part of the writing program" (197). When based on best practices and current research in rhetoric and composition, this influence can align with a WPA's values and lead to helpful reforms; on the other hand, this is not always the case. It pays, then, for WPAs to be aware of what informs general education reforms on our campuses.

As with most aspects of WPA work, such awareness starts with the local, for instance understanding whether (and why) your campus general education program follows a traditional distributive model in which students take a set number of courses from specific disciplines or disciplinary clusters (one from the sciences, two from the humanities, and so on) or a newer integrative model that makes explicit connections among disciplines, whether through individual courses, courses grouped in learning communities, senior capstones, service-learning programs, or portfolios (Hanstedt 12–15). Since WPAs can learn these details only on their home turfs, I have chosen to focus this chapter on what I see as the two other forces we should be aware of. The first looks to the past, to twentieth-century reforms and their impact on college writing instruction—a history that informs what general education is today. The second looks to the present and foreseeable future, to the increasing emphasis on assessment and accountability—particularly as articulated through key external organizations—and how that emphasis will continue to define and constrain WPA work, in both positive and negative ways.

GENERAL EDUCATION AND WRITING INSTRUCTION IN THE TWENTIETH CENTURY

There are three areas of the history of the general education movement that continue to influence writing instruction: (1) its ideological or value-laden aspects, (2) the impact of the communications movement, and, as a result, (3) the questioning of the FYC requirement. I should make clear from the outset that, due to space limitations, the history I offer here is necessarily abbreviated. In addition, it will focus almost exclusively on FYC, in large part because the histories that have been written about college writing instruction and general education's impact on it are themselves almost exclusively focused on FYC. Neal Lerner's *The Idea of a Writing Laboratory* suggests, however, that there is indeed a history of relationships between other kinds of writing programs and general education: for example, situated in a well-known early twentieth-century site of the application of Dewey's instrumentalist philosophy to general education (Miller 79), the University of Minnesota General College Writing Laboratory, founded in 1932, reflected the "hands-on, experimental nature" of the institution and in turn was "a model"—if short lived—"of Deweyan Progressivism that many contemporary writing centers would do well to emulate" (Lerner 31, 89).

This other history of writing instruction and general education has yet to be written, not simply because of the privileging of FYC over writing centers and WAC but because of the complicated institutionalized history of writing in the academy, as suggested by what Yvonne Merrill and Thomas P. Miller (in their own chapter on WPA work and general education) call "maybe the best study of the historical development of general education and writing" (213), David R. Russell's *Writing in the Academic Disciplines: A Curricular History.* Unlike the well-documented rise of FYC in the late nineteenth and early twentieth centuries (Brereton), the forms of writing instruction we would now call WAC and WID were, according to Russell, prevented from taking root until relatively late in the twentieth century because even as academic discourse became dramatically specialized—as unique, disciplinary *discourses*—the development of the modern university was such that faculty remained unaware (willfully or otherwise) of this specialization, hoping instead for the discovery of (or return to) a kind of "academic Esperanto," a wish that general education reform and the development of FYC often enabled (33; see also Downs, this volume).[1]

Traces of such wishful thinking can be found in what is, for many FYC historians, the watershed moment of general education, the publication in 1945 of *General Education in a Free Society* (Harvard Committee), the result of a two-year study by a Harvard general education committee (Miller 134). Kelly Ritter points out that though there were limits to its reach (94–125), the "Redbook," as the report was known, is a convenient lens by which to understand not only central concerns of the mid-twentieth-century general education movement but also the vestiges of these values in twenty-first-century general education programs, including "foregrounding [. . .] broad areas of instruction" and "developing a common two-year liberal arts core" in "a four-year college education," and attempts at "unifying the curriculum, subtly, by institutionally defined morals and ethics" (96).

Such "institutionally defined morals and ethics" indicate that *General Education in a Free Society* (Harvard Committee), like the University of Minnesota General College Writing Laboratory, was hardly value- or ideology-free. According to Gary Miller's useful history, a crucial part of the general education "paradigm" that developed out of the nineteenth-century American college and the research university, and which helps to define it as uniquely American (there is, for example, no equivalent counterpart in European institutions), was the aim of developing in students "the individual and community values associated with a democratic society" (8). Of course, what "democracy" meant over this history was subject to modification. Where it had once, as with Deweyan Progressivism, been "seen as a *process* that encouraged change," after World War Two and during the Cold War, it became "a political ideal that was to be *preserved* in the face of the communist threat," with the focus on "the individual's *responsibility* as a citizen to protect democracy, which was now identified with the *status quo*" (117; see Crowley 162). This latter view is exemplified by the reference to a "Free Society" in the Redbook's official title as well as its concern for the preservation of democracy expressed throughout, which it explicitly links to another locus of general education's democratic impulses, communication. Reflecting what Sharon Crowley holds was a widespread belief among educators that "attributed the onset of the Second World War to a lack of communication—among Americans and between nations" (169), the Harvard report asserts that "Failure of communication between the citizens, or between the government and the public, means a breakdown in the democratic process" (Harvard Committee 68). It is this "rhetoric of war" that, according to Crowley, led to a boom in communications programs and courses, often aligned with general education, in the 1940s (169). The development of general education, then, was as much about producing specific kinds of US citizenry (albeit shifting over time) as it was about promoting broad learning and scholarship.

Moreover, Crowley holds that at many institutions, the armed services had a direct influence on general education and writing instruction through the inclusion of oral communications in composition courses—an unanticipated consequence of which was the displacement of the more traditional use of literary texts that, effectively, "weakened English departments' claim to ownership of the required course by challenging the assumption that literary discourse was its obvious and proprietary subject" (158). As Crowley's observation suggests, the impact of the communications movement on FYC and the field at large can be viewed as beneficial. Similarly, according to Robert J. Connors, this movement shifted a substantial number of mid-century composition textbooks from "static abstractions" to a more "audience-oriented and socially oriented" approach (*Composition-Rhetoric* 289). For Russell, "By encouraging a widespread rethinking of the problems of language instruction," the communications movement ultimately, if indirectly, "led to the WAC movement in the 1970s" (256–57; see also Townsend, this volume). And each of these historians attributes to this movement the interest in rhetoric in the mid-twentieth century (Connors, *Composition-Rhetoric* 160, 204; Crowley 156, 183, 273; Russell 256-57). Perhaps most intriguing is the impact that the communications movement had on the field's professionalization, namely in the founding of the Conference on College Composition and Communication in 1949 (Crowley 182).

But the communications movement also changed FYC, almost to the point of abolishing the course itself if not quite the requirement. Connors notes that Harvard's and other institutions' reaction against what was perceived as the overspecialization of the elective system of the undergraduate curriculum resulting from the rise of the research university "produced widespread withdrawal from the traditional freshman composition course" ("Abolition" 54). As part of this general education reform, the communications movement "proposed to unify what had been separate fields of English and speech by rolling together all four of the 'communication skills'—speaking, listening, reading, and writing." During communications' postwar heyday, "many traditional freshman writing courses were converted into communication courses, often team-taught by English and speech professors" ("Abolition" 54–55).

For the Harvard Committee, however, communications wasn't the solution to "The problem of English composition"—a problem that resulted from composition's "remedial" nature, its lack of a true "subject matter," which therefore "segregate[ed] training in writing from the fields of learning," as well as its focus on "writing literary English or about English literature" (198–99). The committee's solution was to limit the previously yearlong course to one semester and, during the second semester, for "students [. . .] to write frequent themes in connection with their general education course or courses" that would "probably be directed and corrected by the instructors in composition" (200). As Ritter holds, a generous reading would see this plan as a "somewhat forward-thinking [. . .] early version of writing across the curriculum," albeit "without any notion of how that would be supported or enacted" (123). Current FYC directors would no doubt register its many shortcomings, including, through its subordination to general education, the eradication of any disciplinary standing that composition might have had (Ritter 102, 116, 120). As Russell points out, though the resulting course "represented Harvard's first collegewide writing requirement," offered a number of benefits to students, and "was administered by a [general education] committee rather than by the English department," it was taught by TAs and "Composition instruction was still marginalized" through the 1960s when the requirement was dropped (254–55). As with its position in the history of FYC (Brereton), Harvard's contribution to the history of the impact of general education was not always a positive one.

It's important to keep in mind that the intertwined histories of general education and college writing instruction are part of a much larger history of sweeping changes that affected higher education as it shifted from the old college to the modern university at the end of the nineteenth and beginning of the twentieth centuries. Indeed, these histories are intertwined because both FYC and general education are responses to these changes; those nostalgic for the old college might well say that they were both attempts to replace what was lost (writing instruction and breadth) when the new, modern university emerged with its disciplinary specificity and system of electives (Brereton 3, 9; Russell 46–49, 62). As Russell argues,

> Almost from the beginning of the modern university [. . .] there were critics who attacked academic specialization and the narrow compartmentalization of writing instruction. But instead of accepting or confronting specialization, with its thorny rhetorical and political problems, they ignored or sought to transcend it. Reformers from both the left and the right attempted to reestablish an academic community where students and faculty shared a common language, and in many cases, a set of values. "General education" was the single rallying cry of reformers from irreconcilably opposed camps. Predictably, the reformers did not succeed in building a unified academic discourse community, but they did reinforce the

myth of transience by nurturing the assumption that the linguistic millennium would soon come, if only academia would adopt some particular form of general education. (25)

GENERAL EDUCATION AND WRITING INSTRUCTION IN THE TWENTY-FIRST CENTURY

Needless to say, this linguistic millennium has not come to pass. Moreover, many of us continue to confront the problems exemplified by the Harvard Redbook. For example, Yvonne Merrill and Thomas P. Miller report an episode at their institution resembling the solution the Harvard Committee devised for the "problem of English composition"—that it be replaced by "a core curriculum where composition requirements (and resources) would be dispersed into a writing-across-the-curriculum program" (204), and which, like the Harvard plan, was poorly conceived and threatened the autonomy and disciplinarity of writing instruction. As before, "Administrators often want to take a public stand to improve undergraduate education," Merrill and Miller warn, "and writing instruction can appear to be the place to make a stand because there is nothing more general and nothing more generally criticized" (204).

More pervasive, in part because they take the form of what Russell so aptly calls the "god term" of general education (23), are the ideological values of this reform. Since higher education outside of the US usually focuses on the depth and specificity of disciplines, even our emphasis on breadth says something uniquely American about what we expect a college education to do (Miller 8–32). We can see these values too in the shift from "general" to "liberal" education, the latter of which, according to Hanstedt, also signals a specific kind of citizenry, "people who are independent and flexible in their thinking and capable of responding to the demands of a changing world in civic-minded, deliberate ways" (2). AAC&U takes this civic-mindedness one step further, holding that "A truly liberal education [. . .] fosters [. . .] an acceptance of responsibility for the ethical consequences of our ideas and actions" ("Statement"). Not, of course, that such values are bad. Because many WPAs also support them, they can make for good partnerships between writing and general (or liberal) education programs. Merrill and Miller, for instance, argue that the "civic dimensions" of general education "can be enriched" by the "experiential learning, collaborative inquiry, and deliberate problem solving" of FYC (209). Moreover, as they tell it, such willingness to partner on these grounds helped them avoid the abolition of their program. But good or bad, general (liberal) education always brings with it certain values, and it is important for WPAs to know what they are.

In addition, the mid-twentieth-century call to "roll together" writing with other communications "skills" continues to resonate in this century. As evidenced by WPAs' recent involvement in communications across the curriculum (CAC or CXC) programs around the country, this linkage can prove beneficial. However, what might well give a WPA pause are pressures applied by external organizations, though, in contrast to the "communications skills episode" Crowley documents, they seem to be less well armed than the US military (155). Accrediting agencies such as the Western Association of Schools and Colleges (WASC) and the Middle States Commission on Higher Education[2] include writing skills under the larger "communications" umbrella (Allen 23–27) as AAC&U often does (see, for example, *Communicating* 2–3, 9). A recent discussion on WPA-L, a listserv for writing program administrators, shows once again that such "rolling together" can have potentially negative consequences. One poster from Texas worried about the autonomy of his institution's two-course composition requirement in the face of a new state-mandated curriculum, which, apparently following AAC&U's lead, requires communications but not composition, thus leaving the current requirement vulnerable to competition from other communications-offering disciplines ("Texas").

Where external agencies, particularly regional accrediting agencies, have more extensive influence is with assessment and accountability. These agencies determine only *that* undergraduate institutions should offer general education programs not *what* the programs should consist of (Allen 23; Warner and Koeppel 242). However, they do mandate "that general education programs, like other academic programs, undergo rigorous assessment to determine if they accomplish their stated goals and objectives" (Warner and Koeppel 256n). In turn, these assessment pressures can impact writing programs and WPAs. As Peggy O'Neill, Cindy Moore, and Brian Huot suggest, because of the increasing pressure on higher education institutions "to demonstrate the quality of their programs," the composition director shouldn't be surprised "to be included in institutional assessment" (1; see also Harrington, this volume). Again, this isn't necessarily a bad situation to be in: such involvement can showcase your program and the good work it is doing and, as a result, garner more support. It can also help you steer the larger conversation. As O'Neill, Moore, and Huot put it, "administrators, knowing little about accreditation themselves, will interpret accrediting agency language more narrowly than it should be interpreted—and they just need a department chair or program director who is more knowledgeable to explain why the interpretation can be broader" (78; see Comfort et al.; Merrill and Miller). WPAs at institutions undergoing general education reform might especially listen for references to transfer and skills: As Elizabeth Wardle explains in this volume, both terms tend to be symptomatic of "basic but frequently unexamined assumptions,"—including that learning to write is "a simple matter of skill acquisition and that such a skill, once acquired, should be easily usable in another setting or when completing another task, no matter how different that setting or task might be." It is important to be on guard for such "unexamined assumptions" in order to steer stakeholders in the right direction, as much as possible.

General education reform, then, can provide the means by which to build programs that support writing in ways that align with our own professional values. At my institution, for example, general education reform made possible the revision of our composition sequence, which many of us had long wanted but could not execute as long as our institution remained locked in a general education curriculum that was over three-quarters of a century old. The curriculum revision allowed us to reconfigure our two, two-credit composition courses housed in the English Department as a three-credit first-year composition course housed in English followed by a three-credit writing-intensive first year seminar taught throughout the disciplines. As a result, in contrast to the previous sequence, which was taught by a mix of adjuncts and full-time faculty, all of the courses in the new first-year sequence are taught by full-time faculty, many tenure stream (see Steinberg). Though this plan would not work at many institutions, it does at ours because of our small size and focus on undergraduate teaching. Moreover, benefits of this change extend beyond the first-year sequence to more sustainable WAC and WID discussions, to the kinds of writing students bring with them to the Writing Center, and to the prior writing experiences of our undergraduate tutors.

But I should add that these benefits did not occur by accident. Our campus WPAs and writing faculty were leaders in this curriculum revision from the start, made possible in part by the relatively large size and political clout of our department. Further, as testimony to O'Neill, Moore, and Huot's observations, I was asked to serve as coordinator of this curriculum review precisely because of my prior experience as Composition Director and knowledge of curriculum development and assessment that I had first gained through my involvement with the Council of Writing Program Administrators (CWPA). In other words, general education reform and writing program administration can make for very good partnerships, but they require access, involvement, and effort.

NOTES

1. By the early 1990s, however, Susan H. McLeod could report that nearly half of all postsecondary educational institutions had WAC programs, many of which functioned by way of writing-designated general education requirements (1, 5). More recently, Rita Malenczyk reports that such designations may be on the wane as WAC programs "run up against general education reform" and "WAC directors are deciding that it is in the best interests of both their students and their programs to acknowledge the places where the two intersect, even if that means making writing less obviously visible than it had once been" (97). See also Townsend, this volume.

2. Other accrediting agencies include the New England Association of Schools and Colleges, the North Central Association of Schools and Colleges, the Northwest Commission on Colleges and Universities, and the Southern Association of Schools and Colleges.

WORKS CITED

Allen, Mary J. *Assessing General Education Programs*. San Francisco, CA: Anker/Jossey-Bass, 2006. Print.

Association of American Colleges and Universities (AAC&U). *Communicating Commitment to Liberal Education: A Self-Study Guide for Institutions*. Washington, DC: Association of American Colleges and Universities. 2006. Web. 20 August 2012.

—. "Statement on Liberal Learning." 1998. Web. 20 August 2012.

—. "Liberal Education and America's Promise (LEAP): What is a 21st Century Liberal Education?" n.d. Web. 20 August 2012.

—. "Written Communication Value Rubric." n.d. Web. 20 August 2012.

Brereton, John C., ed. *The Origins of Composition Studies in the American College, 1875–1925: A Documentary History.* Pittsburgh, PA: U of Pittsburgh P, 1995. Print.

Comfort, Juanita Rodgers, Karen Fitts, William B. Lalicker, Chris Teutsch, and Victoria Tischio. "Beyond First-Year Composition: Not Your Grandmother's General Education Composition Program." *WPA: Writing Program Administration* 26.3 (2003): 67–86. Print.

Connors, Robert J. "The Abolition Debate in Composition: A Short History." *Composition in the Twenty-First Century: Crisis and Change.* Ed. Lynn Z. Bloom, Donald A. Daiker, and Edward M. White. Carbondale: Southern Illinois UP, 1996. 47–63. Print.

—. *Composition-Rhetoric: Backgrounds, Theory, and Pedagogy.* Pittsburgh, PA: U of Pittsburgh P, 1997. Print.

Crowley, Sharon. *Composition in the University: Historical and Polemical Essays.* Pittsburgh, PA: U of Pittsburgh P, 1998. Print.

Gladstein, Jill M., and Dara Rossman Regaignon. *Writing Program Administration at Small Liberal Arts Colleges.* Anderson, SC: Parlor Press, 2012. Print.

Hanstedt, Paul. *General Education Essentials: A Guide for College Faculty.* San Francisco, CA: Jossey-Bass, 2012. Print.

Harvard Committee on the Objectives of a General Education in a Free Society. *General Education in a Free Society.* Cambridge, MA: Harvard UP, 1945. Rpt. 1955. Internet Archive Universal Library. n.d. Web. 20 August 2012.

Kinkead, Joyce. "How Writing Programs Support Undergraduate Research." *Developing and Sustaining a Research-Supportive Curriculum: A Compendium of Successful Practices.* Ed. Kerry K. Karukstis and Timothy E. Elgren. Washington, DC: Council on Undergraduate Research, 2007. 195–208. Print.

Lerner, Neal. *The Idea of a Writing Laboratory.* Carbondale: Southern Illinois UP, 2009. Print.

Malenczyk, Rita. "WAC's Disappearing Act." *Exploring Composition Studies: Sites, Issues, and Perspectives.* Ed. Kelly Ritter and Paul Kei Matsuda. Logan: Utah State UP, 2012. 89–104. Print.

McLeod, Susan H. "Writing Across the Curriculum: An Introduction." *Writing Across the Curriculum: A Guide to Developing Programs.* Ed. Susan H. McLeod and Margot Soven. Newbury Park, CA: Sage, 1992. Rpt. in WAC Clearinghouse Landmark Publications in Writing Studies: 2000. *The WAC Clearinghouse.* 23 August 2000. Web. 20 August 2012.

Merrill, Yvonne, and Thomas P. Miller. "Making Learning Visible: A Rhetorical Stance on General Education." *The Writing Program Administrator's Resource: A Guide to Reflective Institutional Practice.* Ed. Stuart C. Brown and Theresa Enos. Mahwah, NJ: Erlbaum, 2002. 203–17. Print.

Miller, Gary. *The Meaning of General Education: The Emergence of a Curriculum Paradigm*. New York: Teacher's College, 1988. Print.

O'Neill, Peggy, Cindy Moore, and Brian Huot. *A Guide to College Writing Assessment*. Logan: Utah State UP, 2009. Print.

Ritter, Kelly. *To Know Her Own History: Writing at the Women's College, 1943–1963*. Pittsburgh, PA: U of Pittsburgh P, 2012. Print.

Russell, David R. *Writing in the Academic Disciplines: A Curricular History*. 2nd ed. Carbondale and Edwardsville: Southern Illinois UP, 2002. Print.

Steinberg, Gillian. "Contingent Faculty Labor Practices in the Yeshiva College English Department: A Case Study." *ADE/ADFL Joint Bulletin*. (Forthcoming). Print.

"The Texas and AACU Common Core.". April-May 2012. Web. 20 August 2012.

Warner, Darrell B., and Katie Koeppel, "General Education Requirements: A Comparative Analysis." *Journal of General Education* 58.4 (2009): 241–58. Print.

*Key: Foster convergences b/w writing
Program + mission*

*Issues I have: Mission should not
be "evolving." Hillsdale, St. John's,
+ Dallas don't evolve their
missions. And that's the only
kind of place - that I'd want
to work at.*

8 What Is Institutional Mission? ✓

Elizabeth Vander Lei and Melody Pugh

Most WPAs first wonder about the institutional mission of colleges or universities when they begin applying for jobs. Scanning online documents for hints about the distinctives that they should emphasize, applicants attempt to demonstrate that they are a "good fit" for an institution. During on-campus interviews, candidates refine their sense of the mission of an institution as they listen to how faculty, administrators, and students talk about the institution and the work of the writing program. Once on campus, new WPAs continue to develop their sense of an institution's mission as they take up the practical tasks of running a writing program, tasks such as negotiating budgets with the dean, creating transfer policies, and training teaching assistants.

The term "institutional mission" may feel dated, and legitimately so, since focus on institutional mission arose in the 1970s and 1980s, when economic and cultural changes pressured colleges and universities to enhance their "organizational effectiveness" (Fjortoft and Smart 429; Mayhew 28–29). Nevertheless, it is important for WPAs to explore how institutional mission influences a writing program and, conversely, how a writing program might influence institutional mission, especially in this historical moment of intense attention to outcomes and assessment. Focusing on institutional mission encourages WPAs to look beyond daily crises toward longer-term concerns such as (1) "the relationship between the institution and the outside world," (2) the relationships among "the institution's internal stakeholders," and (3) "an overarching goal toward which any given individual worker can meaningfully direct his or her energies" (Berg, Csikszentmihalyi, Nakamura 45).

As they attempt to understand the mission of their institution, WPAs encounter four complications. First, writing programs exist

105

within the "complex system of postsecondary and secondary education" that includes "four-year liberal arts and comprehensive colleges, community colleges, two-year colleges, and public as well as private universities" (Long 275). Not surprisingly, these institutions host a variety of institutional missions: missions that may be novel to WPAs, or missions that WPAs experience as "a set of written as well as unwritten rules" (Adcroft and Taylor 288). For WPAs who are new faculty members and administrators, the difficulty of discovering and interpreting these rules is compounded by the higher workload that comes with developing new courses and programs and by pre-tenure publication pressures (Adcroft and Taylor 288). Second, "ownership" of institutional mission is typically complex, as Lauren Fitzgerald notes: "Rather than speaking with one voice (if 'voice' is even the right metaphor), institutions 'express' themselves through the multiple, sometimes contradictory, partial (in both senses) voices of various situated and self-interested parties" (142). Third, institutional mission is a constantly moving target: "institutional missions are constantly evolving as colleges and universities respond to threats and opportunities that arise from within and from outside the institution" (Berg, Csikszentmihalyi, Nakamura 44–45). According to Andy Adcroft and David Taylor, institutions of higher education (and, consequently, their missions) are currently being shaped by significant social forces: globalization, economic recession and consequent declines in families' economic status and in state funding, changing ideas about what it means to be in college, and the erosion of the professional status of faculty (288). And fourth, what an institution says about its mission may differ from how its policies and practices operationalize the institutional mission (Delucchi 423).

Despite the difficulties of understanding institutional mission, we are optimistic not only that WPAs can leverage institutional mission to enhance writing programs but also that WPAs can contribute to the continuing evolution of the mission of their institution. A WPA can begin this work by investigating how her or his institution articulates its mission, how it has enacted that mission, and how that WPA can build on an institution's mission.

ARTICULATING INSTITUTIONAL MISSION

As Fitzgerald suggests above, institutional mission is articulated in multiple ways and for multiple purposes. A WPA's earliest encounter with institutional mission will likely come as a result of its direct artic-ulation in the form of administrative documents designed to commu-nicate the institution's values and goals to both internal and external constituencies, to people who are already invested in the long-term success of the institution and to those considering such an investment, such as prospective students, parents, donors, and faculty members. However, Joseph R. Ferrari and Jessica Velcoff point out that these administrative documents typically reflect the ways that institutional mission functions in the day-to-day work of the college or university's "administrative operations, academic programs and policies, and stu-dent services" (243). In other words, WPAs need to understand how institutional mission is shaped by institutional culture, including a school's history, size, social and religious allegiances, and organiza-tional values.

Administrative documents, such as mission statements, offer a logical starting point for WPAs exploring institutional mission be-cause they serve as the "organization's means of publicly proclaiming for critical assessment the institution's objectives, expectations, and values" (Ferrari and Velcoff 243). Formal mission statements—typi-cally two or three sentences—often come packaged with other strate-gic planning documents such as mottoes, goals and objectives, vision statements, and institutional histories. Taken together, these admin-istrative documents carry the "culture, ethos, and ideology" (Swales and Rogers 226) of an institution. Skeptics have typically stereotyped mission statements as an administrative imposition on faculty mem-bers: Because these documents have to reflect the priorities of both internal and external constituencies, they are often made up of stock phrases with little actual significance to the organization of activities at a college or university (Morphew and Hartley 457; Newsom and Hayes 28). Richard Chait, for example, complains that "the more one seeks specificity, the more various constituencies resist. In the end, vague and vapid goals able to attract consensus are preferable to pre-cise aims that force choices and provoke serious disagreements" (36). In a best-case scenario, however, a mission statement provides a focus for an institution, "a sense of direction for planning, a framework for the consideration and evaluation of activities and progress, a feeling of belonging and motivation, and a means of justifying the institu-tion to its publics" (Davies 80). And developing or revising a mis-sion statement provides opportunity for conversation and negotiation *participate in mission-writing committees* [handwritten margin note]

among the many constituencies that make up an institution (Connell and Galasinski 476). When WPAs participate in these negotiations, they develop a rich understanding of the institution's ongoing purpose, and they find opportunity to better align the mission statement of the institution and the mission of its writing program (see Connell and Galasinski 476; Haynes 65–66; Meacham 21).

The array of administrative planning documents that a school provides to its constituencies—which may include goals and objectives, vision statements, and institutional histories—may seem overwhelming to some and redundant to others, so it is important that WPAs consider why an institution is offering each document. Some schools refer to all of these documents as the "mission." Others scrupulously demarcate goals, objectives, mission, vision, and history. In fact, the literature about institutional mission reflects some disagreement about not only what each of these terms means but also about whether there is value in distinguishing among them. Often, mission and vision statements are viewed as those documents that reflect the institution's distinctive educational philosophy and its long-term aims. The mission and vision are often broader and more abstract statements that set the standard by which a school can evaluate its policies, programs, and performance. In contrast, goals and objectives—which stem from the mission and vision—are often understood as the short-term, concrete, measurable standards that indicate the institution's general direction and what it hopes to accomplish (Davies 81; McKelvie 152). Regardless of how an institution constructs its administrative documents, WPAs can discover more about the institution's mission by exploring the full range of documents that articulate the institution's sense of "what we do (operational aims), who we are (institutional identity) and what we aspire to (vision)" (Hartley 11). Such discovery can help WPAs understand the writing program's role and purpose within the larger institutional structure (Haynes 65–66), plan strategically (McKelvie 155), and assess its methods for measuring desired outcomes (Witte and Faigley 40).

Often, these administrative documents will contain linguistic markers that emphasize the institution's type and draw connections between institutional type and the mission of the institution (see Long 273). For example, Susan VanZanten reminds administrators that "The mission statements of R1 institutions tend to concentrate on the production of knowledge, while those of comprehensive uni-

versities and liberal arts institutions are liable to be more centered on
student learning" (1). Conversely, the mission of a community college
is widely understood as "providing an accessible, adaptable, and af-
fordable 2-year education" (Abelman and Dalessandro 306). Larger
institutions must balance their accountability to the public and to government regulating agencies with the need to support student learning and faculty development. Where administrators may emphasize
the importance of mission to achieving fiscal solvency, "serving the
public" maintains a high degree of importance in both public and
private universities (Morphew and Hartley 426). Sheila Slaughter and
Gary Rhoades argue that the notion of "public good" has somewhat
been replaced by "an academic capitalist knowledge/learning regime"
as colleges and universities integrate into the new economy" (8), but,
as Mark C. Long rightly points out, "influence of the expertise of
individual faculty shapes course offerings [and how mission gets en-
acted]" (qtd. in Simpson). WPAs in large colleges and universities need
to think carefully about how institutional mission delegates attention
to economic and social responsibilities.

However, smaller colleges may have to be even more attentive to
mission. In fact, VanZanten has suggested that "smaller private institutions pay more attention to mission. They have meticulously word-
ed mission statements that establish their distinct identities, unique
values, and distinguishing cultures" (2). Small colleges can make
themselves more visible by emphasizing distinctives in their mission statements, helping them survive in a competitive market and
emphasize the communities that they serve (Mayhew 4–8). Colleges with specialized constituencies, such as historically black colleges
and universities (HBCUs), Hispanic-serving institutions, tribal colleges, women's colleges, and religious colleges, are accountable to both
internal and external constituencies in ways that differ significantly
from the accountability patterns of public colleges and universities.
While their original mission may have undergone a steady evolution
of "translation[s] to fit current circumstances," vestigial traces of that
original mission are likely still to be evident and influential. For example, where the mission of women's colleges historically emphasized
access to education, many now seek to provide a "female-centered
education" and to "keep women at the center of the educational environment" (Langdon 25). Furthermore, Matthew Hartley suggests
that administrators like WPAs can build consensus across academic

programs by directing discussion to the relevance of the original institutional mission: "the founding purpose [acts] as a kind of institutional Rorschach test, inviting institutional members to interpret what it
might mean, and in the process come to consensus about core values,
interests, and needs" (121).

Religious colleges offer an excellent example of the range of factors involved in shaping institutional mission. Fitzgerald points out
that "researching the practices and history of the religiously affiliated
college or university can be [. . .] a 'sanity saver,' especially for faculty
new to such institutions and with backgrounds different from those of
their students and colleagues" (151–52). Playing on the religious tones
in the term "mission," VanZanten describes religious colleges and universities as "mission-driven" institutions that enact their institutional
mission in significant ways through faculty hiring. VanZanten describes four categories: exclusive colleges in which faculty are required
"to belong to a specific church, denomination, order, or theological
perspective;" evangelical colleges, which require faculty to ascribe to
"a general statement of faith;" ecumenical colleges, which hire faculty
who are "committed members of any Christian church, whether Cath-
olic, Orthodox, or Protestant;" and pluralist colleges, which "deliberately cultivate a plurality of religious positions among their faculty"
(6). Given the range of ways that religious colleges may enact their
religious commitments, "knowing even a few of the particulars of our
contexts can explain apparent mysteries and provide coping strategies
for completing day-to-day business" (Fitzgerald 152).

A final factor influencing institutional mission, regardless of the
size, institution type, history, or community affiliation, is organizational culture. Hartley argues that organizations are "organisms" that
develop through both planning and natural unfolding: "Organizations
are communities comprised of individuals and as communities are subject to the vicissitudes of humanity" (49). Yet organizations also often
have an internal coherence. Nancy Fjortoft and John C. Smart identify
four primary institution types that typically occur in academic environments: clans, bureaucracies, markets, and adhocracies (430). The
organizational culture that predominates within an institution will
shape the options for how WPAs can enact the institutional mission.

ENACTING INSTITUTIONAL MISSION

Even in the context of well-considered, well-articulated mission statements, students, faculty, and other stakeholders look for information about an institution's mission in programs, procedures, and coursework (see Ferrari and Velcoff 244). From their first contacts with an institution, such as college viewbooks, students receive messages about their role in the institution's mission (Hartley and Morphew). Once they enroll, students receive additional messages from the presence, description, and funding for programs for particular student populations. For example, if an institution's mission statement emphasizes the creation of knowledge, as many R1 universities do, students might expect to find robustly funded and creatively administered honors programs in which they undertake (often in close collaboration with faculty) independent research projects in rhetoric and composition. At institutions like liberal arts colleges that emphasize a holistic approach to student development, students might experience the institution's mission in writing courses that include service learning. If an institution's mission emphasizes student learning, as many comprehensive universities do, students might expect well-funded programs that support student learning, such as a writing center, and they might also expect procedures that enact the institutional mission, such as placement procedures that direct students toward courses they believe to be appropriate to their abilities. When revising writing programs or seeking funding for new program initiatives, WPAs may find it advantageous to draw connections between these efforts and the institution's mission.

Students experience institutional mission most immediately in the classroom, through curriculum and pedagogy. If the institution's mission emphasizes citizenship, for example, students could reasonably expect that writing courses will emphasize the skills they will need to participate in the forums, hearings, and conversations that fuel a robust democracy; they might look for classroom activities and writing assignments will engage them in discussions of current political debates about public affairs. At institutions that emphasize vocational preparation, students might expect to find courses that focus on workplace writing and opportunities for writing internships. If an institution's mission stresses student learning, students might expect to encounter experienced teaching faculty, innovative pedagogy, and writing assignments that stretch their critical thinking skills. When students value the mission of the institution and they can see how the writing program enacts that mission, they are more likely to value their academic experience. Conversely, if students encounter inexperienced or disengaged faculty or if they experience writing program policies, procedures, curriculum, and pedagogies that are out of sync with the institution's mission (as they understand it), they may question not only the value of what they learn in writing courses but also the overall value of the writing program.

If students experience institutional mission most significantly in the classroom, then writing faculty experience institutional mission most importantly in the writing program. To the extent that WPAs influence the hiring, training, evaluation, and promotion of faculty in a writing program, they influence how writing faculty understand, value, and enact the mission of the institution. Faculty draw conclusions about an institution's mission and their role in it from their working conditions: What the institution values is evident in the availability, size, and location of faculty offices and classrooms (Fugazzotto 292) as well as the resources allotted to supporting faculty teaching and research. Not surprisingly, faculty pay particular attention to institutional mission during reappointment and tenure, as discussions of a faculty member's fit with and contributions to the institution's mission influence decisions about reappointment and promotion. Robert M. Diamond notes that "all too often what are articulated as the priorities of a college or university are not supported by the faculty reward system" (1). In such cases, WPAs should not be surprised that faculty focus their energy on producing what the institution rewards, even if that fails to support, or perhaps undermines, the goals of the writing program. WPAs can encourage faculty to value the mission of the institution by aligning faculty rewards with faculty success at enacting that mission (see Ferrari and Velcoff 245).

BUILDING (ON) INSTITUTIONAL MISSION

When WPAs are able to align the goals of the writing program to the institution's mission, they position the writing program to become a valued part of the university (and thus a justifiable recipient of the university's goods—budget, faculty, facilities). Furthermore, they position themselves to influence the institution's evolving mission. In this sec-

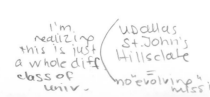

tion we suggest strategies for WPAs to consider as they build (on) institutional mission.

Build your understanding of the institution's mission. WPAs can profit, as Fitzgerald did, from Muriel Harris's advice to "'start with some sort of an ethnography' to investigate the implications of [. . .] context," to surface the "policies, practices, and histories" that mediate faculty-student (and faculty-administrator) relationships (qtd. in Fitzgerald 141). To begin, a WPA could become familiar with key institutional documents (the ones that people refer to) that articulate the school's mission. When learning something of the history of an institution, a WPA is likely to discover the people and communities who view themselves as the "keepers" of the institution's mission as well as those who see their role to adapt the institution's mission to changing circumstances. A WPA should determine the venues for ongoing conversations about institutional mission and how she might gain a voice in those conversations.

Understanding a full range of administrative documents, from the university's strategic plan to archival minutes of key administrative committees, is also useful for WPAs because such an understanding allows the WPA to develop useful assessment mechanisms. John Carver points out how easy it can be to value established activities regardless of how well they support the institution's mission: "Once organizational activity is under way, we are all susceptible to focusing on, talking about, and reporting on our rhetorical positions and our carefully devised methods" (20). Knowing how an institution defines its history, mission, vision, and objectives to both internal and external constituencies, a WPA can strategically develop curriculum, assess programs, and cultivate administrative support for the goals of the writing program.

Explore how external constituencies shape your institution's mission. WPAs can learn much from examining the pressures on the mission of the institution exerted by external constituencies and communities such as legislatures, accrediting agencies, grant-funding institutions, donors, and parents. While these pressures often seem onerous, Gary A. Berg, Mihaly Csikszentmihalyi, and Jeanne Nakamura suggest that responding to these pressures is, in part, an ethical obligation of academic institutions: "However varied the missions may be, our contention is that to survive and prosper, and to enable the good work of the people who work there, a school must live up to a set of ethical guidelines embodied in the mission that express the spirit of a community and constitutes an implicit contract between the institution and the wider society" (42). While these pressures sometimes, perhaps even frequently, result from outdated ideas about pedagogy and curriculum, they shape the mission of academic institutions to fit the needs and the values of the society that supports the institution (44). Conversely, these external pressures may also restrain academic institutions from deviating from their core values. For example, "An increased need for revenues is perhaps the most pervasive force that institutions currently face, and they may resort to strategies for raising needed funds that are not in line with an institution's existing mission" (44).

Foster convergences between the goals of the writing program and institutional mission. Directing attention to the writing program, WPAs might begin by assessing how the writing program currently engages with the institutional mission. For example, they could explore how the writing faculty understand the mission of the institution and how faculty imagine that they enact that mission (see Diamond and see McKelvie for sample instruments). This assessment can also provide data about the morale among writing faculty, since faculty commitment to the institutional mission correlates to their commitment to the institution as a whole (Ferrari and Velcoff 246). To develop faculty commitment to the mission of the institution, WPAs might consider developing a mentoring program that includes faculty rewards "based on the institution's missions and values" (Ferrari and Velcoff 244; Simpson). WPAs can continue by drawing clear connections for students between the institution's mission and features of the writing program like procedures, curriculum, and pedagogy.

Shape institutional mission. By considering the writing program's connection to the culture and the use of material resources of the university, WPAs will be able to position the writing program to support and shape the mission of the institution. If, for example, a writing program's courses are part of the general education requirements, the WPA is positioned to influence decisions about those requirements and, in so doing, influence the institution's evolving sense of its mission (see also Fitzgerald, this volume). Administrators of writing programs who employ a large number of teaching assistants or adjunct faculty may also be able to influence decisions about compensation and working conditions for these instructors (Witte and Faigley 46–47).

Less a Conclusion Than a Caveat

Like most scholars studying institutional mission, we value clarity and consensus in institutional missions and are inclined to accept Ferrari and Velcoff's conclusion that "colleges and universities with institutional missions that are clearly understood and embraced by administrators and faculty report effective strategic planning [. . .] marketing [. . .] useful assessments of outcomes and goals" (244). We would like to conclude, however, by offering the following caveat. As with all things, WPAs should consider not only the rhetorical possibilities but also the limitations of clarity and consensus when working with institutional mission. We concur with Fjortoft and Smart that "[some] institutions are equally successful with vague and inconsistent missions" (442). Indeed, in the context of vague institutional missions, WPAs may find freedom to develop curriculum and encourage pedagogy that reflects current scholarship and that takes full advantage of the particular talents of their writing faculty. They may find it relatively easy to adapt the outcomes of a writing program to evolving student interests and emerging opportunities. As with most issues that WPAs face, understanding and using institutional mission provides us opportunities to engage the full range of our rhetorical skills.

Works Cited

Abelman, Robert, and Amy Dalessandro. "The Institutional Vision of Community Colleges: Assessing Style as Well as Substance." *Community College Review* 35 (2008): 306–35. *JSTOR*. Web. 19 August 2012.

Adcroft, Andy, and David Taylor. "Developing a Conceptual Model for Career Support for New Academics." *International Journal of Teaching and Learning in Higher Education* 22.3 (2009): 287–98. Web. 26 June 2012.

Berg, Gary A., Mihaly Csikszentmihalyi, and Jeanne Nakamura. "Mission Possible?: Enabling Good Work in Higher Education." *Change* 35.5 (2003): 40–47. Web. 25 June 2012.

Carver, John. "Managing Your Mission: Advice on Where to Begin." *About Campus* 4.5 (2000): 19–23. Print.

Chait, Richard. "Mission Madness Strikes Our Colleges." *Chronicle of Higher Education* 18.18 (1979): 36. Print.

Connell, Ian, and Dariusz Galasinski. "Academic Mission Statements: An Exercise in Negotiation." *Discourse & Society* 9 (1998): 457–79. Print.

Davies, John L. "Institutional Mission and Purpose." *Universities: The Management Challenge*. Ed. Geoffrey Lockwood and John L. Davies. Philadelphia, PA: The NFER-NELSON Publishing Company Limited, 1985. 80–101. Print.

Delucchi, Michael. "'Liberal Arts' Colleges and the Myth of Uniqueness." *The Journal of Higher Education* 68.4 (1997): 414–26. Print.

Diamond, Robert M. *Aligning Faculty Rewards with Institutional Mission: Statements, Policies, and Guidelines*. Bolton, MA: Anker, 1999. Print.

Ferrari, Joseph R., and Jessica Velcoff. "Measuring Staff Perceptions of University Identity and Activities: The Mission and Values Inventory." *Christian Higher Education* 5.3 (2006): 243–61. Web. 26 June 2012.

Fitzgerald, Lauren. "*Torah U'Madda*: Institutional 'Mission' and Composition Instruction." *Negotiating Religious Faith in the Composition Classroom*. Ed. Elizabeth Vander Lei and bonnie kyburz. Portsmouth, NH: Boynton/Cook, 2005. 141–54. Print.

Fjortoft, Nancy, and John C. Smart. "Enhancing Organizational Effectiveness: The Importance of Culture Type and Mission Agreement." *Higher Education* 27.4 (June 1994): 429–47. *JSTOR*. Web. 21 June 2012.

Fugazzotto, Sam J. "Mission Statements, Physical Space, and Strategy in Higher Education." *Innovative Higher Education* 34 (2009): 285-98. *SpringerLink*. Web. 21 June 2012.

Hartley, Matthew. *A Call to Purpose: Mission-Centered Change at Three Liberal-Arts Colleges*. New York: Taylor & Francis, 2002. Print.

Hartley, Matthew, and Christopher C. Morphew. "What's Being Sold and to What End? A Content Analysis of College Viewbooks." *The Journal of Higher Education* 79.6 (November 2008): 671–91. *JSTOR*. Web. 21 June 2012.

Haynes, J. K. "Linking Departmental and Institutional Mission." *New Directions for Higher Education* 119 (2002): 65–68. Web. 9 August 2012.

Langdon, Emily A. "Women's College Then and Now: Access Then, Equity Now." *Peabody Journal of Education* 76.1 (2001): 5–30. Web. 19 August 2012.

Long, Mark C. "Center and Peripheries: Guest Editor's Introduction." *Pedagogy* 10.2 (2010): 271–82. Print.

Mayhew, Lewis B. *Surviving the Eighties*. San Francisco, CA: Jossey-Bass, 1979. Print.

McKelvie, Brenda D. "The University's Statement of Goals: An Idea Whose Time Has Come." *Higher Education* 15.1/2 (1986): 151–63. *JSTOR*. Web. 25 July 2012.

Meacham, Jack. "What's the Use of a Mission Statement?" *Academe* 94 (2008): 21–24. Web. 25 July 2012.

Morphew, Christopher C., and Matthew Hartley. "Mission Statements: A Thematic Analysis of Rhetoric Across Institutional Type." *The Journal of Higher Education* 77.3 (2006): 456–71. Print.

Newsom, W. A., and C. R. Hayes. "Are Mission Statements Worthwhile?" *Planning for Higher Education* 19 (1990): 28–30. Print.

Simpson, Cheryl M. "Examining the Relationship between Institutional Mission and Faculty Reward for Teaching Via Distance." *Online Journal of Distance Learning Administration* 8.1 (2010). Web. 21 June 2012.

Slaughter, Sheila, and Gary Rhoades. *Academic Capitalism and the New Economy: Markets, State and Higher Education*. Baltimore, MD: Johns Hopkins UP, 2004. read (book)

Swales, John, and Priscilla Rogers. "Discourse and the Projection of Corporate Culture: The Mission Statement." *Discourse & Society* 6.2 (1995): 223–42. Print.

VanZanten, Susan. *Joining the Mission: A Guide for (mainly) New Faculty*. Grand Rapids, MI: Eerdmans, 2011. Print.

Witte, Stephen P., and Lester Faigley. *Evaluating College Writing Programs*. Carbondale: Southern Illinois UP, 1983. Print.

9 What Is Pre-College Credit?

Kristine Hansen

Pre-college credit is an umbrella term covering three kinds of educational programs high school students can participate in prior to matriculating at a college or university. In many—but not all—cases, students who participate in these programs do so with the expectation that they will be awarded college credit hours for their efforts and will be allowed to bypass courses once they arrive on campus. Because state policy makers increasingly insist that high school graduates must be more "college-ready," high schools are adding pre-college credit programs to their curricula to meet this goal. In this chapter, I describe three common means of earning pre-college credit:

- Advanced Placement (AP);
- Concurrent enrollment (also called dual credit), including early college high schools;
- and International Baccalaureate (IB).

I also explain the pros and cons of each program, describing factors WPAs should be aware of as they consider whether to award credit to new students and/or to waive first-year composition (FYC) courses.

ADVANCED PLACEMENT

The oldest of the pre-college credit programs, Advanced Placement (AP), was created by the College Board in 1954. It took the form of tests administered to students from elite schools that prepared students for highly selective colleges in the east. The aim of the tests was to determine which students among an already selective group were prepared to bypass typical first-year courses and move directly into advanced ones. Over the ensuing fifty-eight years, the College Board has worked aggressively to increase student access, offering AP programs in thousands of high schools in every state and even in foreign countries for the children of American expatriates. In 2012, about two million students took 3.7 million tests in more than thirty different subjects (Pope), earning the nonprofit College Board more than $292 million, since each test cost $87 (College Board).

AP includes two English tests: (1) Literature and Composition and (2) Language and Composition. These are the most frequently taken AP tests, and both are widely used to exempt students from FYC. In 2011, over 780,000 students took one or both of the English exams (College Board). Each exam has a series of multiple-choice questions comprising 45% of the grade and a set of three "free-response" essay questions accounting for 55% of the grade. Students have sixty minutes for the computer-scored multiple-choice section; they have 120 minutes to handwrite the three human-scored impromptu essays. Students' scores on the multiple-choice and essay questions are converted by ETS statisticians into a single composite score on a 1–5 scale. According to the College Board, a score of 5 means a student is "extremely well qualified" for advanced college work; 4 means a student is "well-qualified"; 3, "qualified"; 2, "possibly qualified"; and 1, "no recommendation." Generally, students take an AP course in order to prepare for an AP test, but they can take a test without the corresponding course. Likewise, they can take AP courses without taking the tests.

The older of the two tests, Literature and Composition, focuses on canonical works of literature. The multiple-choice test examines students' ability to recognize formal properties of literature, such as genre, point of view, tone, and figurative language. For two of the three timed essays, students read a short text and analyze it. For example, in 2012 students read Sir Philip Sidney's poem "Thou Blind Man's Mark," then analyzed "how poetic devices help to convey the speaker's complex attitude toward desire." The third essay, called the "open question," uses a broadly applicable prompt, and students choose the work they write about. The prompt in 2012 instructed students to analyze how "cultural, physical, or geographical surroundings shape psychological or moral traits in a character" and "illuminate the meaning of the [novel or play] as a whole" (College Board).

The quality of writing in the three timed essays about literature has long been considered a way of determining student readiness to bypass and receive credit for FYC. But in recent years many colleges have stopped giving FYC exemption or credit for scores of 3 on this test. Some have stopped giving credit altogether for the Literature and Composition exam because the curriculum of a high school literature course does not align with that of a typical FYC course and because students' ability to write timed essays about literature may not predict their ability to use various writing processes to produce other academic writing—reports, arguments, research papers, multimodal compositions, and other genres now commonly taught in FYC.

The second test, Language and Composition, was established in 1980, in part to answer these objections. Since 2002, thanks to a test development committee that includes college professors of rhetoric and composition, this test has become very different from the literature exam. The multiple-choice test focuses on formal properties of rhetoric to be identified in short passages, such as occasion, purpose, audience, ethos, logos, and pathos. The three essays, like many college writing assignments, emphasize synthesis, analysis, and argument. In 2012, the first essay required students to write a mini-research paper using and citing seven brief sources provided by the test makers. The second essay required students to analyze rhetoric from President John F. Kennedy. The third presented two short quotations about certainty and doubt, asking students to take and support a position on the relationship between the two. Because the Language and Composition exam attempts to measure some of the same outcomes sought in typical FYC courses, some colleges now grant exemption and FYC credit for scores of 5, 4, and even 3 on this exam, while disallowing exemption and/or credit for the Literature and Composition exam. The fact that more students now take this test than the literature exam likely reflects changing university policies.

WPAs trying to influence their institutional policies on AP credit should know that college admissions offices have long weighted AP courses favorably because the courses are touted as rigorous and challenging, and they are usually taught by senior high school faculty who've waited years to get the plum AP assignment. Students who score 4 or 5 on AP tests can take pride in achieving a high ranking on a nationally normed test. Scoring 3 is less prestigious, representing a mediocre performance, but even those students are likely more college-ready than their peers. Parents take pride in their children's precociousness, hoping that AP scores can be exchanged for college credit and, if the children amass enough credits, lead to a shorter stay in college and lower tuition bills. Likewise, legislatures and college administrators think that granting exemptions and credit for AP scores will save money by decreasing the number of sections and seats needed for required courses and helping students graduate faster.

However, the above reasons for granting credit for AP tests are somewhat suspect. Traditionally, students take the Language and Composition test as juniors in high school, when they are sixteen or seventeen years old, in an AP course that is often blended with a state-mandated curriculum in American literature. This fact raises questions about student maturity and equivalence of the AP course with a typical FYC course. Another problem is the kind of writing AP students do. Preparation for AP English tests tends to stress the writing of timed essays rather than the process approach typical in FYC courses. The scant forty minutes students are allowed to write each AP essay encourage formulaic five-paragraph writing. Students who skip FYC on the basis of an AP score may lack familiarity with other genres of writing and experience with processes of revising, editing, peer review, teacher conferencing, and researching college-level library and Internet sources. If a college's FYC course is part of an integrated first-year experience aimed at enculturating students into the intellectual and social life of college, bypassing the course may mean that students miss an important building block in their foundation for success. Moreover, data at one university shows that students who matriculate with numerous AP credits on their transcript graduate only a half semester sooner than students who lack such credits (see Hansen et al., "Are Advanced").

Despite these problems, WPAs usually do not determine the AP policy on their campuses; that decision is often reserved for admissions officers. Some admissions offices accept the College Board recommendation that a score of 3 or higher means a student is qualified to skip introductory courses and receive credit hours for them. Other colleges offer AP students a kind of "empty" credit counting toward total hours for graduation, but not exempting them from particular courses. They thus recognize students' high school efforts without sacrificing the learning and maturation they can experience only at college. WPAs may be able to influence the policy on their campus by carefully studying the experience and writing of students who matriculate with AP scores of 3, 4, or 5 on one or both tests. WPAs should carefully compare the outcomes of their own FYC course with the outcomes of the

AP experience to determine whether they are similar. For example, until 2010 my institution operated under a fifty-year-old policy that waived FYC for scores of 3, 4, or 5 on either test. Carefully gathered empirical data led to disallowing the Literature and Composition exam (see Hansen et al., "Argument" and "Advanced"). Now, only students with scores of 4 or 5 on the Language and Composition exam may receive credit; nevertheless, many are persuaded to take honors sections of FYC to strengthen their writing abilities (see Whitley and Paulsen). Policies on AP waivers and credit should be appropriate for local conditions; comparisons to peer institutions may provide helpful insights.

Concurrent Enrollment

Mix and match the terms concurrent and dual with enrollment and credit and you get four different ways of naming various programs across the nation allowing students to enroll in college courses while in high school. (They are also called "postsecondary enrollment options" and "college in the schools.") Usually students receive credit for both high school and college graduation requirements if they successfully complete the course. Originating in the 1970s, these courses aimed to "address worries about a lack of rigor and innovation at many high schools" and help students become college-ready (Klein). Two U.S. Department of Education studies argue that concurrent enrollment (CE) courses add rigor to high school curricula and provide momentum towards a college degree ("Answers" and "Toolbox"). Other evidence indicates that students who take CE courses are more likely to graduate from high school, enroll in college, persist toward graduation, and earn higher GPAs (Karp et al.; Oregon; Swanson); these benefits are more pronounced for male and low-income students least likely to attend college (Barnett and Hughes). Given the demands of today's economy for more knowledgeable, more skilled workers, state legislatures, who view CE courses as a way to increase the numbers of college graduates, frequently mandate CE courses in the high schools. Unlike the AP programs and tests described above, however, CE programs vary by state and by region.

According to National Center for Education Statistics (NCES) data from 2002–2003 (the most recent data available), 98% of public two-year colleges offered CE programs, as did 77% of public and

40% of private four-year institutions. The same study showed that 72% of US high schools offered CE courses, while only 67% offered AP courses. While AP still has the cachet of more rigor and prestige, CE courses are thought of as offering a "safe" path to credit: The cost to students is usually less than for AP, and there is no nationally standardized test to pass, just a course. Once earned, CE credit is usually widely transferable because of the huge network of articulation agreements between all kinds of two-year and four-year institutions across the nation. As a result, admissions officers at Big State U inspecting the transcript of a transfer student from Downtown Community College may have no way of knowing that the student's FYC credit was actually earned in a CE course at Tiny Rural High School (for more on this phenomenon, see Schwalm, this volume).

There are various models for delivering CE courses, the most common being for high school teachers to teach a college's course at the high schools served by the college—perhaps in a city, a county, or even a whole state. Usually, but not always, the college offering the credit trains the high school teachers and sends liaisons to observe, to consult, and to supervise delivery of the curriculum. According to the NCES, in 2002–2003, 74% of CE courses were taught at high schools, 23% on campuses of postsecondary institutions (usually by college faculty teaching high school students who commuted to the campus), and almost 4% via distance education. The ways of paying teachers for CE courses and of calculating and charging tuition vary so much from state to state that it is impossible to generalize, but many states create financial incentives for high schools to offer and students to take CE courses. Colleges usually earn more tuition dollars by offering CE courses, so they have an incentive to mount CE programs, often extensive ones.

Some CE programs have national reputations for high curricular standards, excellent teaching, and strong student performance. For example, Syracuse University established Project Advance in 1972 to help seven area high schools offer challenging courses to students with "senioritis." Syracuse now partners with 140 selected high schools in five different states, offering approximately 6,600 students a year credit for SU courses. Using a dedicated staff and a generous budget to select and train teachers, Syracuse has certified over five hundred high school teachers as adjunct university instructors and supported their ongoing professional development through institutes, seminars, workshops, and site visits. Continuous evaluation ensures that weaknesses in teachers and courses are identified and strengthened (see Moody and Bonesteel). However, other CE programs are not as admirable; some, frankly, have raised questions about whether the sponsoring college's purpose is really to offer high school students a quality experience or just to generate more tuition dollars. Observers of some CE programs have expressed doubt (see Klein for examples) about teacher credentials, preparation, and supervision; curricular integrity and rigor; parity in assessments; ongoing quality control; and student readiness. According to the Education Commission of the States, as of 2008, only twenty-nine states had written laws specifying requirements for teachers of CE courses. Some require high school teachers to hold the same credentials as college faculty who teach the same course; others require only that high school teachers receive approval from colleges or participate in professional development. Only twenty-nine states in 2008 had regulations ensuring that the curriculum of CE courses is equivalent to that received by postsecondary students. Only thirteen states had policies requiring CE programs to be evaluated periodically (Education Commission of the States).

State requirements describing student eligibility for enrolling in a CE course are also variable. Some states have requirements such as a minimum GPA, test scores, and/or written recommendations from teachers and other school officials. Fifteen states reserve CE for twelfth graders only; twenty allow eleventh graders to participate; two allow tenth graders; and nine states allow (though don't necessarily encourage) ninth graders to enroll (Education Commission of the States). One unique type of CE program must be mentioned in this regard— the early college high school (ECHS). Typically, an ECHS is located on a college campus and draws targeted students as young as fourteen from area high schools to give them an accelerated curriculum, moving them from ninth grade through the second year in college in four years instead of six. The ECHS initiative is supported in part by the Bill and Melinda Gates Foundation to "serve low-income young people, first-generation college goers, English language learners, and students of color, all of whom are statistically underrepresented in higher education and for whom society often has low aspirations for academic achievement" (Early College High School Initiative, qtd. in Schneider). The eventual goal is to have 240 such schools serving 100,000 students. Early data indicate some success with this model: Students who have graduated from an ECHS are more likely to view themselves as able to succeed in college and to persist to graduation (Schneider).

Both ECHS and CE courses raise questions, however, about student readiness and the wisdom of offering students a curriculum they may not be ready for cognitively, socially, emotionally, perhaps even physically. When students are still minors—especially as young as fourteen—concerns naturally arise about their going to college campuses and taking courses with students who are older, perhaps by ten or more years. Though such youngsters might be taught to produce correct, competent writing, their lack of life experiences and readiness to confront some of the questions addressed in FYC courses could spell trouble, as Kelly Ritter notes in this volume. Even when students are taught CE courses in their own high school, some question the validity of the course because of the disparity between the cultures of high school and college. For example, high school classes—even ones being taught for college credit—may be interrupted or canceled for sporting events and assemblies. High school teachers are often required to allow make up work, whereas college teachers usually aren't. Unlike college students, failing high school students usually can't drop a course. Because of the age and minor status of high school students, parents have more say in their lives and are allowed to see their educational records, but the Family Educational Rights and Privacy Act (FERPA—see Ritter, this volume) allows students who are either eighteen or enrolled in a postsecondary institution to restrict access to their educational records. CE programs seem to be in a gray area of this law: Are CE students in high school or in college? Can parents and the high school view their CE course records? Different states and institutions give different answers.

Many questions must still be worked out regarding CE courses, but because they are so popular they are likely here to stay. The question then becomes how to make them as good as they should and can be. Because of the variability in or absence of state policies and standards, the National Alliance of Concurrent Enrollment Partnerships (NACEP) was organized in 1999 to work toward national accreditation standards for CE courses. NACEP restricts its definition of CE to college courses taught during the usual school day in high schools by high school teachers selected and prepared by partnering colleges. NACEP excludes courses in which college teachers go to the high school to teach, courses that high school students take at a nearby college, and AP and IB courses. NACEP "works to ensure that college courses offered by high school teachers are as rigorous as courses offered on the sponsoring college campus." It measures rigor with seventeen accreditation standards, categorized in five areas: curriculum, faculty, students, assessment and program evaluation. The standards emphasize that CE students are to be taught and treated the same as fully matriculated postsecondary students. The NACEP standards are high and cannot be met quickly; a CE program must be in place for five years to gather assessment data before seeking accreditation. As of spring 2012, only eighty-three programs across the nation had achieved NACEP accreditation (NACEP). Because the NACEP standards are generic, Chris M. Anson, a former president of the Council of Writing Program Administrators, has proposed additional standards for writing courses to address pedagogical integrity, programmatic integrity, student needs, faculty development, economic fairness, and fair labor practices. A national discussion of Anson's additional standards must still be conducted.

WPAs who have legitimate concerns about CE programs in the areas from which they recruit students should get involved in state and regional organizations to try to influence the kinds of standards set for CE courses, whether by the state legislature, state office of education, or consortia of postsecondary institutions. WPAs usually don't make institutional policy on CE credit, but they may be able to lobby college admissions officers to create a wise, informed policy for identifying and accepting CE credit. WPAs should recognize that some CE courses are strong and likely comparable to the FYC courses they have designed; but where they have concerns about the breadth and depth of students' writing experience, WPAs might work to create a vertical curriculum and try to require or advise students with CE credit—particularly those who earned the credit at a very young age—to take additional writing courses after they matriculate.

INTERNATIONAL BACCALAUREATE

The International Baccalaureate, or IB, is the name of a nonprofit educational foundation established in Geneva, Switzerland, in 1968 to prepare students for international mobility in their higher education (unless otherwise noted, all information below is drawn from the IB website). To accomplish this mission, IB provides secondary schools with a curriculum and a diploma recognized by universities around the world. It seeks to make an IB education available to students of all ages and currently serves over 1,046,000 students in 3,464 schools in 143 countries. It offers three educational programs: one for children, one for the "middle years," and a Diploma Programme for students aged sixteen to nineteen. I focus here on the Diploma Programme, which in 2012 was offered in 2,378 schools worldwide, 927 of those in the US and Canada. Compared to AP and CE, IB is a small player, but it is the Cadillac in a fleet of economy cars.

The Diploma Programme is a full-time, two-year curriculum with six integrated parts: first language (A1), acquired language (A2), individuals and societies, experimental science, mathematics and computer science, and the arts. Schools that want to offer the Diploma Programme take two or more years to complete a strenuous, two-part authorization process: a feasibility study by the applicant school and a site visit from an IB-appointed delegation to assess the school's capacity to deliver the curriculum. If approved, the school undergoes an evaluation by the IB every five years after authorization. At the center of the curriculum is a three-part experience each student completes: an interdisciplinary "theory of knowledge" course exploring the nature of knowledge across disciplines and encouraging respect for other cultural perspectives; a "creativity, action, and service" experience engaging students in artistic pursuits, sports, and community service outside the school; and an "extended essay," a four-thousand-word composition on a subject of each student's choice, demonstrating the ability to do research and use "writing skills expected at the university."

Teachers in an IB Diploma Programme offer internal assessments of students' homework, projects, notebooks, and labs, typically accounting for 20% of students' grades. The other 80% is determined by external examiners, some five thousand of them hired and trained by the IB in order to ensure "international parity." These examiners evaluate students' theory of knowledge essays and extended essays and score their exams in each subject, awarding scores from 1 ("poor") to 7 ("excellent"). This external grading is criterion-based, not norm-referenced, therefore objective, valid, and reliable across time and place. Students who score at least 4 in all six parts of the curriculum, thus achieving a minimum of 24 points, are awarded the IB diploma. (Students who score below 24 may still get IB certificates for each subject area examined.)

Because the entire Diploma Programme curriculum includes lengthy writing in many genres in addition to the externally evaluated course papers and essay exams, students who come to college with an IB diploma have done much more serious writing than just a few short papers or timed essay exams. Like the pedagogical practices typically used in FYC, those used in IB are process-based—drafting, getting feedback, revising, and editing are emphasized. The preparation of IB students is so good that Harvard offers advanced standing to those who earn the IB diploma with scores of 7 on three higher-level exams, a designation that enables students to complete a bachelor's degree in three years (Harvard College Faculty). Oregon State University offers "automatic admission" and a year of college credit to any student whose final exam score is 30 or higher; it also gives such students a generous scholarship renewable for students who maintain a GPA of 3.0 (Cech).

As IB grows in North America, colleges will see more IB students hoping to exchange diplomas and test scores for FYC exemptions and credit. Although IB students are still something of a rarity on most campuses, WPAs may be consulted by admissions officers for advice on formulating policy. Because IB students should be able to present multiple papers as evidence of their proficiency, their work might be treated in the same ways placement essays are—as indicators of the instruction the students are ready for next. This should prove a pleasant problem for most WPAs wrestling with more common and more vexing questions of AP scores and CE credits. WPAs should realize that pre-college learning can sometimes be a valid substitute for an on-campus FYC course, but they should seek to satisfy themselves that their institution's policies are based on the best information available.

Works Cited

Anson, Chris M. "Absentee Landlords or Owner-Tenants? Formulating Standards for Dual-Credit Composition Programs." College Credit for Writing in High School: The "Taking Care of" Business. Ed. Kristine Hansen and Christine Farris. Urbana, IL: NCTE, 2010. 245–71. Print.

Barnett, Elisabeth, and Catherine Hughes. "Issue Brief: Community College and High School Partnerships." 2010. Web. 3 September 2012.

Cech, Scott. "With World Growing Smaller, IB Gets Big." Education Week. 30 October 2007. Web. 3 September 2012.

College Board. Advanced Placement. Home page. College Board. n.d. Web. 3 September 2012.

Education Commission of the States. "State Notes." 2008. Web. 3 September 2012.

Hansen, Kristine, Suzanne Reeve, Richard Sudweeks, Gary Hatch, Jennifer Gonzalez, Patricia Esplin, and William Bradshaw. "An Argument for Changing Institutional Policy on Granting AP Credit in English: An Empirical Study of College Sophomores' Writing." WPA: Writing Program Administration 28 (Fall 2004): 29–54. Print.

—. "Are Advanced Placement English and First-Year College Composition Equivalent? A Comparison of Outcomes in the Writing of Three Groups of Sophomore College Students." Research in the Teaching of English 40 (May 2006): 460–501. Print.

Harvard College Faculty of Arts and Sciences Student Handbook. Harvard University. n.d. Web. 3 September 2012.

International Baccalaureate Program. Home page. International Baccalaureate. n.d. Web. 3 September 2012.

Karp, Melinda, Juan Carlos Calcagno, Katherine Hughes, Dong Wook Jeong, and Thomas Bailey. The Postsecondary Achievement of Participants in Dual Enrollment: An Analysis of Student Outcomes in Two States. 2007. Web. 3 September 2012.

Klein, Alyson. "Acceleration Under Review." Education Week. 31 July 2007. Web. 3 September 2012.

Moody, Patricia, and Margaret Bonesteel. "Syracuse University Project Advance: A Model of Connection and Quality." College Credit for Writing in High School: The "Taking Care of" Business. Ed. Kristine Hansen and Christine Farris. Urbana, IL: NCTE, 2010. 227–44. Print.

NACEP. Home Page. National Alliance of Concurrent Enrollment Partnerships. n.d. Web. 3 September 2012.

National Center for Education Statistics. "Dual Credit and Exam-Based Courses in U.S. Public High Schools: 2002–03." April 2005. Web. 3 September 2012.

Oregon University System, Office of Institutional Research. Dual Credit in Oregon, 2010 Follow-up: An Analysis of Students Taking Dual Credit in High School in 2007–08. 2010. Web. 3 September 2012.

Pope, Justin. "AP Exams Surge as Tools for High Schools Raising Standards." Huffington Post 5 May 2012. Web. 3 September 2012.

Schneider, Barbara. "Early College High Schools: Double Time." College Credit for Writing in High School: The "Taking Care of" Business. Ed. Kristine Hansen and Christine Farris. Urbana, IL: NCTE, 2010. 141–64. Print.

Swanson, Joni. An Analysis of the Impact of High School Dual Enrollment Course Participation on Post-secondary Academic Success, Persistence and Degree Completion. 2008. Web. 3 September 2012.

U.S. Department of Education. "Answers in the Toolbox: Academic Intensity, Patterns of Attendance, and Bachelor's Degree Attainment." 1999. Web. 3 September 2012.

—. "The Toolbox Revisited: Paths to Degree Completion from High School through College." 2006. Web. 3 September 2012.

Whitley, Colleen, and Deirdre Paulsen. "What Do the Students Think? An Assessment of AP English Preparation for College Writing." College Credit for Writing in High School: The "Taking Care of" Business. Ed. Kristine Hansen and Christine Farris. Urbana, IL: NCTE, 2010. 86–118. Print.

10 What Is Transfer Articulation?

David E. Schwalm

The basic concept of course or credit transfer in higher education has been around for a long time in the United States. If you started college at one school and, for some reason, decided to leave and go to another, you anticipated that the work you had completed at the first school would somehow be counted toward graduation requirements at the second. But you were not sure. You therefore took your transcript to the new school and found (possibly with some difficulty) an advisor or admissions counselor who would show you how your completed course work would—or would not—apply. Often this was a disturbing experience wherein you discovered, perhaps, that only forty of the sixty hours you took at one college would apply toward graduation at a second college and it was going to take you an extra year to graduate. Back in the 1960s, my fiancée (quaint term still in use in the 1960s) had completed two years at one good liberal arts college and then one year at another. Our decision to get married at that point resulted in her needing to transfer to yet a third college. Students this transient were pretty rare at the time, and I vividly remember the frustrating experience of shopping her transcript around to every college in Chicago to find one where she could finish her bachelor's degree in a year. Transfer was possible, but contingent. It was difficult to know ahead of time how it was going to work out.

The concept and practice of "transfer articulation" has blossomed since the 1960s due to the increase in the number and size of community colleges, due to the rapid growth in the number of students going to college, and due to significant changes in student demographics—in age, diversity, gender distribution, geographic mobility, and life circumstances. Of most importance is the fact that transfer—possibly involving multiple institutions—has emerged as a *planned* part of completing a degree for many students. Thus, both meanings of "articulation" come into play. That is, "articulation" implies both a specific link or agreement between the sending and receiving institutions *and* a clear and public statement of the details of the connection. For transfer to be an effective part of educational planning, students need to know *in advance* how the course work they take at one institution is going to transfer to another, insofar as that is possible. Typically, attempting to optimize their investment in education, the student may plan to start at a less expensive two-year college and then transfer to a four-year institution. In some cases, large statewide public education systems either require or encourage most students to follow this plan to optimize the state's educational investments. To this end, the public institutions in a state—sometimes voluntarily and sometimes by legislative mandate—will develop a statewide "transfer articulation agreement" making it very clear how courses will transfer from one institution to another. The objective of transfer articulation agreements is "seamless" transfer, meaning that a conscientious transfer student can choose courses at one school with confidence that they will be both *accepted* and *applied* toward graduation requirements at the target institution so that the transfer student does not need to take more credits than the non-transfer student to graduate. The playing field, it is now believed, should be level for transfer and "native" students.

In what follows, I first discuss the various forms of transfer articulation and the reasons they have become increasingly important in US higher education. I then explore some of the general and specific transfer issues that are likely to arise for WPAs in their administrative roles, along with some suggestions for ways to think about and address those issues.[1]

An aside on a couple of terminological issues before proceeding. First, the distinction between credits or courses *accepted* and *applied* is important. All of the courses a student took at College 1 may be *accepted* by College 2, but not all of the courses may be *applied* toward graduation requirements at College 2. That is, College 2 may accept sixty hours of course work from College 1 but may still require ninety additional hours to meet the 120-hour graduation requirements, leaving the student with thirty hours of unused credit. The goal of transfer articulation is to maximize the number of hours from College 1 that *apply* toward graduation at College 2. Second, as the traditional terms *freshman, sophomore, junior,* and *senior* have become dated, freshmen have become "first-year students," sophomores are "second-year students," and so on. These new terms suggest, however, that four years is the standard time frame for college when, in fact, many students are part-time students with no intention of graduating in four years. If we say that by "first-year student" we mean a student with first-year *standing*, we are still positing four years as the norm. I will try to use the terms *lower-division students* (meaning those with zero to sixty semester hours, usually consisting mostly of general studies courses and "on-ramp"—introductory—courses in their majors) and *upper-division students* (meaning students with sixty-one to 120 semester hours and engaged generally in more advanced courses in their majors and other higher-level courses).

KINDS OF TRANSFER ARTICULATION AGREEMENTS

Largely because of the growth in number and size of community colleges and their role in individual and public educational planning, most transfer students transfer while they are lower-division students or shortly thereafter. Since many receiving institutions require transfer students to take a minimum of thirty upper-division hours in residence to be awarded a degree, the typical transfer point is somewhere after the completion of thirty hours and well before the completion of ninety. Thus transfer articulation agreements are primarily focused on lower-division course work.

General Transfer Policies. All institutions, even those that do not have many transfer students, have a section in their print and online catalogs explaining the general rules of transfer that apply to all potential transfer students. This section will typically explain what kinds of courses are accepted, how many hours can be transferred, how military training, Advanced Placement credits or credits for life experience are treated, what credits are not generally accepted, and so on. This catalog section may be the full extent of what schools will publish about transfer if they do not have or do not desire to have transfer students. Potential transfer students are then evaluated one at a time (as my fiancée was back in the 1960s), usually course by course. This is transfer largely without the "articulation" part, in both senses of the word.

Course Equivalency. Institutions that are more actively engaged in preparing or receiving transfer students go far beyond iterating these basic principles. Most transfer articulation agreements are based on established course-by-course equivalencies for a substantial number of courses commonly taken as general education courses or as lower division "on-ramp" courses in most majors. This is especially true for public systems. In some states, as in Florida, equivalent courses at all public institutions—both community colleges and baccalaureate-granting schools—are required to have the same numbers and prefixes across the state system. Almost all articulation agreements at least start with course-by-course equivalencies. Published course equivalencies are especially useful to students who only want to transfer an occasional course or two. For instance, many Arizona State University students (called "swirlers") occasionally pick up a few courses from one of the Maricopa County Community Colleges and transfer them to ASU. Increasingly, students are also transferring lower division courses taken at ASU to the community colleges toward completion of associate degrees or other community college certifications (often called "reverse transfer," although the phrase is loaded with interesting assumptions about which direction should be considered "forward," whereas the transfer street runs both ways). This is common in urban areas where students often treat all the local public institutions as if they were one big college. Established and published course equivalencies facilitate this activity.

Course-by-course agreements also become problematic when students wish to transfer a substantial number of courses, since the courses not only have to be transferable but also must fit into various kinds of different but overlapping requirement structures, such as general education, major, college, and university requirements. These requirements differ significantly from institution to institution and often step on each other within a single institution. At many baccalaureate colleges, their "native" students have a hard time finding their way through the requirement maze. Imagine a small college eager to attract transfer students in a state like Ohio with a wealth of other small colleges and several competing public systems. Such a college may have to develop and maintain different course equivalency agreements with dozens of other institutions—and that's just considering in-state schools. The same challenge exists for any school that is or strives to be a "national institution," attracting transfer students from across the country. This is where the aforementioned distinction between *accepted* and *applied* becomes important. Transfer students often find themselves with courses that transfer but don't apply—that is, don't meet any requirements at the target school.

Sub-degree Transfer. For this reason, many schools have gone beyond course equivalencies and developed what are called "sub-degree" articulation agreements. For instance, students in Arizona who have completed the general education curriculum at any public, regionally accredited Arizona community college or university will have met the general education requirements at any other public Arizona institution. Called the AGEC, or Arizona General Education Curriculum, this "sub-degree curriculum" is not entirely a course-by-course equivalency. It allows for some curricular freedom and variation among general education programs while there is an overall conceptual fit in terms of scope and outcomes. Schools that actively recruit transfer students from a wide variety of preparing institutions may make a similar offer of accepting general education completion at any school as equivalent to completion at their own, often allowing an even looser fit, as measured by course-by-course equivalency, than Arizona's AGEC. Some state systems, including Arizona's, also have transfer "pathway" agreements with community colleges. A student who wishes to major in, say, psychology can earn a sixty-four-semester-hour associate's degree at the community college, which includes the completion of general education and some lower division major requirements, and the student who conscientiously follows the curriculum is assured of being able to complete the psychology major at ASU in the remaining fifty-six hours. (Pathway agreements encourage completion of community college transfer degrees, the AA and the AS.) This is the "seamless" transfer that articulation agreements seek. Additional special "seamless" articulation agreements are often developed for majors with very specific requirements and few electives, such as nursing and engineering, to support optimization of education resources and to address high employment demand.

Degree Transfer. Even more liberal articulation agreements have been devised to facilitate transfer of students who have earned community college associate of applied sciences (AAS or occupational) degrees. This goes a step beyond "sub-degree" transfer to "degree" transfer.

Such degrees have historically been considered as "terminal" (love the term!) degrees whose curricula are largely driven by specific employment requirements. This is unfortunate because the AAS is the degree most frequently awarded by many community colleges. Typical areas of specialization include fire or police science, medical technology, mortuary science, industrial technology, paralegal services, business, and the like. AAS degrees require as many hours as academic AA and AS degrees, but they tend to have a smaller and sometimes less challenging component of general education courses and a larger number of applied occupational courses than the traditional community college transfer degrees. Often, less than half of the courses in an AAS curriculum would normally be accepted and applied toward baccalaureate requirements in transfer to baccalaureate institutions. With a "degree transfer," a student who has earned an AAS will be granted a block of sixty semester credits for the AAS, with no reference to course equivalencies, and will have to take sixty additional credits (with specific requirements, mostly upper division and including some general education "completion" courses) in order to complete a Bachelor of Applied Sciences in a similar or complementary occupational area—or possibly in a different area if the person is planning to pursue a new career. This is essentially a sixty-hour baccalaureate curriculum that requires and presupposes completion of an AAS for admission. This model recognizes the cumulative educational effect of a student's successfully completing an extensive coherent curriculum. Education is not just courses, after all.

Bundling. With all of these different kinds of transfer articulation programs, there are still students who, because of poor advising, false starts, or many other reasons, accumulate large numbers of credit hours from multiple institutions, often having *enough* credits to meet the graduation requirements of one of the institutions they have attended, but not the *right* credits. There are several regionally accredited universities, specializing in degree completion, who will "bundle" all of a student's credits from various sources (including military training, tests and exams, life experience, and so on) and determine the minimum number of courses a student will need to take to complete one of several generic degrees (e.g., a Bachelor of Arts in General Studies) offered by the institution. These courses often can be completed online from the bundling university or elsewhere. Charter Oak State College in Connecticut and Empire State University in the SUNY system are examples of accredited institutions specializing in degree completion. They are transfer articulation specialists deeply committed to optimizing the student's prior educational experience.

As transfer has changed, over the last fifty years, from a fairly rare occurrence to a planned and necessary strategy for degree completion for large numbers of students, the concept of transfer articulation has developed dramatically from the *ad hoc* course-by-course evaluation of transfer course work my fiancée experienced, to published course equivalency transfer agreements, to equivalency of "sub-degree" curricula such as general studies, to "degree transfers," to the comprehensive and inclusive analysis now done by colleges specializing in degree completion. All of these approaches continue to function simultaneously, in the interests of helping students efficiently to complete college degrees in a way that honors as many of their educational experiences as possible. There is growing pressure to increase the number of people earning baccalaureate degrees; said pressure reflects changes in employment opportunities, even while the economic downturn has reduced the resources available to fund education. Efficiency in transfer has a significant impact on the cost of higher education for both students and higher education institutions.

WHY DOES A WPA NEED TO KNOW ABOUT THIS STUFF?

Transfer articulation has been a source of vexation and conflict in higher education, primarily because it is seen by faculty (mostly) as a limitation on institutional curricular autonomy. Faculty at institutions that are primarily receivers of transfer students often feel that transfer agreements take away their control over both the content and structure of the foundational coursework in general education and in the introductory courses in the major. Often, faculty concern over this loss of control is communicated with insufferable arrogance and insensitivity, and is understandably perceived by faculty at institutions that are primarily preparers of transfer students as disrespect for their courses and their professionalism. (A community college colleague with whom I worked in developing statewide transfer articulation programs once referred to his abiding sense of "anticipatory subjugation" in the negotiations.) Faculty at both preparing and receiving institutions complain that transfer articulation agreements tend to stifle innovative curriculum planning and to favor the most vanilla and inflexible curricula possible. College administrators often find themselves in conflict with the faculty when they promote articulation agreements, either in compliance with legislative mandates or because a robust flow of transfer students is necessary to the college's financial plan—a generous and simple transfer policy provides an advantage in recruiting. This often creates friction between the faculty and the administrators: Faculty see themselves as the defenders of academic quality and administrators as mercenary bean counters; administrators see faculty as impractical idealists and themselves as those who must be invested in the "big picture." Both groups claim that they are working for the benefit of the students, of course.

Enter the WPA, who usually tends to be caught somewhere in between faculty and administrative roles. First-year composition (FYC) courses are the most widely required courses in US community colleges, colleges, and universities and are the courses most frequently transferred from one college to another. They are also courses that do not usually have a lot of friends or champions outside of writing programs. FYC courses, rightly or wrongly, are the heart, if not the whole, of most writing programs, and the WPA is the greatest champion and friend of these courses and of the importance of writing instruction in the college or university. We (I'm really describing myself here) may have a natural tendency to prefer our own concept of what a good composition program is and to be a little suspicious of programs that we are not familiar with or that embody a different concept. Thus, when it comes to accepting courses from other places as being equivalent to our own, we might take the term "equivalent" a little too literally in determining course equivalency, and we might lack a little perspective on how uniformly excellent our own courses are. We may also overrate the importance of FYC courses—especially our very own fabulous courses—to the overall literacy development of our students.

One job just about every WPA has with regard to transfer articulation is determining course equivalencies for individual students who are not covered by any of the general articulation agreements that the school might have with others. Approaching transfer articulation in general from this direction makes it very easy to lose sight of the overall goal of enabling transfer. There is a tendency to look for reasons *not* to grant equivalency. In these instances of individual evaluation, for example, the WPA must determine if a transfer student has to take additional writing courses to meet the school's FYC requirements. Can two quarter courses be used to meet a two-semester course requirement? Also, preparing and receiving institutions may have different policies or standards for awarding credit or placement for Advanced Placement (AP), International Baccalaureate (IB), and CLEP exam scores. The preparing school may have awarded composition credit for a 3 on the AP test whereas the receiving school awards credit only for a 4 or 5. Or an FYC course appearing on the transcript from the preparing college may actually have been a "dual enrollment" course, taught in a high school by the high school teacher and earning both high school and college credit (see Hansen, this volume). Your school may be the third or fourth school the student has attended, and the origins of credit for composition courses may be difficult to trace. What if a course called "Freshman Composition" appears from the description to have been basically a literature course while your equivalent course focuses on research-based writing on non-literary topics? What if you have a standard two-semester sequence for the composition requirement and the transfer student comes from a school that has a "distributed" FYC program integrated into the overall general education requirement? If it turns out that these decisions are made in the transfer admissions office or some similar place rather than by the WPA, what do they use as a basis for deciding? This way madness lies. This is also the approach that promotes both the vanilla curriculum and the frustration of WPAs at schools that prepare transfer students for many different receiving institutions.

When I was a new WPA twenty-five years or so ago, I was initially involved in developing simple course equivalencies, and I drove myself and just about everyone else nuts agonizing over these nuances. It was hard for me to get over them when I was later involved in designing our more comprehensive articulation agreements. New WPAs today—at both preparing and receiving institutions—are more likely than I was to find themselves and their courses and requirements already enmeshed to a greater or lesser degree in an existing web of articulation agreements. For most institutions, transfer articulation agreements are a given, and the trend is away from course-by-course transfer and towards various kinds of sub-degree or block transfers that often ignore the mind-numbing nuances of the course-by-course approach. In these agreements, most of the detailed questions above have been settled or, more likely, ignored in an effort to support the larger goal of facilitating transfer. Thus, the first thing a new WPA should do is to get as comprehensive a picture as possible of the existing "transfer articulation landscape," with an eye to the different kinds of agreements described above. Does your institution welcome transfer students? Are there institutional, legislative, financial, or recruiting incentives driving the institution's transfer articulation agreements? At what administrative level are articulation agreements managed or negotiated? What agreements does the institution have with whom? Does anyone maintain them? Who? What role has the WPA historically played in the development of these agreements? Are there any current controversies about articulation agreements? Have previous WPAs met with any representatives of schools to which you send or from which you receive large numbers of transfer students? Are there any schools with which you should have transfer agreements but do not? Pursuing these, or questions springing from or like these, should give you a fairly comprehensive view of the "transfer articulation landscape" (see also Hezel Associates et al.).

Moreover, researching such questions might be interesting just to see if there is any general theory of transfer underlying these agreements or if it is mostly *ad hoc*. It may also reveal gross inconsistencies, missed opportunities, or ways to streamline things. However, the real purpose of answering these questions is to gain a comprehensive understanding of the pathways by which transfer students graduating from your college can complete their composition requirements, other than by taking your FYC courses. The next challenge is to get a comprehensive view of what your institution does beyond FYC to foster adult academic and civic literacy in all of its graduates. This is really the critical question. If your school is counting on FYC (and maybe general studies) to do the whole thing, that really needs to be addressed—even if you don't have a single transfer student.

We often worry too much about the curricular control that transfer agreements take away from us and not enough about what we do with transfer students once they arrive. Transfer is now an essential part of the process of completing baccalaureate degrees for large numbers of students, and those numbers are only going to grow.

Transfer agreements designed to facilitate rather than hinder transfer are part of the new normal. If we want to have a novel or innovative FYC program we can have it, but we must also design a traditional way in for transfer students and be mindful of how our program will transfer elsewhere. We should assume that faculty in the schools that prepare transfer students are just as professional and just as concerned about teaching writing well as faculty in schools that receive them (heck, some writing faculty are both preparers and receivers). I once did a detailed analysis of all the students who earned a D, E, or W (withdraw) in ASU's English 102 one spring semester, in order to see the composition-course-taking history of the students who were not successful in the course that term. The question was whether transfer students who had taken English 101 elsewhere were disproportionally represented among the students who did not do well in our 102 course. With only one or two exceptions, transfer and native students who struggled in 102 had also struggled in previous composition courses (and in lots of other courses as well), regardless of where they took them. There is no reason to assume that transfer students are any less well prepared as writers than non-transfer students.

But there is also no reason to assume that either transfer or non-transfer students are finished learning to write after completing their FYC courses, wherever they complete them. FYC courses are foundational courses, not finishing courses. They constitute at best about 5% of the baccalaureate curriculum. Thus it becomes increasingly important for WPAs in schools that have transfer students to champion not only the FYC program but also subsequent writing experiences that will develop the writing competency they want to see in college graduates (see also Townsend, this volume). Our students, transfer or not, are where we find them, and our job is to make all of them graduates of whom we can be proud.

NOTE

1. Much of the information provided in this chapter was accumulated during the twenty-five years I spent working on statewide transfer articulation in Arizona. Thus it is difficult to attribute to particular sources. The Hezel report cited, however, is the best and most current source available on transfer articulation and will serve readers well as a starting point for follow-up.

WORK CITED

Hezel Associates, Lumina Foundation for Education, and Western Inter-state Commission for Higher Education. "Promising Practices in State-wide Articulation and Transfer Systems." *WICHE: Western Interstate Commission for Higher Education.* June 2010. Web. 27 March 2013.

11 What Is Transfer?

Elizabeth Wardle

Why do we teach composition courses and administer writing programs? There are many answers to this question, but most writing program administrators (WPAs) would likely say that one reason is because we hope that these courses will help students use what they already know about writing, learn something new about writing, and ultimately be able to successfully tackle new writing tasks in different settings. Yet despite our optimism about the courses we teach and administer, we tend to hear a lot of complaints that what we are doing doesn't help: "What did you teach him in composition? Why can't he write a basic history paper for me?" is the sort of lament WPAs hear regularly. We say similar things, looking over our students' shoulders to ask their high school teachers, "What did you teach them? Why can't they support a claim? Did you really think a five-paragraph theme would help them?"

The fact that we offer writing classes, that other teachers ask us what we teach there, and that we in turn ask high school teachers what *they* teach are all evidence of our deep-seated belief in the phenomenon known most often by the term "knowledge transfer." That we teach first-year composition (FYC) at all is an indicator that we believe in the possibility of writing-related knowledge being transferred to other settings and tasks. That other teachers look for and seem to find no evidence of the writing skills they hope for is an indicator that they, too, believe in the possibility of knowledge transfer. Their questions, and ours to high school teachers, indicate that we hold basic but frequently unexamined assumptions about what transfer of writing-related knowledge is, and how it happens. In particular, these questions and attitudes suggest that teachers of all stripes tend to assume (however unconsciously) that learning something writing-related is a simple

143

matter of skill acquisition, and that such a skill, once acquired, should be easily usable in another setting or when completing another task, no matter how different that setting or task might be. These questions also seem to presume that individuals bear the responsibility for lack of transfer; the underlying message is, "If a student was taught X skill before, she must be lazy or not very bright if she can't use that skill when completing this other task I have given her."

Over a century of research on transfer in general (Perkins and Salomon; Thorndike; Thorndike and Woodworth), and more recent research on writing-related transfer in particular (Beaufort, *College*; Foertsch; Ford; Hagemann; McCarthy), has demonstrated that our unexamined assumptions about transfer could use some serious examination, and that our students and educational settings would benefit if we engaged in this examination. (And by "we" and "our" in that sentence I mean every teacher and administrator in every type of college and university, not just writing teachers.) Writing transfer, it turns out, is a much more complicated matter than our common sense understandings lead us to assume. In this chapter, I examine some of what we know about writing and transfer in order to argue:

- The responsibility for transfer is distributed among individuals and the contexts in which they learn and act, including the tasks in those contexts.
- Basic "skills" do not come close to fully comprising writing knowledge; the entirety of writing-related knowledge is complex and its use in new settings is complex.
- Rhetorical problems are ill-structured, without one right answer, and bringing prior knowledge to bear when solving these problems is not a simple task.
- The word "transfer" masks the complexity of what happens when people use prior knowledge to solve new rhetorical problems.

I conclude by outlining some of the ways that WPAs and the teachers they work with can encourage more frequent and effective transfer of prior writing knowledge.

RESPONSIBILITY FOR TRANSFER, OR LACK THEREOF, IS DISTRIBUTED

David Perkins and Gavriel Salomon, well-known and respected transfer researchers, flatly state that transfer in educational settings is problematic: "Abundant evidence shows that very often the hoped-for transfer from learning experiences does not occur. [. . .] It can," they tell us, "but often does not." This is because educational settings are not designed to teach for transfer, though "Education can achieve abundant transfer if it is designed to do so" (Perkins and Salomon). In other words, our assumption that lack of transfer is an individual shortcoming could be considered a form of wishful thinking. I say it is *wishful* thinking because if our students can't do something we want them to do and it is because they won't or aren't able, then we often think we don't bear any responsibility for that failure, or for creating different curricula that would help them be more successful. Research and theory suggests we aren't going to be let off the hook that easily, though: The responsibility for how people learn and what they are able to do seems to be fairly well distributed (Beach; Guile and Young; Lave and Wenger; Russell; Tuomi-Grohn and Engestrom). Here's just one example of how that can work.

When students learn something, they can learn it rigidly and for the present moment only, or they can learn the concepts underlying it and recognize the potential value of this learning for another setting and task. This basic matter of how material is learned and what future value is placed on it is not an individual problem; it is a school problem. In other words, teachers and curricula and entire educational systems are set up to teach in one or the other of these ways. For example, students in Florida are frequently taught rigid formulas for writing in preparation for our standardized FCAT. They may not be taught to see these formulas as flexible heuristics that could be used in non-FCAT settings, and they are even less likely to be taught that these formulas could be repurposed or generalized to become something else, useful in very different settings. In this case, the educational system itself has trained teachers and students to learn something rigidly and for the present task only. In other words, that system is not designed to teach for transfer. When a student emerges from twelve years of engagement with such a system, is it any wonder when she fails to transfer or even attempt to transfer knowledge from one setting to another?

So while individuals bear some responsibility for using prior knowledge, they do not bear that responsibility alone. We all behave in the ways that we were taught to behave, and if we want students to behave differently when they encounter new rhetorical problems, we need to design educational settings that teach them to solve problems and learn new material in effective and meaningful ways.

This is why transfer researchers and theorists have more recently been engaged in debates about where the locus of transfer is: in the individual (Tuomi-Grohn and Engestrom), in the context (Beach; Hatano and Greeno; Lave and Wenger; Tuomi-Grohn and Engestrom), in the task (Judd, "Relation," *Education, Educational*; Thorndike; Thorndike and Woodworth)? Clearly, there is some combination of responsibility distributed across these, because individuals and contexts never exist independently of one another.

WRITING KNOWLEDGE IS NOT BASIC, AND TRANSFER IS DIFFICULT

Another assumption that could use some examination is our belief that skills learned in one setting are easy usable in another setting. This belief is not true for many kinds of knowledge transfer, and it is even less true when it comes to transferring writing-related knowledge. Perkins and Salomon argue that there are two basic kinds of transfer: near and far. Near transfer is when we need to use something we already know in a very similar way and in a very similar setting (for example, if I learn to drive a stick shift in a car, I can probably fairly easily drive a stick shift in a small pickup truck). Far transfer is when we need to draw on something we know in a different way, or a very different setting (for example, I learned to drive an automatic, and now I need to drive a stick shift in a country where I will be driving on the opposite side of the road).

Rhetoric and composition researchers have not disagreed with these near and far distinctions, but they have helped paint a clearer picture of how complex the situation is for writing-related transfer. First of all, knowledge about writing is both declarative and procedural (Anderson). We can know things *about* writing (for example, that effective writing depends on understanding of audience and constructing of meaning as much as it does on our writerly intentions), and we can know how to *do something* when we write (for example, we can know how to correctly use a semicolon or how to revise for main ideas before revising for punctuation). In many cases, to do something new or difficult with writing, we need to have both conscious declarative knowledge about it as well as an ability to attempt the procedural processes associated with it. Our unconscious declarative knowledge might be impeding our ability to effectively tackle a new writing problem, and may need to be brought to conscious awareness and revised in order to complete the new task successfully. Think, for example, of Sondra Perl's research subject, Tony. Tony's unconscious declarative knowledge about what a writing process can and should look like (do one thing at a time and do it correctly before moving on) needed to be made conscious and reexamined before he could effectively undertake the procedures associated with writing a complex college writing assignment.

While some things related to writing could accurately be described as procedural "skills" (for example, shaping letters and forming words), many aspects of writing are much more complex than the term "skill" would lead us to believe. So *what* is getting transferred from one setting to another, whether those settings are near or far, tends to be fairly complex when it comes to writing. If I have learned how to cite "correctly" using MLA style when writing a fairly simple high school paper in which I was only allowed to use printed books, how do I transfer this knowledge to an upper-level history class where I am being asked to use Turabian and work with both primary and secondary sources of various kinds? Will I easily know without any instruction how to do this? Probably not, if this is my only experience with citation. The rhetorical problem I am facing is much more complex than the experiences and tools I bring with me (another finding Perl alerted us to decades ago in her study of Tony).

RHETORICAL PROBLEMS ARE ILL-STRUCTURED

The complexity of transferring writing-related knowledge can also be linked to the nature of written problems themselves. Cognitive psychologists Patricia King and Karen Kitchener outline two kinds of problems: well-structured and ill-structured (or "messy") problems. The former type of problem has a certain and specific answer, a right answer (for example, $2 + 2 = 4$). The latter type of problem does not have a particular answer. There are many ways to explore and resolve an ill-structured problem, and more than one resolution could be effective. Rhetorical problems almost always tend to be ill-structured, and this is another reason why using prior knowledge to solve them is complicated. Anyone who has ever given the same, fairly simple writing assignment to an entire class of students has seen what solving ill-structured problems looks like in action. Twenty-five students will see the same prompt and begin by interpreting it to mean twenty-five slightly (or greatly) different things. They will draw on their stores of prior knowledge and experiences, all different, to imagine what they might be able to produce in terms of genre, style, tone, length, and organization. Some of them will gravitate toward narrative, others toward exposition. Some will organize using headings or outlines, while others will organize in their heads and then put words on paper. Every choice each student makes is influenced by prior knowledge and experience at every level, from genre to style to word choice to punctuation. It is possible, though unlikely, that each of the twenty-five students will solve the rhetorical problem equally well, but it is absolutely certain that no two written solutions will be exactly alike.

The ill-structured nature of rhetorical tasks helps further explain why transfer of prior writing-related knowledge is difficult. Consider the example I gave earlier of transferring basic MLA citation knowledge for a high school English paper to a complex college history paper using Turabian and primary and secondary sources. It is possible that a student looking at the history assignment might not recognize that anything she has done is similar to this task. As a rhetorical problem, it might seem completely new to her (consider the response of Dave in Lucille Parkinson McCarthy's landmark study, who thought everything he did in every class was completely new, despite the similarities to tasks McCarthy had seen him complete). If a student were able to connect the call for citation in history to her citation experience in English, what would she draw on from that experience? She might draw on that knowledge in ineffective ways, for example, using MLA style in her history paper. Or she might find a way to consider the prior knowledge at the conceptual level, and transform it for her current task; she might be able to imagine that citation is about referencing sources in ways that are acceptable to the audience or discourse community, and that to do so effectively would require learning more about what the discourse community expects. She might remember that to use MLA she opened a handbook and looked up the type of source she cited, and conclude that she could do the same here. In other words, there are many ways that prior knowledge can be brought to bear on ill-structured rhetorical problems, including: not at all, inappropriately, or in transformed and flexible ways.

THE WORD "TRANSFER" CAN ITSELF BE INACCURATE

What our examination of transfer has shown so far is that knowledge about writing is not basic, and that using prior knowledge about writing to solve new and ill-structured rhetorical problems is a complex business. This complexity has led researchers to spend more time thinking about what actually happens when people encounter new writing tasks and attempt to draw on what they already know in order to complete them.

Simple unconscious reuse of prior knowledge in a similar setting, what Perkins and Salomon call "low road" and "near" transfer, is fairly well described by the term "transfer," which connotes a sort of "carry and unload" model of using prior knowledge. There are obviously many things we do each day that can be understood as this kind of unconscious and easy use of prior knowledge (for example, driving), but there are also many other ways to use prior knowledge that are not so straightforward. We know from genre theory, for example, that genres are not rigid templates but frames for social action, and that text types vary in small or large ways from one use to the next. Sometimes writing a report in a new setting requires only small adjustments to prior knowledge and experience, but other times, prior knowledge is not useful without extensive adjustment. This adjustment might be dramatic (for example, the writer might realize that the word "report" is simply a shorthand for conveying information from one person to another, but that in this situation the actual text will be informal and perhaps even non-business-like) or it might be minor (for example, the writer might realize that this current report will take the form of a letter without headings, but the information will still fall into the categories seen in his previous report-writing). At times, writing the new report will require drawing on a number of previous texts the writer has written or read and pulling on all of them to see what this new text is like or "not like" (Reiff and Bawarshi; Rounsaville).

We have a number of case studies in rhetoric and composition that illustrate what these various uses of prior knowledge can look like (Beaufort, *College,* "Five Years Later," *Writing*; Driscoll and Wells; Nowacek; Roozen, McCarthy; Robertson et al.), but we are still figuring out how to talk about what happens in these situations. Some moments of transfer might be described as *repurposing* (Prior and Shipka; Roozen), others as *transformation* (Wardle, "Creative"), still others as *generalizing* (Beach), *expansive learning* (Engestrom), or *integration*

(Nowacek). All moments of far transfer seem to be problem solving of one sort or another, and how we solve problems depends on how we approach and understand them, as Linda Flower and John R. Hayes reminded us decades ago (Wardle, "Creative"). When we present rhetorical problems to our students, or coach them through problems they encounter, it might be helpful to consider the type(s) of transfer that is being asked of them.

The discussion of how to talk about the many ways that people bring prior knowledge to bear to solve problems (i.e., moments of "transfer") is ongoing and complex. It is not a purely semantic argument, however, but one that should be of interest to WPAs. How we talk about something limits and frames how we understand it. If we want to question our assumptions about transfer and expand our conceptions of what happens when students move from rhetorical problem to rhetorical problem, it might be helpful to expand our set of terminologies in order to talk more specifically about what is happening and how and why. For example, we might consider why our students struggle with citation in order to determine what type of transfer is or isn't happening, and to consider how to design specific activities and programs that will better help students engage effectively in that type of transfer.

WHAT CAN WPAS DO?

There is much that we still do not know about writing transfer and how or why it happens or does not. But there is a lot that we do know. We certainly know enough to be able to think more carefully about how we design our writing programs and how we set up our own courses. There is much more extensive information elsewhere about how we might better "teach for transfer" (see Beaufort, "Five Years Later;" Boone et al.; Perkins and Salomon), but here I will conclude by outlining a few things we can think about and do in order to help facilitate deeper learning for solving ill-structured rhetorical problems across contexts.

 Teach Flexible Approaches to Rhetorical Problem Solving. Our educational structures implicitly and explicitly tell students how to approach rhetorical problems. Do we teach about writing in ways that suggest that rhetorical problems are well-structured when, in fact, they are

Why not be prescriptive **IMP** (this is a good pt for transfer) *non for own safe* **Good Pt**

not? For example, do we teach rigid rules about writing or give rigid instructions for approaching assignments? If so, then we are suggesting that rhetorical problems can be well-structured with one right answer. If students ask us how many sources are needed in a paper, do we give a rigid answer ("Exactly ten, and three of them must be books") or do we ask students to figure out the answer by examining the problem itself ("How much information is there about this topic? How much information does your audience need? What is the usual way that texts like this are sourced?")? How we talk about writing and conventions for writing sets up an orientation for rhetorical problem solving. If we teach students to expect that for each rhetorical problem there is someone who will tell them exactly what to do, then we are not setting them up for effective rhetorical problem solving. In other words, we are not teaching them to repurpose, generalize, or transform knowledge for new problems. We are teaching them to find one answer and use it, even without knowing why. Perkins and Salomon remind us that literate learning happens "through thorough and diverse practice." When we give guidelines that suggest such thorough and diverse practice is not necessary because there are rigid rules and correct answers that can be invoked instead, we are misleading our students.

true

In order to examine how you and the teachers you work with orient students to approach rhetorical problems, you might look at the language in your assignment sheets. Do you give rigid and acontextual guidelines? Or do your assignments ask students to really think through problems rhetorically?

Incorporate Strategies that Encourage Transfer. Various researchers have outlined strategies to help students better use prior knowledge. If we can become familiar with these, we can integrate them deeply across our curricula. Such strategies include:

- *Teaching concepts and heuristics rather than rigid rules.* Mike Rose reminds us that teaching rigid rules can lead to writer's block, while teaching flexible heuristics can help students usefully approach new rhetorical tasks.
- *Teaching students to explicitly abstract principles* (Gick and Holyoak; Perkins and Salomon). Andrea Lunsford provides an example of how to do this when she advocates giving students a variety of sentences that include semicolons and asking them to abstract

the principle for using semicolons, rather than giving students a list of rules about semicolons.

- *Teaching students to actively self-monitor during difficult writing tasks* (Belmont et al; Perkins and Salomon). Flower and Hayes' finding that writers have monitors can be a useful tool when teaching for transfer. Teachers can help students examine what their monitors are telling them to do during writing tasks, and then guide students to develop their self-monitoring in useful ways. For example, "Is your monitor telling you to recursively edit spelling? Instead, self-monitor and tell yourself to keep writing until the idea is fully on the page" or "Ask yourself what you have written before that is like this new task." This self-monitoring is related to the strategy of *arousing mindfulness*. "Mindfulness refers to a generalized state of alertness to the activities one is engaged in and to one's surroundings, in contrast with a passive reactive mode in which cognitions, behaviors, and other responses unfold automatically and mindlessly" (Langer, qtd. in Perkins and Salomon).
- *Teaching rhetorical awareness.* Self-monitoring and mindfulness seem connected to the more specific literacy strategy of rhetorical awareness. The ability to analyze rhetorical situations, and to read and plan rhetorically, has been shown to be helpful across seemingly disparate contexts (Wardle, "Understanding").
- *Using metaphors and analogies* (Perkins and Salomon). Helping students consider new tasks and knowledge in light of what they already know or have done before can help them make connections. Mary Jo Reiff and Anis Bawarshi, as well as Angela Rounsaville, have fleshed out this idea with genres, asking students to consider what the new genre is like or not like.

Work to Facilitate Integrated Vertical and Horizontal Structures that Facilitate Transfer. While we can always do more to improve our own courses and programs, we must acknowledge that habits of mind, approaches to problem solving, and writing knowledge are acquired across time in multiple settings. Thus, the one course or set of courses we administer is necessary but not sufficient to encouraging transfer. To have a maximum impact on student learning and transfer of knowledge, we must work with our colleagues across disciplines and continue to argue for and help implement WAC and WID programs.

ᛣ

Knowing that writing is complex and transfer of writing-related knowledge is difficult, we can work with our writing programs to help integrate accurate conceptions of writing into courses and assignments, and we can work with colleagues across the university to suggest means by which they can better encourage students to bring prior knowledge to bear in useful ways. Perhaps most importantly, we can remember that meaningful transfer in educational settings always involves some measure of learning, which means our work is never done. We can never expect students to arrive in our classes with all the knowledge and tools they will need to tackle a new and challenging task. Thus, if we want students to usefully transfer what they know, we have to be serious and unrelenting about our own responsibility as reflective teachers.

WORKS CITED

Anderson, John. *Language, Memory, and Thought*. Hoboken, NJ: John Wiley and Sons, 1976. Print.

Beach, King. "Consequential Transitions: A Developmental View of Knowledge Propagation Through Social Organizations." *Between School and Work: New Perspectives on Transfer and Boundary-Crossing*. Ed. Terttu Tuomi-Grohn and Yrgo Engestrom. New York: Pergamon Press, 2003. 39–61. Print.

Beaufort, Anne. *College Writing and Beyond: A New Framework for University Writing Instruction*. Logan: Utah State UP, 2007. Print.

—. *"College Writing and Beyond*: Five Years Later." *Composition Forum* 26 (2012). Web. 1 December 2012.

—. *Writing in the Real World: Making the Transition from School to Work*. New York: Teachers College Press, 1999. Print.

Belmont, J. M., E. C. Butterfield, and R. P. Ferretti. "To Secure Transfer of Training Instruct Self-Management Skills." *How and How Much Can Intelligence Be Increased?* Ed. Douglas Detterman and Robert Stenberg. Norwood, NJ: Ablex, 1982. 147–54.

Boone, Stephanie, Sara Biggs Chaney, Josh Compton, Christiane Donahue, and Karen Gocsik. "Imagining a Writing and Rhetoric Program Based on Principles of Knowledge 'Transfer': Dartmouth's Institute for Writing and Rhetoric." *Composition Forum* 26 (2012). Web. 1 December 2012.

Driscoll, Dana, and Jennifer Wells. "Beyond Knowledge and Skills: Writing Transfer and the Role of Student Dispositions in and beyond the Writing Classroom." *Composition Forum* 26 (2012). Web. 1 December 2012.

Engestrom, Yrgo. *Learning by Expanding: An Activity-Theoretical Approach to Developmental Research,* 1987. Helsinki: Orienta-Konsultit. Print.

Foertsch, Julie. "Where Cognitive Psychology Applies: How Theories About Memory and Transfer Can Influence Composition Pedagogy." *Written Communication* 12.3 (1995): 360–83. Print.

Ford, Julie Dyke. *Knowledge Transfer across Disciplines: Tracking Rhetorical Strategies from Technical Communication to Engineering Contexts.* Diss. New Mexico State University, 1995.

Gick, Mary, and K. J. Holyoak. "Schema Induction and Analogical Transfer." *Cognitive Psychology* 15 (1983): 1–38. Print.

Guile, David, and Michael Young. "Transfer and Transition in Vocational Education: Some Theoretical Consideration." *Between School and Work: New Perspectives on Transfer and Boundary-Crossing.* Ed. Terttu Tuomi-Grohn and Yrgo Engestrom. New York: Pergamon, 2003. 63–81. Print.

Hagemann, Julie. "Writing Centers as Sites for Writing Transfer Research." *Writing Center Perspectives.* Ed. Byron L Stay, Christina Murphy, and Eric Hobson. Emmitsburg, MD: National Writing Centers Association Press, 1995: 120–31. Print.

Hatano, G., and Greeno, J. G. "Commentary: Alternative Perspectives on Transfer and Transfer Studies." *International Journal of Educational Research 31* (1999): 645–54. Print.

Judd, C. H. "The Relation of Special Training and General Intelligence." *Educational Review 36* (1908): 28–42. Print.

—. *Education as Cultivation of Higher Mental Processes.* New York: Macmillan, 1936. Print.

—. *Educational Psychology.* New York: Houghton Mifflin, 1939. Print.

King, Patricia, and Karen Kitchener. *Developing Reflective Judgment: Understanding and Promoting Intellectual Growth and Critical Thinking in Adolescents and Adults.* San Francisco, CA: Jossey-Bass, 1994. Print.

Lave, Jeanne, and Etienne Wenger. *Situated Learning: Legitimate Peripheral Participation.* New York: Cambridge UP, 1991. Print.

Lunsford, Andrea. "Cognitive Development and the Basic Writer." *College English* 41.1 (1979): 449–59. Print.

McCarthy, Lucille Parkinson. "A Stranger in Strange Lands: A College Student Writing Across the Curriculum." *Research in the Teaching of English* 21.3 (1987): 233–65. Print.

Nowacek, Rebecca. *Agents of Integration: Understanding Transfer as a Rhetorical Act.* Carbondale: Southern Illinois UP, 2011. Print.

Perkins, David, and Gavriel Salomon. "Transfer of Learning." *International Encyclopedia of Education.* 2nd ed. Boston, MA: Pergamon Press, 1992. Web. 1 December 2012.

Perl, Sondra. "The Composing Processes of Unskilled College Writers." *Research in the Teaching of English* 13.4 (1979): 317–36. Print.

Prior, Paul, and Jody Shipka. "Chronotopic Lamination: Tracing the Contours of Literate Activity." *Writing Selves/Writing Societies.* Ed. Charles Bazerman and David Russell. Fort Collins, CO: The WAC Clearinghouse, 2003. Web. 1 December 2012.

Reiff, Mary Jo, and Anis Bawarshi. "Tracing Discursive Resources: How Students Use Prior Genre Knowledge to Negotiate New Writing Contexts in First-Year Composition." *Written Communication* 28.3 (2011): 312–37. Print.

Robertson, Liane, Kara Taczak, and Kathleen Blake Yancey. "Notes Toward a Theory of Prior Knowledge and Its Role in College Composers' Transfer of Knowledge and Practice." *Composition Forum* 26 (2012). Web. 1 December 2012.

Rose, Mike. "Rigid Rules, Inflexible Plans, and the Stifling of Language: A Cognitivist Analysis of Writer's Block." *College Composition and Communication* 31.4 (1980): 389–401. Print.

Rounsaville, Angela. "From Incomes to Outcomes: FYW Students' Prior Genre Knowledge, Meta-Cognition, and the Question of Transfer." *WPA: Writing Program Administration* 32.1 (2008): 97–112. Print.

Russell, David. "Activity Theory and its Implications for Writing Instruction." *Reconceiving Writing, Rethinking Writing Instruction.* Ed. Joseph Petraglia. Mahwah, NJ: Erlbaum, 1995. 51–77. Print.

Roozen, Kevin. "Journalism, Poetry, Stand-up Comedy, and Academic Literacy: Mapping the Interplay of Curricular and Extracurricular Literate Activities." *The Journal of Basic Writing* 27.1 (2008): 5–34. Print.

Tuomi-Grohn, Terttu, and Yrgo Engestrom, eds. *Between School and Work: New Perspectives on Transfer and Boundary-Crossing.* New York: Pergamon Press, 2003. Print.

Thorndike, E. L. "Mental Discipline in High School Studies." *Journal of Educational Psychology* 15 (1924): 1–22. Print.

Thorndike, E. L. and R. S. Woodworth. "The Influence of Improvement in One Mental Function Upon the Efficiency of Other Functions." *Psychological Review* 8 (1901): 247–61.

Wardle, Elizabeth. "Creative Repurposing for Expansive Learning: Considering 'Problem-Exploring' and 'Answer-Getting' Dispositions in Individuals and Fields." *Composition Forum* 26 (2012). Web. 1 December 2012.

—. "Understanding 'Transfer' from FYC: Preliminary Results of a Longitudinal Study." *WPA: Writing Program Administration* 31:1–2 (2007): 65–85. Print.

12 What Is Assessment?

Susanmarie Harrington

Talk of assessment swirls around college campuses now. Calls for accountability regarding student performance are reverberating from K–12 up into higher education. Assessment is everywhere, and regardless of your own background with assessment, you will likely find yourself called into campus conversations about it. There is a tradition of assessment practice and theory within rhetoric and composition; this makes WPAs valuable resources for other campus administrators seeking faculty participation or leadership in assessment efforts. Furthermore, there are generally small class sizes in writing programs—and first-year composition programs serve many first-year students. This makes writing classes an attractive site for assessment when campus administrators wonder how to get access to students. Writing is also one obvious way for students to demonstrate what they know, which makes writing programs of interest to the campus. These are just a few factors that bring WPA work into contact with assessment initiatives on campus, creating opportunities for a WPA to work beyond his or her own program. Whatever your own scholarly and administrative priorities, you will find an ability to participate with authority in conversations about assessment to be an asset for you and your program.

At the same time, assessment might seem more of a burden than an opportunity. Not all WPAs have experience or training in assessment, and you might feel that assessment is beyond your immediate area of expertise. Some of the factors I identify above as reasons that writing programs are attractive to campus assessment efforts—such as the access they provide to first-year students during the year—can seem more opportunistic than principled. As this collection illustrates, WPAs deal with many, many roles and issues; you might feel that assessment is simply one more thing you don't quite have time to get to. Assessment can seem like a challenge—and, if imposed by an external audience, it can appear to challenge what we are doing in our classrooms or programs. On top of all this, faculty don't always joyfully volunteer to participate when talk of assessment surfaces. So assessment can feel like a mixed bag. In this chapter, then, I want to offer some core truths about assessment, designed to demystify assessment and give you a framework for making smart choices about its role in your professional life and your writing program. Fundamentally, assessment becomes a scary burden when we can't or won't make choices about it. Setting up your WPA work so that you're in charge of—or heavily influential in—the way assessment is framed on your campus is the best way to make assessment work a real resource for you and your colleagues.

This chapter isn't going to provide a primer in strategies for writing assessment. Assessment methodologies are always evolving, and the best assessments are designed to fit particular contexts. There are many other sources that can help you discover particular assessment methods or designs: Peggy O'Neill, Cindy Moore, and Brian Huot's *Guide to College Writing Assessment* and Bob Broad's *What We Really Value: Beyond Rubrics in Teaching and Assessing Writing* offer excellent introductions to the history, theory, and practice of writing assessment; Peggy Maki's *Assessing for Learning: Building a Sustainable Commitment Across the Institution* is an excellent introduction to assessment more broadly. What I aim to provide here is a guide to the principles and frameworks you'll need to set up in order to ask questions about assessment. By outlining some of the qualities of good assessment, I hope to offer you the chance to integrate assessment thinking and practices into multiple aspects of your work and identity.

ASSESSMENT TELLS STORIES

Consider these examples:

- At the close of the spring semester, a writing program's administrative committee brings together faculty teaching first-year composition to read student portfolios from the first course in a two-course composition sequence. The reading sessions start with three basic questions inspired by an early 1990s conference presentation given by Kathleen Blake Yancey and Meg Morgan about an assessment they implemented at the University of North Carolina at Greensboro: What do you see here that you are pleased about? What concerns you in this portfolio? What's not in the portfolio that you wish were there? The faculty spend two days reading portfolios. Over the course of the reading period, participants are surprised to discover the prevalence of researched writing in the portfolios, and somewhat disturbed by students' reflections on that research, which suggests that a dominant purpose for research was to find a quotation to support a position the writer already held. The surprise here came from the fact that the program's first-semester course did not address research (or so faculty thought); research was a prime focus in the second-semester course (offered in the spring), and the first-semester course focused (they thought) on close reading of texts assigned to everyone in the section. In addition, the research practices the program sought to foster in that second course were much more tied to inquiry and curiosity than to finding support for already-existing positions. The upshot? A series of workshops and conversations the following fall that began by revealing the portfolio readers' widespread concerns about research. The result of that? A frank conversation about what students needed that resulted in an overhaul of the curriculum.

- At a community college, faculty teaching composition courses take a few extra minutes at the end of the semester to fill out an additional form for every third portfolio on their roster (Adler-Kassner and O'Neill 112–14). Using just a few of the program's thirteen common goals, faculty use a checklist to quickly rate the portfolio's level of achievement, and most add a few (voluntary) discursive comments. Each year, the department decides which of the program's common outcomes will be highlighted in the assessment; over five years, virtually all of the outcomes will be assessed. Program administrators total the ratings from all sections and report to the administration on the ways in which the program's students meet proficiency in those areas. They also bring results back to the faculty, who have changed the way they teach in response to what they have learned. Each year, the department plans for the future, given what they now know about student learning in the highlighted areas. Seeing that students were unevenly citing sources, they attended to citation differently in class, developing new teaching approaches after conversation about the assessment results. Eventually, the faculty decided to collapse and revise the program outcomes, moving from thirteen outcomes to just five. The portfolios had been introduced—under faculty leadership—as a way to develop an assessment to replace a standardized exam. Over time, they became a means of complying with the campus' assessment directive as well as a means of reflecting on the curriculum.

Each of these assessment activities lets someone tell a story about student writing. In the first case, the story is about student writing, but more importantly, about faculty response to student writing. Knowing that everyone in the room—from part-time faculty to long-time program administrators—shared the same concerns about research that focused only on finding single quotations to drop into a text (rather than research that focused on understanding a debate) let the assessment participants go out into the program with a striking story. The fall workshops weren't something the program directors imposed from on high; they were conversations that the assessment participants wanted everyone in the program to have. In the second case, WPAs were able to tell stories about program efficacy—they had a narrative about how successful the program was in terms of helping students meet particular goals. Perhaps even more importantly, they had a story to tell each other about how students were citing sources, and that story led faculty to change how they taught that skill. In subsequent iterations of the assessment, faculty could see whether their changes made any difference in how students performed.

So assessment tells a story: It provides a narrative about writing, and teachers, and students. Assessment provides information about what kinds of behaviors writers exhibit; it provides information about what kinds of thinking writers do; and it provides information about what kinds of reading reveals good writing.

Assessment Lets People Make Decisions

The illustrative assessment examples above show that assessment narratives are useful to administrators. But they are also useful to the program itself. In every one of these cases, the information generated from the assessment went back into the program. Key to the design of any assessment is a sense of what the information provided by the assessment will make possible. Good assessments should be done *in order to facilitate the design or improvement of program activities.*

As assessments enable you to tell a story about your program (or course), assessment lets you understand what's happening; that understanding, in turn, permits you—or your colleagues—to take action. It's these ongoing actions that make assessment so valuable. In the examples above, the most significant moments are actually those that followed the assessment: the changes in curriculum that evolved from the discussion of assessment results. In the first example, some of the decisions made had an impact on the entire writing program: Faculty development workshops were designed, and curriculum and textbooks changed, in order to create a curriculum that faculty would teach. Working out why faculty had encouraged independent research in the first-semester course involved exploring a lot of unspoken assumptions in faculty's teaching practices: The writing program's organizing committee had a year's worth of work following that assessment, a year's worth of work and conversations with faculty. In the second example, changes were no less dramatic: a collapsing of program outcomes that provided a much sleeker focus for the program. Yet some of the stories emerging are rather small ones, stories about how students cite sources (as opposed to a grand narrative about how well students write).

The size or scope of the stories is important, for grand stories don't always permit focused actions. However, assessments that focus on very particular aspects of writing will open opportunities for WPAs or individual teachers to act. Assessment provides information that faculty can use to make students' experiences better. That's really the key point for using assessment well: We learn things through assessment that help us do our jobs better. In the classroom, assessment for students should help them understand their own work better. At the program level, assessment should help us do our administrative work better.

Assessment conversations should start with a sense of why the assessment is being performed. It's easy to get sucked into questions about what assessment technique should be used, or how much money is available for assessment, but the very best question to ask in the face of an assessment demand is *who will do what with the information that we generate?* In asking that question, you keep the focus on the continued development of your program.

ASSESSMENT IS ONE OF THE MOST CRUCIAL THINGS WE DO

We are past the point when we can say that assessment is only the job of people whose research area is assessment, or that assessment is only the job of the campus assessment office (if there even is one). Assessment today needs to be everyone's job, for many reasons, the least of which is the fact that your institution is required by accreditors to have some kind of assessment system in place (see also Fitzgerald, this volume). As Linda Adler-Kassner argues, the dominant public narrative about writing asserts that higher education fails to prepare students for a changing economy ("Company(ies);" see also chapter 6 in Adler-Kassner and O'Neill). Her work explores the relationships among educational foundations, policy groups, and standardized test companies. There are powerful economic and political pressures being brought to bear on higher education in general and writing programs in particular (see also O'Neill and Gallagher, this volume). We need to tell a different story about writing, one that honors the ways writing is complicated. Writing involves thinking, research, rethinking. It involves development that proceeds over time, but not in a linear fashion.

The Conference on College Composition and Communication's (CCCC) "Writing Assessment: A Position Statement" focuses on the ways writing assessments should be framed and implemented. The "NCTE-WPA White Paper on Writing Assessment in Colleges and Universities" offers a philosophical and political framework that can be used to bolster the intellectual work of framing assessment as research and inquiry that can serve important local needs. As Linda Adler-Kassner and Peggy O'Neill illustrate in the closing chapter of their book, working on writing assessment frequently involves compromises. Addressing big political issues is a daunting task for any of us, but our assessment activities enable us to plant seeds in broader discussions on campus. Designing our questions and bringing our data to light lets us tell other people what we see when we look at our programs, and what changes we are making over time in our programs.

Assessment Is Rhetorical

Assessments, like all texts, have audiences, purposes, and settings. As WPAs, we can direct our attention to defining the audience, purpose, and setting of assessments within our program, and we can also consider the ways in which our programs can participate in assessment projects that serve broader needs for the campus or institution. Just as your background with research can help you embrace assessment, so too can your background with rhetoric help you embrace assessment. Assessment is one vehicle for communicating about your program, internally and externally.

We can see the ways in which any assessment serves an audience by considering the different settings for assessment. Assessment occurs at an informal and daily level in the classroom; it occurs at a highly standardized and formalized way for national accreditation processes or for disciplinary evaluations like a licensing exam in psychology or education.

WPAs can be involved with almost all of these. First, consider the setting. Who's involved in each setting? In the classroom, individual teachers and students. What do they need to know or want to know? Students want to know how they will be graded and what work will be most valued. At the campus level, administrators may want to know what outcomes guide your program and how you evaluate the effectiveness of your program. Administrators may also need to communicate to others beyond the campus about student learning. By understanding what different audiences for assessment need to know, and what sorts of decisions those audiences might be in a position to make, you can use assessment to help provide information. If you do all this while keeping in mind the narrative about writing that *you* want to promulgate, and while keeping in mind the questions that are most important to you as an administrator, you will weave assessment into the life of your program.

Assessment and Accountability Aren't the Same Thing

Assessment is frequently coupled with the term *accountability*. My provost, in remarks about general education, sometimes notes that developing an assessment program along with our evolving general education work will enable us to be accountable for our work. With the implementation of the No Child Left Behind Act, assessment and accountability have become fused in the K–12 sector. (The state of North Carolina's writing assessments are overseen by the Accountability Services Division of the State Board of Education; West Virginia's state board has an Office of Assessment and Accountability; and New Mexico's Assessment and Accountability Division of the state's Public Education Board oversees assessment there. Your state likely has something similar.) In the world of higher education, the Voluntary System of Accountability (VSA) is a consortium of public colleges seeking to provide common "College Portraits" for those interested in comparing institutions—and one required component of the portrait is the use of a standardized critical thinking test. The notions of assessment embedded with calls for accountability frequently coincide with calls for the use of standardized tests, tests which are said to be both objective and comparative.

These calls for accountability that are so dominant in the news are rooted in a sense that teachers—that we—really aren't doing our jobs. No wonder faculty are hostile to calls for assessment activity when the invitation to join in such work contains an implied insult. Accountability assumes that left to their own devices, teachers—and students—will not work to common standards, and that teachers are simply lazy and/or entrenched in old and ineffective ways of doing things. There is a juggernaut of policy and public conversation that seems to want to make the case that schools are failing, that college graduates aren't ready for the workforce, that students can't write, that students don't write, and that they can't read. Writing, in this discourse, is defined rather narrowly as something that can be tested via standardized exams (and frequently scored by computer algorithms, which gets into a whole 'nother kettle of fish!). Writing, in an accountability framework, tends to be defined in terms of correctness at the word/ sentence level or in very general terms such as *clear* and *organized*. General terms, such as *analysis* or *organization*, are presumed to have a common and standard meaning, But as Chris M. Anson et al. discovered in their analysis of the ways disciplinary faculty defined writing expectations in their own fields, the meanings of these common terms vary enormously from field to field. The accountability discourse, with its emphasis on limited definitions of what counts for good writing and a limited notion of what skilled writers need to learn and do, ignores what we know about how writers develop over time. (See also Doug Downs's and Elizabeth Wardle's chapters in this volume.)

Our assessments can help us generate types of stories that counter this narrative. Longitudinal studies of college writing development suggest that writing development happens in nonlinear ways: Lee Ann Carroll's investigation revealed the ways students put differing levels of work into their advanced writing tasks; Carroll and Richard Haswell (*Gaining Ground*) note the ways student writing tasks are different, and more challenging, as college goes on; studies at Harvard and Stanford reveal the complexities of students' relationships with feedback on writing (Harvard Writing Project) and the wide range of tasks that students take up over their four (or more) years in college (Fishman et al.). Our assessments create different stories, about capable students making writing choices and about students receiving instruction in the disciplinary ways of thinking that undergird their majors. See, for example, the many dimensions of the critique that design students must learn (Anson et al.).

Assessment and Evaluation Aren't the Same Thing

Evaluation is another word that comes up in conjunction with assessment. Evaluation suggests a finished state, an objective analysis that will let someone come up with a judgment about the state of the program—i.e., either this program works or it doesn't. There might, therefore, be times when you wish to seek an evaluation of a program. An example from my own experience: After reading Haswell's work on prototypes and writing assessment, I changed the approach we used to rating student writing samples to simplify the system. Rather than having two readers for every placement text, I had the system stop after one reader if that reader judged the student writer was ready for Comp 1. However, if the reader thought that the writer's needs fell outside Comp 1 (in honors or in basic writing), then a second reader stepped in. We did an evaluation of that program, intended to determine whether the new system was placing students adequately (surveying teachers about whether or not students seemed to be well-placed) and doing a statistical analysis of the relationship between the old system and the new. This evaluation let us know that our system was indeed, working (Harrington). This wasn't an assessment: It didn't generate information that we folded into the ongoing work we did. It was, rather, an evaluation, one that let us know we had made a good system that worked in the moment.

Another example: Asked for ways to demonstrate the effectiveness of the MIT Writing Center, Neal Lerner investigated the relationships between student GPAs and use of the writing center. No significant relationships emerged, but when Lerner added in a different set of variables (controlling for high school grades, SAT scores, and first-year GPA), a "powerful relationship" between writing center visits and grades in composition courses as well as overall first-year GPA was found. (O'Neill, Moore, Huot 117–18). This sort of work tends more toward evaluation: It provides some evidence for a story about whether a writing center has an effect on students or not. It's not assessment, though. The audience for that story is outsiders who want to know whether the writing center works. Assessment is directed more at a disciplinary or internal audience: people who want to know *how* the writing center works in order to *make further decisions* about how to develop the writing center and its tutors. (For more about writing centers and their function within an institution, see Lerner, this volume.)

To sum up: Evaluation asks whether a course or program is effective, and the audience for evaluation is most often external. Assessment is a formative process, providing information for an inside audience who is interested in continued development of a course or program.

THE ASSESSMENT QUESTION SHOULD BE THE FIRST THING YOU DECIDE; THE ASSESSMENT TECHNIQUE IS AMONG THE LAST THINGS YOU DECIDE

Assessment is, as Huot says, research. It is this point about assessment that can help you embrace assessment as a wonderful part of your job (see also Donahue, this volume). Research is something that graduate school provides training in; for tenure-line WPAs, research is likely a significant expectation for tenure. So considering assessment as research—rather than as burden—will help you see assessment as a priority. As Huot notes, the general emphasis on testing and technologies of writing assessment

> [h]as obscured the essential purpose of assessment as research and inquiry, as a way of asking and answering questions about students' writing and the programs designed to teach students to write. The primary consideration in assessing student writing should be what we want to know about our students. (148)

Faced with a request to do assessment, you can easily get drawn into planning means of collecting student work or strategies to score student essays or portfolios or conversations about what sort of assessment method is appropriate. Resist such thinking until you have addressed the foundation of the assessment: *What do you want to know?* And *how will knowing that enable you to do your job better?* As Lerner points out in his work on writing center assessment, it is important that we ask questions about how writing centers affect student development. The same is true of our courses. As the CCCC's "Writing Assessment: A Position Statement" asserts:

> Writing assessment is useful primarily as a means of improving teaching and learning. [. . .] Best assessment practice is informed by pedagogical and curricular goals, which are in turn formatively affected by the assessment. Teachers or administrators designing assessments should ground the assessment in the classroom, program or departmental context. The goals or outcomes assessed should lead to assessment data which is fed back to those involved with the regular activities assessed so that assessment results may be used to make changes in practice.

Thinking of assessment as a way to research your program keeps your focus on activities that are useful. Broad's dynamic criteria mapping illustrates the ways that assessment activities can uncover meaningful disagreements among faculty about expectations for student work—and then can provide opportunities for negotiating those disagreements and deciding how to work with them. Any assessment activity that is driven by your sense—or your faculty's sense—of true curiosity will result in information you can use. And when that happens, everyone benefits.

WORKS CITED

Adler-Kassner, Linda. "The Company(ies) We Keep: Tactics and Strategies in Challenging Times." 2012 Writing Program Administrators Conference. Council of Writing Program Administrators. Albuquerque, NM. 19 July 2012. Plenary Address.

Adler-Kassner, Linda, and Peggy O'Neill. *Reframing Writing Assessment to Improve Teaching and Learning.* Logan: Utah State UP, 2011. Print.

Anson, Chris M., Deanna P. Dannels, Pamela Flash, and Amy L. Housley Gaffney. "Big Rubrics and Weird Genres: The Futility of Using Generic Assessment Tools Across Diverse Instructional Contexts." *Journal of Writing Assessment* 5.1 (2012). Web. 6 May 2013.

Broad, Bob. *What We Really Value: Beyond Rubrics in Teaching and Assessing Writing.* Logan: Utah State UP, 2003. Print.

Carroll, Lee Ann. *Rehearsing New Roles: How College Students eelop as Writers.* Carbondale: Southern Illinois UP, 2002. Print.

Conference on College Composition and Communication. "Writing Assessment: A Position Statement." March 2009. Web. 6 May 2013.

Fishman, Jenn, Andrea Lunsford, Beth McGregor, and Mark Otuteye. "Performing Writing, Performing Literacy." *College Composition and Communication* 57.2 (2005): 224–52. Print.

Harrington, Susanmarie. "New Visions of Authority in Placement Test Rating." *WPA: Writing Program Administration* 22 (1998): 53–84. Print.

Harvard Writing Project. "A Brief Guide to Responding to Student Writing." Harvard College Writing Program. 2007. Web. 12 June 2013.

Haswell, Richard. *Gaining Ground in College Writing: Tales of Development and Interpretation.* Dallas, TX: Southern Methodist UP, 1991. Print.

—. "Rubrics, Prototypes, and Exemplars: Categorization and Systems of Writing Placement." *Journal of Assessing Writing* 5.2 (1998): 231-68. Print.

Huot, Brian. *(Re)Articulating Writing Assessment for Teaching and Learning.* Logan: Utah State UP, 2002. Print.

Lerner, Neal. "Writing Center Assessment: Searching for the 'Proof' of our Effectiveness." *The Center Will Hold.* Ed. Michael Pemberton and Joyce Kinkead. Logan: Utah State UP, 58–73. Print.

Maki, Peggy. *Assessing for Learning: Building a Sustainable Commitment Across the Institution.* 2nd ed. Sterling, VA: Stylus, 2010. Print.

National Council of Teachers of English and Council of Writing Program Administrators. "NCTE-WPA White Paper on Writing Assessment in Colleges and Universities. " April 2008. Web. 11 February 2013.

New Mexico Public Education Department. Assessment and Accountability Division. July 2011. Web. 11 February 2013.

O'Neill, Peggy, Cindy Moore, and Brian Huot. *Guide to College Writing Assessment.* Logan: Utah State UP, 2009. Print.

Public Schools of North Carolina. Accountability Services Division. n.d. Web. 3 May 2013.

Voluntary System of Accountability (VSA). 2011. Web. 11 February 2013.

West Virginia Department of Education. Office of Assessment and Accountability. n.d. Web. 11 February 2013.

Part 3: Personal Questions

13 What Is a Writing Instructor?

Eileen E. Schell

The title of "writing instructor" can be used to describe an array of individuals who teach postsecondary writing courses; however, it is important to remember that writing instructors' professional lives, expectations, expertise, pay, and working conditions may vastly differ. Thus, it is perhaps best to begin this chapter with some analysis of the complexities surrounding instructor status. As Holly Hassel and Joanne Baird Giordano argue, we need to "recognize that contingent faculty is not a blanket category" (Arnold et al. 415).

INSTRUCTOR: WHAT'S IN A NAME?

Consider the following varied portrait of writing instructors that you might conceivably work with in a given writing program:

- a female instructor with a master's degree in English who has taught writing part-time (two courses per semester) for thirty years while raising children and putting them through college. Her income has been secondary to that of her tenured faculty spouse who teaches literature in your department;
- a recently minted male PhD in English literature who took a lectureship (4–4 load) in your department while he searches for a tenure-track appointment;
- an accomplished MFA graduate and published feminist poet who teaches part-time in your department and others in the area while she manages a small literary press and continues with her writing and public readings;

- a tenured linguistics professor who teaches writing occasionally to show solidarity with the composition faculty, and who has been teaching for almost forty years;
- an MA student in English who recently graduated with a BA from a small liberal arts college and is twenty-two years old without any experience in the classroom; you, along with a handful of colleagues, are responsible for orienting and supervising her first semester as a teaching assistant (TA).

As the WPA, your job is to make sure that these different groups of instructors are prepared for the task of teaching writing. Since writing instructors are referred to by various employment categories and acronyms at different institutions, it is useful to consider the typical classes, categories, ranks, and backgrounds—such as the ones mentioned above—that you might encounter as a WPA.

Contingent Instructors

Contingent instructors are those who teach without the job protections and material and economic privileges of tenure: part-time faculty, lecturers, non-tenure-track faculty, as well as those answering to other monikers. Writing instructors, along with teaching assistants, are a large and growing segment in higher education, with some institutions having only contingent faculty staffing writing courses. The 2007 Association of Departments of English Ad-Hoc Committee on Staffing reports that according to the 2004 National Survey of Postsecondary Faculty (NSOPF), "an estimated 46,200 people are employed in non-tenure-track positions in English" (11). Within that number, an estimated "37,500 are employed part-time and 8,700 full-time" (11). Breaking down this data further, we find that of the 46,200 non-tenure-track postsecondary faculty members, "about 6,650 (14.4%) hold doctorates; about 5,590 (12.1%) hold MFAs. A majority—60.9%, or more than 28,000—hold a master's degree other than an MFA" (11).

Within this larger category of contingent faculty, however, you may find distinct differences in employment status and contractual obligations, which affect how these faculty members perceive their responsibilities, rewards, and roles. I highlight below some of the more typical designations you might encounter within the broad rubric of contingent faculty.

Part-time or Adjunct Instructors. Part-time and adjunct instructors are a dynamic, multi-faceted class of workers. These instructors teach one to two classes per semester or quarter or possibly more depending on what counts as a part-time load at your institution. These instructors are sometimes hired in the fall and laid off in the spring due to lower student enrollments. Their credentials, preparation, training, and expertise may vastly differ depending on the hiring criteria at your institution. [*what a useless statement*]

In addition to their varied teaching loads, experience, and preparation, part-time or adjunct instructors—as indicated earlier—bring different individual and structural reasons for teaching at your institution. Some part-time/adjunct instructors may be "moonlighters" pursuing a full-time career or vocation elsewhere and teach around their other obligations. Some may be working parents who need a flexible schedule so they can care for young children or, increasingly, for elderly parents. Some are PhDs or MAs who teach part-time or in adjunct positions while searching for a full-time job. Some may be PhDs or MA-holders who operate as "freeway flyers," driving from campus to campus or navigating from virtual campus to campus to string together enough part-time teaching to equal a full-time job (for more on labor classifications see Gappa and Leslie; Schell, *Gypsy*). Thus, "part-time" or "adjunct" can be a misleading label, since some part-time faculty members are full-time employees across institutions.

Full-time, Non-tenure-track Instructors. Full-time, non-tenure-track instructors typically teach what is considered to be a full load of courses, often a 4–4 or 3–4 per year at colleges and universities or a 5–5 or more loads at community colleges. Full-time, non-tenure-track instructors often have yearly or multi-year contracts, but some teach on semester-to-semester contracts. As noted earlier, these faculty members may have doctoral degrees, MFAs, or MAs.

A non-tenure-track position may be the best position that an instructor can obtain in a difficult career market in their field. It also may be a position that allows an instructor to remain with a spouse or partner employed in a specific geographic area. Also, it is important to remember that some non-tenure-track instructors (or part-time in-

structors) may be graduate students finishing degrees who no longer
have TA funding.

Within specific departments, there may be designations or ranks
attached to non-tenure-track status such as senior lecturer or senior
instructor with tenure-like protections such as security of employment
designations. In addition, non-tenure-track faculty may have administrative or service obligations. In fact, you may be a non-tenure-track
WPA yourself—a situation well documented in Alice Horning and
Debra Frank Dew's edited collection on untenured WPAs.

Teaching Assistants

In addition to the varied groups mentioned above, teaching assistants
are, on occasion, referred to as instructors; however, their status is
distinctly different as they are simultaneously enrolled full-time in a
degree-granting MA or PhD program while holding a teaching assistantship. TAs are considered to be teacher "apprentices" who are supported through formal advising and mentoring structures that other
classes of instructors are not likely to have access to (see Reid, this
volume). You, as the WPA, are likely to be in charge of TA training,
whether as an individual or as a member of a mentoring team (see
Reid, this volume).

Tenure-line or Tenured Faculty

Perhaps the most autonomous of all classes of writing instructor is the
tenure-track or tenured faculty member. This group is often a rare
breed at many large state universities—indeed, only a handful may be
teaching required writing courses (including you if you are on the tenure track) at large institutions. Far more common are tenured/tenure-
track faculty who teach writing courses at small liberal arts colleges
and community colleges where all tenured/tenure-track faculty often
participate in teaching writing and see it as part of their main mission.

Staff Members

Perhaps comprising the smallest number of writing instructors are
full-time staff members who have teaching as part of their staff responsibilities. They may be administering writing centers or WAC

programs or supporting other endeavors at the university as they teach a few writing courses.

As Kelly Ritter notes in the lead chapter in this volume, students are "not us," but we cannot say with total confidence that writing instructors are not like "us," as the possible writing instructor profiles I have indicated above demonstrate. In short, writing instructors, no matter what rank, *are your colleagues.* Their work and their contributions must be, as Sue Doe et al. argue, "understood as essential, meaningful and even central to the function of colleges and universities" (432).

ENCOURAGING A COLLEGIAL INSTRUCTOR CULTURE, ONE BASED ON INVITATION AND INCLUSION

Many writing instructors in your unit may be old hands who will tell you that *they have been teaching longer than you have been alive,* something I was told by a few instructors when I became a WPA at a large state university at age thirty. To be quite blunt, experienced instructors may know more than you do (gasp!) about the students and about what it means to teach at that institution and in that particular locale. These instructors may regard a new WPA, especially a young or inexperienced one, with some suspicion. Yes, you may know more about the scholarship in the field, but institutional and classroom-based practical knowledge also has a value.

As a WPA, you may—or may not—share some of the same background, professional training, and assumptions about the best approaches to teaching composition as some of the writing instructors you work with. In that mix, it's not your job, to put it crudely, to come in and convert the so-called natives to your viewpoint and perspective, although such a missionary culture tends to prevail in some WPA circles; ironically in a field where we privilege diversity and inclusion, we often don't hold the same values in our professional work cultures. You will have to find ways to establish a *shared and mutual pedagogical culture and community* that successfully bridges and addresses differences in knowledge, training, and approaches or that at least attempts to do so through conversation and dialogue.

Figuring Out Work Expectations

When you become a WPA in a department or program with many instructors, one of the first ways you can prepare for your work is to find out what is and is not *in print* about instructors' duties and responsibilities. Some departments are characterized by highly structured employment contracts, including collective bargaining agreements (see Kahn, this volume). There may be strict job classifications with lists of duties and responsibilities, firm start and completion dates, and yet expectations may differ from class-to-class of instructors. On the other hand, some employment contracts, especially in a non-union environment, are informal, with few expectations, duties, and processes spelled out, an issue to contemplate as you consider ways to improve working conditions for instructors.

In addition to learning about instructor contracts and work expectations, you can begin to consider ways to tap into instructors' vast pool of experience and knowledge about students, the university, the community, their fields of study, and the day-to-day practices and pedagogies of the writing classroom. You can begin this process by inviting instructors to a series of "get acquainted" coffees or luncheons sponsored by department funds. Or if you don't have such funds, ask your chair or dean for them, or just ask instructors to bring their own lunch and talk with you about their experiences and goals for teaching writing. Ask your instructor colleagues what they would like to see you and the program accomplish in terms of curriculum and professional development opportunities. Also, you will want to encourage instructors to let you know about their professional accomplishments (conference papers, publications, community involvement) and publicize those accomplishments to your department colleagues and dean.

In addition to getting to know the instructors you work with, get to know the teaching documents they have produced over the years. Read over instructors' syllabi, evaluations, program reports, and any other available teaching-related documents. This is a large investment of time, but it is an important way to understand the teaching culture(s) of the unit and the strengths, weaknesses, and contributions of your instructor colleagues.

GOVERNANCE AND LINES OF AUTHORITY

As you learn more about the instructors you will be working with, consider the processes and procedures that you allow you and others to hire, supervise, mentor, and evaluate writing instructors as well as what governance powers they have. What is the influence of the office of the WPA, real and perceived, in these matters (see also Kahn, this volume)? What role do instructors play in the governance processes in your department? Familiarize yourself with department or program by-laws, and note how the WPA and writing instructors in your unit are included or omitted in those by-laws. What are your voting rights and areas of influence? What are instructors' voting rights and inclusion in matters of governance?

Generate a list of questions and concerns you have about the writing program's, WPA's, and instructors' scope of influence and authority as specified in those by-laws and note areas of needed reform and inclusion. Discuss these ideas with your department chair, dean, or provost (or whomever you report to) and come up with a plan for needed reforms and a way to carry them out.

In addition, consider what committees or program structures allow you to carry out your work. Ideally, the work of a writing program and a WPA is guided by a series of knowledgeable and informed stakeholders. Your department may have a standing composition committee or writing committee that includes a range of writing faculty (or English department faculty) who work on the writing curriculum and matters related to instructor evaluation and professional development. Ideally instructors will be included as representatives to such a committee or have a voice and/or a vote on matters pertaining to writing curricula, professional development, and their employment. If this is not the case, you as WPA will likely be central to helping transform that situation, as I will indicate in the labor reform section of this chapter.

HIRING AND ORIENTATION PROCESSES

One of the most important roles a WPA can play in the formation of a productive workforce of instructors is to be active in instructor search, orientation, and professional development processes. It should go without saying that searches for writing instructors should be fair and aboveboard, following the guidelines for fair hiring practices recommended at your institution and by professional associations such as the American Association of University Professors (AAUP), the National Council of Teachers of English (NCTE), the Modern Language Association (MLA), and the Conference on College Composition and Communication (CCCC). However, all too often, institutions may lack or relax guidelines for conducting instructor searches, fostering haphazard, last-minute search processes whereby a single WPA or chair hires instructors right before the semester when the budget is approved and enrollments are confirmed. Often these conditions are beyond the WPA's control—you may have just been told by your dean or chief academic officer what the enrollments are going to be for the fall or spring and you have to hire a last-minute new group of instructors to cover the courses.

Your goal should be to create the fairest possible hiring processes within the economic constraints of your institution and to also lobby to improve the way instructors are hired, oriented, supported, and paid. With respect to hiring contingent faculty, job ads should be placed in local, regional, and national publications and a search committee should be constituted that consists of more than the WPA. Ask for a curriculum vitae (CV) and a letter of application plus a statement of teaching and a sample syllabus or two. Ask questions that probe the candidate's teaching history, qualifications, and philosophy of writing instruction. Keep the CVs on file of candidates that were qualified but that you could not hire due to no position being available and return to them if a position opens up at the last minute.

Once instructors are hired, you, as WPA, should be ready to help orient instructors to their duties. You will want to develop—if there is not such material already—a standard group orientation outline and schedule. You will want to provide new instructors with an overview of the program, the student demographics at your institution, information about the offices that support their work with students, and sample and required teaching materials such as textbooks, learning outcomes, a common syllabus (if there is one) or sample syllabi to model different approaches, and sample writing assignments and student essays. Ideally, there should be time for group workshop sessions on syllabus structure, writing assignments, and writing assessment. If the instructor is hired early enough in advance of the semester, you may want to suggest that he or she sit in on a summer writing class taught by an experienced instructor. The same privilege should be afforded any new tenure-line faculty or staff who will be teaching writing. Your institution may also have a university-wide orientation that new instructors can attend. New TAs will have a TA practicum to support them, and that practicum will take different shapes depending on the population you will have and the structures/resources available to support them (see also Reid, this volume).

A larger issue with the orientation of new instructors is how much freedom or autonomy they have to develop their own materials within curricular guidelines. You should be clear with instructors about what is expected in your writing program/department—that they use a standard syllabus their first year—or that they may have the freedom to design their own materials within certain constraints. Remind new instructors that you are there as a resource, and where possible, assign them a peer mentor and explain what kind of evaluation processes they can expect within their first year and beyond.

FACULTY DEVELOPMENT

Some writing programs and English departments have well-developed structures of faculty development in place for varied groups of instructors. Other programs are more laissez-faire and give instructors a textbook and wish them luck with the semester. Your goal should be to figure out strategic ways to invest time and resources in improving and capitalizing on the knowledge base of instructors in your program/ department, for all the reasons that Stephen Wilhoit and Carol Rutz specify in their chapter on faculty development.

If there is a well-established structure for professional development in your program, work with that and evaluate what else needs to be done to improve it. If there is nothing or very little in the way of professional development, you may want to start out small—offer a monthly practicum or workshop where instructors can come together to share and discuss assignments, sample papers, common classroom problems and challenges, and discuss relevant articles on writing pedagogy.

While some instructors may not be able to attend every session, you can keep them informed through minutes, archived articles and materials on Blackboard, or though audiotaped or videotaped sessions. Make it *impossible* for the instructors you work with to be pedagogically disengaged by offering multiple mediums and incentives for participation. If your program budget allows for it, offer food and drink at these sessions.

If instructors opt out of such professional development sessions, you and your department/program can make it a condition of instructor employment contracts that they attend and participate. Getting this written into a contract, however, is easier said than done. Instead, encourage instructors to come and share their knowledge and learn from colleagues, and, where possible, compensate them for their time. In fact, encourage and find funds for instructors in your unit to attend and present at workshops or writing conferences, whether in-house/on-campus ones that you might sponsor or regional or national ones.

EVALUATION AND SUPERVISION

The evaluation and supervision of instructors is a key job for a WPA and/or composition/writing committee. When possible, you or a faculty or peer mentor will want to visit and observe the classes of new and returning instructors and review instructor teaching evaluations on a regular basis. Also, a teaching portfolio can be used during contract renewal processes to present a reflective account of teaching that goes beyond classroom observations and evaluations (Stock et al.). Where possible, these evaluation processes can be tied to a reward system of merit pay and rank advancement. Key to a strong system of evaluation is encouraging an attitude of reflection, inquiry, and ongoing investment and growth into one's own teaching practices. Thus, evaluation and supervision must be tied into a strong program of professional development and participation.

CONCLUSION: IMPROVING WORKING CONDITIONS

It has been argued that WPAs, on the one hand, are change agents and activists (see Adler-Kassner) and, on the other hand, that we are a managerial class (see Bousquet, Scott, and Parascandola), what James Sledd referred to derisively as "boss compositionists." Regardless of where you stand or find yourself institutionally in this debate, by becoming a WPA you have entered, perhaps unknowingly and unwillingly, into an ongoing debate over the labor and working conditions of those who teach writing. Studies of the working conditions of writing instructors from the late nineteenth century to the present indicates that instructors are overworked, underpaid, and disrespected, and this discourse has only strengthened of late (see Berlin; Bousquet; Campbell; Connors; Crowley; Hopkins, "Labor" and "Cost"; Lonn; McDonald and Schell; Schell, *Gypsy*; Schell and Stock; Taylor; Thompson). At the same time, professional organizations from AAUP to NCTE to MLA and CCCC have instituted position statements and guidelines about improving working conditions for those teaching writing as well as other subjects off the tenure track. Meanwhile, instructors themselves are working to improve their working conditions through unionization and through local, regional, national, and international coalition and caucus building.

In my book *Gypsy Academics and Mother-Teachers: Gender, Contingent Labor, and Writing Instruction*, I noted four of the most common strategies for improving working conditions in writing programs and English departments:

- The reformist solution: working within the system to reform current conditions, one of the most popular strategies that WPAs embrace (see, for example, Hansen 31–42).
- The conversionist solution: converting part-time/non-tenure-track positions into tenure-track ones, a solution that AAUP and other organizations have advocated and which does not seem to be gaining much traction. In fact, the biggest gains have been with converting part-time to non-tenure-track positions or tenure-track positions to non-tenure-track ones.
- The collectivist solution: instituting collective bargaining where possible. Where not possible, instituting collectives or caucuses to work toward a collective strategy of employment reforms.
- The abolitionist solution: abolishing the writing requirement so that the class of instructors is eliminated or minimized. This is another solution that has not been commonly followed except at institutions where writing requirements are not present.

Of these solutions, the reformist and collectivist ones have proved to be the most popular for changing labor conditions. Adjunct/part-time/non-tenure-track unions are on the rise and have improved working conditions in states where unionization is possible. Accounts of these unionization and organizing efforts are encapsulated thoughtfully in the scholarship on academic labor organizing as well as in articles in our field and Seth Kahn's chapter in this volume (see also Berry;

Bousquet; Schell, "Toward"). In addition, WPAs and instructors have a long history of improving working conditions, focusing their efforts on improving compensation, contractual length, coalitions, and conditions of work—what I call the four Cs (Schell and Stock).

[handwritten margin note: isn't it up to the WPA?]

With one or more of the many statements on instructor working conditions from AAUP, NCTE, MLA, or CCCC guiding a group or committee, a WPA and a group of instructors can conduct a survey of instructor needs and concerns and begin to set an action agenda— whether it involves a focus on improving compensation, contracts, evaluation processes, or participation in governance. What this action agenda will be and how it will play out is an open question that you will need to begin to explore and test with your colleagues and other stakeholders. Partnerships with university colleagues outside your unit—university senate committees and student governance organizations for instance—may be helpful. Increasingly, students are catching on to the importance of instructor working conditions, realizing their education depends upon such conditions.

There are no easy answers, one-size-fits-all solutions, or guarantees for how to improve working conditions and the workplace environment for instructors, but there is a common element: a department/program and university investment in the stabilization and professionalization of the working conditions of teaching-intensive faculty working off the tenure track, for their working conditions are students' learning conditions.

WORKS CITED

Adler-Kassner, Linda. *The Activist WPA: Changing Stories about Writing and Writers*. Logan: Utah UP, 2008. Print.

Arnold, Lisa, Laura Brady, Maggie Christensen, Joanne Baird Giordano, Holly Hassel, Ed Nagelhout, Nathalie Singh-Corcoran, and Julie Staggers. "Forum on the Profession." *College English* 73.4 (March 2011): 409–27. Print.

American Association of University Professors (AAUP). "Contingent Appointments and the Academic Profession." 2003. Web. 31 August 2012.

Association of Departments of English Ad Hoc Committee on Staffing. "Education in the Balance: A Report on the Academic Workforce." 2007. Web. 6 May 2013.

Berlin, James. *Rhetoric and Reality: Writing in American Colleges 1900–1985*. Carbondale: Southern Illinois UP, 1987. Print.

Berry, Joe. *Reclaiming the Ivory Tower: Organizing Adjuncts to Change Higher Education*. New York: Monthly Review Press, 2005. Print.

Bousquet, Marc. *How the University Works: Higher Education and the Low Wage Nation*. New York: New York UP, 2008. Print.

Bousquet, Marc, Tony Scott, and Leo Parascondola, eds. *Tenured Bosses and Disposable Teachers: Writing Instruction in the Managed University*. Carbondale: Southern Illinois UP, 2004. Print.

Campbell, Oscar James. "The Failure of Freshman English." *English Journal* 28 (1939): 177–85. Print.

CCCC Executive Committee. "Statement of Principles and Standards for Postsecondary Teaching of Writing." *CCC* 40.3 (1989): 362–65. Print.

Connors, Robert J. "Overwork/Underpay: Labor and Status of Composition Teachers since 1880." *Rhetoric Review* 9.1 (1990): 108–25. Rpt. in *Selected Essays of Robert J. Connors*. Ed. Lisa Ede and Andrea A. Lunsford. Boston, MA: Bedford/St. Martin's, 2003. 181–98. Print.

Crowley, Sharon. *Composition in the University: Historical and Polemical Essays*. Pittsburgh, PA: U of Pittsburgh P, 1998. Print.

Doe, Sue, Natalie Barnes, David Bowen, David Gilkey, Ginger Guardioia Smoak, Sarah Ryan, Kirk Sarell, Laura H. Thomas, Lucy J. Troup, and Mike Palmquist. "Discourse of the Firetenders: Considering Contingent Faculty through the Lens of Activity Theory." *College English* 73.4 (2011): 428–49. Print.

Gappa, Judith, and David Leslie. *The Invisible Faculty: Improving the Status of Part-Timers in Higher Education*. San Francisco, CA: Jossey-Bass, 1993. Print.

Hansen, Kristine. "Face to Face with Part-Timers: Ethics and the Professionalization of Writing Faculties." *Resituating Writing: Constructing and Administering Writing Programs*. Ed. Joseph Janangelo and Kristine Hansen. Portsmouth, NH: Boynton/Cook-Heinemann, 1995. 23–45. Print.

Hopkins, Edwin M. "The Labor and Cost of Composition Teaching: The Present Conditions." *Proceedings of the NEA*. 1912. 747–51. Print.

—. "The Cost and Labor of English Teaching." *Proceedings of the NEA*. 1915. 114–19. Print.

Horning, Alice, and Debra Frank Dew, eds. *Untenured Faculty as Writing Program Administrators*. West Lafayette, IN: Parlor Press, 2007. Print.

Lonn, Ella. "Academic Status of Women on University Faculties." *Journal of the American Association of University Women* 17 (Jan-March): 5-11. Print.

McDonald, James C. and Eileen E. Schell. "The Spirit and Influence of the Wyoming Resolution: Looking Back to Look Forward." *College English* 73.4 (2011): 360-78. Print.

NCTE College Section Working Group on the Status and Working Conditions of Contingent Faculty. "Statement on the Status and Working

Conditions of Contingent Faculty. *College English* 73.4 (March 2011): 356-359. Print.

Schell, Eileen E. *Gypsy Academics and Mother-teachers: Gender, Contingent Labor, and Writing Instruction.* Portsmouth, NH: Boynton Cook/Heinemann, 1997. Print.

—. "Toward a Labor Theory of Agency in Higher Education." *Works and Days.* 21.1-2 (2003): 313-37. Print.

Schell, Eileen E., and Patricia Lambert Stock, eds. *Moving a Mountain: Transforming the Role of Contingent Faculty in Composition Studies and Higher Education.* Urbana, Illinois: NCTE, 2001. Print.

Sledd, James. "Why the Wyoming Resolution Had to Be Emasculated: A History and a Quixotism." *Journal of Advanced Composition* 11.2 (1991): 269-81. Print.

Stock, Patricia Lambert, Amanda Brown, David Franke, and John Starkweather. "The Scholarship of Teaching: Contributions from Contingent Faculty." Schell and Stock, 287-323. Print.

Taylor, Warner. "A National Survey of Conditions in Freshman English." *Rpt. in The Origins of Composition Studies in the American College, 1875-1925: A Documentary History.* Ed. John Brereton. Pittsburgh: U of Pittsburgh P, 1995. 545-60. Print.

Thompson, Stith. "A National Survey of Freshman English." *English Journal* 19.7 (1930): 553-57. Print.

14 What Is Faculty Development?

Carol Rutz and Stephen Wilhoit

Faculty development has long been recognized as an essential aspect of writing program administration. For example, in 1992 the Council of Writing Program Administrators (CWPA) published the "Portland Resolution: Guidelines for Writing Program Administrator Positions," which includes faculty development on its comprehensive list of writing program administrator (WPA) responsibilities and identifies several faculty development activities that may be required of WPAs: designing and running faculty development seminars, training tutors, evaluating teaching performance, designing pedagogical workshops, and teaching for-credit courses in writing instruction. In its 1998 statement, "Evaluating the Intellectual Work of Writing Administration," CWPA reaffirms that faculty development, "when it truly accomplishes its purpose of improving teaching and maintaining the highest classroom standards, is one of the most salient examples of intellectual work carried out within an administrative sphere." Even as recently as 2012, the CWPA summer workshop for writing program administrators included on its agenda "Hiring Practices, Faculty Development, and Faculty Evaluation." This focus on faculty development makes sense: Unless WPAs personally teach every class in a writing program, they need to prepare other instructors for those classes.

Yet teacher training is just one part of faculty development. According to William J. Carpenter, faculty development in its most general sense "refers to programs and activities designed to improve the overall quality of college and university teaching staffs" (157). More specifically, faculty development entails promoting the "total development" of each faculty member in a program, fostering and supporting his or her growth "as a person, as a professional and as a member of an academic community" (Sorcinelli et al. 1). The Professional and

Organizational Development Network in Higher Education (POD) reflects this understanding of the term when it asserts that faculty development programs should address each faculty member's needs as a teacher, a professional, and a person. POD's definition offers a convenient framework for discussing the role faculty development plays in writing program administration.

Faculty development is best thought of as a long-term, mutually beneficial enterprise. Clearly, promoting a faculty member's instructional, professional, and personal growth takes time; WPAs cannot hope to accomplish these goals quickly. Instead, writing instructors develop their capacities gradually through study and experience, a process WPAs can help foster and guide. Also, faculty development is not a one-way exchange of knowledge, the WPA sharing his or her expertise and getting nothing in return. WPAs who succeed in faculty development enter into mutually beneficial, collaborative relationships with other writing instructors (Willard-Traub 442–43). Promoting their growth aids your own as a WPA by encouraging self-reflection and exposing you to other faculty members' knowledge, experience, and questions (see also Schell, this volume).

WHY IS FACULTY DEVELOPMENT IMPORTANT?

In "Embracing Our Expertise through Faculty and Instructional Development," Beth Brunk-Chavez observes that faculty development enables writing programs "to improve nearly every aspect of instruction, promote student learning, and establish a strong, unified community of instructors" (153). First, any writing program is only as strong as the faculty who teach in it: The best-designed writing program will not achieve its goals if the program's instructors are not able to meet those goals effectively. Faculty development enhances instructors' teaching skills, better enabling them to deliver the curriculum, achieve the program's goals, and promote student learning. Faculty development also promotes a sense of community in a writing program. As instructors work together to improve their pedagogical skills, enhance their professional status, and better understand their personal experiences as teachers and scholars, they develop a sense of camaraderie, unified purpose, shared responsibility, and mutual support.

WHO DO WPAS ASSIST AS FACULTY DEVELOPERS?

As a WPA committed to faculty development, you will work with a wide range of instructors across the curriculum and beyond your institution. Most of your faculty development efforts as a WPA will, however, be devoted to working with faculty and staff who teach writing in your department or program. These instructors can be full-time faculty, part-time faculty, lecturers, or graduate teaching assistants (see Schell, this volume, for a further discussion of who typically teaches writing in higher education). Some programming will be appropriate for all of the instructors in your department or program. At other times, you will need to tailor programming to meet the specific needs of particular groups of instructors: An experienced full-time faculty member may not need the same type of development that a new, inexperienced TA requires.

If your institution has a WAC or WID program (see Townsend, this volume), as a WPA you will likely help to train the faculty and staff who teach in it, regardless of their home department (in fact, you may be in charge of that program). These faculty typically have no background in rhetoric and composition, but still play a crucial part in the literacy education of your institution's students. Developing faculty and staff outside your department or program can be both exciting and daunting. You will find yourself drawing on and sharing knowledge and assumptions you have long acted on tacitly and learning to see your field of study anew through the eyes of instructors learning it for the first time. You may also receive requests from local high schools to help train their teachers, especially if your institution is part of the National Writing Project (NWP—see Banks, this volume). Even if your institution does not participate in the NWP, high school administrators frequently ask local WPAs to help their staff better understand college writing requirements and teach writing more effectively. If your institution offers a dual enrollment program that involves writing classes, you will work very closely with the high school teachers who deliver that course (see also Hansen, this volume).

What Topics Might You Cover as a Part of Faculty Instructional Development?

Faculty development involves promoting the growth of each faculty member as a teacher, professional, and person. Compiling a comprehensive list of the topics related to instructional development of faculty is impossible: Though many topics are commonly addressed and easy to anticipate, others will arise unexpectedly as you work with faculty. One of the more common aspects of faculty development WPAs will address involves course preparation, including textbook selection, syllabus construction, or assignment design. The focus is on preparing faculty to teach the particular writing classes they have been assigned. Depending on the faculty member's experience and the nature of the writing program itself, WPAs might also spend considerable time establishing the goals of the particular composition courses, their relationship to other writing courses in the department or at the university, and the theory of composition serving as the course's foundation.

As you work with faculty in a writing program, you will also pay considerable attention to classroom teaching techniques. The topics you address might include how to present material effectively, how to lead class discussions, how to manage time, how to work with difficult students, how to answer student questions, or how to incorporate readings in the classroom, just to mention a few. What you cover as a part of faculty development in this area will largely be determined by the group of instructors you are working with. Novice instructors may need help learning basic instructional techniques while more experienced faculty may need help refining their pedagogy or adapting it to writing courses. Faculty outside of rhetoric and composition frequently require extra assistance in this area. Instructors in other disciplines often claim that while they can tell good writing from bad in their field, they do not know how to "teach" students to write effectively. As you work with these teachers, you will need to find ways to help them articulate their tacit understanding of their field's discourse conventions and develop practical instructional activities for their classes.

Creating effective, interesting, and challenging writing assignments is an acquired skill. Whether working with new or experienced faculty, expect to devote attention to helping them create effective writing assignments, compose graded and ungraded writing prompts, and craft writing tasks that promote student learning. Both new and experienced writing instructors frequently find responding to and evaluating students' texts daunting as well. First, they frequently confuse or conflate the two; they do not draw useful distinctions between responding to student writing to promote effective revision and evaluating final drafts. As a WPA, you will help faculty establish appropriate ways to respond to and evaluate student writing and establish clear evaluation criteria and grading rubrics.

Increasingly, WPAs work with faculty inside and outside writing programs on assessment-related projects. You may be asked to teach faculty how to articulate and assess student learning outcomes (especially those related to writing) or how to conduct program assessment. Chairs and deans look to WPAs to take the lead on developing faculty assessment skills due to the expertise they have developed through years of evaluating student writing (see Harrington, this volume).

New technologies, too, are constantly impacting writing instruction. Computers and the Internet have radically changed how students research topics and present their arguments in the last few decades and the pace of change is unlikely to slow. As part of their faculty development role, WPAs must help instructors learn about and experiment with these ever-changing instructional technologies. As will be discussed below, often WPAs partner with others—such as the staff in instructional technologies or the campus teaching and learning center—to prepare demonstrations and workshops to familiarize faculty with these new technologies and to encourage their use.

Finally, as instructors gain confidence and experience, WPAs can promote their faculty's personal development by encouraging them to formulate a philosophy of instruction to guide their teaching. Inexperienced instructors give little thought to this aspect of teaching. Over time, though, they will begin to develop their own ideas about the proper goals of writing instruction, the best pedagogies to employ, and most appropriate relationship to establish with their students. WPAs can support this type of growth by welcoming and encouraging it.

WHAT TOPICS MIGHT YOU COVER AS A PART OF FACULTY PROFESSIONAL DEVELOPMENT?

In "Professional Development for Writing Program Staff," Carpenter notes that while instructional development initiatives "usually focus on the local context, the particular program within the particular institution," professional development initiatives "have as their primary purpose introducing faculty members to the knowledge and methods of the larger professional communities found in higher education. They seek to enhance faculty members' understanding of the ways in which professionals present themselves and their knowledge to others in their field" (158).

A large faculty development responsibility for WPAs is informing instructors and administrators of the key roles writing, writing instruction, writing assessment, and the writing program play at their institution (see also Vander Lei and Pugh, this volume). WPAs know the long history of the academy defining composition classes as "service" courses with little institutional value and due little institutional respect. One aspect of faculty development for the WPA is to encourage instructors and administrators to challenge this perception, based on the essential role writing instruction plays in students' education. As a WPA, you will be responsible for promoting the professional status of composition among faculty and administrators at your institution.

With their strong backgrounds in composition theory, history, and practice, WPAs are also the experts on writing research at their institutions. Consequently, one of their faculty development responsibilities is helping to keep the instructional staff informed of recent trends and emerging research in the field. As Carpenter maintains, this task is essential to expanding the perspective of writing instructors beyond the individual institution (158). Writing faculty and staff need to see themselves as members of a vibrant community of scholars and practitioners engaged in a dynamic field of study. If faculty and staff within and beyond the writing program are to base their teaching on current research and best practice in the field, as WPA you must play a central role in disseminating this information. Furthermore, as writing faculty and staff become increasingly aware of current research in the field, they may want to engage in research themselves. Rhetoric and composition have long histories of promoting teacher-researchers who publish the results of their studies in a wide range of venues. WPAs can aid their faculty's professional development by encouraging and supporting their research agendas and helping them find effective publication outlets for their work.

Another way WPAs can promote the professional development of their faculty is to urge them to join professional organizations, attend conferences that focus on rhetoric and composition, or join writing-

or teaching-related listservs. Instructors unfamiliar with rhetoric and composition are unlikely to know how to join professional discussions in the field or meet colleagues outside their institution with similar interests and challenges. WPAs can easily share this information.

WHAT TOPICS MIGHT YOU COVER AS PART OF FACULTY PERSONAL DEVELOPMENT?

As POD points out, faculty development extends beyond one's teaching and professional lives. If you expand the definition of faculty development to include support of the whole person, then some attention must be paid to supporting the personal development of faculty. The personal aspects of faculty development can include the following topics.

Teaching writing can be taxing—inexperienced instructors may find it especially time- consuming and frustrating. WPAs can help writing instructors establish a comfortable, healthy balance between the demands of work and their private lives (see also Hesse, this volume). New TAs often have a hard time finding this balance, devoting too much time to class preparation and grading and not enough time to their studies or to life away from campus with family and friends. WPAs who address this as an important issue certainly aid their staff's personal development.

Additionally, anyone who teaches a writing course may face a lack of confidence, no matter how long he or she has been an instructor. For many teaching assistants, everything about teaching writing is new, and they need your help and guidance to become confident teachers (see Reid, this volume). Faculty who are not members of your department often face similar issues, even if they have been teaching in their own field for years. When asked to teach writing, they may feel unprepared and unqualified, which adversely affects their performance. Even faculty in your department who have taught writing for years may become stressed or lack confidence if they are asked to adopt new approaches to teaching writing, especially those involving technology. As part of a faculty development program, WPAs can act to boost their colleagues' confidence and relieve their stress.

How Does Faculty Development Work Get Done?

Faculty development work takes a number of forms, all of them adapted to the usual range of rhetorical situations: audience, purpose, institutional context, time sensitivity, and exigency. An annual multi-day workshop for new teaching staff will speak to different needs than the hallway encounter with a frustrated colleague. In all cases, the faculty development activity will speak to faculty learning. We can make a rough division of faculty development types, grouping those that are formal learning opportunities and those that are more supplemental or casual.

Formal Faculty Development. By far the most common faculty development venue is the workshop. According to Elaine Maimon et al., the workshop phenomenon itself was born of a pre-WAC effort at Carleton College. Harriet Sheridan, then Carleton's dean, called faculty together for two-week stints in the summers of 1974 and 1975 to read foundational literature (e.g., Aristotle's *Rhetoric*) and work together on approaches to teaching writing in the context of introductory courses in all disciplines (Maimon et al., 142).

As common as workshops are now, they required a cognitive shift for faculty that may be difficult for us to appreciate today. Instead of listening to an expert lecturer, which would have been the default for professional training at that time, faculty found themselves in a specialized classroom situation that assumed their equal responsibility and participation. Sheridan may not have been aware that her gatherings represented a paradigm shift in ongoing faculty development; nevertheless, the model quickly caught on, and any faculty development plan will likely include workshops.

Workshops vary in purpose, audience, and so forth, but we can point to two broad categories: the one-time event and the workshop that is part of a series or, as we prefer, a curriculum for faculty. The one-time event may be driven by a local situation; for example, a workshop can introduce a new assessment plan that will involve faculty participation or serve as the basis for a departmental retreat to consider reorganizing the major. On many campuses, certain workshops occur regularly—for instance, the preservice workshop for new teaching staff or an annual assignment design workshop for first-year seminar teachers (see Reid, this volume).

Careful planning for either kind of workshop will include the following (at minimum):

- Timely invitations to members of the target audience with details of time, place, amenities, and expectations of attendees.
- A written agenda.
- Copies of materials (readings, handouts, bibliographies, a list of attendees, and so forth) for everyone.
- A modicum of presentation, with more time devoted to group work, focused discussion, problem solving, and other active learning techniques.
- Plenty of time for discussion and questions.
- At least one tangible artifact (a syllabus, assignment, list of goals, idea for an article) that each participant can have in hand as he or she leaves the room.
- An evaluation instrument tailored to the audience and the purpose of the event.
- Refreshments.
- If possible, a stipend or some other reward.
- Follow-up from the leader(s) on comments from evaluations as well as key points raised or specific requests made for additional help during the event.

Workshops can be scheduled well in advance and advertised on a website, providing a convenient signup mechanism and reminders for attendees. One-time workshops will be clear about their singular status, whereas workshops offered as part of an ongoing series will announce the general purpose, with details about this year's offering, e.g., "This semester's WAC workshop focuses on 'Writing With Numbers,' and next spring we will work on 'Responding to Student Writing.'"

Workshops may or may not feature speakers from outside the institution or, perhaps, one or more faculty with expertise in the workshop's topic. Speakers can provide formal faculty development in other ways as well. An institution may ask departments and programs to pool funds for a nationally-known speaker to present to the campus at large. Some schools have convocation series, endowed lectures, and other ways to schedule, fund, and deliver public talks—with or without opportunities for faculty, students, and staff to interact with the visitor. Individual departments can bring notable scholars to campus for the benefit of their colleagues and majors. Such experiences can enrich a typical course in inspiring ways.

Speakers drawn from the campus may be equally successful, especially if sponsored by an institution's teaching and learning center or other unit responsible for showcasing effective teaching. Two typical examples would be (1) a faculty panel on current research in the field or (2) an institutional researcher's review of recent National Survey of Student Engagement (NSSE) data related to high impact teaching practices (see Paine et al., this volume).

Depending on the book chosen, reading groups for faculty can generate powerful discussion, offer faculty thoughtful, research-based reasons to try new approaches, or simply build community. A schedule of meetings at two- or three-week intervals allows participants to do the reading and learn from one another. If the institution can purchase the books, so much the better.

Online resources are sometimes overlooked as a means of formal faculty development. For example, the Science Education Resource Center, or SERC (http://serc.carleton.edu), is a grant-funded organization that collects teaching activities, offers workshops at various sites across the US, and invites faculty to contribute their own teaching materials. Originally designed for geoscientists, SERC's materials now range widely, including pages devoted to writing assignments in various disciplines. Purdue University's Online Writing Lab (OWL) is another resource for students and faculty (http://owl.english.purdue.edu/owl/).

Informal Faculty Development. One-on-one consultations are the most common form of informal faculty development. The conversation on the way to the gym or the thoughtful e-mail exchange followed by a coffee break can open up avenues of support, reassurance, and even policy revision. WPAs are wise to listen to colleagues, offer advice and support, and, where necessary, help make a question or problem more visible to the institutional hierarchy.

Conference support can make a difference, especially for young colleagues who are not yet confident about submitting proposals on their own behalf. Resources that allow them to attend, learn, and begin to form a professional network may foster a faster track for scholarly output.

Assessment activities, such as reading placement exams or student portfolios, can jump-start faculty members' understanding of their students' abilities and, in the case of portfolios, their experience of writing on campus in general. Few of us have opportunities to read student work we have not personally designed and assigned; sampling student work from other courses—within and outside of our own departments—exposes faculty to the demands placed on students. In addition, thoughtful attention to colleagues' assignments inevitably produces good conversation and may engender a revised assignment or whole course.

PARTNERS IN FACULTY DEVELOPMENT

As noted above, the WPA can expect to be involved in a range of programs and audiences that requires attention to collaboration across departments, colleges, and other institutional divisions. At the very least, WPAs can expect to work with department chairs, TA training teams, directors of graduate studies, faculty in various departments, librarians, IT liaisons to academic units, the teaching and learning center staff, and administrators of outreach programs such as extension courses or dual enrollment.

In all faculty development situations, WPAs should model good teaching and innovative pedagogical techniques for their various audiences, particularly in workshop settings. When the WPA asks faculty—explicitly or implicitly—to be students for a workshop, the WPA is challenged to offer her very best teaching skills and materials for a "class" of smart, well-prepared "students" who are also colleagues.

Part of the challenge lies in the need to respect disciplinary assumptions as well as genres, conventions, authoring practices, and varying expectations of undergraduate and graduate students. Some of the best work in faculty development integrates individual specialists into the institution as a whole, celebrating their particular practices, respecting those of other departments and programs, and finding ways to strengthen the institution's capacity for teaching and, therefore, student learning.

Works Cited

Brunk-Chavez, Beth. "Embracing Our Expertise through Faculty and Instructional Development." *WPA: Writing Program Administration* 34.1 (2010): 152–55. Print.

Carpenter, William J. "Professional Development for Writing Program Staff." *The Longman Sourcebook for Writing Program Administrators*. Ed. Irene Ward and William J. Carpenter. New York: Pearson, 2008. 156–65. Print.

Council of Writing Program Administrators. "Evaluating the Intellectual Work of Writing Administration." 1998. Web. 27 July 2012.

—. "'The Portland Resolution:' Guidelines for Writing Program Administrator Positions." 1992. Web. 27 July 2012.

—. "Hiring Practices, Faculty Development, and Faculty Evaluation." Albuquerque, NM. July 15–22, 2012. CWPA Workshop, Institutes, and Conference.

Maimon, Elaine, Barbara F. Nodine, Gail W. Horn, and Janice Haney-Peritz. "Beaver College." *Programs that Work: Models and Methods for Writing Across the Curriculum*. Ed. Toby Fulwiler and Art Young. Portsmouth, NH: Boynton/Cook-Heinemann, 1990. 137–51. Print.

Professional and Organizational Development in Higher Education (POD). "What Is Faculty Development?" 2007. Web. 22 July 2012.

Sorcinelli, Mary Dean, Ann E. Austin, Pamela L. Eddy, and Andrea L. Beach. *Creating the Future of Faculty Development: Learning from the Past, Understanding the Present*. Boston, MA: Ankor, 2006. Print.

Willard-Traub, Margaret K. "Writing Program Administration and Faculty Professional Development: Which Faculty? What Development?" *Pedagogy* 8.3 (2008): 433-45. Print.

15 What Is TA Education? ✓

E. Shelley Reid

You probably already have at least one answer to this question, because in the program you know best, one set of resources and spaces has already been defined for you. It's pretty straightforward: Your program's practicum/workshop/seminar/mentorships/in-services take(s) place over 1/3/14/57/125 weeks to help train/educate/certify/supervise the graduate teaching assistants/associates/instructors who are studying English/literature/film/creative writing/composition/linguistics/biology for 1/2/4/8 years while they teach 15/20/38/56 students per semester in your first-semester/second-semester/disciplines-based/technical/ digital writing class(es) based on their 0/1/3/7 years' previous experience working for a writing center/middle school/ESL department in Hungary/US college writing program/trade magazine/community literacy agency during which they never/once/sort-of/frequently encountered principles and scholarship related to the teaching and learning of writing. Simple, really.

However, you've probably also deduced that teaching assistant (TA) education comprises more, and is more complex, than just its structural framework. It's a specific subset of faculty development (see Rutz and Wilhoit, this volume) that focuses on the education and support of novice or relatively inexperienced teachers who are positioned as students in your program (and who are not entirely unlike the undergraduate students described by Ritter, this volume) to help them prepare to move into independent classroom teaching. Supporting new teachers is demanding and inspiring work, work that starts to make more sense once you set some realistic goals, decide on some core principles (see Adler-Kassner, this volume), and map out the features of the larger landscape.

THE PEDAGOGY COURSE: MISSION IMPOSSIBLE?

TA education is often synonymous with "the TA course/workshop," which Anne Trubek has without too much hyperbole called "impossible to teach" (160). Joe Marshall Hardin suggests that such a course typically must serve as at least three courses: "a teaching practicum, a composition pedagogy course, and a course in composition theory" (38). In it we must both strongly reassure and significantly discomfit our students; treat them as experienced professionals and as novices; and prepare them for tomorrow's class and for one ten years down the road. We must describe clear steps for scaffolding writing learning for a semester or two and explain why such learning does not happen sequentially, quickly, or at a uniform pace. And often, we have to function very distinctly as both approachable mentors and authoritative supervisors/professors for our students.

Moreover, even the limited time we are granted to work with TAs is not always fully ours. As our students, TAs must to some degree "answer to us" in a way that other faculty need not, but they still may feel pulled away from pedagogical learning by coursework from their chosen field or by daily demands from their new students. Their learning may be further hampered by the timing of our workshops or courses, whether we are asked to rush new teachers into the classroom at the start of their first semester of graduate school, or to walk them through more abstract learning without a classroom to practice in. (Nobody has yet created a program with my preferred schedule: two weeks of structured TA education, then a week when they teach, then—*with regular time in the universe stopped*—two more weeks of study, and then—the universe spinning again—another week or two of teaching.) We are either providing relevant information significantly in advance of teachers' ability to try it out in the classroom, or asking for their thoughtful inquiry during the "What do I do on Tuesday?" chaos of their first time teaching composition. In addition, teachers, like writers, need to learn everything at once; since we are always aware of what we have not yet addressed, we feel the impossibilities daily.

Once we admit that our task is impossible, though—at least by some definitions—it gets easier. We can set some priorities based on our understandings about writing-learning and teaching-learning, our views of the field of rhetoric and composition, and our long-term goals for new writing-teacher colleagues, and then measure our success against those priorities.

In Principle: Redefining TA Education

Particularly given institutional pressures, it can be easy to get caught up in the truly impossible goal of quickly "producing" new teachers who meet all core standards to deliver a curriculum, rather than helping new faculty begin to become reflective, lifelong learners of pedagogy and of writing-teaching. There are other resources to help you generate comprehensive lists of knowledge to be covered (see the CCCC and TYCA statements noted in the works cited, as well as Rose and Finders; Ward and Perry; and Yancey). However, to aid you in resisting the discourse of coverage and quick competency, I want to suggest five principles to help you focus your efforts as you begin your work with new teachers.

 TA education integrates multiple kinds of learning. Learners need both declarative knowledge (knowing *what*) and procedural knowledge (knowing *how*); recent scholarship also emphasizes students' need for metacognitive knowledge that helps them assess, adapt, and apply their own learning (Ambrose et al. 192–200). From this start, we might tease out a few more specific learning goals for composition teachers (see Table 1); for each, I'll provide an example of something a new teacher might want to share or do with students during the first two weeks of first-year composition:

Table 1

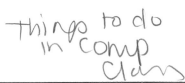

Kind of learning	Field-specific knowledge	FYC application
Declarative knowledge about...	Composition and rhetoric as a field	Introduce concepts of audience and genre to students
	Effective pedagogical practices	Design a session integrating conceptual and experiential learning about responding to audience needs
	How writers learn	Use freewriting and peer response to help writers narrow and support initial claims
Procedural knowledge of (competencies in)...	Writing (reading, researching, revising) strategies	Recognize and articulate strengths and weaknesses in student drafts
	Effective pedagogical strategies	Use initial and follow-up questions to deepen students' analysis of a model essay
	Strategies for instruction in, assessment of and feedback on writing	Provide supportive and revision-directed comments on student drafts
Metacognitive knowledge of...	One's own writing and teaching practices	Draw on one's own struggles with revision to provide specific suggestions to students as they revise

In addition, TAs need to learn strategies for managing their new roles as teachers (Ward and Perry 119–20)—and for handling professional frustration and failure, since Christine Farris notes that "teaching may be the first thing in [TAs'] academic lives that has not gone really well from the beginning" (101). Finally, George Hillocks also argues that to be successful, teachers need to develop a deeply-seated constructivist epistemological stance and an optimistic approach to student learning (134–35). Of course it's not possible to bring new writing teachers to competence or confidence in all these areas quickly, but the solution isn't to teach them class management techniques now and principles of student learning and development later, or the other way around. Since these kinds of learning enable and reinforce one another, a pedagogy course is stronger when we deliberately integrate all of them.

TA education incorporates students' prior knowledge. Composition TAs are not blank slates: They come to us as experienced writers and "senior student[s]" (Sprague and Nyquist 295); they have spent many years in classrooms developing theories about writing, learning, and teaching. Most of them can already capably help undergraduates learn to write better, a fact that we (and they) sometimes lose track of. While there are important accounts of new writing teachers' "resistance" to "indoctrination" (see Ebest; Hesse; and Welch, for instance), it can be helpful to identify some resistance as an ordinary struggle to match prior experiences with new learning, and thus as more inertial than active—and to acknowledge that some of their resistance, under another name ("critical thinking"), is valuable to us as teachers. Moreover, new teachers *need* conscious access to their prior knowledge in order to correct it, if needed, and to connect new knowledge to it (Ambrose et al. 29). Thus the more we deliberately call TAs' attention to their earlier practices and assumptions, the more we will know about the challenges we all face, and the easier it will be to help them integrate new knowledge with strong foundations and to strengthen their confidence as new teachers. Still, research suggests that TAs tend to rely on previous experience, but that they do not always closely examine or reconceptualize it in light of new ideas (Estrem and Reid, "What") or know how best to apply that experience in understanding how their students learn to write (Dryer). Without devaluing their prior knowledge, then, we need to support them early in their careers in the process of examining, connecting, and sometimes adapting or reforming previous beliefs or practices.

3 *TA education emphasizes reflective problem solving.* Teaching writing requires us to manage a series of balancing acts. A particular teacher, student body, or program curriculum may make one approach (collaborative learning, say) seem quite reasonable, but every pedagogical choice provides us some gains at some cost (more student engagement with less precision in learning). New teachers need to explore the principles and limitations of an approach (what's supportive and problematic about teaching a five-paragraph essay structure?) and they need to identify situations in which that approach may be more or less conducive to student learning. They thus need specific practice in solving writing-teaching problems: diagnosing a problem, assessing the possible options, making an informed choice, and evaluating the results. In particular, new TAs may need encouragement to work on *learning* problems as well as what Meg Morgan calls "managerial" problems such as disruptive students, since the former may not seem as visible or urgent to new teachers. When they participate in a repeated cycle of reflective practice, TAs will more strongly link new ideas to prior knowledge and make that new knowledge accessible for use in future teaching situations.

4 *TA education is an "uncoverage" enterprise.* Pedagogy educators rarely have any difficulty coming up with enough content for a writing pedagogy course. However, we cannot possibly cover everything new teachers need to know, and for their new learning to take root and transfer out, students will require time to discover and wrestle with new knowledge to make sense of it for themselves (Reid, "Uncoverage"). Thus Jeff Rice's argument that a pedagogy course shouldn't include a separate unit on "technology" but instead should always integrate questions of media and tools with those of language (279) seems generally applicable: TAs will benefit more from learning how to think deeply about a few teaching problems (like assessing writing or designing productive class meetings), with attention to contextual complexities, than from having multiple issues cascade past them in a torrent. This challenging principle applies even when one has only a brief workshop with which to prepare TAs for their first days in the classroom; it applies to concepts that undergird the local curriculum as well as to core con-

cepts in composition and rhetoric. New teachers who learn deeply will be better decision-makers in their first-semester classrooms—where, even with the tightest of common syllabi, a WPA cannot control all the variables—as well as in their future work as writing teachers or in other professions.

TA education extends learning over time and across modalities. An uncoverage, problem solving approach necessitates space and time for extended learning. We know intuitively and through research (see Reid, Estrem, and Belchier) that the inoculation model we decry for writing instruction is similarly not useful for TA education. Learning to teach is an extended process, and our TAs will need to spend several years in a learning mode for new concepts and strategies to take hold. Jo Sprague and Jody D. Nyquist describe an arc of four stages—unconscious incompetence, conscious incompetence (a natural point of frustration and perhaps "resistance"), conscious competence, and unconscious competence—along which new teachers travel (297–301). Often TAs need to develop an initial set of skills along that arc to a point of confidence before they can develop other skills, so their learning path needs to be recursive. Moreover, new teachers will benefit from having multiple venues in which to encounter and reinforce key concepts. They can learn from senior and peer teachers in guided and informal conversations, during online discussions and face-to-face workshops, from observing class sessions and being observed, while reading about others' teaching principles and writing reflectively about their own teaching. If we build on this principle, the pedagogy *course* can become a TA education *program*, and the "impossibility" of TA education can lessen significantly.

Shirley K Rose and Margaret J. Finders argue not just that teacher educators need to develop their own principles, but that the process of developing and articulating principles—"[their] own reflective practice as teacher educators"—is crucial to their success (80). The time you spend engaging with your local circumstances, uncovering your own prior knowledge, and learning about current students, with guidance chapters like this one and information from the field at large, will help not just to define TA education for your program but also to increase your effectiveness in that program.

Integrating Other Elements of
Your Education Program

Beyond the pedagogy workshop or seminar, TA education merges with other faculty development or *writing pedagogy education* efforts (Estrem and Reid "Writing"). Obviously, we should draw connections with tutor education programs (see Lerner, this volume) or specialized education, like that for teachers of technical writing or online writing courses. Since most TAs are in a multi-year learning mode, WPAs should strive to connect even less obvious efforts to their overall principles in order to reinforce and extend TAs' education.

Begin before the beginning. If your department allows your input in the selection process for TAs, you should use it not just to assess applicants' qualifications but also to engage all applicants in learning early on. You can provide applicants with information about the TA education program, require a separate statement about their preparation for and interest in teaching writing, and request written (or, in an interview, verbal) comments on sample student essays. If your department assigns assistantships without (much of) your input, you can still ask to provide prospective students with written information in advance of an assistantship offer, require applicants to submit a statement or comment on essays even if that writing won't be evaluated for quality, or make yourself available for quick e-mail or video-chat consultations: Any of these will help establish the principles and even begin the process of TA education in your program.

Support peer mentoring programs. Peer-based learning in a TA education program can be an excellent way to reinforce seminar and workshop learning for mentees *and* mentors, whether the program relies on consultative, observational, supervisory, or co-teaching arrangements (see Hansen et al. and Weiser for some examples of programs). A good principle to remember is that a mentoring *program* is an institutionalized requirement, and the WPA should thus take the responsibility of outlining specifically what the goals and responsibilities of mentors and mentees are. Specifying that mentors should invite their mentees to coffee "at least once a semester" and that they should inquire about one thing going well and one challenge in the mentee's teaching sets a baseline that allows everyone to benefit from a professional discussion even if there is no "love connection." Likewise, while it may not seem necessary to say that a new teacher should not show up to observe a mentor's class unannounced, or in the middle of her ham on rye, or barefoot, describing what you mean by "professional behavior" can help everyone gain the most education from their mentoring relationship.

Even first- or second-year teachers can usefully be consultants for or observed by peers—on a single occasion or across a series of meetings—if they have some minimal preparation and clear guidelines. Their pedagogy may not be practiced, but it will be within the reach of other new teachers, and the simple experience of being in another composition classroom is crucial for TAs who are trying to acquire a pedagogical repertoire. If your program uses senior TAs as assistant directors or co-teachers, they will need additional education and support in order to set goals, design guidelines, and discuss strategies to manage their shifting roles with their peers. Just as new teachers can and should be taught, new mentors can and should be mentored in a way that encourages informed, reflective problem solving related to your TA education goals (Reid, "Mentoring").

Integrate and sustain discussions, in-services, and workshops. Many TA education programs shift from "formal" to "informal" structures at the end of TAs' first semester or year of teaching: seminars become discussion groups, discussion groups become office chats in the "I have a student who..." genre, analyses of scholarship become hallway talk of program lore. Yet since teacher educators argue that new classroom teachers need several years to develop and solidify their core principles and practices, it makes sense to regard all ongoing space for teacher-conversation as an opportunity for extending TA education according to your principles. Both quick-start and delayed-start TAs can benefit from ongoing structured discussions after their pedagogy course—in person or online, led by a faculty member or an advanced peer—that encourage them to connect teaching principles to classroom practices and to assess and reflect on alternative ways of teaching writing. Even when ongoing TA education consists primarily of stand-alone workshops (supporting a new technology or a program assessment, for instance), teaching-learners will benefit when workshops are overtly linked to questions from their prior education and designed with attention to declarative, procedural, and metacognitive learning. You can tap more-senior TAs for leadership roles in these sessions (and provide guidance in creating an integrated learning environment) and thus help them articulate their principles and acquire confidence as teachers.

BALANCING ACTS IN TA EDUCATION

The multiple responsibilities of a WPA can create challenges as you develop and sustain a TA education program. You may find yourself facing a "right vs. right" dilemma (Rudney and Guillaume, 86–87), in which you need to widen the framework to see what other constituencies, principles, or resources would be affected before you act. As you formulate plans and outcomes for your whole program, it's important for you to be aware of possible conflicts, and to be clear—to yourself and to TAs and colleagues—what role you are playing at what point, and with what goals.

Formative vs. supervisory roles. You cannot assist a new teacher unless you know where he or she is struggling, so class observations and informal discussions, in a formative role, are crucial. Yet if you also hold the power to assign a course grade, write a recommendation letter, or terminate a contract, any teacher, especially a new one, is likely to be less than frank with you about his or her frustrations or weaknesses. You cannot avoid this conflict entirely, but you can minimize it: You can try declaring some class observations as no-written-record zones, allowing re-observations for the purposes of summative evaluation, preparing peers or other faculty to do some of the formative mentoring (or the summative observations) using specific guidelines, and/or making clear the criteria for any summative evaluation to reduce TAs' stress and uncertainty.

Consistency vs. innovation in curricula. Regardless of the freedoms you grant other faculty in your program to design writing curricula, you may have good reasons to grant first-time teachers less freedom. An abundance of choices will slow down and can overwhelm a novice; new teachers may lack sufficient repertoire or judgment to create a different-but-equivalent curriculum; and there are benefits to having a cohort of new TAs share responses to a common set of teaching problems. Yet for the same reasons you may encourage undergraduates to write about topics they are interested in—they will bring more knowledge, enthusiasm, and innovation to the task, and they will learn strategies for operating independently—you may find it beneficial to look for ways to support new teachers in trying out at least one pedagogical project of their own.

Supporting students. As a WPA, you need to provide quality education for all of the undergraduates in your writing courses; as a teacher educator, you need to ensure that graduate students succeed in their pedagogy course(s) as well as in their broader graduate studies. WPAs are usually quite sensitive to labor issues and to the challenges of working with faculty whose primary identity is not as composition teachers. When all of the parties involved are "your" students, though, the advocacy lines sometimes blur. As you work with TAs on course designs, responses to student complaints, or time management strategies—hoping to change the habits of new teachers who spend more time *or* of those who spend less time than you would recommend on grading student essays, for instance—you may need to shift your sense of greater responsibility from one group of students to another, and to make clear to TAs which stance you are taking and why.

Acquiring resources. You may find you want to change the structures that initially defined "TA education" at your school. Although asking for additional composition program resources is never easy, seeking additional time or funding for TA education poses its own challenges. TAs' time is finite, so if you need more of it (a little more for learning communities or peer observations; a lot of it for another seminar), someone else will have to have less of it: their families, their researching selves, their other professors. This may be one of very few negotiations in which an increase in resources that flow to composition could directly lessen resources flowing to your tenure-line faculty colleagues—or in which you might be asked to reassign resources from one composition constituency to another. Since your roles as WPA, TA educator, and departmental colleague may conflict, you will want to gather local, peer-institution, and scholarly data; look for allies in and beyond the department (What do faculty at your school's teaching and learning center recommend?); and form careful arguments. The cause is just, but the road may be long.

CONCLUSIONS

What's impossible about TA education is to do everything perfectly, or even with a reliable sense of completeness and logical consistency, in a few months or even a few years. I hope you have let go of that notion, and instead have begun to think about what you want most to *embark upon* as an educator of new writing teachers. What kinds of teachers do you want the new TAs to grow into over the next several years, and what do you want to do now to help plant the seeds and nurture their initial growth? This is not a decision about lowering your standards; your administrator side is still responsible for assuring that hundreds or thousands of undergraduates learn important skills and strategies about college-level writing. It's a decision, as in any complicated teaching situation, about selecting your standards for initial learning about composition pedagogy and then helping all your new TAs really, thoroughly rise to them, using everything you know about supporting the hardest, most layered kinds of learning—and then extending the learning space so that you can add another set of standards and repeat the process. When we redefine what successful TA education means, for us and for new teachers, we allow for a richer, more enjoyable, more productive experience for everyone involved.

WORKS CITED

Ambrose, Susan A., Michael W. Bridges, Michele DiPietro, Marsha C. Loveett, and Marie K. Norman. *How Learning Works: 7 Research-Based Principles for Smart Teaching.* San Francisco, CA: Jossey-Bass, 2010. Print.

Conference on College Composition and Communication (CCCC). "CCCC Position Statement on the Preparation and Professional Development of Teachers of Writing." 1982. Web. 15 August 2012.

Dryer, Dylan B. "At a Mirror, Darkly: The Imagined Undergraduate Writers of Ten Novice Composition Instructors." *College Composition and Communication* 63.3 (2012): 420–52. Print.

Ebest, Sally Barr. *Changing the Way We Teach: Writing and Resistance in the Training of Teaching Assistants.* Carbondale: Southern Illinois UP, 2005. Print.

Estrem, Heidi, and E. Shelley Reid. "What New Writing Teachers Talk About When They Talk About Teaching." *Pedagogy* 12.3 (2012): 447–78. Print.

—. "Writing Pedagogy Education: Instructor Development in Composition Studies." *Exploring Composition Studies: Sites, Issues, and Perspectives.* Ed.

Kelly Ritter and Paul Matsuda. Logan: Utah State UP, 2012. 223–40. Print.

Farris, Christine. "Too Cool for School?" *Preparing College Teachers of Writing.* Ed. Betty P. Pytlik and Sarah Liggett. New York: Oxford UP, 2002. 97–107. Print.

Hansen, Kristine, Phillip A. Snyder, Nancy Davenport, and Kimberli Stafford. "Collaborative Learning and Teaching: A Model for Mentoring TAs." *The TA Experience: Preparing for Multiple Roles.* Ed. Karron G. Lewis. Stillwater, OK: New Forums Press, 1993. 251–59. Print.

Hardin, Joe Marshall. "Writing Theory and Writing the Classroom." *Don't Call It That: The Composition Practicum.* Ed. Sidney I. Dobrin. Urbana, IL: NCTE, 2005. 35–42. Print.

Hesse, Douglas. "Teachers as Students, Reflecting Resistance." *College Composition and Communication* 44 (1993): 224–31. Print.

Hillocks, George. *Teaching Writing as Reflective Practice.* New York: Teachers College Press, 1995. Print.

Morgan, Meg. "The GTA Experience: Grounding, Practicing, Evaluating, and Reflecting." *The Writing Program Administrator's Resource.* Ed. Stuart C. Brown and Theresa Enos. Mahwah, NJ: Erlbaum, 2002. 393–410. Print.

Reid, E. Shelley. "Mentoring Peer Mentors: Mentor Education and Support in the Composition Program." *Composition Studies* 36.2 (2008): 51–80. Print.

—. "Uncoverage in Composition Pedagogy." *Composition Studies* 32.1 (2004): 15–34. Print.

Reid, E. Shelley, Heidi Estrem, and Marcia Belchier. "The Effects of Writing Pedagogy Education on Graduate Teaching Assistants' Approaches to Teaching Composition." *WPA: Writing Program Administration* 36.1 (2012): 32–73. Print.

Rice, Jeff. "The New Media Instructor: Cultural Capital and Writing Instruction." *Don't Call It That: The Composition Practicum.* Ed. Sidney I. Dobrin. Urbana, IL: NCTE, 2005. 266–83. Print.

Rose, Shirley K, and Margaret J. Finders. "Thinking Together: Developing a Reciprocal Reflective Model for Approaches to Preparing College Teachers of Writing." *Preparing College Teachers of Writing.* Ed. Betty P. Pytlik and Sarah Liggett. New York: Oxford UP, 2002. 75–85. Print.

Rudney, Gwen L., and Andrea M. Guillaume. *Maximum Mentoring: An Action Guide for Teacher Trainers and Cooperating Teachers.* Thousand Oaks, CA: Corwin Press, 2003. Print.

Sprague, Jo, and Jody D. Nyquist. "A Developmental Perspective on the TA Role." *Preparing the Professoriate of Tomorrow to Teach.* Ed. Jody D. Nyquist, Robert D. Abbott, Donald H. Wulff, and Jo Sprague. Dubuque, IA: Kendall/Hunt, 1991. 295–312. Print.

Trubek, Anne. "Chickens, Eggs, and the Composition Practicum." *Don't Call It That: The Composition Practicum.* Ed. Sidney I. Dobrin. Urbana, IL: NCTE, 2005. 160–82. Print.

Two-Year College English Association (TYCA). "Guidelines for the Academic Preparation of Two-Year College English Faculty." 2004. Web. 15 August 2012.

Ward, Irene, and Merry Perry. "A Selection of Strategies for Training Teaching Assistants." *The Allyn and Bacon Sourcebook for Writing Program Administrators.* Ed. Irene Ward and William J. Carpenter. New York: Longman, 117–38. Print.

Weiser, Irwin. "When Teaching Assistants Teach Teaching Assistants to Teach: A Historical View of a Teacher Preparation Program." *Preparing College Teachers of Writing.* Ed. Betty P. Pytlik and Sarah Liggett. New York: Oxford UP, 2002. 40–49. Print.

Welch, Nancy. "Resisting the Faith: Conversion, Resistance, and the Training of Teachers." *College English* 55.4 (1993): 387–401. Print.

Yancey, Kathleen Blake. "The Professionalization of TA Development Programs: A Heuristic for Curriculum Design." *Preparing College Teachers of Writing.* Ed. Betty P. Pytlik and Sarah Liggett. New York: Oxford UP, 2002. 63–74. Print.

16 What Is A Union?

Seth Kahn

According to the September 2012 *Directory of U.S. Faculty Contracts and Bargaining Agents in Institutions of Higher Education*, your odds of finding work on a campus represented by one or more faculty unions are significant, increasing, and likely to continue to increase (Berry and Savarese). On its website, the CUNY-Hunter National Center for the Study of Collective Bargaining in Higher Education and the Professions, which publishes the *Directory*, summarizes its major findings, two of which are especially germane to this piece:

- A total of 368,473 faculty members are organized into 639 separate bargaining units and distributed across 519 institutions or systems of higher education on 1,174 campuses. The current total represents an increase of 49,969 faculty members, which is a 14% increase compared to the total published in the 2006 *Directory*.
- Ninety-three percent of organized faculty are employed in public institutions. Slightly more than half are full-time, while under half have tenure-track status (Berry and Savarese).

Under current labor law, full-time tenured/tenure-track faculty can unionize only on public university campuses, although as recently as July 2012, *Inside Higher Ed* reports potential challenges to the *Yeshiva* decision precluding faculty at private universities from collectively bargaining (Jaschik; see also Malenczyk). Contingent/part-time/adjunct faculty can unionize on both public and private campuses.

All of this is to say that at some point in your career, you have a good chance of working in a collective bargaining environment. Although I'm a union member and labor activist, my agenda isn't to convince you to support unions. Unions are designed to protect workers from capricious management[1], but in doing so can sometimes make administrative work very complicated in ways that non-union environments don't face. Chains of command can get longer and more intricate. What seem like clear lines of decision-making authority may obscure the real sources of responsibility. You're working with long, complicated documents that only a lawyer could love, and that govern the processes by which *everything* happens. On a campus like mine, you'd be governed by a contract that also governs thirteen other campuses, and thus may not be especially responsive to your needs. You'll see what I mean as you read further.

My primary purpose is to introduce some of the issues that arise in union environments, and secondarily to suggest ways of approaching them; the idea is to represent some of the thought processes you might find helpful to follow as situations arise. I won't be very specific about suggestions, as collective bargaining agreements (CBAs) vary widely in terms of content and specificity. Plus, I serve as the grievance chair/contract enforcement officer for my local union chapter, so the last thing I want to do is give you bad advice based on a contract I'm not familiar with. In a nutshell, all my advice will revolve around one simple (simplistic!) notion:

KNOW YOUR CONTRACT(S)!

That simple notion quickly kaleidoscopes. That I had to offer the provisional plural is one clue. Another clue is the heft of any academic collective bargaining agreement[2] and the time it takes even the most committed reader to keep all the potentially relevant parts of it in your head at once. There are key parts of your agreement that you'll probably need to be more familiar with than the bulk of it, and much of this chapter is given to pointing those out. I'm going to follow the order of the agreement I work under, which governs all faculty (full and part-time, tenured, tenure-track, and adjunct) working conditions across the entire Pennsylvania State System of Higher Education (PASSHE): hiring/appointment, evaluation, (non)renewals, workloads, and investigation of complaints against faculty. I've chosen these issues because they're the ones that have most often arisen in my work as a WPA and as grievance chair, and in discussions in professional venues. At the end, I'll address some issues that collective bargaining agreements usually don't cover, such as whom to turn to for help with problems beyond the contract.

Before getting into specifics, there's one point I need to make explicit about working with complex documents like union contracts, and it's probably true of documents like faculty handbooks (for those of you who aren't on union campuses) too. Collective bargaining agreements have lots of moving parts—that is, seemingly unconnected sections/clauses of contract language will impact each other in ways that can be very oblique, sometimes even inconsistent. Our contract, for example, has language in one article that defines workload one way, and language in another article that defines overload based on a different way of calculating workload. Until you get very used to these kinds of problems, your best strategies for dealing with complicated questions are these. First, trust your instinct; if a question occurs to you about an issue, and you even begin to wonder whether that issue impinges on another, it probably does. If it occurs to you, as a WPA, to wonder how your supervisory responsibilities connect to your workload calculations, check. Second, if you can't figure it out by looking at the language, *ask somebody*. As much as unions can make our lives complicated, one of the payoffs is that somebody within the union structure usually knows the answers to those kinds of questions and is elected/appointed as the go-to person.

KNOW YOUR CONSTITUENCIES, INCLUDING WHICH ONE YOU'RE PART OF

So let's start here. It's crucial to start by understanding—and more importantly keeping track of—membership in the bargaining unit(s). There are campuses on which only tenured/tenure-track faculty belong to a union; others on which full-time and contingent faculty belong to a single union; others on which each constituency belongs to a different union; others on which teaching assistants are unionized. You, as a WPA, may or may not belong to one of those units, depending on your appointment (faculty or staff, public university or private) and your state's labor laws. Depending on the lines of authority in the agreement(s), the status of your department chair (faculty or administration, bargaining unit member or not) may matter also.

Each of those possibilities has its complications. Obviously, if each constituency works under a different contract, you have more to remember (or to remember how to find) in terms of not just each agreement, but of which applies to whom and when. However, if more than one group (say, tenure-track and contingent faculty) work under the same contract, it's possible that the language required to govern both is more oblique because it has to do double duty, or that a contractual stipulation becomes onerous. An appropriately messy example: Our CBA includes "trigger language" that makes adjunct faculty eligible for a departmental vote to convert them into tenure-track positions after five consecutive years of full-time employment. That language is included in the "Appointment of Faculty" article, though, rather than the article that governs position conversions, and as such creates serious tension within departments over procedural and philosophical questions about hiring into tenure tracks. Worse, the language in the article only requires that departments develop a "procedure" (APS-CUF 21) for conducting the vote, but offers no instructions for what the procedure needs to look like, or what kinds of criteria to apply to candidates.

If you and/or your department chair belong to the bargaining unit, you might be protected from faculty filing grievances against you; under our system's CBA, for example, faculty cannot grieve other faculty except for discrimination. As I was drafting this chapter, I did some informal surveying of faculty union members and discovered not one contract that allows faculty to grieve other faculty, even across bargaining units, even if the faculty who would be grieved are carrying out formal supervisory responsibilities. However, that protection only extends so far, and in many cases a faculty member who wants to grieve something you did will have to involve your department chair (if chairs are managers in your structure) or your dean. Different CBA language can complicate lines of reportage and authority, and it's best if you sort that out before you have a problem!

In short: A little frontloaded work keeping track of who is governed by which contract is likely to make your life much easier later.

Hiring/Appointing

In my opinion, hiring and staffing decisions are the second most difficult (after renewals/non-renewals) to make. Again, depending on the structure of your campus and your position, you may not have much, if any, authority over hiring in your writing program, and that's especially true if you have graduate students teaching. In my former WPA position, I had literally nothing to do with making those decisions; I shared WPA responsibilities with another faculty member who oversaw a contingent faculty search process, and the department chair used that committee's results to recommend new hires to the dean. Because almost all of our tenured/tenure-track faculty also teach general education writing courses, and because we're fortunate to have a very large group of compositionists in our department, our WPAs were never required to represent the program even in tenure-track searches.

Your context is likely to be very different. You'll almost certainly play a larger role in hiring decisions, even if the role is token or advisory, and you'll find both upsides and downsides to that increased presence. On a union campus, the odds are very high that you'll find a very detailed hiring protocol—which may be mandated by your union contract or may be a college or departmental policy, but is likely to be just as legalistic no matter which—and I can't emphasize enough how important it is to follow it. The protocol my department follows is probably not much different from most, with a couple of exceptions: (1) Our Office of Social Equity (OSE), which oversees diversity training, discrimination complaints, EEOC issues, and so on, has to vet every hiring plan to ensure the recruiting of a diverse candidate pool—the requirements of which can add time and expense to a search; (2) OSE also requires explicit, detailed rationales for the elimination of each candidate from the hiring pool—which may not sound like a lot of work until you multiply the two minutes per candidate times the hundreds of applicants you don't hire; (3) per the union contract, no candidate can be hired without receiving a majority vote of approval from the hiring department or unit; and (4) unsuccessful tenure-track hires set off all kinds of complex processes for hiring adjunct faculty, or re-running searches, or encouraging departments to reopen their applicant pools, most of which happen far above the level of a WPA.

There are three important points to make about hiring processes. First, put bluntly, the last thing you want to do as a WPA is jeopardize a hire, or a line, or a candidate by failing to follow the rules. Especially in an era where management is looking to reduce costs—and arguably faculty complements—at every turn, risking a hire by cutting corners is not a good idea. Second, depending on the collective bargaining structure, it's very, very important to understand variations between protocols for hiring tenure-track and contingent faculty—or in a setting like mine, where contingent and non-contingent faculty belong to the same bargaining unit, understanding that the same rules apply to both. So, for example, departments across our whole system hire contingent faculty all the time without majority votes by the hiring departments, and that's simply not supposed to happen. It does, however, and in many cases it's entirely understandable: Last-minute openings pop up because of medical leaves, or what have you, and taking the time to conduct a department ballot (not to mention what happens if the candidate is voted down) is burdensome. Finally, if you're on a campus that employs contingent faculty—and if you have much, if any, actual hiring authority—you'll face complicated decisions about hiring full- or part-time, how those staffing decisions fit with budgetary, workload, and other staffing concerns, and so on—many of which your CBA will also govern. Remember, as I said earlier, that union contracts have lots of interrelated moving parts, and you think a question/issue/problem might relate to another part of the document, it probably does.

EVALUATION

As a WPA, I wasn't responsible for overseeing evaluation of writing program faculty; at the time, my department had an assistant chairperson who supervised all evaluation, and in a department with approximately fifty tenured/tenure-line faculty and as many as twenty contingent faculty, that's a lot. All untenured faculty, tenure-line or not, full-time or part-time, are evaluated yearly—classroom observations, student evaluations, a committee report, a chair's report, a dean's report. Tenured faculty undergo the same evaluation every fifth year post-tenure. There are complex rules governing who can evaluate whom, who can or cannot participate in evaluation committee work, how student evaluations are administered, what happens if a component of the evaluation process gets botched, and so on; the "Performance Evaluation" article of the CBA is one of the longest and most complicated in the entire contract.

I've come to understand that evaluation can be the most labor-intensive aspect of a WPA's work, especially if you're in a program with lots of contingent faculty and graduate students. Union settings tend to make the work of evaluation more systematic, but as a result, probably even more labor-intensive. Since collective bargaining agreements are, at heart, about ensuring equitable treatment, the odds are your agreement will require you (or somebody) to evaluate all bargaining unit members no matter how much or little they teach.

Because I wasn't responsible for evaluation as a WPA, I conducted an informal survey of the WPA-L and Adj-L listservs in June 2012 to get a sense of how widely evaluation requirements vary in unionized settings. The results, for our purposes, show that the variations are significant. At one end is a program like mine—except that supervising the evaluation process wasn't the WPA's problem—that requires every untenured faculty member to be evaluated every year. Like many institutions, mine is moving toward hiring as many part-time contingent faculty as possible as an ostensible cost-saving maneuver. As our management replaces full-time contingent faculty with half- or quarter-time contingent faculty, the evaluation burden multiplies accordingly. At the other end, an adjunct faculty member who asked that I not identify her campus reports that in five years of full-time work, she's never been evaluated. Most contracts mandate somewhere in between—some calling for yearly evaluations, some bi-annual, occasionally tri-annual. There are sharp differences among the types of evaluations performed for contingent and non-contingent faculty, and for graduate student instructors, on those campuses where different contracts (or standards for constituencies who aren't unionized) are in force.

Obviously, the more faculty undergoing evaluation, the more complex it is for the department, and for you if you're responsible for doing/organizing it. By the way, don't underestimate the complexity of managing those evaluations if they're not yearly. Keeping track of who's due when, and who's available to do observations or evaluation reports, can be messy—especially if your contract allows for exceptions/extensions, and/or if your management isn't very diligent about making sure programs stay on cycle. It's very easy for even the most organized person to lose track of seventy different people all on different evaluation schedules. Additionally, if you're on a campus with a union that uses procedural violations as pretexts to grieve evaluations that faculty don't like, you may be giving them fodder. Just be careful.

One other point about evaluations, coming directly out of an issue that's arisen in my system over the last couple of years: Although I've focused heavily on mechanical and procedural kinds of issues so far, those issues are intimately connected to the ethics of proper and rigorous evaluation. For example, I explained earlier that our union contract has "trigger language" that makes contingent faculty eligible for departmental votes to convert them into tenure-track faculty after five years of consecutive full-time service. In several departments around campus, including my own, as these conversion votes become more common, the lid has popped off a can of worms—faculty are realizing that in light of not very rigorous evaluations, they don't have reliable information to base their votes on, and in some cases seem to be overcompensating for that problem by simply refusing to vote for any conversions. The individual ethics of that decision aside, it's a problem best addressed by making sure evaluations are done well and according to protocol. Even in simpler situations, the point holds: Whoever is responsible for making renewal/non-renewal decisions needs evidence on which to make them. Likewise, quality evaluations minimize the risk of arbitrary and capricious decisions about staffing.

If you find the sometimes-distended rules and protocols irritating, keep in mind their purpose—to maximize transparency and protect faculty from arbitrary decisions.

Renewals and Non-Renewals

The person you know is harder to let go than the person you don't know is to hire. Concluding that somebody no longer should have a job in your program may or may not be hard, but executing that decision should be. It's easier, at least in theory, if you've hired and evaluated carefully and ethically; at least your odds of getting and keeping good people are higher.

Those points are true whether your environment is union or not. Union contracts can help you, as a WPA, better make these decisions—or recommendations, if that's all your contract allows. They can also exclude you from any meaningful authority or role in the process at all.

In most union environments, the renewal/non-renewal process varies by status and rank. In ours, contingent faculty are non-renewable without explanation; probationary tenure-track faculty in their first two years are as well; in years three through five, the decision not to renew is grievable if a department or manager violates the evaluation protocol, or if the decision is deemed *arbitrary and capricious*. That is to say, management can not renew, or renew, contingent faculty and very new probationary faculty and never have to say a word about why they've reached that decision. Non-renewals involving faculty closer to tenure require more justification.

Some version of this language probably exists on most campuses, union or not. The main effect of a collective bargaining agreement, I would argue, is that it clarifies the limits of your authority in renewal decisions as a WPA. If you have nothing substantive to say about the decisions, it's better for you to recognize that and avoid banging your head. If your dean, or whoever, tends to take your recommendations at face value, your obligation increases to be careful and thorough.

As a final note: A handful of unions have negotiated agreements similar to one my system recently opted out of, which puts time limits on contingent faculty appointments. In our system, until 2007 when we ratified a contract that removed the policy, contingent faculty were not allowed to teach, even part-time loads, for more than four consecutive semesters without having to take a semester off. Of course many departments rehired people after they'd taken that fifth semester off, which was allowed, but that policy enabled some departments/ programs to be somewhat less than diligent about hiring, evaluation, and renewal decisions because they knew they could simply not invite somebody to return after a mandatory semester away. All I can say about that is—if your agreement has a provision like that in it, please don't let it mitigate the need to be on top of careful hiring, evaluation, and renewal processes.

WORKLOAD

So far, I've attended almost entirely to issues regarding how you work with your staff. The next, *workload*, is much more focused on you and your own position. It's no secret to any WPA that job responsibilities tend to creep; a union contract should, but can't always—or as precisely as we'd like—prevent that creep, but it can help you manage it and protect yourself.

With that in mind, a point that's also true for WPAs in non-union environments: The first order of business is to push for as clear and specific a job description as you can. A collective bargaining agreement may help you formulate it. At the very least, the generally extensive protocol for faculty evaluation supports your claim that you need specifics; how can you be evaluated properly if there's no limit to what you might be asked to do? Even beyond the language of your contract, if there's a question about whether something is "your job," there may well be grievance or arbitration history that can help you find out. One of the benefits of a union campus is that rules must (at least in theory) apply evenly across departments and units. In a field where we often struggle with legitimacy issues even in our own departments, that form of equity can be very helpful to invoke.

I am not, by the way, advocating that you never do any work not described specifically in your job description. I'm advocating as much clarity as possible between what you *must* do in order to keep your job and move forward (if there's anywhere to move), and what you *choose* to do. The larger your program, the more faculty and sections you supervise, the less clear the lines of authority through your program/ department up into management—all those factors increase the likelihood of workload creep, and you already have enough to do.

Investigation of Complaints Against Faculty

Every collective bargaining agreement, and presumably every faculty handbook, establishes a protocol for investigating complaints against faculty: charges of unfairness/discrimination, grade complaints, various forms of misconduct, and so on. The structure of your contract and your campus may leave you out of that protocol, sending such complaints to your department chair, for example; but they may not, and the likelihood that you'll need to be prepared for that process is probably high. Thus my most important piece of advice is to learn the details of that protocol; my second most important piece of advice is to enforce it as stridently as anything you've ever done. In my experience, a poorly conducted investigation of faculty misconduct causes more (or worse) headaches (or worse) than any other breach of protocol.

Early in this chapter, I made the point that multiple bargaining units, or multiple constituencies within a bargaining unit, can make things even more complicated than the substance of the issues would suggest. Investigations of faculty misconduct, I think, are the most difficult in that regard. If your bargaining unit represents both the complainant and the recipient of the complaint, you—as WPA, and if you're neither of those—could be caught in all sorts of political and procedural problems. Don't be afraid to say so. If you have even a glimmer of a sense that your ability to administer your program might be compromised by your role in one of these kinds of investigations, you should be able to step out; if you're a member of a union, you should be able to get support for that decision. If the investigation involves members of multiple bargaining units, there's a good possibility that the protocols will differ, but the investigation will be answerable to both. At that point, all I can say is—you're responsible only to the agreement that governs you and your position. It's somebody else's problem to oversee and resolve a disagreement between unions. Short version: Don't hesitate to duck; there are some problems that aren't yours to solve.

Final Thoughts; or, Advice That Doesn't Fit Anywhere Else

I have two other bits of advice, more interpersonal than contractual, I need to offer as a closing note. First, as I suggested at the end of the opening section, on a union campus there should be a go-to person (usually your grievance chair, or contract enforcement officer, sometimes any member of your executive committee) who can help you sort out slippery contract language, who can let you know—or help you find out—if there's history around the issue, or in the worst case can help you grieve and solve a problem. I hope I can speak for grievance chairs everywhere when I say, we do this work so you can get support. Ask for it! On the flipside, though, I expect I can also speak for most of us when I say, remember how annoyed you get when students ask you questions you already answered in the syllabus? At least try to find the answers to your questions in the contract/handbook language before you come to us.

Second, along similar lines, your campus is likely to have people in management positions who can help you when a union can't—because the situation involves members of another unit, perhaps, or because multiple union members are involved. Befriend the labor relations specialist in your human resources department as quickly as possible. If you're an avid reader of *Dilbert* cartoons, you may be as skeptical as I was about HR employees. Don't you believe it. Your labor relations specialist may well be the only person on your campus who can address seemingly intractable situations. You probably also have an EEOC/diversity/equity officer on campus, and you should get to know that person too, for much the same reason.

Because there are as many writing program structures as there are union contracts, I've made no effort to be exhaustive here. I know, after many years of participating on the WPA-L listserv, that there are prominent issues among WPAs that I've said nothing about: training/supervising graduate TAs; assessment burdens/mandates; placement procedures—any or all of which intersect with issues I have raised (hiring/firing, evaluating, workload, and so forth). My hope is that the issues I have focused on offer instructive models for thinking about others, or at least some productive ways of framing your own thinking about them.

NOTES

1. Readers interested in a historical/sociological view of faculty collective bargaining, particularly as it relates to professionalization, might refer to Gary Rhoades's 1998 *Managed Professionals: Unionized Faculty and Restructuring Academic Labor.*

2. You can access the entire CBA for our union (APSCUF: Association of Pennsylvania State College and University Faculties) at http://apscuf.org/members/contracts.php. The *Directory of U.S. Faculty Contracts and Bargaining Agents* (Berry and Savarese, cited early in this chapter) is another important resource).

WORKS CITED

Association of Pennsylvania State College and University Faculty (APSCUF). APSCUF Faculty Collective Bargaining Agreement 2007–11. Approved 11 October 2007. Web. 7 September 2012.

Berry, Joe, and Michelle Savarese. *Directory of U.S. Faculty Contracts and Bargaining Agents in Institutions of Higher Education.* Series II, Number 2. New York: National Center for the Study of Collective Bargaining in Higher Education and the Professions, September 2012. Print.

Jaschik, Scott. "Has Faculty's Role Eroded?" *Inside Higher Ed.* 9 July 2012. Web. 7 September 2012.

Malenczyk, Rita. "Doin' the Managerial Exclusion: What WPAs Might Need to Know About Collective Bargaining." *WPA: Writing Program Administration* 27.3 (2004): 23–33. Print.

Rhoades, Gary. *Managed Professionals: Unionized Faculty and Restructuring Academic Labor.* Albany: SUNY P, 1998. Print.

17 What Is the Writing Center?

Neal Lerner

This chapter starts with a short quiz—please select the best possible response:

A writing center is

a. A place where poor writers are sent to get their problems diagnosed and texts fixed.

b. A window into literacy learning—and all of its struggles, politics, policies, and ideologies.

c. An oasis of congenial staff and friendly advice amidst the harsh, evaluation-driven atmosphere of the writing classroom.

d. A site for research into composing practices, student development, language use, cultural and political identities, and learning and teaching.

e. An under-resourced and often-overlooked-but-vital system of student support.

f. A reminder that institutions of higher education admit students who are not adequately prepared for the reading and writing practices they will need to do.

g. A symbolic—and potentially substantial—indication that institutions of higher education are doing something to support under-prepared students.

h. A site where students and their texts are regulated to conform to the expectations and standards of academic English.

i. A site ripe with possibilities to counter the hegemonic expectations and standards of academic English.

j. All of the above.

If you chose "j. All of the above," consider yourself a writing center expert! If you chose any other response, well, you are not wrong; the one-hundred-plus-year history of writing centers in American higher education demonstrates a pervasive "all-things-to-all people" quality. This quality seems endemic to literacy education and its cultural, political, and ideological complexities—and writing centers are a key site for literacy learning, simultaneously embodying education as a way to transmit status-quo values and the possibilities for education to transform the status quo. While this contradiction might seem a source of frustration, it also offers tremendous possibilities for writing center work and has been a source for a rich variety of scholarship.

This chapter introduces writing program administrators (WPAs) to writing centers as complex sites for literacy learning in American higher education. It is important to note that while writing centers are a growing, and in some cases long-standing, presence in K–12 settings (Farrell; Fels and Wells; Kent), as well as outside the US, given space constraints, this chapter focuses on postsecondary writing centers in the US.

WHAT IS THE HISTORY OF WRITING CENTERS?

Writing centers—or their predecessors known as writing *clinics* and *laboratories*—are not a new idea. Indeed, Stephen M. North ("Idea") identifies Socrates in an Athenian marketplace as perhaps the first writing center tutor. In American higher education, the idea of teaching writing as a "laboratory subject" was first trumpeted in the 1890s and was in relatively widespread use by the early twentieth century (Carino; Lerner, *Idea*). While one manifestation of the concept of "laboratory methods" was the use of class time for hands-on practice (Kitzhaber), another was the creation of outside-of-class options for students to get additional instruction in writing. In his 1929 survey of freshman English practices nationwide, Warner Taylor of the University of Wisconsin identified six "English Clinics" in current use (31). By the 1930s, stand-alone writing clinics or laboratories had been created at the University of Iowa, Dartmouth College, and the University of Minnesota, among other locations (Lerner, "Writing Laboratories"). This trend continued through the first half of the twentieth century, and by 1949 and the founding of the annual Conference on College Composition and Communication (CCCC), six out of the first seven meetings featured workshops on writing laboratories or clinics (Lerner, *Idea* 2).

Amidst this relative heyday for one-to-one teaching of writing, several persistent tensions would come to define writing centers, both past and present. One is that as large enrollment increases in American higher education brought more under-prepared students to our nation's campuses, writing labs and clinics were created to individualize instruction for this group, essentially an admission that previous whole-class approaches were not effective. More under-prepared students, however, created a crisis of sorts, whether for a university's reputation of "excellence" or for an individual writing instructor's workload. The lab or clinic as a solution to this problem could potentially stigmatize less-prepared students and the entities created to deal with them. Thus, the lab or clinic as a medicalized approach for the disease of poor writing is as pervasive an idea in the literature of this era as was the lab or clinic as an opportunity to offer much-needed instruction. This tension between the clinic as punishment for language transgressors and possibility for literacy education has come to define the history of writing centers (Lerner, "Punishment and Possibility"). Elizabeth H. Boquet ("'Our Little Secret'") describes this contradiction as one of writing centers as sites of literacy instruction versus writing centers as a type of individualized pedagogy. As sites or places, it was easy enough to mark writing centers with a remedial label. As pedagogy or practice, however, writing center work represents individualized instruction that has been shown to be the most effective instructional approach (Bloom) and has the potential to challenge long-standing ways of teaching chosen largely based on their efficiency in delivery, not on their effectiveness (i.e., whole-class lecture). Contemporary writing centers, largely born out of the Open Enrollment era of the 1960s (Boquet "'Our Little Secret'"), often continue to exist within these tensions, particularly as they grow to serve writers and teachers across the curriculum and engage in the continual process of educating faculty that student error is a developmental, cultural, and social phenomenon, rather than a mark of "disease."

Creating a contrast with classroom practices is also a long-standing factor in writing center history. As a 1950 CCCC workshop described, "The writing laboratory should be what the classroom often is not—natural, realistic, and friendly" ("Organization and Use" 18). While this contrast has much to do with teaching practices found in the writing center, it also stems from staffing decisions, more specifically the reliance on undergraduate peer tutors, as I describe in the next section.

Who Works in the Writing Center?

Writing center staffing might include full- and part-time faculty, professionals, graduate students, undergraduates, or a mix of all of these groups, but undergraduate staffing defines the bulk of contemporary writing center staffs (Ervin). This pattern stems from several sources: First, simply, is budget. It costs much less to employ undergraduates on an hourly wage than to hire a professional staff—and if those students are on federal work-study money, it does not have any impact on the writing center budget. Second, however, is the justification that undergraduate peer tutors are in a unique position to offer non-authoritative assistance (Bruffee). While the equality of this relationship has often come under question (see, e.g., Kail and Trimbur), the strong reliance on undergraduate peers has potential impact beyond the results of an individual session. More specifically, the undergraduate writing center tutors themselves have much to gain from their experience, including benefits far beyond graduation and into their careers (Hughes, Gillespie, and Kail). Moreover, an undergraduate staff can create a strong culture of writing within an institution.[1]

To prepare undergraduates for their work in the writing center, many institutions require that potential tutors take a semester-long course, and a wide variety of tutor training texts are also available to fill this need (e.g., Geller et al.; Gillespie and Lerner; Murphy and Sherwood; Ryan and Zimmerelli). This preparation, a mix of theory, practice, and reflection, is quite similar to preparing graduate student teaching assistants to teach in the classroom (see Reid in this volume). An additional feature, however, is that many undergraduate writing tutor training courses are also positioned as writing courses, often a strategic decision to allow the course to satisfy multiple requirements but also to stress the experiential learning that is at the heart of writing center practice.[2]

The strong presence of undergraduates in writing centers is also manifested in their scholarship, one of the unique features of writing center studies. For example, *The Writing Lab Newsletter*, now in its thirty-sixth year of publication, regularly features articles by undergraduates (https://www.writinglabnewsletter.org), and *The Writing Center Journal*, a peer-reviewed bi-annual publication in print since 1980, recently featured an issue devoted to undergraduate scholarship (http://www.cas.udel.edu/writing-center/journal/). Other avenues for undergraduate writing center scholarship include *Praxis: A Writing*

Center Journal at the University of Texas at Austin (http://praxis.uwc. utexas.edu/), as well as the National Conference on Peer Tutoring in Writing or NCPTW (http://www.ncptw.net/), which has run annually since 1984. Overall, undergraduate peer tutors' contributions to knowledge making in writing center studies—as well as their contributions to the day-to-day practices of writing centers—manifests many of the values higher education holds dear but does not always deliver.

WHAT ARE THE THEORETICAL FOUNDATIONS OF WRITING CENTERS?

Writing center history and practice have evolved from and continue to shape a set of theoretical understandings of the work. While these theories are not terribly different than the foundation for classroom teaching of writing, the one-to-one nature of writing center work is perhaps the clearest manifestation of theory in practice or praxis. For a WPA, understanding this theoretical orientation is essential to viewing the writing center as a site with tremendous opportunity for knowledge making, as well as for institutional reform.

At the theoretical center of writing center practices is the belief that learning to write is a social process (Ede; Lunsford). Thus, rather than the romantic ideal of the isolated writer calling upon an elusive muse, writing center tutoring is predicated on the idea that interaction is at the heart of any act of writing. In one sense, this interaction is based in rhetorical theory or the idea that any writer needs to consider purpose, audience, context, and content for any writing task. In another sense, the basis for these beliefs draws on developmental learning theory, particularly the ideas of Soviet psychologist Lev S. Vygotsky, who saw writing development as starting with the social and moving to the internal, rather than the opposite. Vygotsky is also influential in his notion of the "zone of proximal development," or the idea that learners are capable of higher achievement if working alongside a more experienced peer or instructor, whether in a writing center or as part of a writing fellows program. Contemporary social theories that influence writing center practice frame learning as taking place between an expert and a novice (e.g., Collins, Brown, and Newman; Lave and Wenger). Writing center tutors have expertise in teaching writing and academic literacies—whether through their experience as writers or the specific training they might receive—and students are novice writers with the intention of learning expert strategies. Further, a student's role in writing center sessions is ideally active and participatory, a kind of learning by doing that is essential to social theories of learning and the development of expertise (see also Boquet, *Noise*; Geller et al.; Shamoon and Burns). Writing center tutoring is also not merely potentially beneficial for student writers but is instead mutual. After all, students usually have expertise in their topic or content (or in the context for their writing task) and in writing center sessions are "teaching" that content to the novice writing center tutor.

writing as process

The theory that writing is a process is also essential to writing center practices. Ideally, a writing center is involved at any point in a student's writing process: early in the process when a writer is brainstorming ideas or engaging in classical rhetoric's notion of *invention*; or at a different point in the process when the rhetorical demands of *arrangement* are in focus and the writer is determining how best to organize content for a given audience and purpose; or at the point when a writer needs to engage in revision, best enabled through feedback; or when a writer is focusing on style and rewording sentences and making language-level corrections. Given many writing centers' association with remediation and helping only struggling writers—as well as prevalent faculty and student perceptions that feedback is equal to correction—a common misnomer is that writing center tutors mostly help students correct their near-final texts before handing in those papers to their instructors. It often takes a strong effort of public relations to inform an academic community that all writers need feedback at all points of a composing process.

This theoretical foundation forms the basis for tutorial practice, though at times practice itself seems to contradict theory (see Hobson, "Writing Center"). As I describe in the next section, the ideals of tutoring as a conversation among peers and the introduction of technology into the mix challenge commonly accepted notions of practice and, in turn, develop new theory.

WHAT DOES WRITING CENTER TUTORING LOOK LIKE?

At the heart of a writing center session is conversation about student writing (North 446). While "conversation" is a term that implies shared responsibility, mutual turn-taking, and symmetric power relations, most guides to writing center interactions assume that at first student tutors will more likely see their roles as editors of their peers' writing, a role to which they are often quite accustomed and accomplished (e.g., Gillespie and Lerner; Murphy and Sherwood; Ryan and Zimmerelli). To move tutors to a more facilitative role, most guides offer question-asking as the preferred type of tutor interaction in writing center sessions as opposed to directives and strong handling of a student's text (Brooks). Also, setting an agenda is particularly important (Newkirk), as what happens in a session is a negotiation between a student's goals and the tutor's sense of responsibility within the ethos of a particular center. For example, most writing centers stress in their mission that they do not edit or proofread students' texts, that they're not a drop-off service for papers to be corrected or cleaned up; instead, writing center tutors work with students to teach them how to best to improve a text. The long-range goal is the development of students as writers, captured succinctly by North in his oft-repeated adage that "in a writing center the object is to make sure that writers, and not necessarily their texts, are what get changed by instruction. In axiom form it goes like this: Our job is to produce better writers, not better writing" (438). In practice, this ideal is complicated by several factors:

1. Students' experiences with and expectations for writing center interaction (usually shaped by their experience with classroom writing teachers, many of whom have played a very directive role).

2. The role of time (Geller), whether that's the time allotted for a session (anywhere from twenty minutes to one hour at most writing centers) or the time before a student's paper is due.

3. The context for a student's writing, whether that's a particular class assignment (and the student's level of commitment to that class), a non-class task such as a resume or statement of purpose, or whether the visit to the writing center is required or voluntary.

The use of technology is an additional feature that potentially complicates any *pure* notions of writing center work as merely a conversation between tutors and student writers. In particular, synchronous and asynchronous online tutoring is now part of the repertoire of many writing centers. In some instances, that simply means offering e-mail response to students' papers, or in others, it means consulting in some sort of virtual environment (McKinney). These practices offer an interesting challenge to long-standing writing center ideals. For example, if the goal of a writing center session is to create conversation with students about their writing, how does one create "conversation" when response is done by e-mail consisting only of a student paper with some contextual notes and questions and a consultant's response? Similarly, how is the hands-off-student-papers approach (lest one succumb to the temptation to edit) challenged when that student's paper itself is largely driving an online tutoring session? Such circumstances have offered opportunities to reexamine many accepted tenets of writing center pedagogy and to consider if online consulting gives rise to completely different approaches to working with students and their texts (McKinney; see also Hobson, *Wiring*; Sheridan and Inman).

Of course, online technologies have not only influenced the teaching of writing; they play an increasingly strong role in students' production of texts, as multimodal composing has become an increasingly common activity in first-year composition and beyond. The response of writing centers to these practices has, on the whole, been slow to take shape (Pemberton). Nevertheless, many writing centers now offer response to multimodal assignments, and are increasingly forming partnerships with educational technology colleagues to address both composing and technology issues.[3]

WHAT IS THE WRITING CENTER'S ROLE IN THE INSTITUTION?

If my point in this chapter hasn't been clear, let me summarize: Writing centers are vital and complex places for literacy learning, as well as research on that learning. Unfortunately, their institutional role might be seen as rather simple—a place for weak writers to get their texts fixed. For WPAs, however, the writing center is a key ally for building and maintaining a writing program. Whether that work involves supporting all writers (whether students, staff, or faculty), or offering a venue for research into literacy practices, the writing center has much to offer.

A vexing issue to realizing this potential is determining the status of the writing center director (WCD), namely whether or not the director should have faculty or administrative status. According to the Writing Centers Research Project 2001–2002 survey, writing center directors most often held positions as tenured or tenure-track faculty (42%), followed by non-faculty or professional staff (32.64%). Still, the majority of those reporting (58%) were non-tenurable faculty or staff (Ervin; see also Balester and McDonald for additional survey data). Hopefully this staffing pattern has changed in the last ten years, and certainly a writing center director with administrative or non-faculty status can thrive in particular contexts, but in many institutions such staffing decisions broadcast a clear message that directing the writing center is not true intellectual work. Publishing writing center research beyond writing center-specific publications and into more mainstream composition journals is a long-standing challenge (Boquet and Lerner), but this challenge is made that much more formidable when potential researchers are not afforded the resources, time, and intellectual space that faculty status often allows.

Writing centers have also displayed a remarkable capacity to collaborate with other institutional partners, for example, as part of writing across the curriculum programs (Barnett and Blumner), learning commons (Bennett), or in partnership with libraries (Elmborg and Hook). Such collaborations increase the writing center's value to the institution, ultimately resulting in increased learning opportunities for students. Thus, as an ally in a writing program's efforts to be central to all writing endeavors for an institution, the writing center is key.

How Can a WPA Support the Writing Center?

What can a WPA do, then, to ensure that the writing center's potential will be realized? One move is simply to become familiar with resources, particularly the International Writing Centers Association or IWCA (http://writingcenters.org) and twelve regional writing center associations (WCAs). Each of these regional WCAs holds annual conferences. The IWCA itself holds conferences every two years, with every other year in conjunction with the NCPTW. These meetings provide key opportunities to find and learn from writing center professionals from a wide variety of contexts.

In addition to the venues for writing center scholarship I mentioned earlier in this chapter—*Writing Center Journal*, *Writing Lab Newsletter*, and *Praxis: A Writing Center Journal*—the listserv WCenter (wcenter@lyris.ttu.edu), first established in 1991, continues to be a forum for writing center professionals to address concerns and discuss common issues. In terms of locating resources, a comprehensive bibliographic source for writing center scholarship—including all articles that have appeared in *Writing Center Journal* and *Writing Lab Newsletter* and every dissertation or thesis written about writing centers up to 2011—is the CompPile database (http://comppile.org/). Within CompPile are also specific research bibliographies on specific writing center-related topics, including an annotated list of articles on writing center tutoring published from the late nineteenth century to 1977 (Lerner, "Chronology").

Finally, the WPA can support the writing center director's work both to provide instruction in writing and to offer the writing center as a key research site. On most campuses, the number of rhetoric and composition specialists is few, and the administrative and intellectual work of writing program administration might not be immediately recognized or adequately rewarded. Further, the institutional standing of WPAs as compared to WCDs is often unequal (Balester and McDonald). The opportunities, however, are many for the WPA-WCD partnership to argue for recognition and resources, and to establish the central role of teaching and learning writing within the institution.

NOTES

1. For WPAs, this outcome is one of many reasons why outsourcing writing tutoring to for-profit providers—e.g., http://www.nettutor.com—precludes the potential impact a writing center might have on an institution.

2. An additional role for writing center tutors is to work with students in individual classes, often called a "Writing Fellows" program (see Hughes and Hall; Zawacki). The WAC Clearinghouse at Colorado State University is also an excellent resource on this subject (http://wac.colostate.edu/fellows/).

3. Many writing centers also use technology to reach a wide audience, whether that is to offer podcast series (e.g., the University of Wisconsin-Madison at http://writing.wisc.edu/podcasts/ and Texas A&M at http://writingcenter.tamu.edu/c/podcasts/) or an extensive array of handouts or online resources (e.g., the Purdue OWL at http://owl.english.purdue.edu/).

WORKS CITED

Balester, Valerie, and James C. McDonald. "A View of Status and Working Conditions: Relations Between Writing Program and Writing Center

Directors." *WPA: Writing Program Administration* 24.3 (2001): 59–82. Print.

Barnett, Robert W., and Jacob S. Blumner. *Writing Centers and Writing Across the Curriculum Programs: Building Interdisciplinary Partnerships.* Westport, CT: Greenwood, 1999. Print.

Bennett, B. Cole. "Private Writing, Public Delivery, and Speaking Centers: Toward Productive Synergies." *Praxis: A Writing Center Journal* 9.1 (2012). Web. 10 July 2012.

Bloom, Benjamin. "The 2 Sigma Problem: The Search for Methods of Group Instruction as Effective as One-to-One Tutoring." *Educational Researcher* 13.6 (1984): 4–16. Print.

Boquet, Elizabeth H. *Noise from the Writing Center.* Logan: Utah State UP, 2002. Print.

—. "'Our Little Secret': A History of Writing Centers, Pre- to Post-Open Admissions." *College Composition and Communication* 50.3 (1999): 463–82. Print.

Boquet, Elizabeth H., and Neal Lerner. "After 'The Idea of a Writing Center.'" *College English* 71.2 (2008): 170–89. Print.

Brooks, Jeff. "Minimalist Tutoring: Making the Student do all the Work." *Writing Lab Newsletter* 15.6 (1991): 1–4. Print.

Bruffee, Kenneth. "Peer Tutoring and the 'Conversation of Mankind.'" *Writing Centers: Theory and Administration.* Ed. Gary A. Olson. Urbana, IL: NCTE, 1984. 635–52. Print.

Carino, Peter. "Early Writing Centers: Toward a History." *Writing Center Journal* 15.2 (1995): 103–15. Print.

Collins, Allan, John Seely Brown, and Susan E. Newman. "Cognitive Apprenticeship: Teaching the Crafts of Reading, Writing, and Mathematics." *Knowing, Learning, and Instruction: Essays in Honor of Robert Glaser.* Ed. Lauren B. Resnick. Hillsdale, NJ: Erlbaum, 1989. 453–94. Print.

Ede, Lisa. "Writing as a Social Process: A Theoretical Foundation for Writing Centers." *Writing Center Journal* 9.2 (1989): 3–15. Print.

Elmborg, James K., and Sheril Hook, eds. *Centers for Learning: Writing Centers and Libraries in Collaboration.* Chicago, IL: American Library Association, 2005. Print.

Ervin, Christopher. "The Writing Centers Research Project Survey Results, AY2000–2001." *The Writing Lab Newsletter* 27.1 (2002): 1–4. Print.

Farrell, Pamela. *The High School Writing Center: Establishing and Maintaining One.* Urbana, IL: NCTE, 1989. Print.

Fels, Dawn, and Jennifer Wells, eds. *The Successful High School Writing Center: Building the Best Program with Your Students.* New York: Teachers College Press, 2011. Print.

Geller, Anne Ellen. "Tick-Tock, Next: Finding Epochal Time in the Writing Center." *Writing Center Journal* 25.1 (2004): 5–24. Print.

Geller, Anne Ellen, Michele Eodice, Frankie Condon, Meg Carroll, and Elizabeth H. Boquet. *The Everyday Writing Center: A Community of Practice*. Logan: Utah State UP, 2007. Print.

Gillespie, Paula, and Neal Lerner. *The Longman Guide to Peer Tutoring*. 2nd ed. New York: Pearson/Longman, 2008. Print.

Hobson, Eric. H., ed. *Wiring the Writing Center*. Logan: Utah State UP, 1998. Print.

—. "Writing Center Practice Often Counters its Theory: So What?" *Intersections: Theory-Practice in the Writing Center*. Ed. Joan A. Mullin and Ray Wallace. Urbana, IL: NCTE, 1994. 1–10. Print.

Hughes, Brad, and Emily B. Hall. "Guest Editors' Introduction." *Across the Disciplines* 5 (2008). Web. 10 July 2012.

Hughes, Bradley, Paula Gillespie, and Harvey Kail. "What They Take with Them: Findings from the Peer Writing Tutor Alumni Research Project." *Writing Center Journal* 30.2 (2010): 12–46. Print.

Kail, Harvey, and John Trimbur. "The Politics of Peer Tutoring." *Writing Program Administration* 11.1–2 (1987): 5–12. Print.

Kent, Richard. *A Guide to Creating Student-Staffed Writing Centers, Grades 6–12*. New York: Peter Lang, 2006.

Kitzhaber, Albert. *Rhetoric in American Colleges, 1850–1900*. Dallas, TX: Southern Methodist UP, 1990. Print.

Lave, Jean, and Etienne Wenger. *Situated Learning: Legitimate Peripheral Participation*. Cambridge, UK: Cambridge UP, 1991. Print.

Lerner, Neal. "Chronology of Published Descriptions of Writing Laboratories/Clinics, 1894–1977, WPA-CompPile Research Bibliographies, No. 9." *WPA-CompPile Research Bibliographies*. July 2010. Web. 10 July 2012.

—. *The Idea of a Writing Laboratory*. Carbondale: Southern Illinois UP, 2009. Print.

—. "Punishment and Possibility: Representing Writing Centers, 1939–1970." *Composition Studies* 31.2 (2003): 53–72. Print.

—. "Writing Laboratories Circa 1953." *The Writing Lab Newsletter* 27.6 (2003): 1–5. Print.

Lunsford, Andrea. "Collaboration, Control, and the Idea of a Writing Center." *Writing Center Journal* 12.1 (1991): 3–11. Print.

McKinney, Jackie Grutsch. "New Media Matters: Tutoring in the Late Age of Print." *Writing Center Journal* 29.2 (2009): 28–51. Print.

Murphy, Christina, and Steve Sherwood. *The St. Martin's Sourcebook for Writing Tutors*. 4th ed. Boston, MA: Bedford/St. Martin's, 2011. Print.

Newkirk, Thomas. "The First Five Minutes: Setting the Agenda in a Writing Conference." *The Longman Guide to Writing Center Theory and Practice*. Ed. Robert W. Barnett and Jacob S. Blumner. New York: Pearson, 2007. 302–15. Print.

North, Stephen M. "The Idea of a Writing Center." *College English* 46 (1984): 433–46. Print.

"Organization and Use of a Writing Laboratory: Report of Workshop No. 9." *College Composition* and *Communication* 2 (1951): 17–18. Print.

Pemberton, Michael. "Planning for Hypertexts in the Writing Center . . . or Not." *Writing Center Journal* 24.1 (2003): 9–24. Print.

Ryan, Leigh, and Lisa Zimmerelli. *Bedford Guide for Writing Tutors.* 5th ed. Boston, MA: Bedford/St. Martin's, 2009. Print.

Shamoon, Linda K., and Deborah H. Burns. "A Critique of Pure Tutoring." *Writing Center Journal* 15.2 (1995): 134–52. Print.

Sheridan, David, and James A. Inman, eds. *Multiliteracy Centers: Writing Center Work, New Media, and Multimodal Rhetoric.* Cresskill, NJ: Hampton, 2010. Print.

Taylor, Warner. "A National Survey of Conditions in Freshman English." *Bureau of Educational Research.* Bulletin, No. 11. Madison: U of Wisconsin, 1929. Print.

Vygotsky, Lev S. *Mind in Society: The Development of Higher Psychological Processes.* Cambridge, MA: Harvard UP, 1978. Print.

Zawacki, Terry Myers. "Writing Fellows as WAC Change Agents: Changing What? Changing Whom? Changing How?" *Across the Disciplines* 5 (2008). Web. 10 July 2012.

Part Four: Helpful Questions

18 What Is a Writing Program History?

Shirley K Rose

A *writing program history* is a narrative about development or change in the work of a particular writing program in a particular institutional context. Although disciplinary histories of writing instruction are often grounded in the work of particular writing programs, these disciplinary histories typically seek to develop narratives and counter-narratives of large-scale changes in curricular designs and instructional practices. These accounts can help to establish the broader disciplinary, social, and cultural contexts in which individual programs undergo change. Writing program histories, however, focus on specific programs, with special attention to the ways they have responded to factors in their particular institutional contexts such as institutional type and mission, student demographics, the program's location within the institution, and writing program faculty characteristics.

Disciplinary histories can inform program histories, just as program histories can inform disciplinary histories. For example, for many years the writing program at Harvard in the late nineteenth century was assumed by many to be representative of disciplinary practices, in part because few histories of programs at other institutions were available. Recent historical research on writing programs at other kinds of institutions, such as that collected in *Local Histories: Reading the Archives of Composition*, edited by Patricia Donahue and Gretchen Moon, has enabled historians to develop a much better understanding of the range and diversity of structures and practices. Similarly, Brent Henze, Jack Selzer, and Wendy Sharer's study of the Penn State composition program in the 1970s, *1977: A Cultural Moment in Composition*, illustrates the ways in which study of events in a particular writing program's past can inform an understanding of a broader disciplinary and professional history and can, as well, be aided by an awareness of the cultural, social, and institutional historical context.

Although WPA biographies are often integral to writing program histories, an account that focuses on an individual figure responsible for leading a program, without attention to other program participants, is not a writing program history. Barbara L'Eplattenier and Lisa S. Mastrangelo's collection *Historical Studies of Writing Program Administration: Individuals, Communities, and the Formation of a Discipline*, includes several chapters devoted entirely or in part to providing biographies of WPAs at various kinds of institutions whose work contributed to developing theory and praxis in the discipline of rhetoric and composition, but these are, in most instances, focused on single figures rather than on dynamic events involving a broad range of participants.

Nor is the history of writing program administration the same thing as a writing program history. Susan H. McLeod's chapter on the history of writing program administration for her monograph in the Parlor Press series Reference Guides to Rhetoric and Composition focuses on the emergence of the WPA as a professional figure and on an evolving role definition for WPAs over the past three decades, discussing the changes in writing programs over time as the context from which WPAs' work arises. However, program history is not the central concern.

WHY ARE WRITING PROGRAM HISTORIES USEFUL?

Within a writing program, an account of its past has value for former, current, and future participants in the program, but it is also useful outside the program. A writing program's history can inform the current work of that program. Knowing how and why specific practices such as curricular models, administrative structures, and policies were originally designed can help current participants in the program recognize how the program has developed and carried out its mission in the past, and to understand as well why current practices that might seem problematic were initially put in place. Outside the program, a history of its development can serve to make the ongoing work of the program—the work of its teachers, students, and administrators—more visible to program stakeholders who may have misconceptions or misunderstandings about the program. A history of one program's work can also provide insights for participants in other writing programs that share similar characteristics. A WPA will always need to understand the past of her or his writing program in order to make good decisions about leading the program in its future direction. Furthermore, histories of specific local programs will help us construct the connections that constitute the larger networks of past relationships among programs and institutions. David Gold's recent *College Composition and Communication* essay, "Remapping Revisionist Historiography," points to several exemplars of such local archival research that do not "merely describe a local scene, but use the local to illuminate larger historical questions" (26).

A program history is an account of a program's past activities and practices that is grounded in evidence. Without program histories, WPAs must rely on gossip, rumor, and hazy memory at the local level, and sometimes sketchily drawn conjecture about broader national contexts, to construct a narrative of how things came to be the way they are.

METHODOLOGIES FOR DEVELOPING WRITING PROGRAM HISTORIES

There are three basic methodologies for developing writing program histories: oral history, archival research, and documentation strategies. Oral histories seek narratives from former participants in the program and reflect their particular perspectives and experiences. Interviewees for oral histories are not typically expected to document or provide other evidence for their claims about the writing program's past, and their perspectives can be significantly constrained by the limits of their participation in the writing program, but subjects of oral histories can provide invaluable assistance in making connections among and establishing larger contexts for events in a program's past. The more informal stories that are often circulated repeatedly as "gossip" in a writing program about a crisis in the program's past are important for the WPA to attend to as well, since these stories can be an indicator that the program is still traumatized by the event—although in many cases determining the historical facts about the incident may be less useful than probing current interpretations of the event. A program history might be warranted if it can serve to "set the record straight" and put the matter to rest.

Historical methodologies grounded in archival study may use one of two strategies or a combination of both: working from an already assembled archive of relevant materials or seeking out specific kinds of materials. With the first approach, an historian of a writing program might seek to construct an account of the program by drawing on the materials in a found "cache" of documents and other artifacts—a box forgotten in a closet or a file drawer of a former program director, for example—examining the materials with no highly specific question in mind, but drawing on a specialized knowledge base to inform her or his interpretation or reading of materials and refining the research question as he or she proceeds. With the second approach, a program historian would formulate a question, speculate about the kinds of documents that might contain information that would contribute to an answer to that question, then go in search of such documents. For example, an historian who wanted to understand how the focus of a writing program's first-year composition sequence had changed over the past fifty years might begin by looking for catalog descriptions of courses and formal curriculum proposals. Documentation strategies take a proactive approach, developing a comprehensive approach to gathering relevant extant materials from a variety of sources and designing and implementing creation, collection, and arrangement practices that will help ensure the presentation of relevant documents and materials for a broad range of research purposes. (The section "Developing a Documentation Strategy" later in this chapter offers a few guidelines for writing program administrators or other participants who might wish to develop a documentation strategy for a particular writing program.)

WHO CONSTRUCTS WRITING PROGRAM HISTORIES?

Many writing program histories have been written by current or former participants in the program. There are several reasons for this: For one, the questions about a writing program's practices that would prompt an investigation of the program's past typically arise from experience in or with that program; another reason is that program participants are most likely to have access to the materials that would inform a program history. Most writing program historians have considered their status as program participants an advantage, as their familiarity with the program informs their understanding of the archival materials and other resources they work with. Because writing programs have, historically, been under-documented, this contextual knowledge can be particularly valuable, despite the possibility that familiarity with a program's current practices will contribute to an unwarranted confidence about the origins of those practices.

Turnovers in program leadership and the relative transience of many program participants—students and teachers—also make writing programs vulnerable to having common sense histories imposed. For example, suppose a writing program director who was an active contributor to the task force that developed the "WPA Outcomes Statement for First-Year Composition" had offered, to the task force, the goals statement that he had articulated for the first-year composition program at his university as an example of how outcomes could be stated. Suppose his local program's goals statement had been taken as a starting point for discussions and negotiations in the collaborative process of drafting and redrafting, revising and editing that program's "outcomes statement." Further suppose that, less than a decade later, the similarities between his own program's still unrevised goals statement and the "WPA Outcomes Statement" were to be explained in an assessment report by his successor as the result of "basing the program's goals on the 'WPA Outcomes Statement.'" This common sense history based on common sense assumptions and a knowledge of the profession's history might serve the writing program and its new director well in a specific rhetorical situation, and would probably do no damage; but it would nevertheless be an inaccurate account of that particular program's history and an inaccurate account of the development of the "WPA Outcomes Statement" as well.

WHAT MATERIALS INFORM WRITING PROGRAM HISTORIES AND WHERE CAN THEY BE FOUND?

As mentioned above, broader disciplinary histories, histories of writing instruction, histories of higher education, and general cultural and social histories as well as histories of other writing programs can be valuable resources for writing program historians or can lead them to other useful resources. Histories of writing instruction will often focus on examinations of teaching materials such as rhetorics, readers, and handbooks, as Jean Ferguson Carr, Stephen L. Carr, and Lucille M. Schultz do in *Archives of Instruction: Nineteenth-Century Rhetoric, Readers, and Composition Books in the United States*. For materials specific to a particular writing program, however, an historian will need to consult local formal and informal archival repositories. Formal repositories for specific programs would usually include only the institution's college or university archives, which typically keep records such as course catalogs and minutes of college and university-level committees and groups involved in governance. Depending upon the individual repository's practices and policies, the holdings might also include the papers of former faculty, administrators and staff, and famous students. Some may have even established a schedule for collecting writing program records, although this is relatively unusual.

Working in the Archives, a collection edited by Alexis E. Ramsey, Wendy B. Sharer, Barbara L'Eplattenier, and Lisa S. Mastrangelo, includes several very useful accounts of writing program research projects that have depended at least in part on materials in collections maintained by formal archival institutions. A researcher might need to spend some extended time in such an archive before recognizing the materials in its collections that could contribute to a writing program history; in "Journeying into the Archives: Exploring the Pragmatics of Archival Research," Katherine E. Tirabassi has described how she "saw firsthand how artifacts already housed within a university archive could be reimagined with a fresh perspective by a researcher asking a different set of questions than those implied by the archive's established categories" (170). In some cases, staff in a college or university's formal archives can be an invaluable resource for locating relevant materials outside the formal repository, as Thomas Masters describes the help professional archivists at Wheaton College, University of Illinois–Chicago, and University of Illinois–Urbana Champaign gave him in his chapter "Reading the Archive of Freshman English" for the same collection.

Some program information is available at national clearinghouses or archives. A few writing programs have deposited some of their records and papers in the National Archives of Composition and Rhetoric at the University of Rhode Island (for more information, see http://www.uri.edu/artsci/writing/nationalarchives.shtml). Formerly housed at the University of Louisville, the archives that constitutes the Writing Centers Research Project is now located at the University of Arkansas at Little Rock and includes oral histories and written records of writing center history for the purpose of preserving writing center history and facilitating research on writing programs. However, most writing programs' records—those that are kept at all—are housed in informal archives: among former directors' papers, teachers' records, and staff files in closets, bookshelves, file cabinets, and cupboards in program offices. Some program faculty will have kept records, but because writing program teachers are often contingent faculty, they are relatively transient, taking their records with them or discarding them before they leave, and those who teach in the program for a long time are often crowded into cubicles or share desks and do not have sufficient office space for storing records.

Because the records that are kept often reside in an informal archive, the ownership of which can be difficult to determine, research based on these records can raise some ethical issues. In his 2009 *College English* article, "'What's in a Name?': Institutional Critique, Writing Program Archives, and the Problem of Administrator Identity," Steven J. Lamos addresses the ethical issues that arise when a research project is grounded in materials residing in a "hidden" archive—that is, an archive that is not an official repository for institutional or personal records that have undergone a formal process of review by a professional archivist or other official custodian. Specifically, Lamos focuses on the question of how to name administrators who played a role in shaping institutional practices and who articulated explanations and rationales for those practices in the course of carrying out their responsibilities. As Lamos points out, it is not simply an issue of whether or not to potentially embarrass an administrator who might still be an active professional colleague by offering a critique of a memo or proposal he or she authored; it's also a matter how to meet one's responsibility to other researchers who need a clear "paper trail" and how best to assure an appropriate focus on institutional dynamics rather than individual identity.

WRITING PROGRAM ADMINISTRATORS AS ARCHIVISTS

In her 2012 *Rhetoric Review* essay "Archival Research in Composition Studies: Re-Imagining the Historian's Role," Kelly Ritter has argued for viewing the archivist's role as more like an ethnographer's than like an historian's, because her or his work is to represent the archival record rather than to construct a narrative from it. Because relatively few writing programs have extensive archives, many WPAs will find they are in a position to contribute significantly to the development and maintenance of their program's archival records. They can do so in two ways: providing archival processing for existing records and developing documentation strategies to assure the generation and maintenance of materials for a long-term archive for the future. Processing existing archival materials involves several steps, all of them recursive to some extent at successive levels of processing: acquisition, evaluation, description, arrangement, and preservation.

WHAT TO KEEP

Making decisions about what to keep and what to discard is critically important for several reasons. First, practically speaking, not everything can be kept, due to space limitations. Second, the more there is to describe, arrange, and preserve, the longer that process will take and the less likely it is to be completed so that the records are accessible and available for research. A program's WPA is in a good position to make informed decisions about which materials to keep, but might want to assign the task to a group of program teachers who are eager volunteers, an undergraduate student intern interested in archival practices, or a graduate student interested in conducting a directed study in writing program administration. Some decisions to discard will be easy—duplicates, dirty materials that might contaminate other materials or illegible materials, and materials that are archived elsewhere (such as college catalogs). Other decisions will be more difficult, but can be informed by general guidelines. Examples of materials that should be kept include minutes of the writing program's standing and ad hoc committees and other materials related to the committees' work, such as proposals and reports, descriptions of the program's work in curriculum development and faculty development, reports and related records for assessment projects, and records related to changes in administrative structures. Research conducted under Human Subjects Review of Institutional Research Boards (IRB) will already have specific procedures for storing and discarding data, but some standard guidelines include these: Student writing should not be kept without signed permissions from students; rosters and records of individual students' grades should not be kept unless access can be restricted; teachers' instructional materials can be kept, although for an extensive collection of an individual teacher's work the program archives might want to obtain a signed deed of gift for the collections.

How to Keep It

Placing paper records in acid-free file folders, clearly and simply labeling contents, and indicating dates is the basic process for making the archive manageable and accessible. A filing system based on chronology is likely to be the most useful for the long term. Other materials not easily accommodated in file folders need to be clearly labeled—for example, a book containing a chapter about an assessment project conducted within the writing program might be easily separated from the rest of the archive without a label indicating the reason for its inclusion. Materials that are especially fragile should be placed in acrylic sleeves, for example, and oversized materials should be stored appropriately, with a note about their existence and location included in the main body of the records.

Digital records such as e-mail and data sets should be transferred to storage media that are accessible. Although archival professionals prefer that digital records remain in their original format, often they are also backed up to a more stable and/or more accessible format. Currently the standard format for digital records is CDs or DVDs, but due to rapid developments in technology, formats quickly become obsolete and decisions about preservation of digital records need to be reviewed frequently. Many repositories are making more and more of their collections available online in digital format—often as images of the original paper records. Few writing programs will have the resources to do this with their old records, although it could be a consideration in decisions they make in designing documentation strategies for long-term future program archives. For guidance on standard practices for establishing and maintaining a writing program-sized archive, see Laura M. Coles's *A Manual for Small Archives*.

Developing a Documentation Strategy

Work with writing program archives usually convinces WPAs and other program participants that they need to be more proactive about assuring that the writing program's work is documented and the documents maintained and preserved in the long term so they are available for future research. Developing a documentation strategy is one of the best ways to go about assuring that records are created and kept for the future. A documentation strategy will identify the kinds of records that need to be created; how, when, and from whom they will be collected; and how, where, and by whom they will be maintained.

All of the kinds of records identified above under "what to keep" should be put on a schedule for creation and collection if these are not already being systematically created and archived. Establishing a regular schedule for developing this information in the first place can prove invaluable for a writing program even in the short term, whether or not it is ever consulted for developing a writing program history at any point in the future.

A WPA should always have at hand in as simple and accessible format as possible the information outlined below. To develop this list, I used the suggested outline for a writing program's self-study provided by the Council of Writing Program Administrators' Consultant-Evaluator Service, because it identifies information that is critical to understanding a writing program's work—the same information a future historian of the program would potentially seek in a program archive:

1. Important program statements, such as mission statements, statement of goals, program philosophy.

2. Lists of courses offered in the program and related course descriptions, who is required to take the courses and relevant placement practices, the sequence of courses or other relationships among them, sample syllabi or standard syllabi, standard program policies.

3. Samples of course texts and readings, samples of writing assignments and samples of student work in response to these assignments (with permission).

4. Documentation related to important program events such as celebrations of the National Day on Writing, convocations, and celebrations of student writing.

5. Lists of teaching staff and their ranks, along with any public information about compensation.

6. Explanations of procedures and instruments for evaluating instruction.

7. Descriptions of hiring procedures for program teaching staff.

8. Descriptions of assessment methods and results.

9. Information about numbers of sections of courses offered and enrollments.
10. Copies of annual reports and other narratives of program work.

Collocations of "fast facts" such as these, the various reports and datasets from which they are drawn, and the reports and proposals to which they contribute all have a place in a writing program's archival holdings.

The notion of a proactive collection strategy was first introduced within professional archival studies by Helen Samuels and was subsequently developed by Larry J. Hackman and Joan Warnow-Blewett in the mid-1980s. The large-scale documentation strategies for geographical regions that they advocated proved unsustainable and unmanageable, but, as Doris J. Malkmus has noted, their principle that development and implementation of a long-term collection strategy should involve members of the community whose activities were being documented has had a lasting impact on archival theory and practice and can inform a WPA's efforts to establish a usable record of a writing program's work. (For an example of the way a documentation strategy might be developed for a writing program, see the chapter by Cinthia Gannett, Elizabeth Slomba, Kate Tirabassi, Amy Zenger, and John C. Brereton in *Centers for Learning: Writing Centers and Libraries in Collaboration*. In "It Might Come in Handy: Composing a Writing Archive at the University of New Hampshire," they describe how they have worked together to establish and maintain an archive that documents the collaboration between the library and writing programs.)

WRITING PROGRAM HISTORIES AS RHETORICAL WORK

Constructing a writing program history is rhetorical work. Louise Wetherbee Phelps's speech given to members of the Syracuse Writing Program in 1996, "Telling the Writing Program Its Own Story: A Tenth-Anniversary Speech" (published in Rose and Weiser's *Writing Program Administrator as Researcher* collection) is one example of such work in a very particular rhetorical situation. Histories make arguments for cause and effect relationships among events and for their significance to participants and other stakeholders, past and present. Though it takes time, effort, and material resources, WPAs can contribute to assuring that this rhetorical work rests on credible evidence.

The very acts of assembling that evidence and ensuring it is accessible to future users make implicit arguments for the value of the teaching and learning that takes place in our writing programs.

Works Cited

Carr, Jean Ferguson, Stephen L. Carr, and Lucille M. Schultz. *Archives of Instruction: Nineteenth-Century Rhetorics, Readers, and Composition Books in the United States*. Carbondale: Southern Illinois UP, 2005. Print.

Coles, Laura M. *A Manual for Small Archives*. Vancouver: Association of British Columbia Archives, 1998. Web. 31 December 2012.

Council of Writing Program Administrators (CWPA). "WPA Outcomes Statement for First-Year Composition." July 2008. Web. 6 May 2013.

Donahue, Patricia, and Gretchen Moon, eds. *Local Histories: Reading the Archives of Composition*. Pittsburgh, PA: U of Pittsburgh P, 2007. Print.

Gannett, Cinthia, Elizabeth Slomba, Kate Tirabassi, Amy Zenger, and John C. Brereton. "It Might Come in Handy: Composing a Writing Archive at the University of New Hampshire." *Centers for Learning: Writing Centers and Libraries in Collaboration*. Ed. James K. Elmborg and Sheril Hook. ACRL Publications in Librarianship Number 58. 115–37. Print.

Hackman, Larry J., and Joan Warnow-Blewitt. "The Documentation Strategy Process: A Model and a Case Study." *American Archivist* 50 (1987): 12–47. Print.

Gold, David. "Remapping Revisionist Historiography." *College Composition and Communication* 64.1 (September 2012): 15–34. Print.

Henze, Brent, Jack Selzer, and Wendy Sharer. *1977: A Cultural Moment in Composition*. West Lafayette, IN: Parlor Press, 2007. Print.

Lamos, Steven J. "'What's in a Name?': Institutional Critique, Writing Program Archives, and the Problem of Administrator Identity." *College English* 71.4 (2009): 385–410. Print.

L'Eplattenier, Barbara, and Lisa S. Mastrangelo, eds. *Historical Studies of Writing Program Administration: Individuals, Communities, and the Formation of a Discipline*. West Lafayette, IN: Parlor Press, 2004. Print.

Malkmus, Doris J. "Documentation Strategy: Mastodon or Retro-Success?" *American Archivist* 71.2 (2008): 384–409. Print.

Masters, Thomas. "Reading the Archive of Freshman Composition." *Working in the Archives: Practical Research Methods for Rhetoric and Composition*. Ed. Alexis E. Ramsey et al. Carbondale: Southern Illinois UP, 2012. 157–68. Print.

McLeod, Susan H. *Writing Program Administration*. West Lafayette, IN: Parlor Press, 2007. Print.

Phelps, Louise Wetherbee. "Telling the Writing Program Its Own Story: A Tenth-Anniversary Speech." *The Writing Program Administrator as Re-*

searcher: Inquiry in Action and Reflection. Ed. Shirley K Rose and Irwin Weiser. Portsmouth, NH: Heinemann-Boynton/Cook, 1999. 168–84. Print.

Ramsey, Alexis E., Wendy B. Sharer, Barbara L'Eplattenier, and Lisa S. Mastrangelo, eds. *Working in the Archives: Practical Research Methods for Rhetoric and Composition.* Carbondale: Southern Illinois UP, 2012. Print.

Ritter, Kelly. "Archival Research in Composition Studies: Re-Imagining the Historian's Role." *Rhetoric Review* 31.4 (2012): 461–78. Print.

Rose, Shirley K, and Irwin Weiser, eds. *The Writing Program Administrator as Researcher: Inquiry in Action and Reflection.* Portsmouth, NH: Heinemann-Boynton/Cook, 1999. Print.

Samuels, Helen. "Who Controls the Past?" *American Archivist* 49.2 (1986): 109–24. Print.

Tirabassi, Katherine E. "Journeying Into the Archives: Exploring the Pragmatics of Archival Research." *Working in the Archives: Practical Research Methods for Rhetoric and Composition.* Ed. Alexis E. Ramsey et al. Carbondale: Southern Illinois UP, 2012. 169–80. Print.

19 What Are *The Administration* and *The Budget?* (And Why Are We Talking About Them Together?)

Irwin Weiser

In this chapter, I have the opportunity to write about two often vilified, mysterious, and frequently misunderstood aspects of academic life: "The Administration" and "The Budget." I use both scare-quotes and capital letters deliberately, to suggest that faculty often talk about administration (and administrators) and budgets as if they were both *other*, and as *other*, to be viewed suspiciously—as if cloaked in mystery, at best. "The Administration," in fact, is often thought to be an uncaring and distant threat. However, in what follows, I assume that I have a sympathetic audience, since WPAs are (as our "A" reminds us) administrators, though we're usually not the people we mean when we talk about "The Administration," a point I'll return to shortly. As administrators, whether we manage budgets ourselves or not, it is to our benefit to understand something about them, because budgets—and every administrator who controls them—determine what we can or cannot do. With a healthy budget, we can think boldly, develop new programs, hire faculty. With a meager budget, we are constrained in every imaginable way.

THE ADMINISTRATION

Some administrators are people like us: academics who for a variety of reasons have assumed leadership positions of a variety of kinds, as department heads or chairs, deans, provosts, vice presidents for research, and presidents of institutions. They typically hold terminal degrees and have earned tenure and promotion, and for those reasons, they have experiences that enable them to understand teaching, research, and engagement, even when some of those activities are no longer part of their daily lives. Some—and this is often the case with department heads and chairs and deans—expect to return to their faculty roles after serving as administrators. Others find themselves taking on new administrative roles that may remove them from the active faculty more or less permanently.

Other administrators are not like us: They are not academics, but hold expertise and training in a variety of fields—finance, accounting, marketing, public relations, development, human resources, facilities management, information technology, and so on. But they are also still people ;-) and their administrative duties can both facilitate our work and create challenges for us. Because they have not lived the faculty life, they may not understand what it means to teach and research, and they generally have very little insight into what faculty do or what the goals and challenges of administration from the academic side of campus mean. In working with them, academic administrators (chairs and deans and provosts) need to be effective rhetors, learning their perspective and learning the means of persuasion that support effective communication and achieving the academic goals of the institution, something increasingly difficult in times of tightening budgets and competition for resources.

"The Administration" often refers to anyone who is not part of our own particular unit, generally beyond our own department and program. At some universities, there is a specific definition or role that identifies a job as "administrative." In higher education, there are definitions of the amount of effort that constitutes a person being counted as a "full-time" administrator. The common definition comes from the U.S. Department of Education's National Center for Education Statistics, through IPEDS, the Integrated Postsecondary Education Data System. Executive, Administrative, and Managerial personnel are defined as:

> [. . .] persons whose assignments require management of the institution, or a customarily recognized department or subdivision thereof. Assignments require the performance of work directly related to management policies or general business

operations of the institution, department or subdivision. Assignments in this category customarily and regularly require the incumbent to exercise discretion and independent judgment. Included in this category are employees holding titles such as: top executives; chief executives; general and operations managers; advertising, marketing, promotions, public relations, and sales managers; operations specialties managers; administrative services managers; computer and information systems managers; financial managers; human resources managers; purchasing managers; *postsecondary education administrators such as: presidents, vice presidents (including assistants and associates), deans (including assistants and associates) if their principal activity is administrative and not primarily instruction, research or public service, directors (including assistants and associates), department heads (including assistants and associates) if their principal activity is administrative and not primarily instruction, research or public service,* assistant and associate managers (including first-line managers of service, production and sales workers who spend more than 80 percent of their time performing supervisory activities); engineering managers; food service managers; lodging managers; and medical and health services managers. (National Center for Education Statistics, emphasis added)

What I find particularly interesting about this definition is the 80% figure, at least as it is interpreted at my institution. Because universities are often criticized for growing their administrations, it is possible to adjust appointments to avoid having what appears to be administrative bloat. Anyone with an appointment of under 80% is not officially an administrator for IPEDS reporting purposes.

Most typically, "The Administration" starts with deans, who are, unlike department heads or chairs, not considered "faculty," at least in regards to governance, despite their being included in the IPEDS definition above. "The Administration" includes those people—such as assistant or associate deans—who work in the dean's office, though they, if they are faculty, continue to have faculty rights and responsibilities.

"The Administration" is also those people to whom deans report—provosts and their associate and assistant provosts—and the people (or often the person—the president)—to whom the provost reports. That's more or less the academic hierarchy, but the hierarchy, if that's even the right term for it, is full of dotted lines and ambiguities. While it is generally the case that some people report to others (and serve at the pleasure of those others who are responsible for appointing and evaluating them), it is not always so clear whether the various associate and assistant provosts and various non-academic vice presidents are peers of the academic deans or further up the hierarchy. Does the vice president for development, who typically reports directly to the president, work *for* the academic deans or *with* them or do they "work" *for* her or him? It's often a fluid relationship.

What all of these various administrators have in common is that they work on behalf of the institutional mission, a mission that itself is rarely singular, as Elizabeth Vander Lei and Melody Pugh point out elsewhere in this collection. While educating students is a shared mission across institutions of higher education, different institutions may focus on a specific student body, based on their mission to serve for example, students from a local community, or students of a particular race or ethnicity (African-Americans, Native Americans, Hispanics), or students who share a set of religious beliefs, or students with particular vocational aspirations. Beyond educating students, some universities place more emphasis on research than others, and some place substantial emphasis on external engagement and service. Teaching, research, and service constitute the foundation of every institution of higher education, but some institutions value each equally while some emphasize one or perhaps two of the three.

Because administrators' responsibilities vary, their interests, though often complimentary, sometimes compete. Often administrators closest to the educational mission find themselves responding to decisions made elsewhere that have implications for their work—for example, how many students to admit in a given year, or the percentage of the first-year class to be made up of international students. As WPAs, we are often on the front line as implementers of these decisions, because most of these students will take one or more of the writing courses we administer, though we generally have no part of the decision-making process. When the numbers of students rise, we have to accommodate them, and when they rise significantly, we may have to add sections, work with other offices on campus to find classrooms, hire instructors, and the like. When the numbers fall, we also have to be nimble enough to address that, which means being prepared to reduce course offerings and lay off instructors or reduce their teaching assignments.

And of course, these kinds of changes have budget implications, which I will discuss later.

As I mentioned earlier, we WPAs are administrators, but for the most part we are administrators who see ourselves primarily as faculty, and we often define our administration as teaching—or at least work in support of teaching—because we develop curriculum and instructional policies, mentor and supervise instructors, and perform other teaching-related activities.

WPAs "administer" from a variety of positions in postsecondary institutions, and they administer a number of different kinds of programs and courses.

- WPAs may be faculty within a department, typically an English department, but with increasing frequency a writing department (variously named). In these most common cases, they report to a department chair or head (see also Kahn, this volume).
- WPAs may be faculty holding a tenure home in a department, but may administer an independent writing program (comprehensive or specialized such as a WAC program) that is not part of the department. In such cases, they may report to a dean, associate dean, provost, associate provost, or other non-departmental administrator.
- WPAs may administer all of writing instruction within their department, program, or institution, or they may be one of a group of WPAs, each of whom has responsibility for a particular aspect of writing instruction: first-year composition, professional writing (variously identified), or a writing center. The reporting lines in such instances vary. If their roles are independent from one another, they are likely to report to the department head or chair, but it is sometimes the case that one person serves as the director of all writing activities and these other directors report to her or him.

THE BUDGET

Administrators often, but not always, have responsibility for a budget. Ironically, while they have responsibility, they often have limited authority or control over it, particularly as they administer further down the hierarchy I described earlier. That is, on the academic side, the provost typically has more authority over resources than do the deans, who (may) have more authority than do department heads or chairs. I will discuss various kinds of funds and how they generally can be used, but first, I want to dispel a persistent budget myth:

> Not all administrators are sitting on pots of money (but some probably are and a lot of it is probably non-recurring).

I also want to point out that there are a number of different models for "The Budget" in higher education, a few of which I'll discuss here.[1]

Incremental (Historic): Incremental budgeting is perhaps the most common model used in higher education. Each year's budget is based on the previous year's, typically with an annual increase, though in difficult financial times, perhaps occasional decreases. Larry Goldstein points out two underlying assumptions of incremental budgeting: "the base [. . .] has been rationalized in previous budget cycles" (163) and "basic aspects of programs and activities do not change significantly from year to year" (164). To some extent the second assumption holds true, because the largest portion by far of any academic unit's budget is salaries and benefits, and unless there are significant budget reductions that preclude hiring or force reductions in personnel, this particular "basic aspect" does not change. However, other costs can fluctuate, as for example when the cost of telephone and Internet connections, often passed on to individual units, is increased.

The first assumption is potentially more problematic. Unless a mechanism is in place for systematic review of the original rationale for the operating base, units may find that significant increases in enrollment or other growth do not result in equally significant increases in the budget. This particular limitation has led to an increase in the popularity of the next two models.

Responsibility Centered: Under responsibility centered budgeting (RCB), each unit receives the revenue it generates from tuition and fees, gifts, endowments, and so on, and is responsible for all of its own expenses, including its share of utilities and the like. There's also usually a "tax" to create a central pool of funds to cover deficits and provide for institutional initiatives for which revenues do not exist or are insufficient.

Enrollment-Based: An enrollment-based budget is a variation on responsibility centered budgeting. Revenues are allocated by the central
administration to academic units based in part on the role those units
play in teaching and the enrollments (often measured in student credit
hours or weekly student credit hours) they accommodate. Both enrollment-based and RCB models have the potential to be more equitable
than incremental models because they respond to the contributions
units actually make to the mission of an institution, based in part
on the revenues those units generate. It is, for example, commonly
recognized that composition is a huge revenue generator for the university because so many students take it and the expenses of offering
it are very modest. Rarely, however, are writing programs budgeted at
anything close to even the tuition revenue they bring to the university.
An RCB model or enrollment-based model could be a boon to English
departments or writing programs as well as to departments that offer similar high demand/low instructional cost courses, such as oral
communication and language courses. There are, however, recognized
drawbacks to this model, which can encourage doing the most teaching for the least money, thus creating over-reliance on teaching assistants and contingent faculty, or competition among units to bolster
enrollments in order to generate revenue.

Initiative-Based: Essentially, an initiative-based budget model involves
reallocation of resources among units based on initiatives that may be
centrally initiated or may be initiated in response to a call for proposals
from the central administration. Some examples include the development of interdisciplinary teaching or research centers or the institution
of a new honors college. While these new initiatives may be desirable
and appropriate, their implementation is costly and generally there are
insufficient central funds available for them, so funds are reallocated
to support them. A variation of initiative-based budgeting may involve
the requirement by central administration that each unit identify a
small percentage of its operating budget each year to support new initiatives. In effect, such requirements encourage creative thinking, but
many administrators are finding it especially difficult to fund new
initiatives when their operating budgets are shrinking and they are
struggling to support their fundamental mission.

Zero-Based: In its pure form, zero-based budgeting requires that each year or budget cycle begin with the assumption that units have no budget and that they must propose an appropriate level of funding. This model is rarely used at an institutional level because some funds have to recur—for example, those that pay tenured faculty and most other salaries and wages, as well as some supply and expense (S&E) costs. What is more common is a blended model in which some funds recur or are carried over and other funds disappear at the end of a fiscal year or budget cycle. The downside of this model, and one reason why it has been abandoned at many institutions, is that knowing the money will disappear if it is not spent encourages wasteful end-of-the-year spending. Conversely, when administrators know that unspent funds will be available to them in subsequent years, they are able to be more forward-looking and strategic about funding requests.

ᴺ°

In reality, most budgets are a blend. For instance, at Purdue, the budget model is historic and incremental, but there are elements of RCB—we pay for our phones and Internet lines and other equipment and supplies from an S&E budget that is part of that historic budget, but that is rarely increased. What I've identified as enrollment-based budgeting can be thought of as RCB if enrollments determine the budget base for instruction and instructional support, but items like telephones, technology, and the like are funded centrally (see Zierdt, 352, for an example at Minnesota State Mankato). At Purdue, we are beginning to see some attention paid to enrollments as part of our funding, largely because the college runs an annual "instructional shortfall" because the historic budget has not addressed enrollment increases in foundational courses that serve all students.

The monies that constitute an institution's budget come from a variety of sources:

- Tuition and fees (including financial aid packages students receive that are applied to tuition and fees and administered by the institution).
- Private fund-raising, often the backbone of scholarship programs, named professorships, buildings, and the like.
- Revenue generating operations: bookstores, student unions, restaurants, housing and food services, athletics—many of which

are self-supporting but may not contribute substantially to the general operating funds available to the rest of the institution.

- Externally funded research and its products, including indirect costs, royalties, licensing agreements, and so on.
- Foundation grants.
- Endowments generated by private fund-raising or institutional self-investment of a portion of its resources (often a major funding source for private institutions, but increasingly important for public institutions, as state support shrinks). These funds are invested for the long term, with revenues stemming from interest or dividends. Frequently, a significant portion of the income from the endowment investment is reinvested to perpetuate and build the principle.
- For public institutions, state support (in ever-diminishing quantities).

Typically these resources fund the operating budget, the portion of an institution's budget that is used for its day-to-day operations, as well as the capital budget, the funds used for long-term capital investments in buildings and infrastructure. In public institutions, capital budgets are sometimes supplemented by the sale of bonds approved by the legislature.

Not all resources are created equal. Some resources are restricted; that is, they can only be used for specifically stipulated purposes. For instance, at some institutions, there are separate budget lines for salaries and wages and for supplies and other expenses, and the funds in those lines can't be shifted from one line to another—i.e., they are not *fungible* (with thanks to David Schwalm, from whom I first heard the term in a presentation at the CWPA conference in Houghton). Many institutions have restrictions on the uses of tuition or state funds— typically not for entertainment, especially not for alcohol. Very often, gifts to a university are restricted: Donors give funds to support a particular college or to support a scholarship or a named professor—or the athletic department—and those funds cannot be shifted to another use without the express consent of the donor.[2] Some resources are unrestricted, giving the institution, college, department, or program much more latitude in how they can be spent, but often still not on some entertainment expenses, which may have to be paid by a separately funded foundation. When students from your alma mater interrupt your dinner to solicit donations during the annual or semi-annual telefund, they are seeking unrestricted gifts to the university. Those gifts usually "belong to" the president to do with as she or he pleases, unless you specify where you want the gift directed. When you receive an annual fund solicitation from the dean of the college or the head of the department where you earned your degree, they are hoping for an unrestricted donation that will allow them to support whatever they deem most important.

Administrators love unrestricted funds.

In addition, some funds are recurring and some are non-recurring. Recurring funds, obviously, are those monies that are budgeted year after year. These include the salaries for continuing employees, some basic level of support for supplies and expenses, and income from endowments. Non-recurring funds are not part of the continuing budget of a unit. They come from salary savings when a faculty member receives a grant or fellowship that allows her to buy out part of her time, from reserves that occur when a faculty or staff member resigns or retires and either is not replaced or is replaced by a person who earns less than the former employee, and so on. Non-recurring funds can also include carry-over from a previous year because that carry-over cannot be assumed to occur annually. Support from donors, both restricted and unrestricted, is non-recurring (though income from endowments is recurring, if not constant since it is based on investment returns). Understanding the difference between recurring and non-recurring funds can help explain why it is often easier to get funds for a one-time project or a non-tenure-track instructor than for a continuing program or tenure-track faculty member.

Budget responsibility varies widely across institutions, in part based upon the budget model that is used, but in part based upon how various administrators who have budget authority decide to distribute that authority. Of course, there is always a "Budget" for the institution and there are always "budgets" for colleges and support units within the university and for departments within the colleges, but not all administrators have budgets, particularly in a difficult economic period; small budgets for faculty or student support programs often are among the first to be reduced or eliminated. In some institutions, whether by policy or long-held practice, budget responsibility remains in the hands of administrators for specific budgetary units—colleges and departments, for example. For administrators of programs within larger units—for instance, for WPAs—there are pros and cons to having a budget.

The benefits to having a budget are:

- You have some authority over resources, which may allow you to pursue new initiatives without seeking the funding from other sources every time you want to do something.
- Depending on the budget model at your institution, you actually may be one of those mythical administrators sitting on a mythical pot of money.
- You can plan, as long as your budget model isn't zero-based—and even if it is, you can still plan based on what you know is likely to happen—in other words, even zero-based budgets can be thought of as historical in many instances.

On the other hand, there are complications caused by having budget authority:

- You are going to have to live within your budget. If it is responsive to enrollment changes, it will fluctuate, and you will still be expected to make do. If you do not and wind up with a deficit, someone further up the line will have to cover it, at least temporarily, and you either will have to develop a plan to eliminate the deficit and work within your budget or to make a case for why the deficit was unavoidable and why you must have an increase in order to carry out your responsibilities.
- You will not escape external pressures on your budget, especially in challenging financial times. It may be reduced even when enrollment increases. In other words, having a budget doesn't mean you are adequately funded, as I have just suggested.
- Managing a budget diverts time and energy away from administering the writing program—from working on curriculum and staff development, for example. If you don't have a budget—or responsibilities for it—it becomes someone else's responsibility to assure that you have resources—a department chair, dean, provost—and your responsibility to advocate for more, without having to explain why you can't operate within the budget you don't have. As a WPA for many years, I never had a budget and thus never had to live within one. When enrollment increased, I got more money, and since our baseline budget has never been adequate to meet enrollment demand, "The Administration"—

in this case the Office of the Provost—paid for the additional instructors.

Whether you have a budget that you are responsible for or not, it is unlikely that you have the resources you need to accomplish what you want to accomplish, so it is important to be constantly tuned-in to funding opportunities that fall outside the normal budget. Many institutions support non-recurring internal funding opportunities; Are there instructional or professional development programs that provide small grants? Library grants? Instructional technology grants? What stars can you hitch your wagons to? Where's the crisis, the locus of interest on your campus? Exploit it.

And in Conclusion . . .

As WPAs, we learn pretty quickly whether we like being administrators or do not. Many WPAs—some of whom are contributors to this volume—have begun their administrative lives as WPAs and then become chairs of departments or deans or provosts or chancellors or presidents. My own experience as a WPA, department head, and dean has taught me much, not only about administrative structure and budgets, both of which I continue to learn more about daily, but also about working with, for, and on behalf of other people. Having some insight into administration and budget complexities enables administrators at every level to understand in the bigger picture of higher education and their place in it.

Notes

1. There are two commonly quoted sources of information about university budgeting, Larry Goldstein's *College and University Budgeting: An Introduction for Faculty and Academic Administrators*, and Ginger LuAnne Zierdt's "Responsibility-Centred Budgeting: An Emerging Trend in Higher Education Budget Reform." While my discussion of budget models is based on their often overlapping work (Zierdt frequently cites Goldstein), the terminology and definitions I use are common parlance.

2. The development office, which generally oversees the solicitation and the acceptance of gifts, is very careful in its use of acceptable language for restricted donations, making sure that the funds can be put to other uses acceptable to the donors if at some time the circumstances under which the

gift was given change. For instance, a gift to support in perpetuity a particular award could go unspent if at some time that award is discontinued. The agreement thus has to include an alternative use, typically to be determined by the administrator leading the unit to whom the gift was given and in keeping with the donor's original intent.

WORKS CITED

Goldstein, Larry. *College and University Budgeting: An Introduction for Faculty and Academic Administrators*. 3rd ed. Washington, DC: NACUBO, 2005. Print.

National Center for Education Statistics. "Glossary." Integrated Postsecondary Education Data System. Web. 27 June 2012.

Schwalm, David. "Playing with Fire." Council of Writing Program Administrators Conference. Michigan Technological University. Houghton, MI. 18 July 1997. Presentation.

Zierdt, Ginger LuAnne. "Responsibility-Centred Budgeting: An Emerging Trend in Higher Education Budget Reform." *Journal of Higher Education Policy and Management* 31.4 (2009): 345–53. Web. 12 June 2012.

20 What Is NSSE? ✓ *Survey on student engage at univ level*

Charles Paine, Robert M. Gonyea, Chris M. Anson, and Paul V. Anderson

The National Survey of Student Engagement, or NSSE (pronounced "Nessie"), provides information, strategies, and other resources that can help you assess and improve your writing program. However, NSSE's reach extends beyond the boundaries of your program. For leaders in higher education across the United States and Canada, "student engagement" has emerged during the past fifteen years to become one of the most important "organizing constructs for institutional assessment, accountability, and improvement" (Kuh 5). It's not just researchers who value this construct but also university leaders, such as deans, provosts, presidents, and other decision makers. There is widespread agreement that when schools, programs, and teachers can increase student engagement, their students tend to succeed at higher rates. As a WPA, you'll be presenting arguments to these leaders for resources and commitments; if you can back up your arguments with assessment results that show you're increasing student engagement, you will strengthen your argument.

Each year, NSSE (a project of the Center for Postsecondary Research at Indiana University) collects information from over half a million students at over five hundred baccalaureate-granting institutions across the US and Canada. For each participating school, NSSE administers its survey to first-year and senior-level students and provides the school with a variety of reports that estimate how students are spending their time and what students report they are gaining in terms of learning and social development. The survey also collects demographic data and other information. NSSE also provides participating schools with student-identified data files of all responses, which institutional researchers can use to conduct their own further analyses.

What does all this have to do with you—a WPA? After all, the resources NSSE provides mostly focus on the institution as a whole, and you are most interested in what's happening within your writing program. Also, your office of institutional research (OIR) may not give you direct access to the data, and in fact your school may not even make available the reports generated by NSSE (though most do). However, you can use three strategies to leverage NSSE results and methods. First, you can work with your OIR to help you conduct program assessment. Second, you can use NSSE-like survey methods to conduct your own research about your program. Third, you can combine the first two strategies. This chapter provides a primer on the concept of student engagement and briefly discusses all three of these strategies.

DEFINING STUDENT ENGAGEMENT

As its name implies, NSSE surveys and analyses are designed to assess student engagement, but what does this term mean? Consider first the non-technical sense of engagement. When we're engaged in an activity, we stay involved and devote time and effort to that activity. Imagine two students, Ann and Beth, who are taking similar economics courses taught by different professors. Ann is highly attentive to the entertaining lectures of her economics professor; she spends time and effort reading the material before class, listens intently, and never misses class. Beth's professor lectures less often but assigns in- and out-of-class active-learning activities and assignments; and while also spending time and effort on readings, listening intently, and never missing class, Beth applies course concepts to a variety of ill-structured problems by discussing, collaborating, and debating with her classmates. (On the meaning of "ill-structured," see Wardle, this volume.) Ann and Beth are both "engaged" (their involvement, effort, and time are equal), but they are engaged in different ways because their professors have presented them with different opportunities.

In terms of student engagement, Beth is engaged in more and different ways, and therefore higher education research would predict that Beth's chances for success in college are greater. While Ann and Beth may be equal in terms of motivation and effort, Beth's "quality of effort" is superior because her professor teaches in a way that encourages Beth to experience "educationally purposeful activities." These are activities that research has shown to lead to greater levels of student success (perceived and actual gains in learning, persistence, and graduation rates). So we can define the term this way: Student engagement is a construct that represents the degree to which: (1) students devote time and effort to educationally purposeful activities and (2) schools, programs, and teachers organize curricula to support and encourage students to devote time and effort to these activities.

STUDENT ENGAGEMENT AS PART OF THE ASSESSMENT PUZZLE: OUTCOMES VS. PROCESSES

It's important to understand that neither the NSSE instrument itself nor the NSSE-inspired strategies described here provides direct measures of student learning and achievement. Rather, as George D. Kuh explains, "student engagement data are 'process indicators,' or proxies, for learning outcomes" (9). While these process indicators "point to areas that schools can do something about to improve student and institutional learning" (9), they provide only a part of the assessment puzzle and should be linked to other data sources, such as conversations (or more formal focus groups) among faculty, staff, and students, direct measures of achievement (such as portfolio scoring and standardized tests), other surveys, and so forth.

In short, outcomes describe your goals for your students in measurable terms—what you want them to know and believe and what you want them to be able to do. Processes describe best practices and other activities that lead to outcomes. For instance, one of the outcomes listed in the Council of Writing Program Administrators' "WPA Outcomes Statement for First-Year Composition" is "Respond appropriately to different kinds of rhetorical situations." A corresponding process indicator would ask students how often they participated in activities that experts in the field consider best practices for helping students achieve this outcome—how often they repurposed work for different audiences, participated in group and individual rhetorical analyses, wrote reflections on the rhetorical choices they made for a certain project, and so forth.

Most assessment efforts in higher education focus almost exclusively on outcomes rather than processes, because they help answer the bottom-line *what* question: What do students know and what can they do? The problem is, outcomes measures don't always tell you what's driving your results or how to improve. That's where gathering process data can help—by providing a window into students' activities and helping answer the *why* question: Why are students achieving as they are? Are students engaging in the activities that will help them attain our outcomes? In other words, by helping you understand what is driving your outcomes results, process indicators can provide the information you need for improving your program.

Process measures are important because it's sometimes impossible to change your outcomes-based results rapidly. If you're monitoring only outcomes, it can be hard to, so to speak, "see the needle move," but when you implement a programmatic change in practice, you can tell more rapidly whether the processes really are changing. For instance, if you were the WPA for a large program that had recently made a curricular change to use more student-based texts in the classroom, you could create a survey that asked students how often they read other students' work. The difference between outcomes and processes is analogous to a person on a diet measuring not just pounds and inches (outcomes) but also keeping track of daily caloric consumption and exercise (processes). Just as dieters tend to be more successful when they document daily processes as well as outcomes, you can be more successful in evaluating your program and implement changes for improvement if you document both processes and outcomes. NSSE and NSSE-based strategies can help you with the process part. Still, it's essential that you remember that NSSE data and other process measures are self-reported data that do not directly measure student learning; they make up just one tool in your assessment toolbox that you will need to augment and link with other kinds of assessment.

Using NSSE Surveys and Data

Because NSSE provides a wealth of excellent online resources (including many recorded webinars) that explain their services and how to use them, we'll provide just a bird's eye view of the surveys and reports that NSSE makes available.

Schools that choose to participate in NSSE pay a fee (priced according to student body size) to NSSE, which works with your university's office of institutional research to administer the survey. All first-year and senior-level students are invited to participate to take the online survey (it is strictly voluntary). NSSE collects data from the survey in the spring and in August sends each institution its "Institutional Report," which includes a variety of overviews and analyses of the data.

Using comparisons to make sense of NSSE data. Non-contextualized results are meaningless. For instance, let's say that 35% of your students are engaged in a certain activity regularly—what does that mean? How would you benchmark that number? Are you happy with that number, or is it something to focus on and improve?

To make sense of your data, you can compare results from your institution or program to results from other institutions or programs and, when available, results from your own institution/program measured at an earlier time. Across-institution/program comparisons help you answer the question, "How does our institution/program stack up against others?" by comparing your results for a given year to results obtained in other contexts for that given year. Across-time comparisons help you answer the question, "Are we improving?" by comparing results from a single context (same school, same unit) across multiple administrations of the survey. (See "Sample Institutional Report" or view the "Your Institutional Report" webinar [Kinzie and Sarraf].)

Driving data down to the program level. NSSE provides data and comparisons at the institutional level, broken down by first-year/senior status (see McCormick and BrckaLorenz), but as a WPA, you will want to get a more focused and narrow snapshot, and to do that you will need to work with the people in your school's OIR, who can help you analyze NSSE data in more fine-grained detail. For instance, you could ask research questions like these: "Do first-year students who are taking Writing 101 in linked-class sections do more peer review than those in non-linked-class sections?" or "Compared to seniors in all other majors, do seniors who are majoring in economics and psychology (the two departments that recently launched intensive WAC/WID efforts) do more writing and report greater cognitive and noncognitive gains?" or "Compared to students whose first language is English, do students whose first language is not English in our FYC courses report more or less interaction with faculty? With fellow students?" The point is, you'll want to use these data, combined with institutional data, to answer local questions that matter for your students, your program, and your school.

OTHER NSSE DATA AND RESOURCES

In addition to the standard survey, NSSE offers a variety of supplemental surveys and services that they can supply to your school. You can also adopt NSSE methods yourself and create and administer your own NSSE-type, process-oriented surveys. You can find out more about all of these services by reading the excellent explanations at the NSSE website (see NSSE, "Customizing" and "Using").

The Faculty Survey of Student Engagement. FSSE (pronounced "Fessie") complements the NSSE survey with a parallel survey of faculty that measures "faculty perceptions of how often students engage in different activities," their attitudes about the importance of "various areas of student learning and development," and how they organize class time and curricula (Shaw and Cole). It provides another way to compare and contextualize your NSSE results. Also, by better understanding faculty attitudes and perceptions, administering FSSE (or your own FSSE-like survey) can give you data to inform your faculty development efforts (see Rutz and Wilhoit, this volume). Schools that participate in NSSE during the current or previous year can administer FSSE.

The Beginning College Survey of Student Engagement. BCSSE (pronounced "Bessie") offers another way for contextualizing assessment results by measuring "entering first-year students' pre-college academic and cocurricular experiences [. . .] [and] their expectations and attitudes for participating in educationally purposeful activities" (Cole and Qi).

The Experiences with Writing NSSE Module. Beginning in 2013, NSSE began offering NSSE-participating schools the option of appending up to two of six "topical modules" to the end of the standard survey, one of which is called "Experiences with Writing" (NSSE, "Topical"). This set of thirteen questions was adapted from a larger set of twenty-seven questions, which were developed jointly by the Council of Writing Program Administrators (CWPA) and NSSE (Anderson et al.; Kinzie, Gonyea, and Paine). These are particularly useful to WPAs because they were created by experts in writing instruction and writing program administration to reflect what are considered best practices. In fact, our study of these survey questions shows that the questions are relatively good predictors of student success and that the practices reflected by those questions contribute "to students' achievement of three major goals [. . .] [:] practical competence, general education, and personal and social development." You can use these questions and develop your own when you administer your own surveys of student engagement (e.g., the CLASSE described below).

Community College Survey of Student Engagement. CCSSE (pronounced Cessie) is the NSSE counterpart for WPAs who teach in two-year colleges. Although there are currently fewer options for adapting the CCSSE to local assessment needs, you can find out if your school participates and if so what it shows about your students and faculty.

The Classroom Survey of Student Engagement. CLASSE (pronounced "Classie") is an adaptation of the NSSE survey that can be administered for an individual classroom. We mention it last because it describes not just a tool you can use "off the shelf" but a strategy that you can adopt and adapt to your local situation. CLASSE is authorized by but not administered by NSSE (NSSE, "Classroom Survey"). Instead, you first seek the authorization of NSSE to administer the survey (a simple process described on the website) and administer it yourself. Anyone can seek this approval, including those at schools that do not participate in NSSE and two-year colleges. CLASSE actually includes two survey instruments: CLASSEStudent asks students about their activities in a specific classroom, while CLASSEFaculty is similar to FSSE in that it asks the instructor about his or her perceptions, attitudes, and practices.

The CLASSE offers WPAs a particularly powerful tool for conducting local assessment because you administer it, and thus control its content. That is, you can customize it to meet your local assessment needs, which, as many in this volume and elsewhere have argued, is especially important in assessing writing (e.g., Adler-Kassner and O'Neill; Broad; Huot).

FINAL BENEFITS, CAUTIONS, AND GENERAL PRINCIPLES FOR SHARING RESULTS

Like all assessment—including and perhaps especially teacher assessment—NSSE results need to be contextualized for a variety of audiences and purposes. There are benefits and cautions associated with this approach. The NSSE and NSSE-inspired strategies described here ask about specific students' behaviors and teachers' practices, and about what students and teachers have done. These behavior- and site-specific measures might prove highly useful for communicating with those audiences David Shupe calls "internal" audiences (teachers, WPAs, other writing experts) when they are focusing primarily on teaching and program improvement. However—and here's the caution—for Shupe's "external constituencies," behavior-oriented data would need to be framed and shared carefully. These external audiences (institutional leaders, faculty outside the field, and the public) may too quickly collapse results into single scores when they are focusing primarily on proving effectiveness and accountability. (NSSE attempts to preclude such score-collapsing, encouraging stakeholders to focus first on various engagement indicators, "Higher-Order Learning," "Collaborative Learning," "Student-Faculty Interaction," and so on, which combine individual items.) Even so, we believe these approaches could provide novel methods and data sources that can be used for a variety of constituencies, from institutional leaders, to WPAs, to individual faculty members.

Even for their internal uses of assessment results, WPAs need to carefully consider how they will use behavioral-oriented survey results. First, consider how you want to maintain the always precarious balance between (a) control and coherence and (b) freedom, discovery, and individual responsibility. (See Dively for an illuminating narrative of one program's efforts to achieve a prudent and stable balance.) As Wanda Martin and Charles Paine describe the dilemma, WPAs consider the often conflicting values of various stakeholders (students, teachers, the institutions, faculty across disciplines, the public):

> On the one hand, we want to give these teachers—experienced as well as new ones—as much free rein as possible to discover and practice what works best for them and their students. [. . .] On the other hand, we have our own beliefs about what constitutes good writing and good writing instruction, we want to articulate and practice a relatively coherent and stable philosophy of writing, and we are obliged to ensure a degree of consistency across all sections of first-year English. (222)

Results that focus on students' behaviors and teachers' practices might tempt a WPA to tip in the direction of mere surveillance, uniformity, and accountability. After all, teachers with outlying scores can be identified, rewards and penalties could be distributed, and the WPA then becomes (or is perceived to have become) the "program cop." Rather, we suggest you remember best practices for assessment—transparency, involving all faculty in the process, developing clear and reasonable standards of performance, and stressing improvement and professional responsibility over accountability.

Most important, during retreats, meetings, and workshops, behavior-oriented survey data (like all assessment data) should be used primarily to facilitate—not to supplant or to poison—rich faculty discussions about teaching and learning. This is especially important when doing the sensitive work of teacher assessment. Rather than announcing what the data show or asking the data to speak for themselves, invite participants to look for patterns or contrasts between

- the program's survey findings and other findings;
- the program's survey findings and its mission, strengths, and challenges;
- the survey questions and the training they have received about writing instruction;
- his or her students' survey responses and the responses of students in the program generally;
- the responses of a fictitious teacher's students and the responses of students in the program generally.

(For ideas on using survey results to facilitate discussions, see NSSE, *Working with NSSE Data: A Facilitator's Guide*.)

We could not possibly articulate every possible method or purpose for using such data, but it's essential that you take the time to help teachers and others understand the roles, possibilities, and limitations of survey data. Some may mistrust such data entirely, and others may accept it too uncritically. Everyone needs to understand that such data, as one element in a balanced, multifaceted approach, can yield helpful insights for improving programs or improving the effectiveness of individual teachers.

Notes

1. In the standard "Institutional Report" prepared for each institution, NSSE provides three customized comparison groups of institutions and also a major field report, which compares students in categories of majors with students in those same categories at the comparison-group institutions. Each institution chooses its comparison groups.

2. Your office of institutional research will receive a data file from NSSE. They can combine that data with other institutional data they have (student IDs, participation in certain programs, measures of success such as grades and completion, demographic information, etc.) to do more fine-grained analyses.

Works Cited

Adler-Kassner, Linda and Peggy O'Neill. *Reframing Writing Assessment to Improve Teaching and Learning.* Logan: Utah State UP, 2010. Print.

Anderson, Paul, Chris Anson, Chuck Paine, and Robert M. Gonyea. "Consortium for the Study of Writing in College." CompPile. n.p. Mar 2010. Web. 4 Dec 2012.

Anderson, Paul, Chris Anson, Robert M. Gonyea, and Charles Paine. "The Contributions of Writing to Learning and Intellectual Development: Results from a Large-Scale National Study." Forthcoming. Print.

Broad, Bob. "Organic Matters: In Praise of Locally Grown Writing Assessment." *Organic Writing Assessment: Dynamic Criteria Mapping in Action.* Ed. Bob Broad, Linda Adler-Kassner, Barry Alford, Jane Detweiler, Heidi Estrem, Susanmarie Harrington, Maureen McBride, Eric Stallions, and Scott Weeden. Logan: Utah State UP, 2009. 1-13. Print.

Center for Community College Survey of Student Engagement. "About CC-SSE." CCSSE: Community College Survey of Student Engagement. The University of Texas at Austin, n.d. Web. 4 Dec 2012.

Cole, James, and Wen Qi. "Engagement Readiness of First-Year Students." *National Survey of Student Engagement.* The Trustees of Indiana University, 12 Apr 2011. Webinar. 10 Oct 2011.

Council of Writing Program Administrators (CWPA). "WPA Outcomes Statement for First-Year Composition." July 2008. Web. 4 December 2012.

Dively, Ronda Leathers. "Standardizing English 101 at Southern Illinois University Carbondale: Reflections on the Promise of Improved GTA Preparation and More Effective Writing Instruction." *Composition Forum* 22 (2010): n..pag. Web. 10 Oct 2011.

Huot, Brian. *(Re)Articulating Writing Assessment for Teaching and Learning.* Logan: Utah State UP, 2002. Print.

Kinzie, Jillian, Robert M. Gonyea, and Charles Paine. "Using Results from the Consortium for the Study of Writing in College." *National Survey of Student Engagement.* The Trustees of Indiana University, 22 Sep 2009. Webinar. 10 Oct 2011.

Kinzie, Jillian, and Shimon Sarraf. "Your Institutional Report—Step by Step." *National Survey of Student Engagement.* The Trustees of Indiana University, 6 Sep 2012. Webinar. 4 Dec 2012.

Kuh, George D. "The National Survey of Student Engagement: Conceptual and Empirical Foundations." *Using NSSE Institutional Research.* Ed. Robert M. Gonyea and George D. Kuh. San Francisco: Wiley, 2009. 5-20. Print.

Martin, Wanda and Charles Paine. "Mentors, Models and Agents of Change: Veteran TAs Preparing Teachers of Writing." *Preparing College Teachers of Writing: Histories, Theories, Programs, Practices.* Ed. Betty P. Pytlik and Sarah Liggett. New York: Oxford UP, 2002. 222-32. Print.

McCormick, Alex, and Allison BrckaLorenz. "Driving Data Down: Using NSSE Results in Department, School, and Major-Level Assessment Activities." *National Survey of Student Engagement.* The Trustees of Indiana University, 15 Sep 2009. Webinar. 10 Oct 2011.

National Survey of Student Engagement. "About NSSE." *National Survey of Student Engagement.* The Trustees of Indiana University, n.d. Web. 4 Dec 2012.

—. "Classroom Survey of Student Engagement (CLASSE)." *National Survey of Student Engagement.* The Trustees of Indiana University, n.d. Web. 4 Dec 2012.

—. "Customizing Your NSSE Institutional Report: A Guide to Selecting Your Comparison Groups." *National Survey of Student Engagement.* The Trustees of Indiana University, n.d. Web. 4 Dec 2012..

—. "Sample Institutional Report." *National Survey of Student Engagement.* The Trustees of Indiana University, n.d. Web. 4 Dec 2012.

—. "Topical Modules." *National Survey of Student Engagement.* . The Trustees of Indiana University, n.d. Web. 4 Dec 2012.

—. "Using NSSE Data." *National Survey of Student Engagement..* The Trustees of Indiana University, n.d. Web. 4 Dec 2012.

—. *Working with NSSE Data: A Facilitator's Guide. National Survey of Student Engagement,* . The Trustees of Indiana University, n.d. Web. 4 Dec 2012.

Shaw, Mahauganee and Eddie Cole, Jr. "What to Expect from FSSE Participation." *National Survey of Student Engagement.* NSSE, 17 May 2011. Webinar. 10 Oct 2011.

Shupe, David. "Toward a Higher Standard: The Changing Organizational Context of Accountability for Educational Results." *On the Horizon* 16, no. 2 (2008): 72-96. Print.

21 What Is the National Writing Project?

William P. Banks

Over the years, I've worked in various writing program administrator (WPA) positions—assistant director of a writing center while a non-tenure-track faculty member, assistant WPA as a graduate student, associate director of first-year composition (FYC) as a tenure-track faculty member, and currently as the director of a multi-campus WAC program. During my decade-long work as a WPA, I have also been actively involved in the National Writing Project at local, state, and national levels. Despite being engaged in both types of "writing programs" simultaneously, I only recently began to think that the two were having a significant impact on each other, an impact that has gone somewhat unrecognized in the scholarship of our field. Given the increasing collaborations among the National Writing Project (NWP), the National Council of Teachers of English (NCTE), the Council of Writing Program Administrators (CWPA), and the Conference on College Composition and Communication (CCCC), it makes sense that WPAs would want to know more about the NWP and its network of Teacher Consultants. In this chapter, I look briefly at the thirty-plus-year history of the NWP in order to highlight how the goals and values of the organization intersect with those of WPAs in productive and symbiotic ways, and I conclude by noting particular spaces where WPAs might find the work and resources of the NWP particularly beneficial.

A HISTORY OF GRASS-ROOTS EDUCATIONAL CHANGE

The National Writing Project began in 1974 at the University of California-Berkeley with a Summer Institute initiated by James Gray, then teacher-educator in the school of education. *Teachers at the Center: A Memoir of the Early Years of the National Writing Project,* Gray's memoir of those early years, tells a compelling story of how an invested group of teachers, working together, could make a difference in their own professional development experiences and reclaim their power as teacher-leaders in their own schools and classrooms. That first summer, Gray had the idea that rather than a "training" model, where an outsider-expert delivers to captive teachers a neatly packaged, "foolproof" set of handouts, activities, or approved practices, teachers could be leaders in their own growth and development as professionals, could begin to think of themselves as researchers and their classrooms as sites for pedagogical inquiry. To those first summer institutes of the Bay Area Writing Project (BAWP), Gray invited a cadre of smart and accomplished teachers from elementary, middle, and high schools, as well as from the university: teachers like Miles Myers, who would go on to publish an important book on teacher-research with NCTE and be Executive Director of that organization; Bill Brandt from UC's rhetoric department; influential literacy theorist and educator James Britton; and Mary Ann Smith, a young teacher who would eventually leave the elementary classroom to be a leader of the National Writing Project and who would be a key figure in securing federal funding to grow the NWP network in the 1980s and 1990s.

At that first summer institute, Gray established a new model for professional development, which has become the motto of the NWP: "teachers teaching teachers." The idea was simple: Bring together strong teachers, have them share some of their "best practices" with teaching writing, and provide space where everyone in the room can ask questions, challenge assumptions, and collaboratively build better practice by bringing together research and the experiences of a diverse set of classroom teachers. Gray shares the story of one teacher from that first institute, Joan Christopher, who showed up to the summer institute surprised that she wasn't the only one there: "I really didn't think anyone would be there. [. . .] I was thinking maybe I was the only teacher in the world who cared about teaching writing" ("First BAWP"). Those of us who have studied the history of writing instruction in US schools know that *writing* has rarely been the center of the English classroom; teachers often teach it reluctantly, though a more accurate description might that they "assign" writing. *Teaching* writing, of course, is more difficult, and what those teachers showed in their teaching demonstrations ("demos") to each other that first summer is what NWP Teacher Consultants (the name in the network for those teachers who have participated in a summer institute) have held onto ever since: Being a successful writing teacher involves putting research and practice together.

While the NWP began as one site at UC-Berkeley in 1974, by 1976—mostly through word of mouth—the network had grown to fourteen sites in six states, a growth rate that remained somewhat constant over the next fifteen years, during which individual sites worked to secure minimal funding through organizations involved in public education: nonprofits and other foundations, colleges and universities, and state departments of education. Having built a grass-roots network of K–12 and college teachers of writing, sites also raised funds to support the summer institute through in-service contracts with schools and districts. In addition to the summer institute, where teachers teach teachers, NWP in-service projects also reflect the belief that local teachers, who know both local working conditions *and* research on the teaching of writing, are the best people to deliver professional development to schools and districts. Unlike the professional development that textbook publishers and other "nonprofits" supply schools, where individuals or companies come to schools in order to sell the current "cure all" for education's ills and then leave, NWP Teacher Consultants are teachers who live and work in the schools and districts in which they seek to effect a change; likewise, faculty leadership at local sites live and work in the area, often have children who go to the schools they are working to support and improve, and thus have a vested interest in local change.

As of Summer 2012, there were over two hundred sites of the National Writing Project offering institutes of various kinds in all fifty states, the District of Columbia, the US Virgin Islands, and Puerto Rico—and, occasionally, through grants and other partnerships, in sites as diverse as England and Malta. The NWP remains committed to "plac[ing] a writing project site within reach of every teacher in the nation" ("About NWP"). Unfortunately for K–16 teachers and students, dedicated, direct federal funding for the National Writing Project, like that previously offered to Reading Is Fundamental (RIF) and Teach for America, has ended, but based on the strength of the NWP network and the research and investment in assessment that has been central to NWP work for over twenty years, the NWP continues to seek and secure funding through various public and private sources. As such, WPAs are likely to have a site of the NWP on their campuses, which means that WPAs have access to a network of writing teachers in all disciplines and all levels of education. That's a network worth tapping into.

One of the real strengths of the National Writing Project model is its network of teachers, and I suppose it's true that those who have participated in a summer institute and become part of an NWP site often talk about their experience in cult-like terms. They act as though they have found a professional "home," and that's nothing to scoff at in the current educational climate, where policy makers and corporate pressures work very hard to de-professionalize teachers and to render them as expendable as entry-level workers. In the summer institute, teachers find validation for themselves, their interest in writing/teaching writing, and their desire to be better at their profession. More important, teachers learn to be researchers themselves, conducting writing studies in their own classrooms. Having worked with the NWP for nearly fifteen years, I have seen countless examples of teachers who, through their own classroom research, have become stronger, more effective teachers; they become the sort of advocates for writing and for students that we want more of in school environments. They're less likely to take the easy way out, to accept the prevailing narrative of ineptitude that permeates the "Johnny Can't Read/Write" discourses of public education; they work to make change in their schools, and they use their experience as researchers to make better arguments to administrators, parents, and other teachers. Their arguments do not always work, but NWP teachers know that they have a national, digitally-connected network of teachers to support them and to help them discover new research, new methods of teaching, and new means of persuasion for the stakeholders they need to convince.

Connecting WPAs with NWP Sites

While National Writing Project sites are nearly always located at colleges and universities, primarily because summer institutes tend to offer graduate course credit, WPAs should know that the specific location of the sites varies, though they tend to be located in colleges of education or in English departments. At my own institution, we started our NWP site with a faculty member from English and a faculty member from education. Because previous federal funding tied to the NWP required local cost-sharing of resources, we thought it made more sense strategically to share that burden across different departments. WPAs who are interested in connecting with their local sites (or starting one) might consider this approach, one that minimizes individual department contributions and maximizes the site's capacity to reach teachers from throughout the K–16 continuum.

Whether or not they have access to a local site, WPAs can make use of the extensive collection of resources available at the National Writing Project's website (http://www.nwp.org). Embedded in monographs and articles from *The Quarterly* and *The Voice*, WPAs will find information on how to design effective professional development projects, either "one-and-done" type events like Red Mountain Writing Project's "Scholarly Writing Retreat for University Faculty" (Perry), or sustained, long-term projects like UCLA Writing Project's *Creating Spaces for Study and Action Under the Social Justice Umbrella* (Carter, Mota-Altman, and Peitzman). All monographs are available for free as PDFs, as are other publications like Check et al.'s "NWP Professional Writing Retreat Handbook," which showcases what NWP teachers have learned from hosting hundreds of local, regional, and national writing retreats for over thirty years. The website also provides free access to a host of topics ranging from "professional development" and "teaching writing" to "standards and assessment" and "being a writer" ("Resource Topics").

NWP also provides access to two additional social networks of resources: NWP Connect (http://connect.nwp.org/) and Digital Is (http://digitalis.nwp.org/). NWP Connect provides educators with an open, interactive space for sharing teaching ideas and for exploring effective teaching practices related to writing, whether that practice is digitally mediated or not. Currently, there are over four thousand community members who contribute content to the various book groups and teacher networks. Likewise, Digital Is, which began as a project funded primarily by the John D. and Catherine T. MacArthur Foundation Digital Media and Learning Initiative, provides a space for teachers to explore how we "write, share, collaborate, publish, and participate" in today's digitally-mediated environments (http://digitalis.nwp.org/about). Most of the resources on these sites come from NWP teachers and those writing scholars who have worked closely with the NWP for many years. WPAs might find some of the Digital Is projects useful in their teaching or administrative work, or they might consider curating a collection of resources for Digital Is based around their particular research expertise.

SHARING THE WORK OF IMPROVING WRITING

While there are a wealth of print-based and digital resources now available on the NWP website, I want to finish this chapter by noting some of the primary ways that my own thinking about WPA work has been influenced by experiences with the National Writing Project and the various local and national projects I've seen the group develop. These projects have given me a very different sense of what we do when we "train" teachers and how we might reconceptualize that work in more effective, more egalitarian ways. Likewise, I've seen how a shared commitment to K–16 writing can improve teaching at all levels, as well as help teachers make more effective arguments to various stakeholders and policy makers.

Empowering Contingent Faculty. One of the issues that WPAs often face is what to do about the fact that they rarely, if ever, administer a staff of teachers who have extensive training in rhetoric and composition theory and research. More likely, we're working with graduate teaching assistants who are teaching for the first (second, third) time (see Reid, this volume) or with a cadre of non-tenure-track (NTT) teachers whose degrees may have involved little or no background in writing research and pedagogy; or we find ourselves directing a group of very experienced teachers who are unfamiliar with current research. Or we're working with all three at once (see Schell, this volume). These groups represent very different needs, and a "training" model does little more than alienate these different groups in different ways.

Fundamental to the home-grown NWP philosophy is that teachers are professionals; they do not need "training" when it comes to teaching. They deserve spaces where they can build on their knowledge, experience, and expertise in positive and productive ways. Too often, in K–12 spaces, teachers are told their expertise is irrelevant; they will use the current method/worksheet/binder of materials or else; they will teach to the test; they will be held accountable not by their teaching quality or ability but by student scores on standardized tests. Such an atmosphere makes it next to impossible to take chances, to ask real questions, to explore problems that take time to understand or address. Similar constraints exist for graduate students and NTT faculty: The former can be anxious about what they do not know and eager to do what they're told without actually knowing *why* they're doing it; the latter can fear losing their jobs if their student evaluations are low or if they deviate from what the WPA wants. To that end, the Summer Institute (SI) model of professional development is one that I've returned to repeatedly when working with various groups of teachers. Such a model can work effectively both in graduate course work, where graduate students design assignments/writing activities, align them with research from the field, and teach them to their classroom peers, who serve as early responders, and with NTT faculty through Teacher Inquiry Communities (TICs) that serve as year-long (or multi-year) pedagogy and research groups. TIC groups might read a book or series of articles together and explore what happens when they modify their teaching practice based on current research, the members of the group serving as thinking partners. In my experience, these work best when they start small, as an elective group of teachers who want to improve their practice. So the first year, the WPA might recruit five or six teachers, ask what they want to explore, and then join that exploration. The second year, the WPA steps back and lets those five or six teachers become group leaders for new TICs, meeting over coffee with the TIC leaders to see how things are going, finding out what the WPA needs to know so as to improve working conditions or effect changes in the program.

At the core of the SI model is that teachers have questions and concerns about their own teaching, with both content and method, and those questions and felt needs are the best places to start. From them, we discover what we value and how our values shape our work. This model is not necessarily quick or efficient, but it seeks to empower teachers who are often not empowered or valued by the systems in which they work. Happier, more knowledgeable teachers are likely to be more effective teachers, teachers who are constantly growing and expanding their knowledge and ability. Most important, these are teachers who approach their classrooms as spaces of shared inquiry, so they come to see teaching obstacles as opportunities rather than annoyances. In an economic climate where WPAs cannot guarantee continuing employment to even the best of teachers, the only ethical stance to take, it seems to me, is one that seeks constantly to engage teachers as makers of knowledge, teachers who are better at their profession, and who can compete for other positions at other institutions should the need arise.

Crowdsourcing Research and Responsibility. When Congress defunded the NWP (because of new "earmark" regulations, NWP could not continue to be direct-funded), one of the greatest concerns throughout the network was the loss of the network itself. Of course, the research and resources that already existed were not going anywhere, nor were the thousands of teachers who had become better writing teachers through the SI and follow-up Open and Advanced Institutes, writing retreats, workshops, symposia, and national conferences. Rather, we were all concerned about the loss of the person-based network itself; what we'd learned together in the previous years, even before there were Web 2.0 social media for sharing resources, was that individual teachers working alone were not remotely as effective as a sprawling network of engaged, inquiry-driven educators.

As a WPA, I'm in a much better position if I am working through a strong, deeply connected network of teachers who share goals, objectives, and knowledge about writing, research, and pedagogy than if I have constantly to reign in a group of maverick instructors whose closed classroom doors and resistance to my interest or inquiry mean I have little to no understanding of what's happening in the program. Beyond FYC, now that I'm responsible for a WAC program, I see this in even sharper focus: Now I'm working with teachers across multiple campuses, most of whom have never read anything about how to teach writing in their disciplines, so our programmatic efforts to engage these teachers have been about starting where the teachers are, allowing them to showcase what they know, and then finding ways to engage them in inquiry questions related to their courses.

Do teachers have questions/concerns that seem, to me, "old-fashioned" or "retrograde"? Sure. Sometimes, that's because I've already asked those questions or seen research that helped me think through them; but these teachers often have not, and that doesn't make them "old-fashioned" or "backward." Rather, by working through the questions or problems themselves, the teachers take a more inductive approach toward understanding. Sometimes, their findings challenge prevailing "best practices" and my own experiences with teaching or research; other times, they find that there's research out there that claims what their own classroom-based inquiry shows them first-hand. In any case, the teachers themselves are more knowledgeable about research (processes, products, methods), writing, and pedagogy than when they started, and they do not feel that they have been belittled or force-fed a particular way of doing something. In their inquiry design and implementation, we talk about the affordances and constraints of research on writing/writing instruction, and those conversations and experiences become a way to crowdsource knowledge about writing, as well as a way to share responsibility in important ways.

Improving K–16 Articulation. While WPAs know a great deal about composition theory and pedagogy, far too often we are not really connected to writing instruction in K–12 schools. Each sweeping change that moves through K–12 public schooling is a change that impacts the students that WPAs/college faculty will see in their classrooms. One of the things the NWP continues to help me with as a WPA is to understand what changes are being made in public policy around education and how those changes look in actual schools, classrooms, and students' lives (see Gallagher, this volume). Because I see those changes not just in the classrooms near my university but across the country, I also have a sense of whether local policy is aligned or not with national movements or broader interpretations of federal policy, which matters since our university students rarely come from only one school system or area of the country.

In the Summer Institute and other K–16 projects, NWP site directors potentially work with teachers from every discipline and at every level of education. In these institutes, we see what teachers are concerned about, how they teach writing, what they are seeing among their colleagues, and so on. By participating in these spaces and conversations, I find it much more difficult to assume that K–12 teachers are simply *not* doing something, and I have a much better sense of what is feasible in a public school writing context, as well as how college instruction might build on what came before. Knowing where the gaps are likely to be in students' composition experiences helps me to think about what our writing program could/should address and how we might need to scaffold instruction so as to build on previous knowledge and experience. Likewise, because teachers in NWP-style institutes are not talking only to teachers at their grade level or in their own subject area, they have a chance to see how what they're doing does or does not prepare students for writing in other contexts. These discussions—What is writing? How do we teach writing?—tend to be the most interesting when teachers come together in NWP-style institutes, because they help unearth assumptions and values that impact instruction at the most local level: the individual teacher's classroom. Outcomes-based education, whether that's the "WPA Outcomes Statement for First-Year Composition" or the new Common Core State Standards, tell only a very small part of a story, as the outcomes themselves can be met through a seemingly endless set of methods and procedures depending on how those outcomes are interpreted. Effective WPAs should seek out spaces to participate in such conversations and should find ways to engage those conversations with teachers in their own programs. There are many models on the NWP website that can help with facilitating such conversations.

Talking to Policy Makers and Other Administrators. Finally, because the National Writing Project has continually sought funding for various programs since its earliest years, the network has developed a rich collection of heuristics and materials to help teachers communicate their stories, experiences, and needs to those with the power or resources to help them. For example, each spring for nearly twenty years, NWP teachers have traveled to Washington, DC, to meet with their own elected representatives in Congress and to encourage them to fund work around literacy. These teachers provide powerful messages to their senators and representatives about what is happening in their classrooms and in the lives of their students. They follow up with their representatives throughout the year with stories from the classroom, snippets of student work and achievements, and requests for support for their own schools and districts. NWP provides useful template letters for writers less experienced with legislative communications.

As a WPA, I find that I frequently call on my experiences on Capitol Hill and in state and local government offices when I have to talk to my chair, dean, or provost about the writing program and what it needs to be successful. I certainly do not always get what I want, but I have found that effective storytelling, which I learned through NWP congressional visits, remains the most important strategy for connecting to these administrators as people and fellow educators. When I first began meeting with members of Congress, I assumed that numbers and "hard data" were the key, that they wanted to know how

X amount of money invested in the National Writing Project did Y amount of work in improving student writing or achievement. While that information is useful, it's not something that busy people remember nearly as easily as a powerful story. And as Linda Adler-Kassner notes repeatedly in *The Activist WPA: Changing Stories about Writing and Writers*, we know about story.

What the National Writing Project has done for me and for hundreds of teachers and local NWP Site Directors around the country is to provide useful heuristics each year to think through what our message is and to focus that message so that we can provide it quickly and effectively (see "How to Plan for Legislative Visits"). Nothing in the heuristic should surprise WPAs: Research your audience, focus your message, scaffold your approach (arrangement), consider how you will deliver your message. But each year, based on the shifting concerns of Congress and the nation, NWP also provides a list of suggested talking points about which individual sites might have stories to tell. For several years now, we've been reminded to think of stories around digital learning/writing in addition to stories about the impact that our local sites have had on teachers and their students.

How might this strategy work for WPAs? For one, how often do we ask those teaching first-year composition for their stories of successes and struggles? And how do we leverage those stories when we sit in spaces that most contingent faculty and graduate students do not get access to? If someone asked us, "What message do you want the university to know about first-year composition?" or the WAC program, could we articulate a brief and coherent program that's rigorous and relevant to students, the university, and the community? It's fairly easy for a middle manager like the WPA to fall into the dangerous role of speaking and listening only to her or his bosses or like-minded tenure-stream colleagues, but the work of a writing program is strengthened when the WPA can use her or his role to leverage the knowledges, stories, experiences, and concerns of those who do not have access to upper administration. Likewise, the experience of crafting a message with those who are not often listened to or whose opinions are rarely considered helps build a community of writing teachers that can then serve more effectively in grassroots initiatives for improving not only writing instruction but also the working conditions of writing instructors.

We Are All the NWP

While not everyone who is a WPA will be interested in participating in or directing a local site of the National Writing Project, WPAs should take time to explore the vast resources that writing teachers and researchers have made available on the various NWP websites. These materials tell the story of a grass-roots network of teachers who have worked continually to improve the teaching of writing across all disciplines and grade levels over the last thirty-plus years. They contribute to the call that Stephen M. North issued in his foundational text *The Making of Knowledge in Composition: Portrait of an Emerging Field* to pay greater attention to the contributions of classroom teachers, to use those contributions in productive ways in order to research our practice and better understand our collective enterprise. Most important, however, is that WPAs will continue to find in the NWP network the sort of eager, excited teachers of writing that make our work as administrators that much more rewarding. The energy of these teachers alone is something for a WPA to try to cultivate in her or his own program.

Works Cited

Adler-Kassner, Linda. *The Activist WPA: Changing Stories about Writing and Writers.* Logan: Utah State UP, 2010. Print.

Carter, Marlene, Norma Mota-Altman, and Faye Peitzman. *Creating Spaces for Study and Action Under the Social Justice Umbrella.* Berkeley, CA: National Writing Project, 2009. Web. 25 August 2012.

Check, Joe, Tom Fox, Kathleen O'Shaughnessy, and Carol Tateishi. *NWP Professional Writing Retreat Handbook.* Berkeley, CA: National Writing Project, 2007. Web. 25 August 2012.

Council of Writing Program Administrators (CWPA). "WPA Outcomes Statement for First-Year Composition." July 2008. Web. 6 May 2013.

Gray, James. *Teachers at the Center: A Memoir of the Early Years of the National Writing Project.* Berkeley, CA: National Writing Project, 2000. Print.

—. "The First BAWP Summer Institute." *The Voice* 11.1: 2006. Web. 25 August 2012.

National Writing Project (NWP). "About NWP." 2013. Web. 2 January 2013.

—. "How to Plan for Legislative Visits: Ideas for Dividing Up the Work & Setting Up a Timeline." 2012. Web. 25 August 2012.

—. "Resource Topics." 2013. Web. 2 January 2013.

North, Stephen M. *The Making of Knowledge in Composition: Portrait of an Emerging Field*. Portsmouth, NH: Heinemann, 1987. Print.

Perry, Tonya. "The Red Mountain Writing Project Scholarly Writing Retreat for University Faculty." 2012. Web. 25 August 2012.

22 What Is Community Literacy?

Eli Goldblatt

All institutions of higher learning exist within surrounding communities. Whether your school sits in a cornfield or a post-industrial urban landscape, suburban sprawl or an idyllic park of waterfalls and oak groves, you meet your students in a location whose identity grows from a history and a politics not attuned to the academic calendar nor measured by grade point averages. In short, life as an instructor or a writing program administrator unfolds within the larger social drama of a regional economy. Add to this the home situations all students bring with them like gossamer threads trailing behind the U-Haul trucks they drive to dorms or the commuter trains they catch to class, and you have a picture of the complex but often unseen social settings of literacy that influence and sometimes determine our students' understanding of what we purport to teach (see Durst's still relevant study of students' expectations in writing programs).

Professors and graduate students shape their lives around the demands of scholarship and the pressures of an academic career. We can easily forget, in the welter of essay deadlines and section schedules, that life in the academy goes on within a social fabric defined by non-academic concerns and seemingly mundane imperatives. We are reminded of these imperatives most when students annoyingly yearn for a life they believe is more "real" outside school. Indeed, our deans or provosts must take the "outside" into account when donors, legislatures, and the media inquire about what is happening within our groomed campuses or concrete high rises. This isn't necessarily a bad state of affairs, but increasingly the days of the campus life apart from the rest of society seem quaint and self-indulgent. Problems such as crime and unemployment, struggling schools and climate change, overcrowded prisons and overwhelmed soup kitchens are no longer the concern of a few "applied" disciplines and the student activist cadre. To teach writing as a live art is to teach writing as an engaged enterprise, and that means lifting our gaze beyond the curriculum.

Writing teachers, program administrators, and researchers have for some time been developing meaningful projects that connect their classroom commitments to substantial work with organizations and individuals living outside traditional academic circles. The appearance in *College Composition and Communication* of Bruce Herzberg's 1994 article on service learning in writing courses and Wayne C. Peck, Linda Flower, and Loraine Higgens's article on community literacy in Pittsburgh's Settlement House in 1995, followed by the collection *Writing the Community* (Adler-Kassner, Crooks, and Watters) in 1997, called the field of rhetoric and composition to pay attention to the world off the campus. The pedagogical and theoretical approaches to writing associated with Ernest Boyer's 1996 call for the scholarship of engagement have been referred to in our field as service learning (Cushman; Deans), the public turn (Mathieu), community writing (Rousculp), writing across the communities (Kells), the public work of rhetoric (Ackerman and Coogan), and many other formulations. I and others (see Grabill; Long; Rousculp) choose to follow Flower and her associates in calling the tendency community literacy, partly out of loyalty to their founding work and partly because it succinctly links the activist impulse to support politically disenfranchised groups with a rich understanding of literacy developed by Deborah Brandt and other scholars in recent years.

Briefly stated, community literacy refers to projects that involve postsecondary students at any level with work in community settings such as day care centers and schools, prisons and homeless shelters, hospitals and clinics, GED and adult basic education programs. Like the related field of service learning (Butin; Eyler and Giles, "Where's"; Rhoads; Stanton, Giles, and Cruz; Waterman), community literacy asks students both to draw on academic classroom-based learning and also contribute meaningfully to the lives of people not adequately served by the dominant society and not traditionally included in the college experience. Because of the special interests of rhetoric and composition, community literacy projects frequently center on reading and writing in some activist form, including but not limited to tutoring children and adults, composing texts for nonprofits, or participating in research projects helpful to local organizations. Often these arise from a cooperative partnership between an academic unit or individual instructor/scholar and one or more nonprofit groups or agencies that have a stake in the success of the project. In notable cases, projects go beyond single semester efforts, and the principal collaborators join in a truly cooperative mission to sustain and institutionalize the program for the good of all concerned.

The editors of the 2010 *Writing and Community Engagement: A Critical Sourcebook* indicate the movement's energy, diversity, and ambition in the introduction to their excellent collection: "These approaches often cross customary divisions within English studies and forge alliances with diverse others, seizing the power of poetry, publication, performance, community organizing, or multimedia to take writing public and, in the process, transform public discourse" (Deans, Roswell, and Wurr 2). I cannot do more than make a few general observations here about the multiform and restless turn toward public engagement in literacy studies, inviting readers to look at the books I cite as guides to this growing part of rhetoric and composition. Fortunately, Shirley K Rose and Irwin Weiser have already collected essays by and for writing program administrators in *Going Public*, noting: "Public engagement initiatives have the potential to transform our understanding of the 'service' role of writing courses from that of 'serving' other academic programs to 'serving' a much more broadly defined public" (4). For writing program faculty and administrators, engaging with communities outside the campus can lead to a new perspective inside writing programs, too.

One of the central tenets of community literacy among most practitioners is that the principle of reciprocity—sharing power in developing a program and sustaining a collaborative spirit throughout the project—should inform any university/community partnership. To manage such reciprocal relationships, I have argued, each party involved must recognize their own self-interest in the shared project (Goldblatt, *Because*). In the next section I briefly explore the self-interests writing teachers or program administrators might bring to a partnership, considering public engagement as an essential component of an overall conception of college literacy education. I address self-interest not to embrace selfishness but to make motives more explicit so that participants are less likely to make decisions driven by an unexamined agenda. In the succeeding section I consider the comparable range of self-interests a cooperating community partner might bring to a literacy project. The concluding section returns to the question of what relationships postsecondary institutions could have with their surrounding neighborhoods and populations.

COMMUNITY LITERACY FOR WRITING PROGRAMS

Here I focus primarily on the self-interest of higher education partners connected to the educational experience of their students. Researchers and practitioners have written about the advantages and disadvantages of community literacy for career advancement (Cella and Restaino), but there is no space for this vexed and messy subject here. One can surmise all kinds of personal, political, and philosophical reasons why an instructor or director might develop a community-oriented research and teaching agenda, but this too would be a difficult subject to investigate in the confines of the present essay. The mandate to teach our students well and the hope that what they learn will transfer to work they undertake beyond college is perhaps the predominant charge all writing programs share. The focus on undergraduate or graduate learning also can be a major imposition on the operations and ultimate goals of nonprofit community partners, so it is worthwhile both to name the focus on the postsecondary side and indicate the way a writing program's interests can sometimes clash with the self-interest of our partners.

Whether or not students in a writing program work with people off campus, the context of literacy in the immediate area and the larger region of a school can be a powerful factor in the thinking of a WPA. A director in any postsecondary program should consider a question a friend in a local nonprofit once asked me: "What community do your students come from, and what community are they going to?" The answer to this question is never couched exclusively in academic terms. A program must take into account the range of secondary schools students attend before arriving at college, and the majors they typically choose, as important factors in the design of a curriculum. However, the question asks for more investigation about students' attitudes toward literacy, expectations about the place of reading and writing in their work and home lives, experience with Internet and media environments. An orientation toward community literacy is not primarily a political commitment to doing good deeds or righting social inequities; after all, professing English or even rhetoric may not be the best platform for healing the world. Community literacy involves not only a theoretical stance toward literacy as socially embedded but also an honest-to-goodness commitment to acting on that conception, a recognition that a professor and a student are also citizens of a place in a specific time period. Reading and writing have a function for the whole person in a society. A person responds to and shapes words not only as an academic, an economic agent, or an emotional entity but also as a participant within a social network and an implicated subject within a political process.

Brandt's recent work highlights the way writers in work situations fall under surveillance, ghostwrite for their bosses, and internalize discourse strictures that reduce them to corporate scribes, threatening their ability to read and write autonomously in their personal lives. She worries about the effect of "competition and regulation" on what she calls the "the literacy habits of writing-worn Americans" ("At Last" 310). She concludes: "If literacy is to remain an entitlement of citizenship, this may be a time when the field of writing studies must assert what is most threatened in the transformation to knowledge capitalism—the human right to equal value—and the crucial role of literacy in sustaining that right" (310). Laying bare to students the complex functions for literacy in today's economy is a crucial function of community literacy, but social engagement also provides students with a deeper understanding of what Brandt calls elsewhere "attending to the relationship between literacy and civil rights" (*Literacy* 15). Teaching or learning across community settings sensitizes us to the diversity of possible goals for writing and reading instruction that can easily become routinized and standardized in an increasingly rigid higher education environment.

Community literacy projects woven into disciplinary curricula or student life cocurricular activities can thus enrich immensely students' understanding of writing and reading as human behavior. Without a compelling vision of literacy as lifelong, multifunctional, and unavoidably ideological, first-year composition (FYC) or writing in the disciplines courses can become merely stages for skill installation or training grounds for word technicians. Jeffrey Grabill, for example, has applied this deepening perspective quite effectively to technical and professional writing, thus bringing the analysis of ethics and institutional structures into course work that might seem to some the precinct of generic forms and marketing savvy. Both instructors and program designers in postsecondary schools must remember that the "human right to equal value" requires writers to pay attention to what a given use of language reflects about the fashioners and the consumers of words and images. The most effective way to teach such attention is to have writers encounter language in settings that challenge their sense of appropriate use, communicative efficiency, and assumed value.

I do not particularly advocate service or community-based learning in FYC courses, although the results can be promising. As with any curricular initiative, the deciding factor should be the learning outcomes of a given writing program. Students who graduate from underfunded high schools often need course work that acclimatizes them to the habits of mind expected of them in college classes, and even better-prepared students have received instruction tuned to the tests that will get them the admissions and scholarships they desire. In many undergraduate programs, entering students may need instruction that focuses primarily on intellectual controversy and inquiry within a classroom setting. Still, a well-designed program at any level can be successful where, as Thomas Deans says, college students write with "about," "for," or "with" the community. In any community setting, students encounter people who wish to read and write for economic, personal, or advocacy purposes, and this can provide a literacy experience that matters beyond a grade.

One element of service learning pedagogy in the professional literature is readily recognizable to composition instructors. That element is reflection, famously emphasized by John Dewey in books like *Experience and Education* and regularly integrated into common composition practices such as portfolio assessment, process pedagogies, and tutor training. As Janet Eyler and Dwight Giles observe in their review article on quality in service learning programs, "Perhaps the most often appropriated element of Dewey's thinking about experiential learning is the concept of reflection or 'reflective activity' [. . .] Through reflection, action and thinking are linked to produce learning that leads to more action" ("Importance" 59). Writing programs that incorporate community literacy can contribute significantly to students' overall learning experiences because instructors are more comfortable in teaching reflective writing than faculty in disciplines where measuring, analyzing data, or providing services are the primary focus.

MUCH TO DO AND TOO LITTLE MONEY TO SURVIVE

The life of a nonprofit director or coordinator or service provider, no matter what size the organization, is often harried and frustrating. From the tiny group addressing the needs of undocumented immigrants in a ten-block radius, to the relatively huge food distribution network serving those living with HIV in a metropolitan area, the staff must keep the organization running while also handling volunteers, raising funds, promoting the mission of the group, and reminding themselves that those they serve are autonomous and valuable people despite their momentary or chronic needs. Except in the very largest nonprofits, staff and administrators are almost always underpaid. They can be frustrated that they can never adequately fulfill their mission or that their board of trustees doesn't understand the difficulty of their jobs, but nonprofit staffs do what they do not only for a paycheck but for the hope that they will make a difference in other people's lives. Often labor conditions are cramped and supplies scarce, but in well-managed nonprofits the morale of the staff can be high despite poor conditions because they feel appreciated and effective. All nonprofits go through stages where their survival is in question, and many do fail. It's a precarious business, but nonprofit work can be immensely satisfying. For young staffers, a first job working at a soup kitchen or food co-op or disability support office can be a fine way to develop experience in the working world no matter where else their careers may take them. For veteran workers or leaders, nonprofits provide the culminating opportunity in a career devoted to confronting social inequities.

College and university partners must recognize that when they come to a nonprofit executive director with a request to place students in a community literacy project, the offer does not seem like an unalloyed gift from the nonprofit side. Organizations frequently need eager helpers to support a class or provide a service, but volunteers represent a potential strain on a system that may already be overburdened. No matter how eager college students might be, they still need to be trained, supervised, evaluated, and debriefed. An eighteen-year-old with the best intentions might make an inadvertent comment, fail to show for a shift, or neglect a duty that could cause a loss of trust among the served population or endanger a child or give cause for a lawsuit. A neighborhood garden plot could be ruined by a student who forgot to turn a hose off before he rushed off to his evening class, or a storefront theater could be vandalized because a volunteer forgot to lock the back door after a performance. These may not be the common experience in every nonprofit, but they are surely the stuff of bad dreams executive directors have when they allow unpaid staffers to carry some or much of the burden of the daily interaction with the nonprofit's public. Furthermore, in economic hard times directors are more and more absorbed by fundraising campaigns and courting donors; increased demands on managerial attention in a small organization often adds great stress to an already overwrought nonprofit administrator. In short, the request may be tendered in a generous spirit and accepted with enthusiasm, but working with a postsecondary partner can be a great burden on the nonprofit collaborator.

Those of us with advanced degrees and good politics think we enter into a collaboration armed with knowledge of contexts and open minds. However, even if an instructor in a writing program may feel herself or himself to have little status in the field, or to be on the side of the outsider rather than a representative of deans and provosts, we often cannot see how others see us. The very name of our institution may suggest arrogance in the minds of those who have to see students' trash on the street and read about the latest gift to the university library. Full-time faculty may feel that an exceptional course or a community-based research project will help further their careers and couldn't possibly hurt anyone, but courses and publications may mean next to nothing to a director looking to raise his salary for the next three months. Postsecondary instructors may come to a neighborhood organization with an incomplete idea of the needs of the people who come to the center, and may accidentally say something to insult individuals, the program, or the staff simply because underlying attitudes haven't been adequately shared and recognized. If a staff person takes pride in a plan of action he is carrying out, the critical approach an academic brings to the initial planning meetings may be offensive or disheartening even if the college partner meant no harm at all. Even "literacy" has so many meanings in different practitioners' minds that we cannot utter it without a careful gloss on what the term means in the context of a given collaboration.

Clearly cooperative projects between nonprofits and academics can be highly beneficial to both sides, but practically nothing about the relationship should be taken for granted. A nonprofit may be quite interested in a carefully designed assessment project or an inquiry into their organizational history or a successful public relations effort. People in a basic technology class might well enjoy working with a college student on developing a website or learning to read e-mail. As long as both sides continually revisit the process of valuation and understand that often what is gold in one setting is dross in another, academic/community partnerships may thrive. One very good way to learn about the precariousness of nonprofit organizations is for the academic partner to serve on a board or at least a board committee for the community partner. Board work is demanding, enlightening, and terribly bewildering at times, but board experience is invaluable in community literacy (Goldblatt, "Introduction").

SHARED INTERESTS: WHY WE STAY AT IT

Community literacy partnerships require that everyone involved work, at least in part, outside of institutional structures. WPAs who support their instructors in requiring community experience and reflection to complete a first-year course, or business writing teachers who arrange for their students to develop business plans for local merchants in low-income neighborhoods, risk the wrath of deans who would rather students stay safe and predictably on campus. Executive directors may run afoul of their boards if they are found to have "wasted" their staffs' precious time training college students to take jobs that they will leave in only a dozen weeks. Yet, we persist in such work. The work must in some sense satisfy the self-interests of each partner or the projects could not begin, let alone endure. But, having discussed the self-interests separately, I want to return to the shared interests that keep many of us looking for more partnerships across institutional and social divisions.

Community literacy is a framework from which people with remarkably different outlooks, commitments, and backgrounds can come together to discuss, plan, execute, and assess actions that can make shared social spaces more vibrant and equitable. Dewey warns against a narrow specialization of knowledge, which can confer expertise but not judgment (*Democracy* 67). Similarly, Brandt warns that literacy defined and driven by economic value hides the equal human value of those around us ("At Last" 310). Collaborators on the postsecondary side and those on the nonprofit or neighborhood side would, I think, agree that the messy and challenging process necessary for collaboration, and for students and learners of all stripes to work together, requires all parties to look beyond their particular status and, while acting together, come to a new understanding about the efficacy and relationship of knowledge to action. This is what Dewey calls "conjoint activity": "By doing his share in the associated activity, the individual appropriates the purpose which actuates it, becomes familiar with its methods and subject matters, acquires needed skill, and is saturated with its emotional spirit" (*Democracy* 22). "Conjoint activity" is crucial for young writers because students who compose purely for the teacher/judge will never be able to critique and reinterpret on their own, nor will they be able to synthesize other people's assertions into independent arguments. The outcome of collaboration is likewise valuable in the community setting, where people with little political power can come to realize something of their possibilities as they write and read for themselves and their peers rather than for a teacher.

Transformations of this sort may not fill potholes or rebuild houses destroyed by fire, but they can redefine us alongside one another. I had a student in an advanced writing class who came from a rural/suburban area outside of Philadelphia. The students in that class tutored older ESL learners in preparation for the citizenship test. This young woman loved writing but didn't know what she wanted to do for a living. She came back from the second meeting with her learner with a glowing report of her interactions with the elderly Russian man she had been assigned. She had no previous experience with Eastern Europeans or even speakers of other languages. By the time she finished the class she had written an extensive study of how the man learned English words, what they had talked about, but also how their growing friendship affected her. She had lost her own grandfather only a year before, and although this Russian immigrant was nothing like her grandfather, the relationship brought her to consider what she'd learned from both older men. She wrote a series of reflections, poems, lesson plans for teaching English, and speculations on her future. A year later I heard from her that she'd finished her teaching certificate and started teaching high school in a challenging urban school. The remembrance of her grandfather and her Russian "grandfather" remained with her in the years she continued to contact me.

I can think of many stories about students from community learning courses where the experience had a transformative effect on the college learner. I know fewer stories about learners who worked with my students, and most of those stories are about younger kids, who met college tutors and mentors at a crucial time in their development and kept up with them later. The stories I personally know best, however, involve executive directors, fellow board members, and staff people in the organizations I met along the way, helping them write grants, develop policy and programs, reach out to funders and allies. In many ways I have myself gained the most from the various community literacy programs I've worked on because I've made close friends, learned about parts of the city I didn't know, and published articles about my experiences. I like to think I teach better because I've challenged my conceptions of socially contextualized literacy within the unfolding dramas of human striving, hope, and loss that I encounter in community programs. This is a selfish reason to do such work, but it keeps me at it.

WORKS CITED

Ackerman, John, and David Coogan, eds. *The Public Work of Rhetoric: Citizen-Scholars and Civic Engagement.* Columbia: U of South Carolina P, 2010. Print.

Adler-Kassner, Linda, Robert Crooks, and Ann Watters. *Writing the Community: Concepts and Models for Service-Learning in Composition.* Washington, DC: AAHE/NCTE, 1997. Print.

Brandt, Deborah. "At Last: Losing Literacy." *Research in the Teaching of English* 39.3 (February 2005): 305–10. Print.

—. *Literacy and Learning: Reflections on Writing, Reading, and Society.* San Francisco, CA: Jossey-Bass, 2009. Print.

Butin, Dan W. *Service Learning in Theory and Practice: The Future of Community Engagement in Higher Education.* New York: Palgrave McMillan, 2010. Print.

Cella, Laurie, and Jessica Restaino, eds. *Unsustainable: Reimaging Community Literacy, Public Writing, Service Learning and the University.* Lanham, MD: Lexington Books, 2012. Print.

Cushman, Ellen. "Sustainable Service Learning Programs." *College Composition and Communication* 64.1 (2002): 40–65. Print.

Deans, Thomas. *Writing Partnerships: Service Learning in Composition.* Urbana, IL: NCTE, 2000. Print.

Deans, Thomas, Barbara Roswell, and Adrian J. Wurr. "Teaching and Writing Across Communities: Developing Partnerships, Publics, and Programs." *Writing and Community Engagement: A Critical Sourcebook.* Ed. Thomas Deans, Barbara Roswell, and Adrian J. Wurr. Boston, MA: Bedford/St. Martin's, 2010. 1–12. Print.

Dewey, John. *Democracy and Education.* 1916. New York: Free Press, 1944. Print.

—. *Experience and Education*. 1938. New York: Touchstone/Simon and Schuster. 1997. Print.

Durst, Russel. *Collision Course: Conflict, Negotiation, and Learning in College Composition*. Urbana, IL: NCTE, 1999. Print.

Eyler, Janet, and Dwight Giles. "The Importance of Program Quality in Service Learning." *Service Learning: Applications from the Research*. Ed. Alan S. Waterman. Mahwah, NJ: Erlbaum, 1997. 57–76. Print.

—. *Where's the Learning in Service-Learning?* San Francisco, CA: Jossey-Bass, 1999. Print.

Flower, Linda. *Community Literacy and the Rhetoric of Public Engagement*. Southern Illinois UP, 2008. Print.

Goldblatt, Eli. *Because We Live Here: Sponsoring Literacy beyond the College Curriculum*. Cresskill, NJ: Hampton Press, 2007. Print.

—. "Introduction to Enlightened Self Interest." *Reflections: Public Rhetoric, Civic Writing and Service Learning* 11.2 (Spring 2012). 109–13. Print.

Grabill, Jeffrey. *Community Literacy Programs and the Politics of Change*. Albany: SUNY P, 2001. Print.

Herzberg, Bruce. "Community Service and Critical Teaching." *College Composition and Communication* 45 (1994): 307–19. Print.

Kells, Michelle Hall. "Writing Across Communities: Diversity, Deliberation, and the Discursive Possibilities of WAC." *Writing and Community Engagement: A Critical Sourcebook*. Ed. Thomas Deans, Barbara Roswell, and Adrian J. Wurr. Boston, MA: Bedford/St. Martin's, 2010. 369–85. Print.

Long, Elenore. *Community Literacy and the Rhetoric of Local Publics*. West Lafayette, IN: Parlor Press, 2008. Print.

Mathieu, Paula. *Tactics of Hope: The Public Turn in English Composition*. Portsmouth, NH: Boynton, 2005. Print.

Peck, Wayne C., Linda Flower, and Lorraine Higgens. "Community Literacy." *College Composition and Communication* 46 (1995): 199–222. Print.

Rhoads, Robert A. *Community Service and Higher Education*. Albany: SUNY P, 1997. Print.

Rose, Shirley K, and Irwin Weiser, eds. *Going Public*. Logan: Utah State UP, 2010. Print.

Rousculp, Tiffany. "When the Community Writes: Re-Envisioning the SLCC DiverseCity Writing Series." *Writing and Community Engagement: A Critical Sourcebook*. Ed. Thomas Deans, Barbara Roswell, and Adrian J. Wurr. Boston, MA: Bedford/St. Martin's, 2010. 386–400. Print.

Stanton, Timothy K., Dwight E. Giles Jr., Nadinne I. Cruz, eds. *Service-Learning: A Movement's Pioneers Reflect on Its Origins, Practice, and Future*. San Francisco, CA: Jossey-Bass, 1999. Print.

Waterman, Alan S., ed. *Service Learning: Applications from the Research*. Mahwah, NJ: Erlbaum, 1997. Print.

Part Five: Vexed Questions

23 What Is Class Size?

Gregory R. Glau

At the risk of oversimplifying what we as writing teachers are trying to accomplish in our classes, I suspect that most college writing teachers today would agree that students learn to write effectively by receiving rhetorical instruction about audience, purpose, process, and so on, and then by drafting, getting useful, thoughtful feedback from a range of readers on their writing, and then by revising (often several times) their initial drafts, working always to more effectively accomplish a specific rhetorical purpose for a specific audience, in a particular context. We also often have student writers read good examples of the kind of writing we ask them to construct, and to spend some time analyzing how those models "work" to accomplish their own rhetorical goals. We also want our students to become good readers of their own writing (putting themselves into their audience's place, so to speak), so they can learn how to effectively revise their own texts. Additionally, we probably want them to learn how to accept and effectively use feedback from others as well as practicing writing in a range of genres. Let's also add that we often want our student writers to learn how to find, evaluate, and integrate the thoughts and ideas of others into their own writing (and of course, to cite those ideas correctly!).

Quite a task, in other words. And at the heart of any pedagogy that we might want to deploy is *class size*, for the number of students in a writing class directly impacts and in a way controls what teachers can best accomplish as they work to help their students become effective writers.

A Brief Scenario

If you've been a WPA for any period of time, this scenario will be familiar to you: Your teachers—most are teaching assistants (TAs), but you also have a few instructors—buy into your overall goals and objectives (in fact, your school has adopted the "WPA Outcomes Statement for First-Year Composition" as its goals, which gives your goals a good deal of *ethos* as well as a national connection). Student evaluation numbers and comments are consistently good, so it appears that your students are generally happy with the instruction they receive. Your writing program, in other words, seems to be going along nicely. Now, however, as you're gearing up for orientation and just a month before the fall semester is to begin, your dean calls you in and tells you that she wants to increase the number of students in your first-year composition (FYC) classes. From twenty-two students to thirty. This fall. She says that the move is necessary as there is a "huge uptick" in the size of your school's incoming first-year class.

"But you can't," you stammer, "that will never work! The quality of the instruction will go down! My teachers will be overloaded! The students won't learn to write as well!"

The dean then asks, "How do you know? What *is* the right size for writing classes?"

How would you answer that question? Do you have any program data or know of any research that demonstrates that a writing class of ten more effectively helps students become better writers than a class size of fifteen? Twenty? Thirty?

"Well," you finally continue, "the ADE and CCCC position statements say that twenty students is the optimal size for a writing class."

Your dean just looks at you. It's clear that such position statements don't carry much weight.

"And I've done workload calculations," you say, "and adding that many extra students will, over the semester, add weeks' worth of work for my teachers."

Again, the dean looks at you. She seems a little more sympathetic, but it's clear that the workload of your teachers also doesn't carry much weight.

"And the Graduate College says that TAs aren't supposed to work more than twenty hours a week. I think that's a federal law, too, for international TAs," you say.

Again, the dean looks across her desk at you. "The Graduate College," she says, "might have to change its thinking."

No help from the Grad College, either.

Then the dean continues, "And aren't there new technologies that make a lot of what you do in your classes kind of obsolete—can't students do some of what you ask them to do, online? I can point to several colleges and universities that use online modules to help students learn better, more effectively, and, I might add, more efficiently. Why should your writing teachers have to lecture when students can learn the same things with videos? I think they call it 'blended' learning— a mix of in-class and online instruction. In high schools they call it 'flipping the class' or some such thing, where your lectures are online and available anytime to students. And don't you think your students should be more responsible for their own education? Do teachers have to be there for every little part of a writing class? Wouldn't it be better if you moved some of your classroom activities online, and then your teachers would have more time to concentrate on higher-order concerns?"

"Well," you interject, "I know there are studies that show how important individual attention is, and how students like getting feedback on their writing from faculty. And it takes a teacher *a lot* of time to give students useful feedback on how to improve their texts."

"What students like is not the issue," your dean says. "And unless I'm wrong, isn't one of the things you really work on in your writing classes is to have students learn how to give effective feedback themselves? If so, then why does the teacher need to give feedback at all? I can only imagine how much time not giving feedback might save . . ."

Oh, my!

What do you as a writing teacher and as a WPA think about class size? Is smaller always better, or is that a concept that we just kind of hold sacrosanct, without any real supporting evidence?

In *Doing what Comes Naturally: Change, Rhetoric, and the Practice of Theory in Literary and Legal Studies*, Stanley Fish foregrounds the notion that we often just accept things as, well, natural, and I think that he might suggest, as I want to do here, that perhaps we need to examine class size in a little more depth and detail. For class size is one of those concepts that WPAs most often think of in just this way:

- small class size: good
- large class size: bad

No ifs, ands, or buts: We know larger classes are bad and we simply resist any effort to increase the number of students in our writing classes . . . even though we don't have supporting data to prove that smaller class sizes improve student writing. As Alice Horning argues, WPAs have an "absence of detailed, empirical evidence" that smaller classes lead to better writing—a lack of research that "suggests that the national organizations concerned with the teaching of writing should work together and fund and execute studies to support the need for smaller writing classes" (11).

or about anything

This is not to say that education in general does not have any data that supports the notion that smaller classes are more effective for student learning. In her germinal work on class size, Horning reports that the best work [examining class size and academic achievement] "has been done in studies of K–12 education" (13). While your dean may not be convinced by K–12 data, Horning suggests that "it seems fair to extrapolate from such studies to the college level" (13). Horning notes that "there are empirical research studies, albeit not focused specifically on writing, and other kinds of evidence to show that smaller class size in writing courses improves student success" (11). Horning outlines a wide range of studies and points out that:

- Richard Light's "findings show that students find small classes to have the greatest impact on their learning" (15).
- Students report that "individual research experience with faculty make a significant positive difference to their undergraduate experience" (15), according to Kuh et al.'s *Student Success in College*, which draws on the National Survey of Student Engagement (see Paine et al., this volume).

Horning also suggests that writing classes, in particular, engage students and aid their learning (and since writing classes generally are small, the inference is that "smaller classes are better"), when she indicates that Nancy Sommers and Laura Saltz "confirm Light's findings of students' reports of their levels of engagement in classes that entail levels of extensive writing" (16).

However, Horning also notes that she was not able to "find a solid empirical study to demonstrate, once and for all, that smaller classes help students become more effective writers in college" (11).

And there's the rub: As Horning reports, the data seems to indicate that small classes may "engage" students more effectively than larger lecture classes, that smaller classes make for a better educational experience, and that (as Richard Light argues) smaller classes make for better learning . . . however, those same things can be said for all classes, not for writing classes specifically. So as Horning notes, "surveys of engagement and other broad data on student satisfaction [. . .] are not enough to win a fight with the dean's office on any campus" (13).

CLASS SIZE: ASKING THE RIGHT QUESTION

In addition to the paucity of data showing that small writing classes are more effective for students, it seems as if WPAs tend to ask one question, while deans and other administrators often ask an entirely different question. There is, after all, a big difference between these two questions:

1. "Are small writing classes more effective than larger classes at helping students become better writers?" (This is the question WPAs generally want to focus on, just as WPAs generally will argue that smaller classes are more effective.)
2. "What is the optimal size for a writing class that is effective at helping students become better writers?" (This is the question administrators tend to focus on. They often will think of it another way, such as "What is the largest number of students we can put in a writing class and still have it be effective?")

In my own work, for example (which Horning reports on), I learned that when Arizona State University dropped the starting size (the class "cap") of its FYC classes from twenty-three to nineteen students:

- Pass rates improved (which meant that the number of students withdrawing, or getting a D or an F, decreased).
- Student continuation from fall to spring improved.
- Teacher evaluations for all ranks of faculty improved (25).

What those data tell us is just that a drop in class size accompanied a higher student pass rate and that students, overall, appreciated the smaller classes and so gave their teachers higher evaluations.

What it does *not* tell us, however, is that student writing improved. While this data validates our intuitive belief that smaller classes are better, it does not answer the question that deans always ask: What is the right class size for a writing class? Is it nineteen? Eighteen? Twenty-three? A hundred? Five?

We just do not know.

I want to ask you as a WPA to consider the issue of class size through a rhetorical lens: What are you trying to *do*, to accomplish in your writing classes? Are you working to help students with all of the concepts and practices outlined in the opening paragraph of this chapter? In that opening section, I suggested that we want our writing students to

[handwritten marginal note: What FYC/ writing class is for/ teaches:]

- Receive rhetorical instruction about audience, purpose, process, and so on;
- Construct a draft;
- Receive useful, thoughtful feedback from a range of readers;
- Revise (often several times) their initial draft;
- Work to more effectively accomplish a specific rhetorical purpose for a specific audience, in a particular context;
- Read good examples of the kind of writing we ask them to construct;
- Spend some time analyzing how those models "work" to accomplish their own rhetorical goals;
- Become good readers of their own writing (putting themselves into their audience's place, so to speak), so they can learn how to effectively revise their own texts;
- Accept and effectively use feedback from others as well as practice writing in a range of genres;
- Learn how to find, evaluate, and integrate the thoughts and ideas of others into their own writing;
- And of course, cite those ideas correctly!

Do your writing classes focus on some of those concepts? All? Other aspects of writing? Your answers to such questions necessarily drive everything else: curriculum, pedagogy, textbook selection, readings, classroom activities, and so forth. Only once you know and understand what you're trying to accomplish can you then think about anything else, including what might be the optimal class size to best accomplish your goals.

[handwritten marginal note: yes]

In a perfect world, then, a WPA would decide on those program goals (perhaps adapting and adopting the "WPA Outcomes Statement") and then arrange a sequence of classroom readings, writing assignments, feedback and revision opportunities, and other activities that would best help the WPA's particular student population achieve those goals and objectives. Part of such a plan would be to determine the optimal class size so that the largest number of students would improve their writing.

But . . . what really happened is that when you took the WPA position, your class sizes were already set, right? Class size is part of the baggage that comes along with any existing writing program: WPAs inherit it. And the conversations you're now having with your administrators never seem to be about setting class size, or reducing class size, but rather about raising class size (you will hear "We have a larger first-year class than we expected" or "A larger class cap is only temporary" or "A lot of students drop, so if teachers start with a higher class size, they'll actually end up with fewer students"). So while you may have a lot of control over the curriculum (How many papers to assign? What length? How many drafts? Who gives feedback and how and when?), and the textbook, and even what classroom activities your teachers might choose to use, WPAs usually have little or no control over the actual number of students in your writing classes.

While "class size" of course refers to the number of students in any particular class, it seems to me that the issue itself needs to be complicated a bit, in two ways: the *practical* and the *administrative/political* aspects of what "class size" is and what it means to a WPA.

PRACTICAL CONSIDERATIONS

Of course, everyone thinks of class size as just that: how many students are allowed to register into any (in our case, a writing) class. (For data on class sizes for first-year composition classes from more than 230 colleges and universities, see http://comppile.org/profresources/classsize.htm.) Our professional organizations also have statements about what the size of writing classes should be (NCTE/CCCC, for instance, has for years recommended twenty students as a maximum class size for first-year composition classes, fifteen students maximum for basic writing classes). I suspect that very few WPAs actually offer classes with those maximum numbers of students.

Of course it isn't the number of students in a class that is a WPA's concern but rather (1) the workload that those students require for the teacher, along with (2) what effective pedagogical strategies might be employed to help students improve their writing.

Workload is something WPAs can affect, at least to some extent, by controlling the number of writing assignments (and working drafts) students are asked to construct, the times in a semester when a teacher provides feedback (and what kinds of feedback, and how comprehensive that feedback needs to be): essentially, the more teacher feedback, the fewer students a teacher can work with, in a writing class. Horning summarizes Richard Haswell's workload calculations, which argue that writing teachers spend much more time than everyone might think they do (17–18). (For an outline and calculations on how workload can be calculated, see http://comppile.org/profresources/compworkload.htm.) I suggest that WPAs do their own calculations on workload: Each time a teacher interacts with a student's text takes "X amount" of time (always depending on the length and complexity of that text)—and determine what your teachers' workload is, per student. At my university, for example, on average each *extra* student adds between ten and fifteen hours of workload time, over a semester, for a writing teacher; just three more students in a class, then, means writing teachers will work an extra full week over the course of the semester.

ADMINISTRATIVE/POLITICAL CONSIDERATIONS

Your college or university's administrators might seem only to be people who disagree with you about class size, or as Horning puts it, "If you are a WPA, sooner or later, you are going to have a fight with your administration over class size" (11). But administrators are, for the most part, *us*: faculty members who now are "Associate Dean of This" or "Assistant Deans of That." They want students to learn and to succeed and to be retained and to graduate. At the same time, small writing classes are easy targets for administrators who face constant budget issues. So there is always a natural tension between the WPA (small class size = better) and administrators (who want to put the most students into any given class).

In many places (and I hope in yours) this natural tension plays out in a professional manner: Everyone works together and does the best they can. But the issue of class size will continue to play a big role in

[Handwritten marginalia: "will have to fight over class size as WPA"]

[Handwritten marginalia: "Deans want to put many students in every class"]

the life of a WPA, so let's end by asking you to consider your future, to consider what a writing class might soon look like . . .

FUTURE SHOCK

[handwritten: The Future of Writing Instrs]

Today, most often college-level writing classes are small, with twenty to twenty-five students. Teachers get to know their students, and most often work with them individually or in small groups on their writing. Do you see that approach continuing?

Look a few years down the road and consider: What will a college writing class in the year 2020 or 2025 look like? Do you think your writing teachers will still teach small classes with perhaps twenty to twenty-five students to work with? How many and what kinds of papers will students be asked to construct? Will some (many? most?) writing classes be scheduled on the traditional quarter or semester basis? Will some (many? most?) writing classes be self-paced, based on a set of measurable learning outcomes, and if so, what might those be? Will some (many? most?) writing classes be completely online, perhaps self-paced, with "instructional modules" students can watch at their convenience, which essentially eliminates rhetorical classroom instruction and discussion? Or will such digitized instruction be supplemental to what the classroom teacher does (as publishers now offer as ancillaries to the textbooks we use)? Will such digital teaching be supplied by you and your teachers, or by textbook publishers?

Will computers at some point be able to "read" and comment effectively on student writing—which would free writing teachers from the time-consuming work of providing feedback? Can you visualize a Siri-like interface in which the computer might tell (and show) a student writer, "Well, James, this is a good start, but another way to arrange your paragraphs might look like this [show example]. And here's another way [show example]. Which do you think might be the most effective? And it looks as if you make an assertion in this paragraph [show example] that you don't provide any evidence to support . . ." *[handwritten margin note: Siri giving feedback]*

Oh, my!

Today, for example, publishers and other software providers are selling what amounts to rhetorical instruction by way of videos and interactive quizzes that allow students to work at their own pace and at their own schedule. A recent headline in the *Chronicle of Higher Education* reported that "E-Textbooks Can Report Back on Students'

Reading Habits." Administrators see this approach as a way to reduce costs: One doesn't need as much teaching time (and as many teachers) when instruction can be digitized and stored on a server. Software providers tout the benefits of *adaptive learning*, where how accurately a student answers one question determines what feedback and other questions he or she works through—thus improving the whole learning process. That approach also can be applied to the software: Once computers "know" what information students aren't "getting," the software will adapt to provide more instruction, perhaps in a slightly different manner, to help students understand it.

Of course, this approach belies the fact that writing classes are *performance* classes, which require students to take the rhetorical principles they've been instructed in and then *use* those principles as they construct an effective piece of writing. Knowing the definition of *audience*, for example, is not the same as demonstrating an understanding of audience through the creation of a text that accomplishes a particular purpose for a specific audience in a specific rhetorical context.

What writing instruction will look like and include and be in the future is, of course, unknown—but every change and innovation will affect a WPA's concept of and how you deal with class size at your own institution.

Works Cited

Association of Departments of English (ADE). "ADE Guidelines for Class Size and Workload for College and University Teachers of English: A Statement of Policy." March 1992. Web. 28 July 2012.

Conference on College Composition and Communication (CCCC). "Statement of Principles and Standards for the Postsecondary Teaching of Writing." 14 February 2005. Web. 28 July 2012.

Council of Writing Program Administrators (CWPA). "WPA Outcomes Statement for First-Year Composition." July 2008. Web. 6 May 2013.

Fish, Stanley. *Doing What Comes Naturally: Change, Rhetoric, and the Practice of Theory in Literary and Legal Studies*. Durham, NC: Duke UP, 1989.

Glau, Gregory R. "Internal Report on Project 85." Spring 2005. Unpublished report.

Horning, Alice. "The Definitive Article on Class Size." *WPA: Writing Program Administration* 31: 1–2 (Fall/Winter 2007): 11–-34. Print.

Parry, Marc. "Now E-Textbooks Can Report Back on Students' Reading Habits." *The Chronicle of Higher Education*. 12 November 2012. Web. 6 May 2013.

contrasting views of writing:
WPA + CR   everyone else
_____   _____
language used now,   skills-based, transferable,
not practiced for later;   preparatory, placement
about "access"   tests, meant to build
                                 skills for later, focus
Key!! We're generally less   on sentences grammar,
powerful   organ etc.

24 What Are *Institutional Politics?*

*Me: I think
my vision of
writing greatly
expands upon.
rather than
contrasts, this
view.
It is a
transferra-
ble skill,
as is
rhetoric!*

Tom Fox and Rita Malenczyk

Until recently, it was more or less a tenet of WPA discourse—both published and unpublished—that nobody should take a WPA job without tenure. We say "until recently" and "more or less" for two reasons: One, if anecdotal evidence is any indication, said tenet exists only to be ignored. As Doug Downs pointed out in a 2007 CWPA conference session about, for, and attended by untenured WPAs, "Everybody told us not to take WPA jobs without tenure, and of course we all went and did it anyway" (Downs and Reid). Reason number two is identified by Colin Charlton et al. in *GenAdmin: Theorizing WPA Identities in the 21st Century*: It is difficult to sustain the don't-do-it-without-tenure rule—such as it is—when both the material conditions of graduate training and the increased professionalization of writing program administration push against it. More and more graduate students are coming to see and experience "writing program administrator" as one of their professional identities, if not their only professional identity, and the notion of waiting to be a WPA until tenure—when job security and greater institutional status kick in—strikes them as condescending and absurd. As Charlton et al. note: "We find ourselves in fundamental disagreement with arguments that claim we should play it safe. [. . .] The subject position that these arguments create doesn't leave us much room to respond because our critique of these arguments can be dismissed as naïve, unaware, or unwilling to accept the gravity of life as a jWPA" (43; see also Roach).

We agree. And yet. We think it's important for all administrators to bear in mind that they are more vulnerable, in many ways, to outside forces than plain old faculty members are. For WPAs, this is because—as Tom said to Rita back in 1996, when they were on a panel at the Conference on College Composition and Communication

313

(CCCC) together—*composition affects everything*. It's required of all students; it's usually a general education course (as Lauren Fitzgerald and Mary R. Boland remind us in this volume). The administrators to whom the WPA reports want to fill seats; the admissions office, and sometimes the office of academic advisement, typically wants placement to be handled as easily—and as conveniently for the students—as possible. And so on. Sometimes this desire for ease and convenience can be a result of legislative oversight, particularly if you work, as we do, in public higher education (for two different CSU systems, in fact, one on the east coast and one on the west). So the state legislature pressures the university president to make changes not necessarily in line with good practice; the president pressures the provost; the provost the dean; and so on down the line to the WPA—who typically holds a view of language, and writing, very different from the views of the people pressuring him or her. As we will elaborate below, most people outside a department of writing and rhetoric perceive writing to be skills-based, and those skills to be transferable to any context (see Wardle, this volume). When a WPA threatens that view, the threat can get turned around on the WPA pretty quickly.

We don't want to subject readers to any of the WPA narratives the authors of *GenAdmin* so appropriately critique: the hero narrative, the victim narrative, or the advice narrative (Charlton et al. 36–46). As you read what we have to say, you'll understand why: It was the English department and the faculty union, not Rita herself, that saved Rita's job; both of us are in fact now tenured professors; and we just don't have any great advice. Nor are we telling anyone not to take an untenured WPA position. Rita, in fact, did just that, because "writing program director" was her (nascent, at the time) professional identity, and as Tom's narrative will reveal, sometimes tenure doesn't matter. However, we think it's important to understand that what people often call "institutional politics"—the power relations present, yet often hidden, in any college or university—can affect the WPA in any number of profound and sometimes less-than-pleasant ways. We present here, then, in dialogue form, some personal cautionary tales about institutional politics for readers to do with what they will, and to serve as a reminder of the sometimes hidden forces at work in various institutional contexts. While these narratives may be a bit dense, that density is part of our point: All WPAs are deeply embedded in their own rich, complex environments with their own complex power relationships, often replicable nowhere else.

A CONVERSATION

RM: My own confrontation with the reality of what we're calling "institutional politics" came in the second year of my tenure-track appointment as a WPA, when a vice president—to whom I reported at the time—decided that he'd had enough of students actually writing essays for placement, and that we needed to use SAT verbal scores or some other standardized means to place them instead (see Royer and Gilles, this volume). It was a difficult time for the university; there was a lot of faculty hostility toward the president, who was—to put it politely—very hands-on in terms of governance, hiring, and promotion and tenure decisions. Faculty searches, for instance, regularly stalled or failed because the president insisted on meeting, however briefly, every job candidate, or sent candidate lists back to search committees declaring that the candidates were unsuitable. While this control, at least in terms of searches, was sometimes legitimate—in certain cases, it was an attempt to get departments to take what was then called Affirmative Action seriously, and did have the effect of greatly diversifying our faculty—still, there was tension between academic departments and the higher administration, all of whom reported directly to the president and pretty much did his bidding.

It was in this environment that I (hired as a tenure-line assistant professor of English, with reassigned time to direct the writing program) had spoken against our changing the placement process at a meeting, citing what I knew about the invalidity of SAT verbal scores as a predictor of writing ability. The speak-against, at which an associate academic vice president who reported directly to the president, was present, got back to somebody; the VP to whom I reported summoned me to his office and, in a threatening exchange, told me that "we can't afford negative people" (see Malenczyk). While my department chair spoke up for me, I still came to be seen as a troublemaker by the administration and received a letter of non-renewal several months later, despite strong positive recommendations from my department and dean. Ultimately, my job was saved thanks to our union president and a dogged grievance officer—who refused to let somebody be fired without stated cause—and the senior faculty in the English department, who just didn't want to let the president push someone in their department around. But I was pretty much on tenterhooks until I got tenure some four years later, when things had died down.

TF: Marilyn M. Cooper's recent article "Rhetorical Agency as Emergent and Enacted" cites Bruno Latour's description of actors as "troublemakers" (424), which seems also like an appropriate description of WPAs who try to actually do something with a writing program. Writing in the university, despite all the words about its value thrown our way, isn't generally *materially* valued, and to develop a program that treats student writing rhetorically creates trouble. This isn't news. Linda Brodkey's experience at the University of Texas a decade and half ago is only the most public case (see Brodkey).

Tenured or not, WPAs are often caught in untenable positions between their own program's beliefs and values surrounding language and learning and the institutional politics of the university. Our program, for many years, was staffed mostly by lecturers, most of whom were dedicated teachers but only some of whom were interested in what they could learn from the field of rhetoric and composition. Most of the lecturers were long-term, having begun their careers many years before I started. The program had a tradition of letting everyone create his or her own syllabus, without much, or any, coordination. The result was that students in one section might have a dramatically different experience than students in another one. There wasn't much that held us together as a program. Those of us with doctorates in rhetoric and composition or related fields struggled with this arrangement and chafed at the occasional really crazy pedagogy that students reported or we observed. Our program was structured like a little department, with the composition coordinator arranging for meetings, scheduling classes, and visiting each lecturer's class during the semester—except that we didn't have a budget, weren't in charge of hiring, and didn't participate in the review of the lecturers because the department's personnel committee took care of that. It was the old "responsibility without power" situation. We were responsible for the health and wisdom of the program, but had no institutional authority to change any substantive changes.

You can't keep good WPAs down, though. My colleague Judith Rodby led a change that mainstreamed our basic writing program (see Rodby and Fox) and actually captured the budget, too. In the process, she broadened the use of adjunct workshops. However, one change triggers another. We didn't need to staff basic writing courses anymore. True, we added some first-year composition (FYC) courses, but overall, the number of courses available to lecturers dropped.

Around the same time, the university-wide committee on general education reviewed our program and put us on "probation" for lack of multi-section uniformity. Though many of our literature colleagues tried to come to our defense against the tyranny of the university, our own response was "D'oh." I was pleased, in fact, to have a mandate to reform our program from somewhere besides the full-time faculty. We knew that the lecturers detested the idea of a common syllabus, so we (lecturers and full-time faculty) wrote some goals for the program (based on the "WPA Outcomes Statement for First-Year Composition"), and then asked people to form syllabus-writing groups around particular ideas (popular culture, public sphere, writing about writing, and so forth). Faculty could choose which syllabus they would like to teach. Seemed like a good idea, except that we underestimated the gulf between lecturers and full-time faculty. Our chair began to act really nervous around us, and stopped making sense (it happens!), and then we were hit with two grievances, apparently filed by a large group of lecturers. One grievance demanded that we not use information garnered from the adjunct workshop leaders in personnel files and the other demanded that we cease inviting lecturers to voluntary meetings that gave the appearance of being involuntary (seriously, those were the words). Since we never actually evaluated the lecturers anyway, and since no information from workshop leaders would be acceptable evidence anyway, the first grievance seemed gratuitous. The second one had to do with the contract language of the lecturers, who are hired solely to teach and not to develop curriculum.

RM: Oh, God. Here it comes. (Ahem—sorry. Continue.)

TF: Actually, we were "forbidden" to call meetings with the lecturers for a time. We had already contacted our union lawyer about nastiness in the English department. Many of the lecturers were protegés of full-time literature or creative writing faculty, so the lit/comp divide had become especially sharp and we felt like we were working under hostile conditions. The lecturers also needed a union lawyer, so she contacted her regional supervisor, who said he would serve as the lecturers' lawyer. Their lawyer was our lawyer's boss. Things didn't look good.

Let's pause this narrative for a moment and parse out the politics. Who's got power and who doesn't? That's always a good question to start with. Let's start with job security. The lecturers in question had three-year contracts and their evaluation, as we learned, depended on the thickness of their file, not its quality. The reasoning was this: If a lecturer had been rehired over the course of twenty or twenty-five years, then he or she had been performing satisfactorily. So, in fact, the lecturers had more job security in this case than the assistant professors in rhetoric and composition. As a tenured faculty, however, some of us had more job security, because in times of economic desperation, lecturers would lose their job before any tenured or tenure-line faculty. Who, then, had more institutional support? None of us had much, but the lecturers had more. Our insistence on professionalization of the composition program, despite being supported by the general education mandate, threatened the system of "delivering" FYC at a less expensive rate than using all full-time faculty would have cost. Our lecturers were well-paid, working at the same rate as assistant professors and topping out at the associate professor rate; but they teach five courses a semester instead of four. The chair continued not making sense, but with more animus towards us; the dean, also formerly friendly, began to sound ominous; the provost, not ever that friendly, seemed annoyed by the whole flap; and the associate vice president for academic affairs was completely hostile.

Cheaper (but not by that much) course delivery only explains a part of this mess—economic in the last instance. Culture, attitudes towards language and writing in particular, fills out the picture. The everyday struggle of WPAs finds its roots in a view of language, and writing in particular, that sharply contrasts with the view of writing held by the university (see also Boland, this volume). This contrast, as David Bleich argues in *The Materiality of Language*, is between two different visions of language. One, held by most of the university, supported by placement and proficiency tests, grading systems, "learning management systems," and general education policies, understands writing as a skill that prepares students to do something else, later. At Chico State, the first-year composition course is in a group of courses called "Foundations," meaning that students take them first in order to do better in the courses that follow. Writing, in this view, isn't for its own purpose at the time, but is to build a set of skills that are transferable to other contexts at a later date (see Wardle, this volume). The skills themselves are typically imagined to be facility with sentence-level conventions, spelling, the use of transitions, organizational schemes, and documentation. Despite our active presence on campus, GWSI—General Writing Skills Instruction—still ruled (Petraglia). WPAs, often with doctorates from programs that emphasize rhetoric, approach writing instruction with the understanding that language is *used*, not practiced for later. Learning to write occurs with students who are really writing, not practicing.

RM: Also, as Lauren Fitzgerald notes in this volume, the development of general education programs and courses has historically been part of the problem. Citing David R. Russell's work, Fitzgerald notes that "the development of the modern university was such that faculty remained unaware (willfully or otherwise) of the existence of particular disciplinary discourses, hoping instead for the discovery of (or return to) a kind of 'academic Esperanto,' a wishful thinking that general education reform as well as the development of FYC often enabled."

TF: So guess what happened. When we were stuck with a variety of approaches to writing instruction, in the double bind of having to create uniformity and being forbidden to meet with the lecturers who teach the class, the associate vice provost for academic affairs found a document from 1983 that named the outcomes for the class, "Executive Memorandum 99-05." First of all, note the resort to a sacred text instead of actually addressing the problem. Then gasp, as we did, when you examine the text and find a course in the modes of discourse. The AVP-AA, and we assumed the provost, were adamant about using this text to enforce multi-section uniformity, and we were required to submit our syllabi to a review team (which we were invited to participate in, but refused). Most of our syllabi came back with the message "needs work."

Though this episode could be chalked up as an episode in the miniseries of "Those Crazy Administrators," there are predictable moves that point to the institutional politics that are consequential for faculty and students. First, by enforcing—with considerable academic policing—a understanding of writing as skills-based, preparatory, formal, and transferable, the university covertly kept in place acontextual standards of language that reduce access for students of color, re-entry students, and that group of students who find tests and abstract standards perplexing. Second, by inhibiting the power, authority, and respect of the tenure-line and tenured professors of rhetoric and composition, the university reduced our ability to administer a writing program that was based on increasing access for students of color, English language learners, and other disenfranchised students. Third, by sacradizing the Executive Memorandum that told us to teach the modes, our own professional knowledge was ignored and students received outdated and unsupportable pedagogy.

RM: I think it's important right here to remember that—as Douglas Hesse suggested several years ago in his CCCC talk, "Who Owns Writing?"—the field of rhetoric and composition, despite its professionalization, does not control the public discourse of writing. Look at the Common Core State Standards. (And the College Board, which—not my vice president—was, I would claim, my real problem in the placement controversy.) As Linda Adler-Kassner has argued in *The Activist WPA: Changing Stories about Writing and Writers* and in this volume, we can and should continue to try to influence that discourse—but I sometimes picture the discourses of writing as two parallel railroad tracks: One is us, with our professional knowledge. The other is the conversation that takes place outside of the university, led by business interests and legislatures, and able to affect our jobs and programs at the drop of a hat. The state of Connecticut, for example, just passed a bill requiring mainstreaming of all so-called "remedial" students. Now, while this bill does not affect the writing program I direct (our students are already mainstreamed), and while I will say that the legislators, in developing the bill, asked good questions—e.g., "Why can't students receive college credit for courses they're required to take in college?" and "How can you judge someone's writing ability based on an essay they're required to write in half an hour?"—it does affect other programs in the state, and there's not a damn thing those WPAs can do about it except do the best they can to work with it. We are, professional knowledge notwithstanding, part of a larger universe, and we represent only one discourse about writing—and arguably not the most powerful. Moreover, for every dean who appreciates what we do—and gives more faculty lines to specialists in rhetoric and composition because he or she maybe understands the importance of writing and praises our work—there is someone less generous out there. Maybe the two tracks will stop running parallel at some point, but that intersection, I believe, is in the future.

SOME CONCLUSIONS

Believe it or not, we're not trying to scare anyone here; but it's important, we think, to understand that at any moment someone can come along and say "Off with your head!" OK, maybe that's putting it too strongly. We support graduate education in WPA work, all facets of it; we feel that WPAs without tenure can do just fine. But institutional politics? None of us can change that stuff. And institutional politics are unpredictable, sometimes capricious, and can have their consequences—though both of us were, in the end and in the larger scheme of things, pretty lucky. In Rita's case, the union stepped in; she worked like a dog for a while, published enough to get tenure, and is now in fact a full professor; administrations changed, and she is one of the more respected members of the faculty, asked to chair important and complicated searches (gee, *thanks!*). Perhaps most importantly, she has job security, which—given the fact that at this writing, she has three kids on the cusp of college—is of no small importance. Tom is also a tenured full professor, and engages in work as an associate director of the National Writing Project (see Banks, this volume), working with schools and teachers nationwide. His department and university currently seems healthy and supportive. So, yeah, things turned out well for us. But we also want to point out that the intellectual and emotional energy—not to mention the time—spent coming up with arguments and strategies, stewing over the uninformed attitudes of others, and figuring out what to do next would have been much better spent actually, you know, administering a writing program. Or writing an article. Or talking with a student. Or having a nice, uncomplicated glass of wine with a partner or spouse. (On that last matter and why it is important, see Hesse, this volume.)

In any case, WPAs, tenured or not, entering any job should be aware not only of generic facts about what administrators do and who controls the budget at most institutions, or of what type of evidence is likely to convince said administrators (see Weiser, this volume; Glau, this volume). They should also know, as far as such things are knowable, the particular quirks of their own schools. Who is likely to be especially discomfited by having their views of writing challenged or complicated? What is at stake for the other administrators (president, provost, dean) involved? To what extent can, or should, you choose your battles? Stephanie Roach says you can't:

> To do my job, I need to be in the room, all the rooms that might affect or could be affected by my program. [. . .] I need to sweat some of the small stuff, go to workshops, volunteer, reply to calls to review the language of a document. [. . .] It is through this work that I meet the people and learn the language and get familiar with the history and find the policies that help me win material and moral victories for the writing program. If I follow the pat advice to junior faculty, I run the risk of not stumbling (by chance or by strategy) into the right people at the right places at the right times that make a difference for the way writing is viewed and taught on campus. [. . .] I simply couldn't do my job as a WPA. (112–13)

Indeed.

WORKS CITED

Adler-Kassner, Linda. *The Activist WPA: Changing Stories about Writing and Writers.* Logan: Utah State UP, 2008. Print.

Bleich, David. *The Materiality of Language.* Bloomington: Indiana UP, 2012. Print.

Brodkey, Linda. *Writing Permitted in Designated Areas Only.* Minneapolis: U of Minnesota P, 1996. Print.

Charlton, Colin, Jonikka Charlton, Tarez Samra Graban, Kathleen J. Ryan, and Amy Ferdinand Stolley. *GenAdmin: Theorizing WPA Identities in the Twenty-First Century.* West Lafayette, IN: Parlor Press, 2011. Print.

Cooper, Marilyn M. "Rhetorical Agency as Emergent and Enacted." *College Composition and Communication* 62.3 (2011): 420–49. Print.

Council of Writing Program Administrators (CWPA). "WPA Outcomes Statement for First-Year Composition." July 2008. Web. 6 May 2013.

Downs, Doug, and E. Shelley Reid. "Untenured WPAs as Change Agents: When to Rule, When to Run, When to Hide." Council of Writing Program Administrators Annual Conference. Tempe Mission Palms and Conference Center, Tempe, AZ. 14 July 2007. Workshop.

Hesse, Douglas. "CCCC Chair's Address: Who Owns Writing?" *College Composition and Communication* 57 (2005): 335–57. Print.

Malenczyk, Rita. "Productive Change in a Turbulent Atmosphere: Pipe Dream or Possibility?" *Administrative Problem-Solving for Writing Programs and Writing Centers*. Ed. Linda Myers-Breslin. Urbana, IL: NCTE, 146–64. Print.

Petraglia, Joseph. "Introduction: General Writing Skills Instruction and Its Discontents." *Reconceiving Writing, Rethinking Writing Instruction*. Ed. Joseph Petraglia. Mahwah, NJ: Erlbaum, 1995. xi–xvii. Print.

Roach, Stephanie. "Why I Won't Keep My Head Down or Follow Other Bad Advice for the Junior Faculty WPA." *The Promise and Perils of Writing Program Administration*. Ed. Theresa Enos and Shane Borrowman. West Lafayette, IN: Parlor Press, 2008. 109–16. Print.

Rodby, Judith, and Tom Fox. "Basic Work and Material Realities: The Ironies, Discrepancies and Disjunctures of Basic Writing and Mainstreaming." *The Journal of Basic Writing* 19.1 (2000): 84–99. Print.

25 What Is Academic Freedom? ✓

Mary R. Boland

Dear new WPA,

I don't mean to alarm you, but the future of writing instruction, rhetoric and composition, and the free world are in your hands. You, as puny and unprepared as you may now feel, are the steward—cultivator, promoter, and protector—of the study of language use at your institution, a subject intrinsically linked to the conscious making (and questioning) of meaning, to self-expression and reflection, and to academic and civic empowerment. The curricula and pedagogies you support; the institutional arrangements you negotiate or oppose; the care, training, and conditions of work you provide the instructors who work with you—all will affect more students, year after year, than almost any other course or set of arrangements at your institution. You are also the steward of academic freedom, a set of professional principles that enables (or should enable) the rich study and teaching of language use at your institution, rather than its oft-demanded but anemic cousin, "writing skills instruction."

If I am right that you do indeed feel puny and unprepared, it is also likely that you do not especially feel the protections of academic freedom yourself. Tenure is either a long way off or your position lies outside the tenure stream. How, then, can it be that you are the bulwark against the erosion of your disciplinary subject and academic freedom? The answer is simple: It just is. WPAs, then, typically face a catch-22 of mind-blowing proportions. They need to assume authority they don't truly have in order to protect the integrity of a subject matter few see as genuine academic work.

If you are still with me, and I hope you are, then you are probably wondering where you will acquire the superhero powers you will need to succeed as a WPA. Unfortunately, neither the FDA nor the

324

EPA has established the safety of Teflon coating for new WPAs (see Fox and Malenczyk, this volume). However, knowledge is power, and what I offer in the remainder of this chapter are some ways of thinking about the complexities of academic freedom as it relates to rhetoric and composition and to the role of the WPA. Become conversant with these concerns—and think early and often about how you can position yourself within them.

WHAT IS ACADEMIC FREEDOM?

Academic freedom is a concept and a set of codified professional principles intended to authorize and ensure the quality of academic work by protecting it from the undue influence of those outside the disciplines. It is not "law" (although it has a presence in the law as a subset of free speech rights and it has some legal force when academic freedom language is incorporated into a faculty employment contract), and it is not universally granted or guaranteed. It is, however, considered the necessary precondition for all genuinely trustworthy academic work and thus it is perceived as legitimating not only the work of individuals within the university, but "the university," itself. Also, while typically thought of as a set of faculty rights, academic freedom comes with (and is defined by) attendant responsibilities: that the professoriate will practice self-regulation and peer review within our disciplines.

Although the idea of academic freedom applies to both teaching and research in (most) US universities and colleges, it has its taproot in the research ideal. This is important to consider because the rationale for academic freedom establishes a chain of connections and relationships (among subject, research, and teaching) that today we often overlook to our disadvantage. Understanding this history may lend insight into why academic freedom is generally more tenuous in community colleges (in fact, under overt attack at some institutions) than four-year universities, why contingent faculty are often seen as a threat to academic freedom and yet are denied it, and why rhetoric and composition is often treated across institutional levels as if academic freedom need not apply.

AN ALL-TOO-BRIEF HISTORY OF ACADEMIC FREEDOM

By the latter part of the nineteenth century, the classical college in the US was giving way to the rise of the research university, modeled on the German university. Dedicated to the pursuit of scientific (empirical, objective, methodological) research, the German university was founded on a belief that knowledge, regardless of immediate utility, was worth pursuing. Academic freedom rights were essential to this mission; they protected objective science from governmental and ecclesiastical interference, thus assuring the legitimacy of this work.

Like their German counterparts, American reformers believed that science for science's sake was valuable. However, the complexity and growing nature of American society would not allow them to imagine their purposes so narrowly. There was also a strong utilitarian sensibility motivating their embrace of the research ideal that provided grounds for the professoriate to adopt an advisory role to the larger society (a role German faculty did not enjoy) (Lucas 144–45; Metzger, *Academic* 139–45; Veysey 63–68). Of course, notions of "useful" education can be understood in different ways within the terms of democratic capitalism, a fact illustrated by an important disciplinary split that emerged at the time: Hard scientists, particularly those in applied fields, tended to dedicate themselves to producing and transmitting technical knowledge in support of industrial democracy; social scientists, meanwhile, were often dedicated to analyzing and eradicating societal ills, including those associated with the industrial economic system (Veysey 63–68, 73–74). This ideological divergence gave rise to two sets of academic freedom concerns that became the subject of much public struggle and which were both eventually reflected in the American Association of University Professors' (AAUP) "1915 Declaration of Principles on Academic Freedom and Tenure"—the codified starting point for the principles of academic freedom that still pertain today.

The fights that played out over academic freedom had two distinct but equally important moments. The first occurred in the natural sciences and freed scientific work from ecclesiastical judgment. As Walter P. Metzger describes, by 1870, Charles Darwin's work on natural selection had earned the respect of the scientific community. The religious community, however, was not so inclined. This led to friction in the colleges and emerging universities as teachers tried to introduce Darwin's theories to students in schools that were still largely denominational (*Academic* 51). Faculty dismissals ensued and, for the first time, the professoriate responded as a community. Challenging the premises of doctrinal moralism—the dual principles that "only the believer can be believed" and "the truth of any idea is determined by its consequences"—they argued that scientific method, not moral character, guaranteed reliable results and that those outside of science were incompetent to judge scientific matters (Metzger, *Academic* 79–83). The result of this was the association of academic freedom with the idea of scientific professionalism, based upon methodological competence and expert review.

The second battle over academic freedom occurred slightly later in the realm of social sciences and raised questions about freedom of speech, the advisory role of professors within the larger society, and the proper role of administrations as sponsors of academic work. Keep in mind that the late nineteenth century was a time of unprecedented philanthropic outpouring from big business to higher education: Think here of names like Johns Hopkins, Carnegie, Stanford, Rockefeller, and Cornell (Metzger, *Academic* 141). Not surprisingly, the same captains of industry who were promoting the idea of "useful research" to advance technology were outraged by the "disloyalty" of social scientists whose work exposed the social costs of industrial capitalism, especially when such professors spoke publicly (Lucas 194–95). Unfortunately, the emergent tradition of academic freedom had no real force in this situation. As J. Peter Byrne observes, it was much easier for these businessmen to recognize their lack of expertise in the natural sciences than to believe they were inexpert in matters of economy and society; they felt quite justified in quelling any such knowledge that they viewed with suspicion, particularly when it might be costly to business (279). While faculty protested the rolling dismissals of social scientists for their public speech, they gained little ground.

This situation began to change with the founding of the AAUP in 1915, which investigated five violations of academic freedom around the country and based on observations in these cases developed an extended rationale for academic freedom in *all* disciplinary areas. Looking first to German principles for guidance, the AAUP founders adopted the basic tenet that the intellectual freedom of professors is essential to the mission of the university. The three functions for which the university exists, they noted, are to "promote inquiry and advance the sum of human knowledge," "to provide general instruction to students," and to "develop expert advisors for various branches of public service" ("1915 Declaration" 295). The committee reasoned that for professors to fulfill any of these roles, they must be allowed to pursue disinterested investigations into their subject matters and impart their results "without fear or favor" to students and the general public ("1915 Declaration" 294). Recognizing that the gravest danger to this mission was posed by boards of trustees who considered themselves private employers and thus "the ultimate repositories of power" ("1915 Declaration" 292), they argued that trustees must recognize themselves as having a fiduciary duty to the larger public. From this public trust the committee derived the necessary relationship between trustees and the professoriate: "[. . .] The latter are the appointees, but not in any proper sense the employees, of the former. For, once appointed, the scholar has professional functions to perform in which the appointing authorities have neither competency nor moral right to intervene" ("1915 Declaration" 295).

As Metzger notes, this established the American university as a "neutral" institution, one in which "the governing board is not for one constituency but for the whole society and not just for the society-in-being but also for the society-in-prospect—a posterity that [had] as yet no voice" ("Profession" 14). This logic of neutrality thus provided a rationale for including both professional and nonprofessional extramural utterances within its protections. The neutral university need not (because it is not responsible for) and should not (because it is not competent to) validate or invalidate any truth claim, regardless of what it is or whom it might offend (Metzger, "1940 Statement" 15).

The committee also gave a good deal of attention to the issue of freedom in teaching. Noting that "[n]o man can be a successful teacher unless he enjoys the respect of his students, and their confidence in his intellectual integrity," the committee argued that student confidence would certainly be impaired if students have reason to believe that "the teacher is not expressing himself fully or frankly, or that college and university teachers are in general a repressed and intimated class who dare not speak with [. . .] candor" ("1915 Declaration" 296). Although this freedom was conditioned on the scholar setting forth knowledge or conclusions "gained by a scholar's method and held in a scholar's spirit," it did not require that the professor avoid controversial material in the classroom or "hide his own opinion under a mountain of equivocal verbiage" ("1915 Declaration" 298).

The document concludes by outlining the procedural means by which academic freedom is to be secured and protected, including a discussion of tenure. In 1922, the statement gained more persuasive force when the American Association of Colleges, a body that represents administrative interests, signed the statement as a pact partner, agreeing that academic freedom benefitted all parties and was a defining feature of a university (Metzger, "1940 Statement" 19–23). Since then, there have been two restatements of the principles (1925 and 1940), as well as the issuance of interpretative comments at various points, and the number of academic and administrative societies endorsing it has grown substantially. That said, the document itself has shrunk and now stands just under two pages before notes (see "1940 Statement"). While its basic provisions remain intact, the extended rationale for academic freedom that appeared in the original document has given way to an administrative-sounding, at-a-glance guide for academic work. Anyone entering academia would be well advised to read both documents in conjunction with one another.

THE IMPLICATIONS OF HISTORY

As a new WPA, then, what should you take away from this discussion? The most important is this: Academic freedom relies on notions of a *subject matter upon which to pursue disciplined scholarly inquiry.* It is this obligation to pursue new knowledge, along with the expertise that one obtains in becoming a member of a discipline, that historically entitles instructors to freedom in their classrooms. It is also the rationale for faculty governance principles that reserve issues of curricula to the faculty, not to administrators, chancellors, presidents, boards of trustees, or legislators. This however, raises some questions for those of us working in composition studies and particularly those administering a first-year composition (FYC) program: What *is* the subject of composition and who decides?

That we are in the place to even need to ask this is, of course, a historical artifact. The virtual disappearance of rhetoric from the curriculum, Harvard's placement test, the invention of the universal writing requirement to correct "student deficits," the rise of literary study, the abandonment by tenured faculty of the labor intensive work of correcting papers, and the long reliance on non-disciplinary and non-secure teachers to deliver FYC courses have all contributed to the appearance that composition is, even at the first-year level, a remedial class—a skills-based precursor to the real work of college. Obviously, for those of us who have pursued advanced degrees in rhetoric and composition, the idea that there is no "there" there in composition is just crazy. Still, our academic freedom is all too often abbreviated by institutional arrangements that insist composition is mostly about providing students with skills that they should have acquired in high school. In a practical sense, then, the problem of academic freedom for people in composition is a matter of context: Where and how is writing located within the curriculum and within the institution? These things, as often as not, will profoundly influence the definition and status of our subject and your authority as a WPA.

To take only one example, FYC is usually a general education requirement. As such, it is typically defined by an interdisciplinary committee, which will determine the curricular purposes the course will serve and how it will be described (see also Fitzgerald, this volume). Not surprisingly, these descriptions are often out of step with contemporary field-based understandings of the subject of composition and its pedagogy and set the stage for tensions between institutional and disciplinary expectations of writing and writing instruction. For example, at my school, FYC is described simply as a "basic skill" over which students must have a "firm grasp" (CSUSB, *Bulletin* 68). Other areas of the general education program, however, are considered "breadth areas" and located within the structures of larger disciplinary areas: humanities, social and behavioral sciences, and natural sciences (*Bulletin* 68). My point is that the language of the general education requirement typically authorizes the work of FYC and simultaneously delegitimizes it. This will have implications for you, which you will need to negotiate, but to which you should try not to capitulate.

How well you can do this, however, will depend in part on your institutional zip code. Institutionally, writing programs are either located within a disciplinary department, most commonly an English department, or as an independent unit within a college or directly under a provost or dean of undergraduate studies. Occasionally, you will run across that rare and wild critter—an actual academic department of rhetoric or writing (or some titular variation thereof)—where writing and rhetoric are understood to be legitimate disciplines and majors and minors flourish along with first-year writers. No one situation is inherently better than another, however, and the quality of your experience as a WPA will be determined by the local context and culture for writing. Each location offers its own potentialities and vulnerabilities, depending on how well it supports and promotes the rich subject of composition and how well it supports the instructors in the writing program.

So Who's the Boss?

This brings us to one of the oddities of being a WPA. While you may, if in a tenure-track position, earn tenure, many of those who work with you in your program are unlikely to have this opportunity. You are, in other words, what James Sledd has vividly described as a "boss compositionist," so it is all the more important to respect the intended relationship between academic freedom and tenure. As history makes clear, tenure is *not* the precondition of academic freedom; it is its insurance policy. Indeed, without the necessity of academic freedom, there is no rationale for tenure in the first place. Thus, academic freedom does not and should not hinge on rank; contingent faculty should be entitled to academic freedom just as are tenure-track faculty.

While these may seem like straightforward principles to abide by, for most WPAs there are complications. For one thing, not all contingent faculty are the same; you will likely be working with some combination of full- and part-time non-tenure-track faculty, as well as graduate student teaching assistants, and while some of these people will have disciplinary training in rhetoric and composition, many will not (see Schell, this volume). In this position, you will need to be concerned for the wellbeing of your faculty and the conditions of work they experience, for the integrity of your subject matter, and for the experiences with writing and language study that students have (or do not have) in their classrooms. Moreover, as an administrator you are likely to be legally responsible for some of these things (but see Kahn, this volume).

How do you reconcile your role as guarantor of program coherence and pedagogical quality with your role as an advocate of faculty freedom when your faculty may not be even be particularly conversant with the knowledge of the field in which they are teaching? This conundrum has not been lost on the AAUP, which has commented on just this problem and has attributed to it the serious erosion of higher education and learning conditions for students ("Contingent"). Given this, it is no wonder that many WPAs end up producing required program syllabi and limiting text choices for their faculty. Yet lock-step curricula and prefabricated course materials do little to improve things: They won't do if your goal truly is to promote a rich subject matter experience for students and teachers alike. Language use is not a subject that one so much delivers as enacts, so teachers need both subject matter knowledge and the flexibility to respond as that knowledge is taken up and enacted by the community as a whole.

This would seem to lead us back around in a circle: The instructor needs freedom to utilize knowledge he or she still may not have. Here is where understanding the history and tenets of academic freedom may again be a friend. As the AAUP's 2003 statement on contingent labor reminds us: "It is the professional involvement of faculty in academic disciplines that ensures the quality, currency, and depth of the content being offered to students" ("Contingent"). In other words, the right to freedom in teaching presumes and derives from faculty members' engagement in the professional scholarship of their fields. Teachers have a responsibility to disciplinary knowledge that predicates and authorizes their teaching. Institutionalized hiring practices that promote the hiring of unprepared, subject-irresponsible faculty should stop, and to the extent that you, as a new WPA, have control over hiring, you should be very careful about whom you bring on.

This raises a related question: To what degree do you control the terms of contingent faculty contracts in your role as a WPA? Is it possible for you to contractually require participation in ongoing faculty development initiatives or professionalizing activities and in regular program meetings? As AAUP notes, academic work, when healthy, involves: " [. . .] a full range of faculty responsibilities, including teaching activities both in and outside the classroom, scholarly pursuits such as contributions to an academic discipline or maintenance of professional currency, and service that ensures that academic decisions are well informed by the experience and expertise of all faculty. [. . .] ("Contingent"). Clearly, to the extent that you can expect, encourage, and contract participation in professional activities and service, the culture of your program—as well as its curricular substance—is likely to improve.

The difficulty, of course, is that from a contingent faculty viewpoint, expectations like these may be unwelcome for a variety of reasons, not the least being the demands of freeway flying and untenable course loads. Situations like this are sticky, and while the literature on WPA work often points to the ways in which progressive, pro-labor WPAs often discover that the demands of management create unexpected conflicts, seeing some of these tensions through the lens of academic freedom suggests the problem is not labor vs. management; it is more akin to labor vs. disciplinary responsibility. Earlier I used the term "subject-irresponsible faculty," and while I suspect it raised some hackles, I did so to stress this idea: Academics working within a discipline have responsibilities to the enrichment of that subject. This is something that many employment contracts, even thoughtful ones, overlook. For instance, lecturers at my school have one of the best union-negotiated contingent labor contracts in the nation. While this has dramatically increased the stability of the workforce in my department, the contract generally obliges lecturers only to teach their classes and hold their office hours. My department cannot require additional professional development or service; if we wish to offer in-service workshops to improve our programs or to invite contingent faculty to contribute to program development, such participation must be considered voluntary—a principle underscored by my institution's faculty review policies, which make clear that unless hired under special contractual provisions, contingent faculty are only to be reviewed in the area of teaching (CSUSB, "Procedures" 24).

What's a WPA to do?

Let me stress, again, that the rationale for academic freedom teaches that quality instruction is predicated on and presumes professional development and subject matter knowledge. Within the frame of academic freedom, then, professional development is *part* of teaching. While a contingent contract may not allow you to mandate attendance at faculty development sessions, it also may not prevent you from pointing out the ways in which aspects of teaching are being neglected. In this regard, program reviews and periodic faculty reviews, along with classroom observation reports are your outreach tools: They are a means of letting faculty know when their teaching reflects too little contact with your program philosophy and too little contact with the scholarship in the field; they are also a means of holding people accountable for making adjustments. A WPA can thus make recommendations that include becoming acquainted with certain scholarly works in the field, attending faculty development workshops, and working with a more experienced mentor to revise classroom materials. Furthermore, while the WPA may not be able to compel the particular means by which faculty members improve their subject matter knowledge and hence, their teaching performance, the WPA can subsequently comment on whether such issues were addressed and the means of doing so successful.

Of course, contingent faculty may experience such reviews as sticks, not carrots, since by and large the only thing a decent evaluation earns is the opportunity to keep a low-paying job in an institutional situation where, but for the review process, contingent faculty are likely to feel invisible and detached. The only way I know to improve this situation is to improve the context in which evaluation transpires. I am suggesting, in other words, that you champion academic values and procedures in your program, so your faculty will have the opportunity to rise as professionals.

CULTIVATING FREEDOM AND RESPONSIBILITY

There is a difference between being in control and being in charge. If you try to control your program, you will contribute to the de-professionalization of your faculty. Just as without responsibility, there is no freedom, without freedom there is no responsibility. Despite your managerial obligations, then, promoting academic traditions, including those of faculty governance, are likely your best means to cultivate the meaningful teaching of writing in your program. I strongly recommend you read the AAUP's 2003 statement on "Contingent Appointments and the Academic Profession" and bring your program in line with its recommendations as far as is institutionally and contractually possible. Consider, too, how you can use this same statement as a blueprint for animating and establishing a professional academic culture in your department. There are two things that your diverse faculty likely shares in common: (1) concern for students and their learning, and (2) some investment in or desire for an academic life. Your task is to animate these interests within a framework that will mentor faculty to become knowledgeable teachers of writing and participants in professional life. Moreover, if familiarity with the history, rationale, tenets, and problems of academic freedom can empower you, it can empower contingent faculty, as well, reminding them both of their rights and responsibilities as academics. There already exists an extensive literature to help you in your task. I trust, good academic that you are, you will find it.

WORKS CITED

American Association of University Professors (AAUP). "1915 Declaration of Principles on Academic Freedom and Academic Tenure." 1915. 291–311. Web. 11 November 2012.

—. "1940 Statement of Principles on Academic Freedom and Tenure with 1970 Interpretive Comments." 1940, 1970. Web. 11 November 2012.

—. "Contingent Appointments and the Academic Profession." 2003. Web. 11 November 2012.

Byrne, J. Peter. "Academic Freedom: A 'Special Concern of the First Amendment'." *Yale Law Journal* 99.2 (1989): 251–340. LexisNexis. Web. 11 November 2012.

California State University, San Bernardino (CSUSB). *Bulletin of Courses 2012–2014.* 40.1 (2012). Web. 11 November 2012.

—. "Procedures and Criteria for Performance Review and Periodic Evaluation. Vol I: Instructional Faculty." *Faculty Administrative Manual, Section 300.* n.d. Web. 11 November 2012.

Lucas, Christopher J. *American Higher Education: A History.* New York: St. Martin's, 1994. Print.

Metzger, Walter P. *Academic Freedom in the Age of the University.* New York: Columbia UP, 1964. Partial Rpt. in *The Development of Academic Freedom in the United States.* Ed. Richard Hofstadter and Walter P. Metzger. New York: Columbia UP, 1955. Print.

—. "Profession and Constitution: Two Definitions of Academic Freedom in America." *Texas Law Review* 66 (1988): 1265–322. LexisNexis. Web. 11 November 2012.

—. "The 1940 Statement of Principles on Academic Freedom and Tenure." *Freedom and Tenure in the Academy: The Fiftieth Anniversary of the 1940 Statement of Principles.* Ed. William W. Van Alstyne. Spec. Issue of *Law and Contemporary Problems* 53.3 (1990): 3–77. Print.

Sledd, James. "Why the Wyoming Resolution Had to Be Emasculated: A History and a Quixoticism." *JAC: Journal of Advanced Composition* 11.2 (1991): 269–81. Web. 11 November 2012.

Veysey, Lawrence R. *The Emergence of the American University.* Chicago, IL: U of Chicago P, 1970. Print.

26 What Are Educational ✓  Standards?

Peggy O'Neill

Standards, in general, articulate shared goals. They represent a group's expectations for a particular component of education. We often think about standards in terms of student learning outcomes: What knowledge and experiences should students be achieving in this program? However, standards can also apply to other aspects of education such as pedagogy, working conditions, evaluation/assessment, and teacher preparation. The groups that articulate standards may be associated with a discipline, such as engineering, education, or English; a non-profit or special interest group, such as Achieve or Lumina; regional accrediting agencies, such as the Southern Association of Colleges and Schools (SACS); or policy makers, such as state departments of education or school boards. Individual institutions and programs also establish standards, usually connected to their mission. Sometimes standards are followed voluntarily; at other times, they are required or imposed. The link between learning outcomes and assessment has been well established, as illustrated by the National Institute for Learning Outcomes Assessment (NILOA), which "assists institutions and others in discovering and adopting promising practices in the assessment of college student learning outcomes."

LEARNING STANDARDS

Ideally, learning standards are big-picture expressions for students, programs, or institutions related to curriculum and performance, informed by the research and scholarship of the discipline. Educators often divide standards connected to student learning into two types:

content standards and performance standards. Content standards relate to the curriculum—the subject matter knowledge and skills that students are expected to learn and that teachers are expected to teach. These types of standards might be referred to by a range of different terms, such as learning outcomes, aims, goals, or competencies. The "WPA Outcomes Statement for First-Year Composition" is a good example of content standards familiar to writing program administrators (WPAs). These were developed by members of the Council of Writing Program Administrators (CWPA), vetted through the larger group, and finally endorsed by CWPA. They are optional, meaning writing programs aren't required to use them for certification, funding, or accreditation; but, because they are endorsed by the professional association that represents college writing programs, they are considered to represent the discipline's expectations for first-year composition. Although optional, individual instructors or administrators may be required to use them because the program has already adopted them. However, in general programs are free to adopt or adapt them as they find appropriate.

Performance standards, on the other hand, refer to how well students can do something, and usually relate to assessment and levels of achievement. These standards might be simply determining what is considered the minimal competency in an area, or they might discriminate among multiple levels of achievement. While these levels are described discursively, performance standards are most clearly articulated by samples of student work because descriptions of a level of performance—e.g., "excellent," "proficient," "not meeting expectations"—are abstract terms that are interpreted and applied differently in different contexts. For writing, performance standards are typically accompanied by student samples (which are frequently referred to as "exemplars," "anchor papers," or "benchmarks") because the same descriptive language can be used in many different contexts and mean very different things depending on the context. The College Board, for instance, provides samples of scored SAT Writing Test essays on its website so that test-takers (and other stakeholders such as teachers, parents, college personnel, and policy makers) can understand what each score point means in terms of writing expectations, given the prompt and the time constraints, among other situation-specific factors (College Board). Because many types of college-level writing assessments—such as placement, proficiency, or exit exams—are locally designed, individual programs determine the assessment criteria and exemplars when reading the student writing completed for those assessments.

The focus on local assessment and exemplars, and even local performance standards, is considered best practice in composition studies because writing is a context-specific activity. Even when a program uses national exams for a local assessment, such as ACCUPLACER for placement into its first-year composition curriculum, it often uses local examples (as well as local cut scores) to show how those standards play out in its particular context. For instance, a program that uses the "WPA Outcomes Statement" usually operationalizes those outcomes in terms of their particular program and students. They may develop a rubric, criteria, or a set of performance standards based on the "WPA Outcomes" in light of the particular curriculum and students.

There are multiple ways that content standards can inform performance standards, as demonstrated by examples in the CWPA "Assessment Gallery and Resources—Assessment Models and Communication Strategies." Frederick Community College, one of the programs featured in the gallery, clearly articulates student learning goals and then the performance standards used to evaluate the achievement of those goals. Grand Valley State University, another example, uses a required portfolio program to determine exit proficiency for its required first-year composition course and publishes a guide that includes information on the curriculum, grading expectations, the portfolio's content and evaluation, and multiple examples of "good" student writing to illustrate their expectations. About the student writing examples, the editor notes: "Our goal is to select writers who understand their papers' purposes, know what it is they are trying to accomplish in their work, and we look for authors who keep their audience in mind as they write. No matter what your assignment may be, the keys to good writing remain consistent—a solid sense of purpose, focus, and audience (Mulally 36). The editor then describes each of the six sample portfolios and explains why they were chosen to "showcase" the expectations. Grand Valley only shares high quality student samples instead of the gamut of work that may qualify. In this way, the samples aren't illustrating the range of the expectations but rather only the highest levels. This kind of selection, especially when accompanied with the lengthy explanations of why particular samples were chosen for distribution, illustrates both the content and the per-

formance standards. The editor explains, "We invite WRT 150 instructors and students to read and discuss these six portfolios as a way
to generalize about what characterizes good writing in the first-year
writing program at Grand Valley State University" (Mulally 41). The
exemplars are not defining the minimal competency needed for pass-
ing the portfolio at Grand Valley, but rather setting aspirational goals
and clarifying the definition of good writing for the students writing   *great*
in this particular course.

While most WPAs tend to focus on local standards, as in the previous examples, performance standards can also be more general and
come from a professional group or other group of educational experts.
For example, the Association of American Colleges & Universities
(AAC&U), as part of the Valid Assessment of Learning in Undergraduate Education (VALUE) Project, developed a written communication rubric, which was one of fifteen rubrics they created related to
the "Liberal Education and America's Promise" (LEAP) initiative. As   ⟵
Terrel L. Rhodes, AAC&U's Vice President for Quality, Curriculum,
and Assessment who worked on the LEAP initiative, explains, VALUE
rubrics are "broad, generic, institutional-level rubrics" that can be
adapted to individual contexts. The "performance levels reflected in
the VALUE rubrics—capstone, milestones, and benchmark—do not
represent year in school" but rather attempt to express "the capstone
level" and to reflect "the demonstration of achievement for the specific
criterion for a student who graduates with a baccalaureate degree." The
AAC&U also includes examples of student work, which—as Rhodes
notes—are not exemplars but "show how a piece of work demonstrated
for a set of reviewers the level of performance for the specific criterion."
The VALUE rubrics, according to Rhodes, are grounded in the learning outcomes developed as part of LEAP.

Because standards, or learning outcomes, are general statements,
they do not mandate a detailed curriculum—the day-to-day teaching
and learning that happens in classrooms. Instead, they usually identify
a body of knowledge and set of skills and may privilege certain pedagogies, approaches or materials. For example, a program or instructor
can approach the standards in a multitude of ways, assigning various
types of activities and using a variety of texts to facilitate students'
achievement of the "WPA Outcomes."

Ideally, content and performance standards are aligned with each other, as in the VALUE and the Frederick and Grand Valley examples, so that the performance accurately represents the outcomes or learning. Both sets of standards, however, can be broad and general, not tied to a specific curriculum (as in VALUE), or more specific and tied directly to a program, institution, or discipline (as with the Frederick and Grand Valley examples). Because writing is a key component of many different disciplines and is emphasized in many types of programs from first-year composition through writing across the curriculum (WAC), writing in the disciplines (WID), and general education, WPAs often find they need to be aware of content and performance standards at many different levels. For example, an institution's general education outcomes express the learning aims for all undergraduates at a particular institution regardless of major, while a program within that institution articulates specific learning expectations, and maybe even performance standards, for students who complete that program. WAC/WID programs—either formal, designated programs or more diffused models that are not centrally administered—highlight the interdisciplinary interests in writing standards. Figure 1 represents the way a college course may be nested in the educational system, with each circle contributing a different set of standards that can vary according to different factors, including the course level, discipline, and accrediting agencies. Typically, standards associated with a course are most specific and get more general as the circles move out from the center. If a program is part of a public institution, it may also need to meet an additional set of standards specified by state policymakers. These would then influence or specify institutional standards.

Why Do WPAs Need to Know about Learning Standards?

As Figure 1 shows, WPAs need to be aware of a host of different types of learning standards because written communication is an essential component of education across institutions and disciplines. A WPA, for example, could be involved in helping to prepare students to meet disciplinary writing standards in diverse areas from business to engineering to education as well as to meet general education writing standards. For example, the WPA's charge could be related to the WAC program, as John Bean explains (see Seattle University in the CWPA

"Assessment Gallery" for a discussion and examples of Bean's work with assessment of writing and WAC).

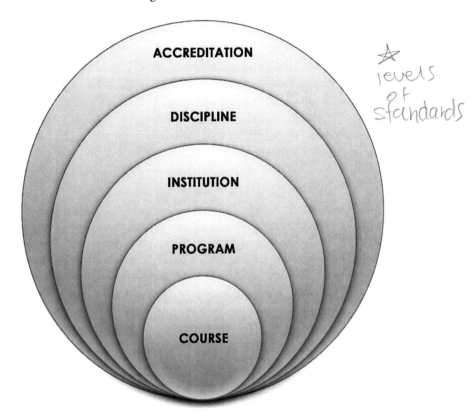

Figure 1.

Or a WPA might be responsible for the writing-related content and performance standards associated with a particular discipline and accreditation for that program. Some WPAs work within disciplines like engineering and business, for example, to teach and assess written communication directly connected to program accreditation, as outlined by accrediting agencies such as ABET (Accreditation Board for Engineering and Technology) or AACSB (Association to Advance Collegiate Schools of Business). For ABET accreditation, programs must demonstrate that they are following the content standards and that the students are meeting them. Linda Adler-Kassner and Peggy O'Neill's *Reframing Writing Assessment to Improve Student Learning* includes several mini-case studies of how WPAs use accreditation-related assessments to enhance student learning. In one example, Professor Jones, a rhetoric and composition professor in a college of engineering, explains her role in preparing the ABET accreditation information that was directly linked to both the content of the curriculum and the assessment of the students (Adler-Kassner and O'Neill 130–36). Other disciplinary accreditors often include written communication as an expected student learning outcome, or they highlight the need for students to develop competency in written communication (e.g., AACSB and the American Speech-Language-Hearing Association [ASHA]). Accrediting agencies of various types have been proponents of linking outcomes and assessment related to writing for over a decade.

WPAs may also be charged with preparing students for certifying exams or state-mandated, minimal competency assessments. This involvement might include teaching specific courses for a program, providing remediation or support for individual students preparing for the exams, or consulting with disciplinary faculty to offer professional development linked to the exams. Some of these exams may relate specifically to writing courses that all students attending an institution of higher education must take, or they may be related to a placement or graduation requirement. Exams such as these usually reflect performance standards that may or may not be directly related to content standards adopted by a particular program or institution. For example, the Collegiate Learning Assessment (CLA) includes externally designed writing-specific performance criteria on its rubric. WPAs at institutions using the CLA should be aware of these criteria (among other aspects of the exam). Some discipline-specific programs require national exams such as the Praxis, which, again, may or may not align with local standards.

Learning standards are useful instruments for WPAs not only in determining the curricular component of their programs but also in assessing those programs. Writing programs are not—or at least should not be—isolated from the larger community. As Figure 1 illustrates, a course and program operate inside of larger communities or institutions. The particular writing course, such as first-year composition, should be informed by the expectations of its writing program, the institution as a whole, the discipline, and even relevant accrediting agencies. WPAs who are familiar with the different types of learning standards relevant for their programs can be strategic advocates for their program's curriculum. Using nationally recognized standards, such as those published by CWPA, can emphasize the need for curricular changes or resources, such as technology support for student learning or professional development for faculty in the program. Critical to developing assessments of writing programs, learning standards articulate the criteria for success as programs determine to what degree students are learning what the outcomes say they should be learning.

OTHER TYPES OF STANDARDS USEFUL FOR WPAS

While learning standards, which mainly address curriculum, are the most common standards WPAs encounter, there are many other types of standards that are relevant to the administration of a writing program. These standards often deal with workplace issues (such as staffing, class size, and instructor support) and other professional issues (such as assessment, teacher preparation, scholarship, tenure, and promotion). As with learning standards, these can be found at multiple levels from local programs to institutions to disciplines to accrediting agencies. They also may be referred to by different names such as "position statements," "principles," or "frameworks." While not all of these statements are standards *per se*, they do articulate the expectations and principles that should guide practice in those areas. Accreditors, for instance, have explicit standards that cover the scope of higher education. In their publication *Characteristics of Excellence in Higher Education*, the Middle States Commission on Higher Education articulates fourteen standards that institutions seeking accreditation must meet. These standards cover all areas of higher education and are divided into two groups: (1) Institutional Context, which includes standards focused on aspects such as mission, administration, and allocation of resources; and (2) Education Effectiveness, which includes those addressing admission and retention, student support services, faculty, educational offerings, general education, and assessment of student learning. While these are very general standards that are applied at the institutional level, WPAs can tap into these in planning a program review, or for creating program standards for faculty qualifications or curricular review. By using the accreditation agency's standards, a WPA will be more prepared for the accreditation reviews that come up periodically and will also be able to demonstrate to the upper administration the way the writing program contributes to meeting the accreditor's standards.

Professional organizations also offer WPAs ways of both evaluating a program and advocating for it. For example, the Conference on College Composition and Communication (CCCC) position statement "Statement of Principles and Standards for the Postsecondary Teaching of Writing" articulates the qualifications, support, and working conditions for writing faculty at all ranks. Other CCCC statements identify criteria for evaluating faculty, while some link more directly to student learning, such as the position statement on "Writing Assessment" that articulates specific guiding principles and their application to assessment of student learning in the classroom or beyond. Some statements are specific to faculty's responsibilities, such as the "CCCC Guidelines for the Ethical Conduct of Research in Composition Studies" or the Association of Teachers of Technical Writers' (ATTW) "Code of Ethics." Professional organizations have many such statements (usually available on their websites) that refer specifically to writing programs. Like learning standards, these statements can be helpful for WPAs in determining how their writing program is situated in the broader context of higher education or the discipline. These types of standards, as with learning standards, also change over time, so WPAs should be sure to check them periodically for updates or additions.

A FINAL NOTE OF CAUTION

Chris W. Gallagher argues that "[f]ocusing on outcomes tends to limit and compromise the educational experiences of teachers and students" (43). While Gallagher realizes that outcomes, and outcomes assessment, are a reality of higher education today, he urges us to "consider carefully (and perhaps reconsider) how we frame and use educational aims in our profession, departments, programs and classrooms" (43). WPAs, as Gallagher contends, need to be critical users of the standards, whether those formulated in a local context or those adopted from other organizations. Standards, especially learning outcomes, are not in and of themselves good or bad. Rather, it is the way they are interpreted and applied that determines their value. The impact of standards on teaching and learning is what is most important. WPAs need to be mindful of how standards are used by them and by other constituencies, and the effects of the use in each particular case. This evaluation must consider both the intended and unintended results—or consequences—of using particular standards. After all, as WPAs, our overarching goal is to promote student learning, whether we are thinking about learning goals, teachers' qualifications, or working conditions.

WORKS CITED

Adler-Kassner, Linda, and Peggy O'Neill. *Reframing Writing Assessment to Improve Teaching and Learning*. Logan: Utah State UP, 2010. Print.

American Association of Colleges & Universities (AAC&U). "Liberal Education and America's Promise." 2012. Web. 23 November 2012.

Association of Teachers of Technical Writers (ATTW). "Code of Ethics." n.d. Web. 23 November 2012.

College Board. "The Essay: SAT Writing Practice Questions." SAT Homepage. 2013. Web. 2 January 2013.

Collegiate Learning Assessment (CLA). "About the CLA: Sample CLA Measures." Council for Aid to Education. n.d. Web. 30 November 2012.

Conference on College Composition and Communication (CCCC). "CCCC Guidelines for the Ethical Conduct of Research in Composition Studies." November 2003. Web. 6 May 2013.

—. "Statement of Principles and Standards for the Postsecondary Teaching of Writing." October 1989. Web. 6 May 2013.

—. "Writing Assessment: A Position Statement." March 2009. Web. 6 May 2013.

Council of Writing Program Administrators (CWPA). "Assessment Gallery and Resources—Assessment Models and Communication Strategies." n.d. Web. 23 November 2012.

—. "WPA Outcomes Statement for First-Year Composition." 2008. Web. 23 November 2012.

Gallagher, Chris W. "The Trouble with Outcomes: Pragmatic Inquiry and Educational Aims." *College English* 75 (2012): 42–60. Print.

Middle States Commission on Higher Education. *Characteristics of Excellence in Higher Education*. 2006. Web. 6 May 2013.

Mulally, Duavan, ed. *WRT 150: A Guide to First-Year Writing at Grand Valley State University*. 10th ed. Allendale, MI: Grand Valley State University, 2011. Web. 4 September 2012.

National Institute for Learning Outcomes Assessment (NILOA). "Our Mission & Vision." Lumina Foundation for Education, The Teagle Foundation, and the College of Education at the University of Illinois. 2012. Web. 6 May 2013.

Rhodes, Terrel L., ed. "Introduction." *Assessing Outcomes and Improving Achievement: Tips and Tools for Using Rubrics*. Washington, DC: AAC&U, 2010. Web. 25 August 2012.

27 What Is Policy?

Chris W. Gallagher

> *You may ask yourself*
> *Well…how did I get here?*
>
> —Talking Heads, "Once in a Lifetime"

It's a well-worn refrain among WPAs: *I never imagined I'd find myself here.* Here: in a conference room, explaining directed self-placement to advisors. Or in the offices of the academic judicial review board, describing the writing program's grading policies. Or on the floor of the faculty senate testifying about the use of test scores to waive first-year composition. Or in the provost's office, explaining why the institution should invest in electronic portfolios. Or in the trustees' boardroom, providing an update on K–16 efforts. Or even in court, testifying about academic freedom; in state senators' offices, giving a briefing about writing assessment; in the state board of education's hearing room, testifying about university articulation agreements; in a U.S. Department of Education office, participating in a task force on writing in the twenty-first century.

But most WPAs do find themselves in at least some of these places, advocating for and against programmatic, institutional, and governmental policies of all sorts. Unfortunately, though, as Edward M. White suggests, most of us are ill-prepared—by disposition and training—for this kind of "extracurricular activity" (183; see also Gallagher). While the WPA community has generated a vast array of resources to help prepare WPAs for administrative work—a national organization, a journal, an annual conference, a dedicated book series, and a robust literature, including work on graduate student and junior faculty administration (see Edgington and Gallaher's WPA-CompPile research bibliography on this topic)—it has been my experience, and the

346

experience of most WPAs I know, that the multi-sited complexity of WPA work is daunting and surprising.

One of the most important things for WPAs to understand is that no program is an island. Policies we create and implement are embedded in and interact with other policies within and beyond our institutions. We must understand what policy is and how it works in order to engage effectively in policy making and with other policy makers.

WHAT POLICY IS AND HOW IT WORKS

And you may ask yourself
Where does that highway go to?
> —Talking Heads, "Once in a Lifetime"

Recently, in the program I help administer, influenced by language theorists in rhetoric and composition as well as language studies, we moved away from our policy of teaching and accepting from students only "standard" edited American English and toward a policy of helping student writers achieve their goals in the dialects and forms that best suit the rhetorical situations they wish to enter (see, for instance, Horner, Lu, and Matsuda; Horner, Lu, Royster, and Trimbur). According to our revised Philosophy and Aims statement, which is posted on our website,

> Our overarching goal in our courses and in the Writing Center is to help students write effectively. We acknowledge that "effective writing" must be defined in the context of writers' goals, audiences' expectations, and situational factors such as available technologies. There is no all-purpose prose that serves writers equally well in all situations. Different academic, professional, and public discourse communities practice different conventions, and these—like the English language itself—evolve over time. In some contexts, in fact, writers are expected to move across dialects within English or even across languages. Thus, instead of teaching students a single "standard" dialect or set of conventions, we help them develop knowledge of and facility with the conventions that characterize (but never fully define or stabilize) the academic, professional, and public discourses and communities they wish to enter. (Northeastern)

What is this policy and how does it work?

Conventionally, a policy is understood as an official statement, adopted by organizational leadership, that guides organizational practice. To this way of thinking, a policy is (or is reified in) a governing document. (In Middle English *policie* referred to governmental or civil administration.) It issues from the administration, directing the actions and behaviors of actors within an organization, thereby shaping the space(s) of the organization. So, for instance, a teacher who teaches students "a single 'standard' dialect or set of conventions" would be in violation of the above policy and presumably told, "We don't do that here."

More recent policy theory, however, encourages us to think of policies not in terms of documents that determine spaces in a top-down fashion but rather as practices that give shape to spaces in dynamic interplay among a range of actors.[1] Even people who are thought to be "merely implementing" policies—teachers and students in classrooms, say—are in fact interpreting and negotiating those policies, and thereby affecting and even changing them.[2] So to understand what my program's policy is and how it works, we would not only analyze its content or its framers' intentions, but also and more importantly what various actors—starting with teachers and students, but extending as well to administrators, disciplinary colleagues in other institutions, accreditors, employers, prospective job candidates, and so on—*do* with it. We would not assume that these actors all have equal power; one thing policies do is construct power relations within spaces, always seeking to serve some interests and not others. However, we would be attentive to how those actors exert their agency, sometimes in ways that undermine the original intent of the policy. We would also seek to understand—since no program is an island—how the policy interacts with other policies within and beyond the institution. How is it enabled and constrained by, consistent or inconsistent with, the language policies of the university, the state, the nation, and the profession?

In short, the policy is not so much an "entity" as it is an "enactment" (Hornberger and Johnson). It works not by making people do things but by being something people *do*: a practice through which people give shape to the spaces they inhabit.

How To "Do" Policy

And you may ask yourself
How do I work this?

—Talking Heads, "Once in a Lifetime"

How does this shift in how we understand policy affect how we *do* policy? Traditionally, policies are understood as levers for operationalizing the will of those who govern—as technologies of control. As documents that create and govern organizational spaces, they must be clear, consistent, and, to the extent possible, "people-proof." They also must be implemented with fidelity to their design and purpose (though *personal* fidelity is not required, so long as actions and behaviors are consistent with the policies). If we shift our lens on policy and think of it as a practice engaged in by variously situated actors, however, our notion of what it means to "do" policy is considerably broadened and made more complex. Now we begin thinking about:

Designing policies to help shape spaces rather than determine actions. Education research indicates that when policy is used as a blunt instrument to leverage certain behaviors, it tends to provoke resentment and subversion (Darling-Hammond; Elmore; McNeill). It is, for reasons we've explored here, a limited technology of control. On the other hand, policy as a practice can and does shape spaces in which effective teaching and learning become more or less likely.

Our writing program's language policy, for instance, makes no attempt to mandate a certain set of teaching strategies; instead, we provide a way of thinking about language that our research and experience indicate to us will be more effective and appropriate for learners in our university. This is not to say that policies should never ban or require particular behaviors; our program's classroom etiquette policy, for instance, bans student behaviors that interfere with others' learning. But effective teaching and learning (like all complex social processes) are not the result of simply prescribing and proscribing behaviors. Teachers and students must be able to exercise their intellect in pursuit of shared goals through a range of possible activities. (In our program, for instance, discourse analysis, genre study, and multimodal composing are just a few ways instructors and students explore "effective" writing across contexts.) Policy helps shape spaces by identifying that range of possible activities.

It also potentially shapes spaces beyond the immediate program. We hope, for instance, that other programs and departments on campus consult our policy and perhaps adopt similar policies. We hope administrators are influenced by our thinking as they shape university policy. We hope the evolving disciplinary conversation about "translingualism" will be informed by attempts such as ours to put some of those ideas into policy (see Horner, Lu, Royster, and Trimbur). These are our hopes; what matters most, however, is what the people situated in these spaces *do* with the policy.

Developing policies with, rather than for, those who are affected by them. For us, what teachers and students in our program do with the policy is the key to determining its value. In a sense, the first thing they did with the policy was to formulate it. Although the program directors literally composed the written policy, it emerged alongside a program assessment process that involved a thorough review of curriculum documents, classroom documents, teacher- and student-generated concept maps, and student writing from our program. This review revealed to the assessment committee and program directors that the program was shifting in various ways, including toward the capacious understanding of the purpose of college writing captured in the statement. Though it would be going too far to suggest that the policy represents an absolute consensus, it captures the current zeitgeist of the program and is in this sense collaboratively authored.

Far from trying to design a "teacher proof" or "student proof" policy, we are asking teachers and students simultaneously to examine and to work with the policy. We have made it an object of discussion at a program workshop; asked teachers to keep it in mind as they design their courses; invited teachers to share and discuss it with their students; and solicited feedback from teachers and students through our assessment process. Because they are most intimately affected by the policy—most centrally involved in the activities the policy seeks to influence—teachers' and students' perspectives are actively sought and will most powerfully influence whether and how the policy is revised moving forward. We will also seek and consider the perspectives of others outside the program, including faculty across the university, administrators, colleagues in the field, accreditors, community members, employers, and so on, and these perspectives may also influence our policy. But because this is an educational policy engaged most meaningfully in the classroom, teachers' and students' perspectives are weighted most heavily.

Approaching policy work as dynamic and ongoing. Our expectation is that our program's language policy *will* be revised, perhaps frequently, based on ongoing conversations and feedback. While the primary purpose of the policy is to help shape the writing program—to lend it some coherence by marking the range of activities that characterize it—it is a mistake to assume that it ensures perpetual organizational stability. In a steady state system, behaviors and activities that characterize the present are expected to characterize the future. This cannot be the expectation of a system as complex as a writing program.

At the same time, we must remember that dynamism does not mean that policy makers can force change quickly and decisively with top-down edicts, simple solutions, and quick fixes. These moves are tempting for a policy maker looking to make her mark, whether it's a WPA who wants to build a distinctive program or a politician who keeps an eye trained on the electoral calendar; but it is just as misguided to imagine that everything will change based on a policy from on high as it is to imagine that nothing will change once a policy is promulgated. This is why our writing program will use the feedback to the current iteration of the policy to revisit it early and often.

Building coalitions to influence policy systems. Even if WPAs engage in policy making in ways I've advocated here, all writing program policies will continue to operate within larger policy systems in which various interests and perspectives—and the institutions and cultural values from which they issue—vie for power. (See, for instance, Linda Adler-Kassner's and Peggy O'Neill's chapters in this volume.) Part of what it means to "do" policy, then, is to attempt to influence these policy systems, institutions, and cultural values such that our policies have force and reach.

This is no small order. Our present culture and the institutions that support it are designed to shut out teachers, academics, and students from educational decision-making. Educators' expertise has been shunted aside in favor of the business, management, and technical expertise of educational services companies, the testing and test prep industry, and philanthropists (see O'Neill, this volume). Teachers, academics, and students are treated at best as merely "stakeholders," equal in status and power to other stakeholders—and at worst as "special interests" looking to protect their unearned prerogatives.

For this reason, it is necessary but insufficient for WPAs to heed the familiar call to "know our audience" and to make more effective arguments to those in power. This admonition assumes our "audience" already exists, ready to listen if only our arguments are good enough. To put it bluntly, the soundness of our arguments about teaching and learning—however well grounded in research and experience—doesn't always matter. We must first *build* audiences to get a hearing for our arguments.

What I'm talking about here is something we don't often think of as "policy work" but is crucial to the policy process: good old-fashioned political organizing (see Adler-Kassner; Adler-Kassner and O'Neill; Fleischer; Gallagher and Turley). Designing policies for our programs and institutions will never be enough. In order to influence policy systems, WPAs need to work as allies with K–12 teachers and students at all levels to put pressure on other policy makers to listen to the perspectives of those who participate most centrally in teaching and learning.

For instance, the WPAs and teachers in my program can marshal compelling (to us) arguments, supported by research and experience, in favor of our language policy: We can challenge the myth of a monolithic "academic discourse" (see Fitzgerald, this volume); we can show how languages and dialects, including "standard" dialects, change over time; we can demonstrate that writers, both while they're in the university and once they graduate from it, will need to be flexible, agile language users; we can show that our approach better prepares them for these demands than a traditional, static approach to "academic writing." But unless and until we can convince university administrators or state and federal policy makers to listen to us on these matters in the first place, these arguments will have no effect on the larger policy systems in which our policy operates. What is needed is a concerted, organized movement by a broad swath of educators and students to intervene in language and educational politics as usual.

This is not the place to present a blueprint for such a movement, but I would make a couple of points. First, we need to leverage the leadership capacity of extant coalitions and networks such as the National Writing Project (see Banks, this volume), the Teacher Leaders Network, and the various student, parent, and teacher organizations that have sprung up to oppose high-stakes standardized testing (such as Students Against Testing and Rog and Joseph Lucido's Educators and Parents Against Testing Abuse). Postsecondary educators, including WPAs, can and should take a larger role in these efforts. Second, a key strategy moving forward is to help policy makers at all levels understand that *top-down policy making doesn't work.* This is, or should be, the clear lesson from No Child Left Behind: Policies can mandate change, but they cannot force improvement (Elmore). When teachers and students are ignored by, rather than centrally involved in, the policy process, educational policy is doomed to fail. Like it or not, teachers and students *do* policy. Policy makers at all levels must be made to understand that their work is to help shape effective teaching and learning environments; to develop policies with those affected by them; and to approach policy as ongoing and dynamic.

CONCLUSION

And you may say to yourself,
My God! what have I done?

—Talking Heads, "Once in a Lifetime"

For many new WPAs, "doing" policy—promulgating it for our programs and attempting to influence it in and beyond our institutions—is understandably daunting. As we've seen, however, policy is a practice requiring capacities with which WPAs are intimately familiar: the ability to listen; to inquire; to appreciate and sort through multiple perspectives; to adapt and revise; to collaborate; to organize. We WPAs may be surprised where our policy work takes us, but we will be better prepared—and perhaps less willing to "let the days go by"—if we keep in mind what policy is and how it works.

NOTES

1. Policy studies is a vast field of inquiry encompassing work in political science, sociology, economics, psychology, law, communications, ethics, and more. It includes scholarship employing a wide range of theories and methods to explore policy discourse, policy analysis, and policy making. It would be impossible to offer even a cursory survey here. For my purposes, though, it is worth noting a general trend in this broad literature away from strictly rational, linear, positivist, technocratic, top-down models and toward inter-

pretive, rhetorical, constructivist, and highly contextual models. Whereas traditional, mainstream policy studies focused on the international and national contexts, privileged the intent of policy makers, and assumed people in any locality would respond as "rational actors," policy scholars have recently shown significant interest in exploring how policies are interpreted, narrativized, and engaged in specific sites of practice by people with distinct values, beliefs, perceptions, and feelings (see, for instance, Entwistle and Enticott; Fischer; Green and Shuttleworth; Liu et al.; Stone; Yanow). There is also a considerable literature on participatory policy evaluation and planning (e.g., Dobbs and Moore; Fischer; Laird; Torgerson; Williams). Both of these foci are evident closest to our disciplinary home, in language policy and planning; the shift from conceiving of "English" as a monolithic structure or system to thinking of "Englishes" as they are practiced in multiple locales has occasioned much interest in "local contingencies" (Pennycook; Ricento; Tollefson) as well as "bottom up" analysis and planning (Canagarajah "Ethnographic" and *Reclaiming*; Hornberger; Hornberger and Johnson; Ramanathan and Morgan).

2. In educational policy, this has come to be known as the "black box" or implementation problem (see Canagarajah, "The Place"; Darling-Hammond; Elmore; Liston, Whitcomb, and Borko).

WORKS CITED

Adler-Kassner, Linda. *The Activist WPA*. Logan: Utah State UP, 2008. Print.

Adler-Kassner, Linda, and Peggy O'Neill. *Reframing Writing Assessment to Improve Teaching and Learning*. Logan: Utah State UP, 2010. Print.

Canagarajah, Suresh A. "Ethnographic Methods in Language Policy." *An Introduction to Language Policy: Theory and Method*. Ed. Thomas Ricento. Malden, MA: Blackwell, 2008. 153–69. Print.

—. "The Place of World Englishes in Composition: Pluralization Continued." *College Composition and Communication* 57.4 (2006): 586–619. Print.

—, ed. *Reclaiming the Local in Language Policy and Practice*. Mahwah, NJ: Erlbaum, 2005.

Darling-Hammond, Linda. *The Right to Learn: A Blueprint for Creating Schools that Work*. San Francisco, CA: Jossey-Bass, 1997. Print.

Dobbs, Lynn, and Craig Moore. "Engaging Communities in Area-Based Regeneration: The Role of Participatory Evaluation." *Policy Studies* 23.3/4 (2002): 157–71. Print.

Edgington, Anthony, and Robin Gallagher. "Junior Faculty and Graduate Student Administration Issues." WPA-CompPile Research Bibliography

No. 1. 2009. Web. 25 August 2012. Elmore, Richard. *School Reform from the Inside Out.* Cambridge, MA: Harvard UP, 2004. Print.

Entwistle, Tom, and Gareth Enticott. "Who or What Sets the Agenda? The Case of Rural Issues in England's Local Public Service Agreement." *Policy Studies* 28.3 (2007): 193–208. Print.

Fischer, Frank. *Reframing Public Policy: Discursive Politics and Deliberative Practices.* New York: Oxford UP, 2003. Print.

Fleischer, Cathy. *Teachers Organizing for Change: Making Literacy Learning Everybody's Business.* Urbana, IL: NCTE, 2000. Print.

Gallagher, Chris W. "Opinion: At the Precipice of Speech: English Studies, Science, and Policy (Ir)Relevancy." *College English* 73.1 (September 2010): 73–90. Print.

Gallagher, Chris W., and Eric D. Turley. *Our Better Judgment: Teacher Leadership for Writing Assessment.* Urbana, IL: NCTE, Forthcoming.

Green, Ann E., and Ian Shuttleworth. "Local Differences, Perceptions and Incapacity Benefit Claimants: Implications for Policy Delivery." *Policy Studies* 31.2 (2010): 223–43. Print.

Hornberger, Nancy, ed. *Indigenous Literacies in the Americas: Language Planning from the Bottom Up.* Berlin: Moulton, 1996. Print.

Hornberger, Nancy H., and David Cassels Johnson. "Slicing the Onion Ethnographically: Layers and Spaces in Multilingual Language Education Policy and Practice." *TESOL Quarterly* 41.3 (2007): 509–32. Print.

Horner, Bruce, Min-Zhan Lu, and Paul Kei Matsuda, eds. *Cross-Language Relations in Composition.* Carbondale: Southern Illinois UP, 2010. Print.

Horner, Bruce, Min-Zhan Lu, Jacqueline Jones Royster, and John Trimbur. "Opinion: Language Difference in Writing: Toward a Translingual Approach." *College English* 73.3 (2011): 303–21. Print.

Laird, Frank N. "Participatory Policy Analysis, Democracy, and Technological Decision Making." *Science, Technology, and Human Values* 18 (1993): 341–61. Print.

Liston, Dan, Jennifer Whitcomb, and Hilda Borko. "NCLB and Scientifically-based Research: Opportunities Lost and Found." *Journal of Teacher Education* 58.2 (2007): 99–107. Print.

Liu, Xinshen, Eric Lindquist, Arnold Vedlitz, and Kenneth Vincent. "Understanding Local Policymaking: Policy Elites' Perceptions of Local Agenda Setting and Alternative Policy Selection." *Policy Studies* 38.1 (2010): 69–91. Print.

McNeil, Linda M. *Contradictions of School Reform: Educational Costs of Standardized Testing.* New York: Routledge, 2000. Print.

Northeastern University Writing Program. "Philosophy and Aims." 2011. Web. 25 August 2012.

Pennycook, Alastair. *Global Englishes and Transcultural Flows.* New York: Routledge, 2007. Print.

Ramanathan, Vaidehi, and Brian Morgan. "TESOL and Policy Enact-
    ments: Perspectives from Practice (Introduction)." *TESOL Quarterly* 41.3
    (2007): 447–63. Print.
Ricento, Thomas. "Theoretical Perspectives in Language Policy: An Over-
    view." *An Introduction to Language Policy: Theory and Method.* Ed. Thom-
    as Ricento. Malden, MA: Blackwell, 2008. 3–9. Print.
Stone, Deborah. *Policy Paradox: The Art of Political Decision Making.* New
    York: Norton, 1997. Print.
Talking Heads. "Once in a Lifetime." *Remain in Light.* Sire Records, 8 Oc-
    tober 1980. LP.
Tollefson, James W. "Introduction: Critical Issues in Educational Language
    Policy." *Language Politics in Education: Critical Issues.* Ed. James W.
    Tollefson. Mahwah, NJ: Erlbaum, 2002. 3–15. Print.
Torgerson, Douglas. "Between Knowledge and Politics: The Three Faces of
    Policy Analysis." *Policy Sciences* 19 (1986): 33–59. Print.
White, Edward M. "English Professor as Public Figure: My Days in Court."
    College English 73.2 (2010): 183–95. Print.
Williams, John J. "Community Participation: Lessons from Post-apartheid
    South Africa." *Policy Studies* 27.3 (2006): 197–217. Print.
Yanow, Dvora. *How Does a Policy Mean? Interpreting Policy and Organiza-
    tional Actions.* Washington, DC: Georgetown UP, 1996. Print.

Part Six: Eternal Questions

28 What Is an English Department?

Melissa Ianetta

There's a joke I've always liked to tell on WPA job interviews:

> *The dean dies. And being a particularly wicked and cruel dean, he goes straight to hell. When he gets to the Inferno's iron gates, he's greeted warmly (get it?) by the Devil himself. "Welcome!" Satan tells him. "We've got just the job for you!" Old Scratch takes the dean to an office—oddly, this office looks just like his office back on earth. His administrative assistant, too, looks just like his long-suffering mortal secretary. Indeed, as Satan runs over his responsibilities, the dean cannot help but think this all sounds just like his previous job. So he asks Satan: "This is just like my last decanal position—how can this be my eternal damnation?"*
>
> *With a gleam in his eye and a whiff of brimstone, the Lord of Flies responds: "Here we have TWO English Departments! BWAHAHAHAHAHAH!!!"*

This one always kills—largely, I think, because it appeals to the self-identities of everyone involved. Deans, for instance, who can feel like they do nothing but deal with the bad behavior of faculty all day, often identify as the martyred individuals who have to cope with the problems around them—for them, an extra English department can seem like hell, indeed. And English faculty, I find, often enjoy identifying as troublemakers—the Socratic speakers of truth and disrupters of the bureaucratic system who righteously vex these sinning administrators. As with the finest job-related jokes, then, the important stakeholders can all find a sympathetic definition of themselves in this opener.

I begin with this joke, however, not only in the hope of providing my reader with a handy icebreaker for that next job interview but also to illustrate a premise often overlooked yet nevertheless central to

359

the success of a WPA who works in an English department. That is, in order to move the members of our departmental audience toward acceptance of our individual program proposals—never mind our intellectual worldview—our rhetoric must work from a focus on their professional identities and disciplinary values and not from our own desires or insecurities. We must learn to understand how *they* would answer the question "What is an English department?" Or, to express my point another way: You'll notice I don't suggest starting an English department job talk with: "Q: How many English department faculty members does it take to change a light bulb? A: "Change a light bulb? We tried that once and it didn't work." Such humor might be true, but it does not offer the auditor a sympathetic role. That is, if a department identifies as righteously wicked or a senior administrator believes himself unduly persecuted by said wicked department, it behooves us to keep such identifications in mind when crafting our own proposals, be they to hire us or, once we are appointed, to support our initiatives.

This assertion may sound, paradoxically, incredibly obvious (Why would one presume to teach a writing teacher audience awareness?) and vaguely insulting (Why should I pander to my colleagues' biases—particularly when those very biases have been known to devalue the work of writing studies specialists such as myself?). Yet, I would argue, the fact remains that it is essential to attend more closely to our departmental contexts and our colleagues' disciplinary notions than our scholarship suggests we have done in the past. Among the "rhetorics for writing program administrators" that this collection seeks to foster, then, I argue that we need to include intradepartmental rhetorics that help us get beyond those longstanding rehearsals of English department inequity that have populated our scholarly descriptions of these departments. Toward this end, in the pages that follow I'll first create exigency by looking to representations of the English department—or the lack thereof—in the scholarship of writing program administration to demonstrate that we have previously paid scant attention to this crucial audience. I will then broaden the scholarly gaze to the wider world of rhetoric and composition by considering Maxine Hairston's "Breaking Our Bonds and Reaffirming Our Connections" as an example of an epideictic rhetoric that is exceptional for the durability of its influence on our field's understanding of the English department—and that has, in one essential way, long been misinterpreted. Finally, I will argue for a reassessment of Hairston's essay by reading her advice for living a life *inside* English—a reading she herself forwards. Such a revisioning, I conclude, will not only help us better understand the history of Hairston's rallying cry but will also allow us to function more effectively in, and with, the department of English.

THE FISH SEE THE WATER LAST: THE ENGLISH DEPARTMENT IN WPA SCHOLARSHIP

In preparing this essay, I turned to those scholarly resources that grounded my own entry into WPA work and was surprised to realize how, collectively, they relegate the entity of the English department to near invisibility. For example, in the index of Irene Ward and William J. Carpenter's *The Allyn and Bacon Sourcebook for Writing Program Administrators*, a resource long beloved by new WPAs, there is no entry whatsoever for English or the English department. Individual essays in the volume, admittedly, such as David Schwalm's "The Writing Program (Administrator) in Context: Where Am I, and Can I Still Behave Like a Faculty Member?" pay a bit of attention to life in English studies:

> Most writing programs [. . .] are located in English depart-
> ments. [. . .] [Y]ou may have colleagues who share your academ-
> ic interest in rhetoric and composition and bring knowledge
> and experience to the program and the classroom, but you
> may also have to deal with cultural differences between the
> "literature faculty" and the "composition faculty," along with
> possible conflicts over resources. In the second case, you may
> well be "the writing person" and you may be working with
> faculty who resent having to teach writing classes. (11)

From this brief account, Schwalm moves on to other issues of institutional context, leaving the reader who came looking for advice related to the English department at a bit of a loss. Admittedly, his comments here are largely correct—the challenges and opportunities in a department where you are the only writing specialist may well differ greatly from those in a department where you have colleagues in your field. Yet the writing specialist who serves as an English department citizen may well be left wanting more. How do you identify, assess, and ne-gotiate these "cultural differences," for one? What are the "resources" that might cause conflict between you and your literary colleagues, for another?

In this same volume, Edward M. White's "Use It or Lose It: Power and the WPA" offers a bit more detail to the WPA adrift in English:

> Power in relation to the English department is [. . .] tangled hopelessly in the dispute over the professional status of rhetoric and composition as a field. If the department is aware of this field, or willing to consider the possibility of it as a field, the WPA gains power as any other faculty member gains power, usually through publication and other professional activity. [. . .] If not, the WPA must find a department that will or prepare to publish in the field of literature. (112)

Many departments' understandings of rhetoric and composition as a discipline have evolved since White first penned this essay in 1991. So most—but not all—contemporary readers will find their departments do expect or, at least, accept that rhetoric and composition specialists will pursue writing research, opening one avenue for the WPA to negotiate with the departmental expectations Schwalm describes. Yet even with White's further explanatory words, the reader is left to wonder how to skillfully determine if the department regards rhetoric and composition with respect, and what other "professional activity" will lead to "power."

However, beyond these essays and a suggestion to consult the *ADE Bulletin* (Hesse 213)—the newsletter of Associated Departments of English, the MLA's professional organization for English chairs—the *Sourcebook* offers little assistance on negotiating the peculiarities of English department culture, and so largely leaves adrift the WPA who is looking for advice on handling his or her departmental colleagues. I am not, however, asserting this omission as peculiar to this foundational work, nor am I limning this gap to criticize this work's editors or contributors; this oversight is not peculiar to this collection but rather is endemic to WPA scholarship. When turning to other often-consulted scholarly works in writing program administration—such as *The Writing Program Administrator's Resource: A Guide to Institutional Reflective Practice* (Brown and Enos) or, more recently, *Untenured Faculty as Writing Program Administrators* (Dew and Horning) and *The Promise and Perils of Writing Program Administration* (Enos and Borrowman)—we find they too offer little systematic or procedural insight into successfully negotiating the English department's rhetorics. In part, this is attributable to the genre of the volumes themselves—both *Untenured* and *Promise* largely rely on individual anecdote, a method that makes the development of any broadly applicable or systematic claims difficult. Partially, too, perhaps this oversight has to do with over-familiarity with our environment—what Nancy Grimm, in a recent consideration of the writing center, referred to as the phenomenon that "the fish see the water last." That is, fish are unaware of the water in which they live, for they have known nothing else. So too, as the majority of WPAs have been educated in English departments, the cultural norms of said departments are a constant in our lives and thus rendered invisible by their omnipresence. Like our students, who can have trouble seeing the rhetorical systems at play in their private, professional, and public lives, we writing specialists can sometimes neglect the discourses and value systems that define our home environments and so miss opportunities for effective rhetorical action.

As this brief survey suggests, then, in WPA scholarship we have avoided an explicit confrontation with the cultural systems, affiliations, and identifications among the disciplines that comprise English departments. We can, however, discern some commonalities in their implicit representation in WPA scholarship, particularly that WPA scholarship written with an English department audience in mind. Some of these commonalities embody assumptions that are troubling in their unhelpfulness for the English department WPA. Two that are especially pernicious in this regard are, first, the looming presence of literature as the all-encompassing Other and, second, the absence in our departmental representations of the other subspecialties that comprise departments of English. We can find examples of both trends in one of the documents foundational to articulating WPA work as scholarly work, that is, "Evaluating the Intellectual Work of Writing Administration," which argues "writing administration can be seen as scholarly work and therefore subject to the same kinds of evaluation as other forms of disciplinary production [. . .] [and so is] worthy of tenure and promotion when it advances and enacts disciplinary knowledge" (CWPA; see also Janangelo, this volume). While the WPA who identifies as a scholar in this area will be quick to agree with both the overarching premise of this piece as well as most of its particulars, it is useful to note the disciplinary anxieties and elisions that are (un)articulated here as well. One the one hand, the document takes as its starting point the hypothetical failure of a particular WPA who is judged by her department's lit-centric standards and is so defined as "A Problematic Case," thus establishing the uneasy relationship between the WPA and the English department that houses her. Also, the WPA herself is at least partially defined by the draconian working conditions of her departmental context—as an assistant professor attempting to gain tenure in a research-intensive department, she serves as the director of composition and the director of WAC, and has taken on the development of several upper-level writing courses. A reader of this document can both wonder at the imaginary martyrdom of this fictional WPA—and can envision a real-world promotion and tenure committee taking comfort that a WPA who only directs first-year composition (FYC) has a much easier time than this "typical" WPA. Thus "Evaluating" defines its representative WPA, at least in part, by her departmental exploitation.

More interesting to a consideration of the English department in administrative scholarship, however, is this statement's representation of a department focused exclusively on composition and literature faculty. It even names the department as comprised of "the broad field of English literature and composition" (CWPA)—nowhere is there any recognition of the other disciplinary specialties that might constitute an English department, such as linguistics, film, journalism, critical theory, English Education, and those digital humanities subfields focused on textual production and consumption. Such specialists can provide strong professional allies—and interesting personal friends. In many ways, then, this foundational document seems an appeal to only our literary colleagues in order to garner their support for the tenure-track WPA who is unsuccessfully reaching across the composition-literature divide. By first focusing on a case study whose working conditions may well be more extreme than those of the WPAs this document purports to support and, second, catering to the assumption that "English really means Literature," our professional organization's position statement—like the scholarship of individual WPAs—inadvertently reinscribes those very enthymemes of WPA victimization and literature centric-ness that so vex us. Surely, then, it is time for WPAs to look beyond the scholarship of our field to answer the question "What is an English department?"

Breaking Our Bonds of Love and Hate

These assumptions about the flashpoints and fissures of English department politics reach well beyond the WPA scholarship or the CWPA statement, however: A focus on the acrimony of literature-composition relations has long been the definitional quality to rhetoric and composition's representations of the English department. Most famously, perhaps, Hairston called for us to "Break Our Bonds" in her 1985 Conference on College Composition and Communication Chair's Address. Hairston's essay is still one of the most well known screeds against our literary colleagues, whom she refers to as the affected "Mandarins of English":

> [I]n traditional departments the system still dictates that the hardest work of the department, teaching freshman writing, remains at the bottom of the social and political scale. [. . .] I see no evidence that this value system is going to change in most universities. I think it reflects an elitist mindset that prefers that which is accessible only to the few and that despises the useful or the popular. The attitude is the same one that made Chinese mandarins grow long fingernails and decree that their women must bind their feet. [. . .] And we have to face the truth that our mandarins think we are ugly because we have short fingernails and big feet. Nothing is going to change that. (Hairston 275–76)

As this incendiary rhetoric might suggest, at the time Hairston's address was "electric;" even today, for scholars such as Susan H. McLeod, "[t]o reread this essay is to be struck by how relevant it still is as a declaration of independence for our field" (525). Hairston's essay has been well-circulated since its publication and its valence continues to influence our conversations today.[1] Commonly, scholars have used this address, as does James E. Porter, to position Hairston as opposing "bridging the gap" between literature and composition (123) or to frame it as a "cal[l] for secession" (Gunner 39). Hairston is thus seen as a firebrand and the earliest prophet of independent writing programs. Yet if we turn back to the actual text we can see that her manifesto in fact reads far more as advice for living in the English department than as an exhortation to leave it.

That is, when we revisit her address itself what we find is that, despite its frequent invocation in discussions of the rise of rhetoric and composition as a discipline separate from English (i.e., literary) studies, Hairston herself does not focus her remarks on this matter. Indeed, she opens her critique with the assertion that "the time has come to break those bonds—not necessarily physically" (273). Rather, she attempts to focus her audience's attention on breaking our bonds "emotionally and intellectually" (273). Thus, much of her essay reads less as a manifesto for escaping the English department and more as an argument for living in it successfully. Certainly, there are analogues for such coexistence in many English departments, where literary studies has long shown its ability to live alongside a number of related disciplines, ranging from linguistics, to film, to journalism. However, while our colleagues in these cognate fields might feel validated by their peers in the traditional areas of literary studies (or, perhaps, are uninterested in such validation), Hairston notes that rhetoric and composition specialists yearn for literature's acceptance. Such yearnings, she claims, are to our detriment: "I [. . .] see us stunted in our growth because we are not able to free ourselves from needing the approval of the literature people. We've left home in many ways, but we haven't cut the cord. We still crave love" (274). Such "cravings" form a core part of many arguments for leaving English departments, as illustrated by the response from McLeod in her description of one department's focus on the dismal treatment of writing teachers:

> At the time [of Hairston's talk], I was teaching composition in an English department that was deeply dysfunctional. It was so fractious that one beleaguered chair remarked that the members probably could not agree on whether or not the sun would come up the next day. [. . .] One thing the literature faculty did agree upon, however, was the place of composition in the department—they wanted none of it. (525)

The rejection of rhetoric and composition by the English department is familiar, certainly. A WPA in the situation McLeod describes, however, might take some small solace from the fact that her department is, at least, consistent in its dysfunctional behavior. That is, a department that treats its individual members hatefully can probably be expected to treat its writing program in a similar fashion. Looking for departmental approval in this situation seems an inevitably doomed enterprise.

Less ominously, and perhaps more commonly, a department that is cheerfully indifferent to one another's scholarship—where the specialist in early African-American film has little interest in the work of the Spenserian and vice-versa—is unlikely to muster much enthusiasm for those in other disciplines, including rhetoric and composition. Such a lack if interest may shock the writing program administrator who spends most of her days involved in the triumphs and trials of the writing program. Nevertheless, success in an English department is often predicated on being mindful that, just as the teaching of writing is central to our conception of the department's mission, so too literary studies is central to our literature colleagues' notion of the English department. Scholars of all stripes can inadvertently assume their work is the center of the academic enterprise writ large. Or, in Hairston's parlance, the wise WPA needs to get over the need for "love." For chasing departmental approbation is a time-consuming, energy-depleting, often fruitless task—and, ultimately, unproductive. To be clear, I am not advising WPAs to endure without complaint poor treatment of their program or themselves. I am, however, urging the reader to consider advice given to me early on in my WPA career: The smart administrator never fights over anything he or she cannot count. Thus one should advocate concerning faculty lines, salaries, course releases, course caps, hours of administrative support, and placement numbers. Such things have the point-at-ability of data and therefore can be framed in evidence-supported arguments. But to fight over one's colleagues' respect for one's field, the departmental perception of one's expertise, or the valuing of one's individual work is likely to be a losing battle because of the lack of objective evidence. It's hard to empirically prove love, or the lack thereof, and, to borrow from another (half-)joking maxim of the administrative job market, if you want gratitude, get a dog—or, preferably, two.

As a flip side of this argument concerning the need to relinquish our desire for professional love, Hairston suggests we need to let go of our more negative emotions too:

> My second suggestion is that we quit wasting our time being angry. Getting angry can be useful at times, particularly if it helps one get rid of illusions and decide to take action, but staying angry consumes too much energy. [. . .] When we let

when we let

wow.

on anger.

people keep us in an uproar, we give them too much importance and risk assuming that they are more powerful than they really are. (278)

She goes on to claim that our time is better spent "building our own reputations and enhancing our status outside of our departments instead of over-reacting to hostility at home" (278). I would suggest, however, that this advice is equally applicable to working with difficult individuals in the English department. That is, the happy WPA doesn't dwell on the lunatics he or she encounters in or out of the department. It is a blessed department indeed that does not have one or two obstructionist faculty members, and oftentimes a WPA is in a position to run afoul of these toxic individuals. Partially, this may be attributable to old wars and old ways of doing things. For some English department denizens, the "world has," as Hairston notes, "changed a great deal in the past decade [. . .] many of them know that they're like dinosaurs standing around waiting for the weather to change, that things are never really going to be the same again" (278). With others, however, the WPA will enter into conflict merely by being an administrator, as would any individual serving as WPA—or as director of graduate study or as chair. The savvy WPA will not focus on the few difficult department members, nor will he or she endow these individuals with the ability to speak for the department as a whole.

Hairston's advice to stop looking for love and refuse to hate is thus valuable for the WPA in an English department, but perhaps her most productive comments are those concerning communication in this environment. She claims, "THEY'RE NOT LISTENING. We are wasting our energy pummeling at them and trying to get them to acknowledge our claims or our merit. As long as we do that, we are playing their game" (278). While Hairston uses this observation to urge writing teachers to make connections outside the English department, I would expand these comments to account for our interdepartmental dealings as well. That is, if we "pummel" them—if we "make our claims" focused on our values and not our audience's, they certainly will not listen. Arguing the primacy of the first-year composition program in the English department's mission is no more likely to persuade literature faculty than a literary scholar's citations to the writing specialist of the longstanding departmental precedent of literature. If you are the WPA in an English department, and they are not listening but you need them to listen, it is your task to make that possible. Often this means negotiating with their desired outcomes in a given situation or explaining how their desires are best—or, at least, partially— met through your proposals. Such communication, too, means the WPA will have to keep explaining the same things—such as program configurations, budgeting realities, and departmental governance processes—eternally. Admittedly, it may seem futile to explain for the nine-hundredth time, for example, why upping the caps in a writing class to match the cap in a large lecture literature survey course is not a move toward parity. Yet such rehearsals of long-standing arguments are part of the WPA's job, just as explanations of the undergraduate course rotation might be a constant task for the director of undergraduate studies. Faculty may not like to listen or to apply critical thinking to their own cherished assumptions, but when we assume roles of administrative leadership anywhere in the university—in or out of the English department—it becomes our job to help them do so.

Ultimately, then, the response to the question posed to me by the editor of this collection—"What is an English department?"—is, in fact, more mundane than any of the representations in WPA scholarship, CCCC keynotes, or even job market jokes. English departments are not solely comprised of powerful Mandarins or provocative Socratic philosophers. They are not places to look for love or foster hate. Like most groups, English departments are a mix of people with a range of interests—and a range of social skills. It is the WPA's task to hear beyond the stereotypes we've helped to perpetuate in our professional discourses and to see our colleagues for who they are and to help them listen to our proposals—and to hear what they say in return.

NOTE

1. Google Scholar, for example, lists eighty-one entries for this work, the most recent published in 2012 (McClure).

WORKS CITED

Brown, Stuart C., and Theresa Enos, eds. *The Writing Program Administrator's Resource: A Guide to Reflective Institutional Practice*. Mahwah, NJ: Erlbaum, 2002. Print.

Council of Writing Program Administrators (CWPA). "Evaluating the Intellectual Work of Writing Administration." 1998. Web. 2 September 2012.

Dew, Debra Frank, and Alice Horning, eds. *Untenured Faculty as Writing Program Administrators.* West Lafayette, IN: Parlor Press, 2007. Print.

Enos, Theresa, and Shane Borrowman, eds. *The Promise and Perils of Writing Program Administration.* West Lafayette, IN: Parlor Press, 2008. Print.

Grimm, Nancy. "Identity and Multiliteracies." International Writing Centers Association 2012 Summer Institute. Seven Springs, PA. 31 July 2012. Workshop.

Gunner, Jeanne. "Identity and Location: A Study of WPA Models, Memberships, and Agendas." *WPA: Writing Program Administration* 22.3 (Spring 1999): 31–54. Web. 8 May 2013.

Hairston, Maxine. "Breaking Our Bonds and Reaffirming Our Connections." *College Composition and Communication* 36.3 (1985): 272–82. Web. 8 May 2013.

Hesse, Douglas. "Understanding Larger Discourses in Higher Education." *The Allyn and Bacon Sourcebook for Writing Program Administrators.* Ed. Irene Ward and William J. Carpenter. New York: Longman, 2002. 299–314. Print.

McClure, Randall. "Resistance is Not Futile: Guiding Writing Programs Through Turbulent Times." *Writing and Pedagogy* 4.1 (2012): 121–34. Web. 8 May 2013.

McLeod, Susan H. "'Breaking Our Bonds and Reaffirming Our Connections,' Twenty Years Later." *College Composition and Communication* 57.3 (2006): 525–34. Web. 8 May 2013.

Porter, James E. "De(con)fining English: Literature, Composition, Textuality." *Journal of Teaching Writing* 121–31. Web. 8 May 2013.

Schwalm, David. "The Writing Program (Administrator) in Context: Where Am I, and Can I Still Behave Like a Faculty Member?" *The Allyn and Bacon Sourcebook for Writing Program Administrators.* Ed. Irene Ward and William J. Carpenter. New York: Longman, 2002. 9–22. Print.

Ward, Irene, and William J. Carpenter, eds. *The Allyn and Bacon Sourcebook for Writing Program Administrators.* New York: Longman, 2002. Print.

White, Edward M. "Use It or Lose It: Power and the WPA." *The Allyn and Bacon Sourcebook for Writing Program Administrators.* Ed. Irene Ward and William J. Carpenter. New York: Longman, 2002. 106–13. Print.

29 What Is *The Intellectual Work of Writing Program Administration?*

Joseph Janangelo

In 1998 the Council of Writing Program Administrators (CWPA) issued a statement on "Evaluating the Intellectual Work of Writing Administration." Since then, that text has become an evocative and defining document. It depicts WPA work as capaciously constellated—inclusive of writing center directors, writing across the curriculum leaders, and writing program administrators. It resonates with many of us who pursue that work as our vocations and careers. The statement is a multitasking text: On the one hand, it is pedagogical in that it offers readers "a source of ideas about the intellectual work of writing administration and about how this work can be evaluated responsibly and professionally." It is also protective in that it explains the "exchange value" of scholarship done by individuals "engaged in such work."

Part of the statement's enduring resonance is that it offers considered advice to all parties, providing ideas for understanding the value of WPA work in multiple institutional contexts and permutations. To that advice, I wish to offer a bit of situated perspective. When asked to explore the intellectual work of writing program administration, my first thought is not to denote worthy topics or specify mandatory areas of focus such as placement and assessment, but to discern useful ideas for conceptualizing, presenting, and explaining WPA work in ways that are professionally rewarding, intellectually intriguing, and personally sustaining. My goal is to suggest strategies that may help you demonstrate professional staying power (doing and presenting the kind of work that institutions deem worth rewarding with job security, promotion, and/or tenure) and ideas for staying interested in, and connected to, your work.

WE DO OUR WORK

I see the intellectual work of writing program administration as akin to "gleaning." Allow me to clarify my metaphor: "to glean" means "to learn, discover, or find out, usually little by little or slowly" (*Dictionary. com*). It also means "to gather (something) slowly and carefully in small pieces" and "to gather (the useful remnants of a crop) from the field after harvesting" (*Collins English Dictionary*). Gleaning involves seeing things as they are publicly perceived—the scraps deemed unusable—and envisioning their value and, then, creating a more noble role and use for them. In terms of WPA work, this can mean paying attention to people, ideas, and artifacts that others have deemed to be too basic for, or unworthy of, intellectual inquiry. Gleaners, however, may see and save; we may tease meaning out of what others call relatively meaningless information, individuals, and/or their experiences. I wish to discuss writing program administration in this context, not as a series of steps to follow but as a constellation of ideas and dispositions that may reveal and heighten the complexity and value of our work.

As gleaners, we do our best to notice and appreciate everyone's contributions, activities and interests in our composition programs and institutions. We mine these experiences (both the ones we offer students and the ones students offer tutors and faculty) for what gets called "data" and more. We also strive to see ourselves at work. In this we ask, *What is it we are really doing when we are doing the obvious or "routine" work we are (or are not) doing?* To ask this question we need to be reflective and creative: In our scholarly pursuits we roam and read outside our disciplines to find ideas that may explain our work from new and perhaps strange perspectives. In our publications—let's use articles as an example—we strategically center and digress from received knowledge.

By "center and digress," I mean we devote attention to what has been published regarding our topic (e.g., undergraduate research) and ask: What is the learning that's said to be central and valuable to undergraduate research and researchers? To honor that knowledge and establish ethos, we may include and discuss that mainstream and expected wisdom, story, and take on our topic. We'll also make sure that some of that work is represented in our citations lest we be thought to be novice or uninformed. Along the way, we become critical and ask where there is need or room for an intervention or new learning. Such work involves alertness and attunement. It means being willing to see things (e.g., curriculum redesign, faculty development) as they are identified in best practices and reified in prestigious publications. It also means being wary of that received knowledge and articulating nuanced inquiries or critiques of it. Such scholarship also helps us wonder publicly what lessons have been too well learned and which practices we might test or rethink.

I pause here to offer some evocative examples of this kind of work. One provocative example is "Big Rubrics and Weird Genres: The Futility of Using Generic Assessment Tools Across Diverse Instructional Contexts" by Chris M. Anson, Deanna P. Dannels, Pamela Flash, and Amy L. Housley Gaffney. These scholars criticize the use of generic rubrics, suggesting that "Although it could be argued that generic criteria provide a starting point by providing language whose heuristic value compels faculty in the disciplines to think about general but sometimes unconsidered concepts such as 'rhetorical purpose' or 'style appropriate to the defined or invoked audience,' there is too much risk that such criteria will 'make do' for everything students produce."

Another trenchant note about assessment rubrics is sounded by Peter Dow Adams who, in a WPA-L thread about assessment called "Crappy Reframed," offers this incendiary insight: "It seems to me over the years that I've seen a lot of assessments that show no significant improvement after a semester of writing instruction. One conclusion is that what we are doing isn't working, but there is also the possibility that we have not developed research tools capable of measuring the kinds of improvements that occur over a fifteen week period."

These scholars question inherited knowledge by seeing and scrutinizing earlier ideas. They also oscillate between what is said to be "true" and what could be learned that may be even truer.

Just as we may toggle among multiple ideas in our scholarship, we must multitrack at work as we strive to extend hospitality to the many constituencies (e.g., students, full-time and adjunct faculty, colleagues, and administrators) we serve. It is small surprise then that oscillation can pervade our working lives. Here I think of Cathy N. Davidson who, in *Now You See It: How the Brain Science of Attention Will Transform the Way We Live, Work, and Learn*, shows us how attention allocation is a multichannel affair. Defending oscillation, she suggests that we can work effectively while experiencing multiple distractions, of which there is generally no shortage in WPA work. Davidson asserts that: "In our global, diverse, interactive world, where everything seems to have another side, continuous partial attention may not only be a condition of life but a useful tool for navigating a complex world" (287). She disabuses us of overrated fantasies of undistracted attention (e.g., Where's my reading day?), saying that "Those blissful episodes of concentrated, undistracted, continuous absorption are delicious—and dangerous" (287). She adds "that sole, concentrated, direct, centralized attention to one task—the ideal of twentieth-century productivity—is efficient for the task on which you are concentrating but it shuts out other important things we also need to be seeing" (287). If Davidson is right, we need to cultivate the ability to work effectively on several things at once. We also need to be *seen* working effectively, which brings me to the next facet.

We Value Our Work

Having done our work, we now explain and present it in ways that are perceived as valuable to our disciplines and institutions. Here I think of one of gleaning's earlier meanings: *glennare*, "make a collection" (Harper). In forming a collection of tenure and/or promotion (T&P)-worthy artifacts, we also accumulate areas of expertise and public reputation for being learned about a given topic. Careful collecting requires time, deliberation and strategy. What do we want to spend our lives working on? How might we assess and explain our work's value? Framing our work is itself vital work. In framing strive for return on investment. Here I recommend thinking in terms of professional outcomes: Whom do you want to be seen as and valued by? Take care to assemble an intentional *oeuvre*; don't let it look like you run from task to task or text to text.

Let's think about framing in the short and long terms. Each semester, you might draw your own version of a curriculum map. What does your evolving collection of work say about your intellectual commitments and investments? How do your administrative texts (e.g., proposals, letters, and workshop materials) depict you as an effective rhetor (Dew) and valuable colleague? Rather soon you will be compiling your work into a T&P document. Here it is wise to consult with your departmental colleagues and draw on the accumulated wisdom of veteran composition scholars.

Such work abounds. Recently, Irwin Weiser offered a clear explanation of possible T&P processes. He helps us understand the "practice" (647) of peer review and the importance of framing our work so that committee members can appreciate its value and worth. Committee members, tasked with reading many applications, will likely value a clear and explicit text that explains your work, its contributions (how it relates to national disciplinary conversations), what it has contributed and how it will evolve. Don't be surprised if you find yourself drawing a rather explicit picture of your work as well as a discussion of the importance of writing program administration (inclusive of writing center and writing across the curriculum work) as examples of campus leadership and rigorous, disciplined scholarship. A preemptive word of advice: Concentrate on making substantial contributions to a few areas. Your intellectual work will be easier to appreciate and extol if it is not spread out across more than three or four areas.

There are experts who can help us describe the links between what we are doing and what's needed on campus. For example, John Schilb offers fine advice for explaining teaching "as places for generating and implementing ideas" (24). Elizabeth Tebeaux helps us document our contributions in relation to institutional mission. She asks key questions like "What has the faculty member done to further the welfare of the institution and contribute to the achievement of its mission?" (194) and "What is the value of the faculty member's intellectual work to students, to the community, and to the institution?" (195)

In "Mentor and Evaluator: The Chair's Role in Promotion and Tenure Review," Richard C. Gebhardt reminds us that "scholarship may be released through a variety of professionally accepted channels" (151). In "Methodologies of Peer and Editorial Review: Changing Practices," Cynthia L. Selfe and Gail E. Hawisher help us understand the possible risks and rewards of online publications. In *A Digital Portfolio*, Cheryl E. Ball persuasively uses the affordances of online discourse to frame and display her work. Mindful of institutional context, Keith Kroll and Barry Alford note that "tenure and promotion review in the two-year colleges presents a different constellation of issues" (57). Individuals engaged in WPA work at two-year colleges would benefit from reading the work of Peter Dow Adams, Carolyn Calhoon-Dillahunt, Malkiel Choseed, Jeffrey Klausman, and Jeff Sommers, to name a few. If you work at a "small college" it behooves you to engage the scholarship of Tom Amorose, Jill Gladstein, and Dara Regaignon, among others. The larger point is to know that you have institutional colleagues beyond your own institution. Make thoughtful use of their insights.

One more thought about explaining the value of your work. In Edna Ferber's Pulitzer Prize-winning novel *So Big*, a character compares life to theatre, calling it "A fine show." He advises that "The trick is to play in it and look at it at the same time" (10). My advice is to conceptualize and stage "a fine show." Build and refine your collection to show yourself becoming and being a successful campus leader and scholar. If you are starting your career, you are in a grand position to employ backward design; you can decide what you want to be known for and as. You can work at seeing yourself and at being seen, even in advance, as a leader.

It's good to merge self-assessment with rhetorical acumen. By this, I mean remember that your audience very likely wants you to be successful and impactful. You can help your readers appreciate the value of your intellectual work by offering them a curated reading experience. One strategy when advocating for your ideas, in meetings or in a promotion review, is to link purposefully to inter/national initiatives (e.g., The Citation Project, The WAC Clearinghouse, and writingcenters.org) and professional affiliates (e.g., CWPA, IWCA, and TYCA). Explaining your allegiances and disagreements in terms of best practices can help you situate your work within larger conversations and may protect you from being perceived as talking out of naiveté or self-interest. Many WPAs want their work to be more visible. My thought is that increased credibility can enhance that visibility.

We Work Intentionally and Inclusively

I see gleaning as intrinsic to supporting inclusion. One powerful image for me is of Jean-Francois Millet's 1857 painting *The Gleaners*, in which the characters are doubled and bent from searching—some might say scavenging—the field for its scraps and remnants. Such bending captures gleaning in another sense: "to gather (grain or the like) after the reapers or regular gatherers" and "to gather (the useful remnants of a crop) from the field after harvesting" (*Dictionary.com*). Here the fit between WPA work and gleaning is quite close. Don't many of our programs serve discarded, overlooked, and undervalued individuals (e.g., basic writing, English Language Learners)? Furthermore, aren't some of our courses and writing centers "staffed" by professionals whose value is often underappreciated, misunderstood, and under-rewarded? Working inclusively means working with new and perhaps disturbing priorities. It means including others' insights, contributions, and needs for the sake of ethical responsibility and programmatic health.

Gleaning takes place in the after-harvesting; one of its synonyms is searching. Let's think about intellectual work as searching. In composing mainstream scholarship (as described in facet one), we might ask: Who cares about Topic X and what has been written about it? Working inclusively might also mean becoming more attentive and hospitable to dissonance. Regarding Topic X, we might ask why, exactly, those who care about X care. What assumptions, investments, fears, or fantasies do they have about the topic? In our gleaning, we might ask who doesn't seem to care (anymore) and why? Proceeding on, we might wonder who could come to care if . . . ? Our gleaning might challenge mainstream knowledge by asking where interesting, perhaps understudied, conversations are occurring and where we might start or fuel some.

"Mapping Knowledge-Making in Writing Center Research: A Taxonomy of Methodologies" by Sarah Liggett, Kerri Jordan, and Steve Price is a provocative enactment of such searching. The authors argue for methodological plurality in writing center research and scholarship (see also Lerner, this volume). They describe disagreements among writing center scholars and contend that "the writing center community has moved beyond the either/or debates of positivists vs. phenomenologists or quantitative vs. qualitative evidence" (54). They argue that "we see this 'considerable disagreement' alongside discernable trends in research interests as characteristic of a thriving research community—one that intentionally seeks to discover, test, articulate, and revise best practices in their search for knowledge" (54). Notice the words "test, articulate, and revise." These scholars remind us that critical scrutiny is the scrutiny that is critical *of* inherited knowledge and critical *to* building new possibilities. This means asking: What is this topic said to mean? What could/did it mean and to whom? What might the next iteration and conversation include?

Inclusion is a catalyst. It provokes/invites us to go back and re-mine our data. It helps us "see" the common wisdom on a topic (e.g., assessment), interrogate its historical streams of input, and scrutinize the reigning observations, assumptions, and claims. As we glean, we promote the incidental, innocuous, and irrelevant story, stance, and sidebar to enhanced dignity and value. Examples of such work include *Race and Writing Assessment*, edited by Asao B. Inoue and Mya Poe; Harry Denny's *Facing the Center: Toward an Identity Politics of One-to-One Mentoring*; and Frankie Condon's *I Hope I Join the Band: Narrative, Affiliation, and Antiracist Rhetoric*. Inclusion can also mean determining our relationship with programmatic "ephemera." The CWPA "Intellectual Work" statement says that "Clearly boundaries must be set; not every memo, descriptive comment, or teaching evaluation embodies the concept of intellectual work." There is much WPA work (e.g., tutor and teacher observations, videos, and mission statements) that could qualify, though, if we let it. My point is to be wary of how we consign things to ephemera. The ephemeral is a designation: Its status reflects decision-making practices that may reveal tacit priorities about what merits being kept or discarded, and what is said to be more or less valuable.

CONCLUSION

I wish to end by touching on ideas of "status" and "value." The *status* of WPA work, as evinced by the scholars cited here, is in-process, to be done, and occasionally undone. It enacts Stewart Brand's idea that we are "always building and rebuilding" and "that finishing is never finished" (11). As for WPA work's intellectual *value*, it is situated in community standards and ongoing audience perceptions. I see our intellectual work as a big and worthy project, one that involves being wary of received wisdom and (re)discovering meaning in our data, constituencies, and commitments.

If this sounds like too much work and a rather perpetual maintenance activity, well, it can be. That's why it's worth doing . . . again and anew. I return to Ferber's idea that "The trick is to play in it and look at it at the same time" (10). Self-awareness and strategy are valuable; so are gratitude, passion, and investment. Ask me to define the intellectual work of writing program administration and I'll say two things. It's the work that needs to be to be done, circulated, celebrated, questioned, and redone. It's also a hybrid challenge, sustenance, and joy. Our intellectual work is not just what we *have* to do. It's also what we *get* to do.

Works Cited

Adams, Peter Dow. "Crappy Reframed." WPA-L. 11 April 2012. Online posting. 28 November 2012.

Anson, Chris M., Deanna P. Dannels, Pamela Flash, Amy L. Housley Gaffney. "Big Rubrics and Weird Genres: The Futility of Using Generic Assessment Tools Across Diverse Instructional Contexts." *Journal of Writing Assessment* 5.1 (2012): Web. 1 December 2012.

Ball, Cheryl E. *Dr. Cheryl E. Ball: A Digital Portfolio*. 2010. Web. 1 December 2012.

Brand, Stewart. *How Buildings Learn: What Happens After They're Built*. New York: Viking, 1994. Print.

Collins English Dictionary. 10th ed. HarperCollins. n.d. Web. 7 January 2013.

Condon, Frankie. *I Hope I Join the Band: Narrative, Affiliation, and Antiracist Rhetoric*. Logan: Utah State UP, 2012. Print.

Council of Writing Program Administrators (CWPA). "Evaluating the Intellectual Work of Writing Administration." 1998. Web. 1 December 2012.

Davidson, Cathy N. *Now You See It: How the Brain Science of Attention Will Transform the Way We Live, Work, and Learn*. New York: Viking, 2011. Print.

Denny, Harry. *Facing the Center: Toward an Identity Politics of One-to-One Mentoring*. Logan: Utah State UP, 2010. Print.

Dew, Debra Frank. "WPA as Rhetor: Scholarly Production and the Difference a Discipline Makes." *College Composition and Communication* 61.2 (2009): 40–62. Print.

Dictionary.com. Dictionary.com LLC. 2013. Web. 2 January 2013.

Ferber, Edna. *So Big*. Garden City, NJ: Doubleday, Page & Company, 1924. Print.

Gebhardt, Richard C. "Mentor and Evaluator: The Chair's Role in Promotion and Tenure Review." *Academic Advancement in Composition Studies: Scholarship, Publication, Promotion, Tenure*. Ed. Richard C. Gebhardt and Barbara Genelle Smith Gebhardt. Mahwah, NJ: Erlbaum, 2007. 147–65. Print.

Harper, Douglas. *Online Etymology Dictionary*. 2012. Web. 2 January 2013.

Inoue, Asao B., and Mya Poe, eds. *Race and Writing Assessment*. New York: Peter Lang, 2012. Print.

Kroll, Keith, and Barry Alford. "Scholarship, Tenure, and Composition Studies in the Two-Year College." *Academic Advancement in Composition Studies: Scholarship, Publication, Promotion, Tenure*. Ed. Richard C.

Gebhardt and Barbara Genelle Smith Gebhardt. Mahwah, NJ: Erlbaum, 2007. 57–70. Print.

Liggett, Sarah, Kerri Jordan, and Steve Price. "Mapping Knowledge-Making in Writing Center Research: A Taxonomy of Methodologies." *The Writing Center Journal* 31.2 (2011): 50–88. Print.

Schilb, John. "Scholarship in Composition and Literature: Some Comparisons." *Academic Advancement in Composition Studies: Scholarship, Publication, Promotion, Tenure.* Ed. Richard C. Gebhardt and Barbara Genelle Smith Gebhardt. Mahwah, NJ: Erlbaum, 2007. 21–30. Print.

Selfe, Cynthia L., and Gail E. Hawisher. "Methodologies of Peer and Editorial Review: Changing Practices." *College Composition and Communication* 63.4 (2012): 672–98. Print.

Tebeaux, Elizabeth. "Afterword: Re-Envisioning Tenure in an Age of Change." *Academic Advancement in Composition Studies: Scholarship, Publication, Promotion, Tenure.* Ed. Richard C. Gebhardt and Barbara Genelle Smith Gebhardt. Mahwah, NJ: Erlbaum, 2007. 191–99. Print.

Weiser, Irwin. "Peer Review in the Tenure and Promotion Process." *College Composition and Communication* 63.4 (2012): 645–72. Print.

30 What Is WPA Research?

Christiane Donahue

> *We are all on the same journey, all trying to say interesting
> things, all falling into bad habits, all struggling to imagine
> the [social] world anew (xii).*

—Andrew Abbott

As this volume has shown time and again, writing program administrators are in complicated positions. They are teaching, directing
programs and writing centers, spearheading curricular initiatives, negotiating complex relationships across institutions, and often working toward tenure. In this context, "research" can take on particular
shapes, benefits, and challenges. How might WPAs "do" research, of
what kind, and with what purposes and approaches? What is WPA
research, what isn't it, and why is it so important to WPA work?

Of course, WPAs do research before becoming WPAs, in most
cases. The research and scholarly inquiry necessary for completing a
dissertation, for example, are paths well trodden. Once a WPA, however, the position tends to call out specific kinds of research, more directly linked to the context of WPA concerns. For the past two years,
for example, the Dartmouth Summer Seminar for Composition Research, designed to foster research in the field, has seen WPAs focused
on issues including: Are students learning better in some conditions?
Does tutoring have an effect on quality of student writing? Are labor
conditions a factor in teaching quality? Does every student writer need
to share the same process? Is there a way to identify what knowledge
or know-how is transferring across writing contexts? Research, in
this case, takes on a distinctively social sciences flavor, emphasizing
data-driven inquiry, replicable-aggregable results, and systematicity.
Charles Bazerman ("Disciplined") has suggested that the key for rhet-

oric and composition is to develop the kind of rigor for which much social sciences research is noted, but without losing the rich complexity of what we study: teaching and learning writing in highly complicated social contexts. Noted social sciences researcher Andrew Abbott suggests that "science is a conversation between rigor and imagination" (3), which supports a version of research resisting the reductions that we fear.

To step back for a moment: What do I mean here by *research*, in particular *data-driven research*? After all, research is something all scholars do, in forms that can seem unrecognizable from one field to another; as Susan Peck McDonald noted in 1989, for example, humanities research and social sciences research are quite different. The one generalizes from multiple instances of data—multiple texts, each one carefully analyzed and all subject to diverse interpretations. The other is conceptually driven; writers "begin with communally-defined abstractions which then drive the selection and discussion of data" (211). *Data* is thus open to interpretation. Some scholars have been quite specific about the field's lack of *replicable, aggregable* research (Haswell, "NCTE/CCCC's War"), while others call for empirical research, equating it with quantitative methods alone. Here, we will consider it as a state of mind as much as an approach, a systematic mindset beginning at points without the end already in mind, seeing where the data take you . . . understanding too that there is numerical data and descriptive (word) data . . . and part of what we try to do when we move in certain directions is to move our word data into numerical form.

On the other hand, what research is not, in this arena, is assessment. These are distinctly different, while equally important, activities for a WPA (see Harrington, this volume). If we take *research* as description and explanation, rather than evaluation for action, we see the framing of this difference.

This chapter will introduce the idea of research for WPAs, acknowledging how devilishly hard research about writing is—especially from a social sciences perspective—but how important it is to telling better, more accurate, and more useful stories than, say, those told by Richard Arum and Josipa Roksa (of *Academically Adrift* fame), as well as to decoding the research stories out there—the ones that tend to land on a WPA's desk from the dean or the provost with a request for action or a well-intentioned "Check this out!" I will briefly explore the history of research in the field, give an overview of methods, offer the key questions with which you might grapple as you carry out this research, and articulate the reasons for it.

HISTORY

For decades, most compositionists have skirted data-driven types of research in favor of humanistic studies of writing (Voss), including close reading. However, data-driven work has come back into sharp focus, in part because of its methodological links with assessment, Quality Enhancement Plans (QEPs), reaccreditation, and broad-brush national discourses of accountability. WPAs find themselves needing to better understand the contours of this work without having had the opportunity to develop the research abilities to do so.

Recently on the Writing Program Administrators listserv (WPA-L), noted scholar Peggy O'Neill critiqued composition's relation to research in general: "We haven't been exactly rigorous when it comes to relying on research for our theories and practices," she commented, pointing out that few compositionists have empirical training or the ability to critique such research. "All methodologies, it seems to me, can tell only part of the story. Knowing what the strengths and weaknesses [are] inherent in methodologies can help us understand more fully what the results mean, what inferences we can draw, etc." Assessment expert Edward M. White chimed in to critique the attitudes compositionists appear to hold about such research: "I've met lots of people in our field who boast of their ignorance of science and statistics. I don't mean the kind of informed distrust of empiricism that Rich Haswell demonstrates, built on wide experience, but a kind of pride that our knowledge is so superior to all others that we need not know anything else."

This story, informally expressed, is far from new; it appears to cycle through our field at regular intervals in tension with its foil, the story of risk from "science-based" research as misleading and limiting (Voss), or of loss, as humanism gives itself over to quantification. Because of our WPA role in institutional accountability discussions and our (most often) English department worksites, we find ourselves at the center of this debate.

While John R. Hayes suggests that empirical methods are not in and of themselves anti-humanist but, instead, tools that help us to address our field's problems and challenges, Russell Durst cites the "increasingly anti-cognitive/anti-social science perspective" of the late 1980s, a sentiment that is clear in work like Ralph Voss's 1983 article in *JAC: Journal of Advanced Composition*, "Composition and the Empirical Imperative," in which he warns against the "chance that composition studies risks a detrimental borrowing of prestige from science" (1) and argues for the deep value of humanistic studies of writing. Ellen Barton points to the same tension, as represented by Elizabeth A. Flynn's 1995 critique of empiricism and Davida Charney's 1996 critique of the absence of a systematic adoption of networks of studies that are in dialogue and can help develop a coherent, ongoing, and shared research agenda. These two narratives are complicated by an additional tension between scholars describing the apparently plentiful research associated with composition studies (Bazerman, "Disciplined"; Durst) or its absence (Anson; Haswell, "Teaching"). Richard Haswell ("NCTE/CCCC's War") and Chris M. Anson have each commented powerfully on the lack of a particular kind of research in US composition studies—data-driven, replicable, aggregable—and the harm that lack might do to our self-knowledge and to our broader credibility in higher education.

The history of assessment also sheds some light on the field's tenuous relationship with data and systematic information gathering. As Kathleen Blake Yancey suggests, that history is a series of waves, from the objective testing of the 1950s through the 1970s, to holistic scoring of essays in the 1970s and 1980s and now to portfolio assessment and pragmatic assessment (again, see Harrington, this volume). These waves help to explain at least in part why earlier encounters with data-driven inquiry raised the concerns we have today.

WHY RESEARCH MATTERS

The primary reason is not specific to WPAs: We do research because it's exciting, it's knowledge-generating, and it's part of our interests and desires (see also Janangelo, this volume). There are reasons specific to WPA work, as well. Research activity situates us with our colleagues in other fields; research is a language spoken in the academy. Via literature reviews and professional events, research keeps our knowledge of current issues quite fresh. WPAs, as leaders, must be constantly situated in the available research. Doing research allows us to transform the field—its work—the future of WPAs. We can move into an era of evidence-based programs, with the right kind of research and development. Finally, perhaps just as importantly, research is a form of faculty development (see Rutz and Wilhoit, this volume) for the faculty in most writing programs in the US, where scholarship is often not a part of writing faculty profiles.

PROCESSES AND APPROACHES: WHAT DOES A WPA NEED TO KNOW?

Here's a consciousness-raising exercise. As a WPA, reflect on this statement from Abbott:

> The social sciences share subject matter, theories, and a surprising amount of methodology. They are not organized into a clearly defined system but take their orientations from various historical accidents. Loosely speaking, economics is organized by a theoretical concept (the idea of choice under constraint), political science by an aspect of social organization (power), anthropology by a method (ethnography), history by an aspect of temporality (the past), and sociology by a list of subject matters (inequality, the city, the family, and so on). (5)

Ask yourself, "As a social science (or—if it were a social science—and why couldn't it be?), what does composition do? What is it organized by?" This will help you to begin almost any research trajectory.

In simplest terms, to do research, you propose a question, design a study, draw inferences, and acquire, treat, analyze, and interpret data; but to both smartly read and effectively produce research in the ways most useful to WPAs, you'll need to develop an approach, a methodology, discrete skills, and a mindset that enables the best command of these elements. Here, I'll discuss some of the key elements of this process. Each of these elements has an appendix with a set of useful questions for WPAs.

Researchable questions are at the heart of effective, thoughtful research. What you might want to know as a WPA researcher might not be what is knowable—or researchable. It might need to be broken into many discrete parts, each its own study. Your questions could grow from assumptions that are themselves worth researching, testing, undoing.

More than all other cautions, think about how you might differentiate questions that begin with the premise that what we do in our programs works and we just need the evidence, from questions that seek to describe and explain, to observe and test, to identify "whether" before moving to "how."

Literature reviews—familiar to us all—can usefully move research forward, helping us to understand who else has asked this question. They can also cover methodological ground: Who else has used my method? To what success, in what context? How have the results been treated and interpreted? Literature reviews, as Howard Becker has suggested, also can deter research. They both constrain our work and offer opportunity. They can get in our way, our willingness to think fresh, dominating our intuitions, making us feel there is nothing left to say. But they also can be generative and heuristic; they can save much time and spark new ideas (Becker 147–48).

Methodological frames and method decisions deeply shape what's possible for WPA research. As Bazerman ("Methods") has pointed out, research methods are simply procedures, tools for proceeding; when those methods become well known and associated with particular disciplines, they are standardized procedures—with more clout and weight. A methodology, for Bazerman, moves us into reflective reasoning about the logic of our inquiry: "Being reflectively methodical and disciplined about methods; understanding the implications and consequences of methods; understanding the relation of data and findings from one method to those from other methods" ("Methods"). This way of thinking about our methods pushes us toward determining as WPAs the shape and nature of the very discipline we support with our programmatic and curricular and faculty development roles.

The heart of method is explanation: Each method is a different way of approaching explanation, a "program of explanation" (Abbott 8). This means that choices of methods are essential to long-term research goals; methods are not so much more or less effective as more or less in line with what a WPA hopes to describe, identify, or explain. Bazerman ("Methods") offers the following questions for working through methods choices:

- What do you want to explain?

- By looking at what? (texts, meanings, individual behavior, individual cognition, social behavior, social cognition, relations, institutional conditions/constraints, consequences, effects of interventions, processes . . .)
- What do you want to measure in order to explain?
- How do you want to measure it? Is that way of measuring possible? If so, is it still interesting?

That final question is perhaps one of the most powerful. While overall choices about methods are a major step in research processes, Becker reminds us that small choices researchers make all along add up to larger effects, and some smaller choices close off future methods at certain process points.

Of course, *methods* is itself a slippery term. Consider, for example, Abbott's analysis of the five "most conspicuously successful" methods in social science research:

- ethnography (a procedure for gathering data)
- historical narration (a procedure for writing up results)
- causal analysis (a general analytic approach)
- small-n comparisons (a choice of data size, very effective for looking further into what the large quantitative results suggested—it improves "reading" of variables and allows for detailed comparisons)
- formalization (a specific analytic approach with purely abstract data) (15).

Each of these hones in on a different part of the research process and affords different analyses, but each is *method*.

We have been talking about methods in the abstract, but concretely now we can consider: methods of data collection, data treatment (turning data into analyzable material), and data analysis (what do the data *say?*) and interpretation (what do the data *mean?*). In the process, I hope to clarify some of the terms often used in relation to these methods: quantitative, qualitative, and empirical. These are terms that apply for all stages of data work. We often hear methods classified as empirical, quantitative, or qualitative. I would argue that the term *empirical* is really a larger descriptor of a research *tradition*, with data collection and treatment falling into quantitative or qualitative categories.

Data *collection*—the actual gathering of whatever it is you then plan to study—is thus most often described as quantitative, qualitative, or mixed. The National Science Foundation (NSF) classifies data collection as either quantitative (questionnaires, tests, database mining, etc.) or qualitative (observation, interviews, focus groups, etc.). Even this, however, is not as simple as it looks. For example, as Christina Hughes points out, "interviews may be structured and analyzed in a quantitative manner, as when numeric data is collected or when non-numeric answers are categorized and coded in numeric form[1]; as research advances, clear distinctions on the level of methods have become harder to maintain.

The NSF makes an interesting case for the power of mixed methods. They suggest that "[d]ata collected through quantitative methods are often believed to yield more objective and accurate information because they were collected using standardized methods, can be replicated, and, unlike qualitative data, can be analyzed using sophisticated statistical techniques," while qualitative methods serve the need for formative recommendations and narrative evaluations. But in fact, they argue, this dichotomy oversimplifies research: The quantitative approach is open to criticism for the potential flaws in data collection bias, flawed instruments, etc., while a qualitative approach can be rigorously set up for working with data. "[A]ll data collection— quantitative and qualitative—operates within a cultural context and is affected to some extent by the perceptions and beliefs of investigators and data collectors."

In addition, mixed methods are more likely to work from multiple sources of data, offering the WPA researcher a stronger foundation for both statistical analysis and thick description. Mixed methods do carry their own debates with them, in particular given the argument that qualitative and quantitative paradigms "have a different view of reality" and should always be considered complementary, not combinable for purposes of cross-validation or triangulation (Sale, Lohfeld, and Brazil 43).

As a WPA develops methods, it is essential to read other studies specifically for their methods, exploring how others have tried to understand your question or explain your issue. (Unfortunately, many currently available studies have not been very transparent with methods, making it difficult to enter into their procedures—in particular their procedures and data treatment and analysis.)

Once you have your data, qualitative *treatment* for empirical research generally will involve segmenting and coding the data, and there are many different ways to tackle this (see, for example, Bazerman and Prior; Geisler), essentially rendering your ordinal data (words) into numerical data. Quantitative data—numbers and what they represent—generally involves prepping what's collected for analysis (for example setting it up in Excel, SPSS, Dedoose, and so on).

Data *analysis* then provides ways of discerning, examining, comparing, contrasting, and interpreting meaningful patterns or themes in the data. There are two broad categories of ways to do this analysis systematically and rigorously: parametrically and nonparametrically. Christina Haas notes that "parametric statistics (e.g., ANOVA, t-test, regression analysis) assume that the groups of people from which a sample, and hence data, are drawn are normally distributed and independent. Non-parametric statistics do not rest on these underlying theoretical assumptions [. . .]" (2). The distinction is important. In the broader research world, nonparametric statistical analyses are considered second cousin to the reigning parametric models (Hughes highlights the "politics of legitimacy" associated with these kinds of choices), but nonparametric statistics most often are best for the kinds of data writing scholars analyze, and are quite powerful in the WPA domain of interaction with other institutional stakeholders. Generally speaking, the kinds of data from which WPA research is built are far more likely to not be normally distributed and independent. Haas also notes that nonparametric statistics can be far more useful for the more typical small-n studies in writing research.

Finally, data *interpretation* is the explanation of the study results and the re-contextualization of the results of that particular study into the larger discussion—with a return to the literature, the institutional framing, and/or the other studies and data out there. This is one of the research phases (recursive, of course) that differentiates research from assessment, and that sharply focuses on contributing to a broader pool of knowledge that evolves over time and offers the epistemological foundation for a discipline—our discipline.

WHAT (ELSE) IS A WPA RESEARCHER TO DO?

Carrying out research projects *is* WPA research. But many linked activities are equally important. As WPA, you will find you need to:

- Talk with colleagues and administrators about your research, including using the language of evidence and data. Your ability to discuss, highlight, engage/critique productively will be key—as well as eventually your ability to produce.
- Read research—a lot. Excellent research, poorly-designed research, research that contradicts what you believe you know.
- Embrace numbers, however difficult that may be at first. That attitude will open up understanding but also the ability to critique. An interesting example: Abbott points out that one of the most frequently-used methods is standard causal analysis, originally meant to help people make pragmatic decisions about courses of action, not to explore "why" or "how" but rather to say, "because we know x is correlated with y, if we do z we'll improve the situation." This approach wasn't meant to help "understand why and how things happen." But according to Abbott it is now used largely with a narrative (explanatory) function: "x is caused by y."
- Manage the time commitment to research carefully, identifying early in your position the ways in which you will protect the time for research. WPA work is far from conducive to that protection, though it is also highly conducive to fostering interesting research questions. Your WPA research agenda can well serve your scholarly career alongside your programmatic responsibilities and your institutional interactions. Indeed, assessment as a component of your WPA work can both generate research questions and offer you support for linked research work.
- Partner with other colleagues, departments, and offices. Learn to craft interdisciplinary research projects in which various participants' strengths complement each other. Network with colleagues at other institutions. Ferret out support for your research: undergraduates, graduate students, Institutional Research Offices . . .

WPA research is essential research. It changes us as WPAs, changes the nature of our interactions with colleagues within and beyond our programs, changes the rigor of our thinking and the creativity of our imaginations, and over time, changes the epistemological foundations of our field.

NOTE

1. I strongly recommend Christina Hughes, "Qualitative and Quantitative Approaches to Social Research," on this question. *Find*

WORKS CITED

Abbott, Andrew. *Methods of Discovery: Heuristics for Social Sciences.* New York: Norton and Company, 2004. Print.

Anson, Chris M. "The Intelligent Design of Writing Programs: Reliance on Belief or a Future of Evidence." *WPA: Writing Program Administration* 32.1 (2008): 11–36. Print. *Read*

Arum, Richard, and Josipa Roksa. *Academically Adrift: Limited Learning on College Campuses.* Chicago, IL: U of Chicago P, 2010.

Barton, Ellen. "Review: Empirical Studies in Composition." *College English* 59.7 (1997): 815–27. Print.

Bazerman, Charles, and Paul A. Prior. *What Writing Does and How It Does It: an Introduction to Analyzing Texts and Textual Practices.* Mahwah, NJ: Erlbaum, 2004. Print.

Bazerman, Charles. "The Disciplined Interdisciplinarity of Writing Studies." *Research in the Teaching of English* 46.1 (2011): 8–21. Print.

Bazerman, Charles. "Methods and Methodology: Practices, Principled Choices, and Post-facto Reflections." Dartmouth Summer Seminar for Composition Research. Hanover, NH. 2 August 2011. Presentation.

Becker, Howard. *Writing for Social Scientists.* Chicago, IL: U of Chicago P, 1986. Print.

Charney, Davida. "Empiricism is not a Four-Letter Word." *College Composition and Communication* 47 (1996): 567–93. Print. *read*

Durst, Russell. "Writing at the Postsecondary Level." *Research on Composition: Multiple Perspectives on Two Decades of Change.* Ed. Peter Smagorinsky. New York: Teachers College, 2006. 78–107. Print.

Flynn, Elizabeth A. "Feminism and Scientism." *College Composition and Communication* 46.3 (1995): 353–68. Print.

Geisler, Cheryl. *Analyzing Streams of Language: Twelve Steps to the Systematic Coding of Text, Talk, and Other Verbal Data.* New York: Longman, 2003. Print.

Haas, Christina. "Non-Parametric Statistics: A Brief Description and Rationale for Writing Researchers." Dartmouth Summer Seminar. Hanover, NH. 7 August 2011. Presentation.

Haswell, Richard H. "NCTE/CCCC's Recent War on Scholarship." *Written Communication* 22.2 (2005): 198–223. Print. *read*

—. "Teaching of Writing in Higher Education." *Handbook of Research on Writing: History, Society, School, Individual, Text.* Ed. Charles Bazerman. New York: Erlbaum, 2008. 331–46. Print.

Hayes, John R. *Reading Empirical Research Studies: the Rhetoric of Research.* Hillsdale, NJ: Erlbaum, 1992. Print.

Hughes, Christina. "Qualitative and Quantitative Approaches to Social Research." *The University of Warwick Department of Sociology.* 2006. Web. 15 August 2012.

National Science Foundation. *User-Friendly Handbook for Mixed Method Evaluations.* 1997. Web. 29 August 2012.

O'Neill, Peggy. "Arum and Roksa." WPA-L. 15 July 2011. Web. 9 May 2013.

Peck, Susan McDonald. "Data-Driven and Conceptually Driven Academic Discourse." *Written Communication* 6.4 (1989): 411–35. Print.

Sale, Joanna, Lynne Lohfeld, and Kevin Brazil. "Revisiting the Qualitative-Quantitative Debate: Implications for Mixed Methods Research." *Quality & Quantity* 36 (2002): 43–53. Print.

Voss, Ralph. "Composition and the Empirical Imperative." *JAC: Journal of Advanced Composition* 4.1 (1983): 5 –12. Print.

White, Edward M. "Arum and Roksa." WPA-L. 15 July 2011. Web. 9 May 2013.

Yancey, Kathleen Blake. "Looking Back as We Look Forward: Historicizing Writing Assessment." *College Composition and Communication* 50 (1999): 483–503. Print.

Appendix: Heuristics for Research Stages[*]

Situating your research:

- What are the major research programs in writing and composition research?
- What are they explaining, if anything?
- What do you know about your topic—how have you approached your literature review? Has that constrained you or afforded opportunities?
- What might you do differently?

Identifying your project's contours:

- What do you want to explain?
- By looking at what? (texts, meanings, individual behavior, individual cognition, social behavior, social cognition, relations, institutional conditions/constraints, consequences, effects of interventions, processes, etc.)

- What do you want to measure in order to explain?
- How do you want to measure it? Is that way of measuring possible? If so, is it still interesting?

Collecting data:

- What data are you collecting, and why?
- What else might you need?

How much is too little, too much?

- What data collection methods have others used to understand/study/explain your question?
- Have you found them to be explained in a way that allows you to imagine replicating them?

Treating and analyzing data:

- What treatment and what kinds of analysis of your data are you thinking you'll do?
- Why?
- What data treatment and analysis methods have others used to understand/study/explain your question?
- Have you found them to be explained in a way that allows you to imagine replicating them?

* Adapted from presentations by Charles Bazerman

31 What Is Principle?

Linda Adler-Kassner

Throughout this collection, you've read about the complexities, joys, and sometimes struggles of WPA work. You've probably gotten a sense of some the realities of it, as well. The diversity of activities and expectations linked to WPA activities is captured in the title of Diana George's edited collection, *Kitchen Cooks, Plate Twirlers, and Troubadours*—they involve a lot. A lot of activity, a lot of movement, a lot of conversation with people inside and outside of the institution. You've probably also realized being a WPA involves a lot of choices. Sometimes, these concern issues you have some pretty strong feelings about. For instance: You hear (second-hand) that your department chair has ordered a set of grammar exercises that she might want to have introduced in writing classes because she thinks students "can't write" when they're out of those courses, but she also wants to invest more money in the writing center. You learn that the dean is thinking of increasing class sizes, but decreasing teaching loads for some (and only some) lecturers by one course a year. You find that your program is being offered more TA lines, but in order to take advantage of them, you're going to need to let some long-time adjuncts go.

But sometimes—more often than not, really—WPA work doesn't involve these kinds of charged challenges (or the other moments about which people write to listservs with subject lines like, "Help!") Instead, being a WPA revolves around the day-to-day work of administering writing programs. This is a combination of balance of exciting opportunities (that you can help to create, like developing ways to showcase the program and its students, undertaking assessment projects that inform the development of curriculum, creation of new courses), and seemingly mundane activities, like course scheduling, making sure enrollments are where they need to be, and so on.

394

As a WPA, you'll need to decide how you (and, perhaps, others in your program) are going to handle all of these moments, whether they're charged decision points or seemingly "simple" questions about who should teach what course, in what room, at what time. It's important to note, however, that even these less complicated decisions are related to important issues—resources; location; positioning of the program, its faculty, and maybe even its students. And whatever choices you make related to these decisions means that you're privileging some things and letting others go. If the program chooses to work on one thing—say, developing a celebration highlighting student work—those are resources of time, personnel, and maybe even money that can't be used elsewhere. If an assessment focuses on one thing, it's also not looking at something else. As when we teach writing courses, as WPAs it's critical to remind ourselves that we, too, need to make conscious choices and reflect on the implications of those choices. Our *real* challenge, then, is to find a way to make these choices strategically. This is where principle comes in.

Principles are those beliefs and values that lie at the core of what we do. They represent ideas and values that are absolutely foundational for our work—for your work as a WPA and for the work of writers, faculty, and writing in your program. They are those "die on your sword" elements, the lines that you absolutely won't cross in making the decisions, choices, and sometimes compromises that comprise the everyday life of the WPA. Without working from principle, your actions—and, possibly, the actions of those in your program—are without foundation. An apt metaphor here might be a skyscraper. Without a firm foundation, the skyscraper can't stand; it just won't hold up its own structure. On the other hand, a skyscraper also has to be fairly flexible on top of that foundation. If it's too rigid, it will break in strong winds, earthquakes, and so on. Strength and flexibility are predicated on a strong foundation—and for WPAs, this foundation must consist of the principles underscoring our own work and that of our program.

STRATEGIES WITHOUT PRINCIPLES

Many years ago I attended a lecture about Paul Wellstone, the Minnesota Senator (and former political science professor) whose untimely death inspired the creation of Wellstone Action, a nonprofit that trains progressive community organizers and political candidates.

On a blackboard at the back of the room—I think coincidentally—was a quote I've since returned to many times: "Strategies without ideals is a menace, but ideals without strategies is a mess" (Llewellyn qtd. in Adler-Kassner, *Activist* 5). I'll come back to this idea of "ideals without strategies" in a moment. For now, it's the first part of the quote that's important, "Strategies without ideals is a menace." Here, substitute "principles" for "ideals." As a WPA, you'll encounter situations that require strategic thinking and some strategic compromises almost every day. You need to decide where the limits of your principles lie and what kinds of compromises you're willing to make. Principles will underscore the key questions you'll encounter as a WPA. These include (but are not limited to):

What kind of a WPA do you want to be? Do you want to work collaboratively with others—in your program, on your campus, and/or in the community? Or do you want to (or need to) work independently, representing the work of writing and writers and your program independent of those others? Whatever your response to this set of questions, you might say to yourself, "Of course, I want to [one or the other, or something that's not listed here]." But in fact, your response is neither obvious, nor commonsensical—it comes from principles that you hold about leadership, collaboration, participation, work with others, and so on.

What kinds of alliances do you want to build? Do you want to make connections with administrators? Other departments? Offices that serve students outside of academic affairs (or whatever division your writing program is located in)? Nonprofits off campus? One thing is certain: You can't make connections with everyone, so you need to make some priorities and do some thinking. Who are the most important folks with whom to build connections? Who are the next most important? After that? Here, too, the decisions that you make are informed by principles—about making connections, about who is important, and so on. I'll come back to this point shortly.

What kinds of compromises are you willing to make, if any? As the "controversial" questions that opened this essay illustrate—questions, by the way, which are drawn from actual experiences of WPAs—this is a job that virtually always requires compromise. It's at this juncture, especially, that principles are critical.

Here's an example: Let's say one of your principles is that defining what writing is and what is important in writing for students is a discussion that should be shared among writing teachers at all levels. From this principle, you seek to build alliances with local schools. The local schools are, by mandate (district, state, federal) heavily invested in teaching to the Common Core State Standards (CCSS) (see also O'Neill, this volume). You're invited to a working session to think about how secondary students can best work on "college and career readiness" (the mantra at the center of the CCSS). Specifically, you've been invited to contribute to the development of standardized, templated assignments that lead to repeated practice with the creation of the three "genres" (and those quotes are intentional) included in the CCSS Anchor Standards for Writing—argumentative writing, expository/informational writing, and narrative writing. These assignments will help students practice for the mandatory assessments that accompany the Common Core. You have read through the CCSS intended to delineate these anchor standards in action and recognize them as enormously prescriptive. As part of the invitation, the district office has also shared drafts of the criteria that will guide the machine-scored assessments used to evaluate students' work.

If you're like me, there's a lot here to find problematic. If one of your principles is that definitions of "good literacy" should be grounded in local contexts and shaped by students, faculty, administrators, and others in those contexts (Broad; Huot), the entire premise of the CCSS is a challenge. Additionally, the "college and career readiness" frame has been created by enormously powerful organizations and is based in a story that says that teachers (K–16) don't know what students need, so private entities will either respond to the question or strongly guide teachers' work with the questions (Adler-Kassner, "Companies"; Hesse). The three "genres" that students will practice with in the CCSS are what Paul Prior called "domesticated genres," forms of writing that exist only in the classroom and nowhere else (see Prior in Soliday); at the same time, the CCSS documents represent these genres as ones that will function across contexts, reflecting the kind of "general skills writing" that many researchers and teachers in our field (e.g., Bawarshi and Reiff; Bazerman; Downs and Wardle; also see Devitt for a discussion of genre pedagogies) have demonstrated is not only not useful but can also be detrimental to students' abilities to analyze writing in context and instructors' awareness of the need to unpack conventions of writing in context. Machine-scored assessments are bound to contribute to a further narrowing of the boundaries of these genres (Whithaus). You're also not sure who will be included in this group: Will there be teachers who will actually have to *teach* these things there? Or will it just be administrators and you, the "college representative"?

On the other hand—and this is a big, heavy, strong other hand—you know that this is the only way you're going to be able to make connections with K–12 colleagues and the school district that is near/surrounds your campus. Would that there were an easy answer to situations like this—but if you're like me, there's not. So again, you need to decide: What are your principles? And if multiple principles come into play in a situation like this, which one(s) are most important? Enacting strategies in a situation like this one *without* considering those principles can be highly problematic.

This, then, is why "strategies without [principles]" is a mess. It's critical to have a set of core ideals at the center of one's actions—lest one's actions reflect multiple principles, multiple ideals. It's also critical to continually reflect on those principles, checking them against situations that we identify in our administrative, teaching, research, and everyday life experience. Again, I'll provide just a short example. During the summer of 2012 I read a book by an educational historian/sociologist named David F. Labaree called *Somebody Has to Fail: The Zero Sum Game of Public Schooling*. Among its other astounding qualities, this book led me to think about my own principles and those of our field in relation to some very, very big picture issues that we currently face.

Painting with an excessively broad brush, I'll just say that Labaree examines several simultaneous and contradictory movements that have run through American education since the founding of the common school in the mid-nineteenth century. Among these movements are ones that position education as a public good that should be accessible to all, and ones that position education as a private good that should foster privilege. My own principles—and yours, too, probably—lead you to say, "Of course, education is a public good! Naturally! Education for citizenship, for democratic participation, for equality and social justice—that's what we're all about." At the same time, Labaree points out that movements to standardize education across all institutions, all schools—movements, in fact, something like (though not exactly like) the Common Core State Standards—reflect this conception of education. While many in our field object to the Common Core for reasons apart from the content of the standards (the process has been driven largely by educational operators with enormous amounts of money; the voices of actual educators were severely marginalized during the process of their creation; the assessments that will drive the standards, especially among one consortium, are controlled by the same large-money entities), we also chafe at the idea of common standards for learning.

Does this mean, then, that we in part think of education not as an entirely public good—a bit, perhaps, as a private good? Of course the entire *system* of postsecondary education in the US, differentiated as it is by institutional mission (see also Vander Lei and Pugh, this volume), reflects the idea of education as a *private* good in many ways (though the idea of mission-differentiation in a state like California, with a master plan that guides students toward particular kinds of schools based on their previous achievement, also reflects the idea of education as a public good in other ways). Since this is a conundrum I'm currently mulling myself, I don't have a response. What's important and productive for my own thinking about instances like this, though, is that they lead me to think through my principles very carefully. This might lead to a revision of those principles, or a restatement of principles in relation to actions. Because for me, as for others who act on principle, it's critical that those principles and actions be as aligned as we can possibly have them be.

PRINCIPLES WITHOUT STRATEGIES

Identifying principles, as I've suggested, is critical to WPA work; but as the second part of that quote from the back of the law school classroom says, "[principles] without strategies is [*sic*] a mess." That's because if one identifies principles but doesn't think about how to act on those in a way that is simultaneously consistent and flexible, the principles really won't matter because you won't accomplish anything. When many of us think about these kinds of ideas, we go to Michel deCerteau's work on strategies and tactics. DeCerteau defines "strategy" as a position occupied by the very powerful and "tactics" the activities that the "other" uses to circumvent or try to seize ground in the face of strategy (xix). As I'm using them here, though, strategies and tactics reflect definitions that come not from cultural theory, but from community organizing. "Strategies" are those long-term visions that we have that are closely linked to principles and values; "tactics" are the activities that we undertake to enact those strategies. As Erik Peterson, a community organizer for Wellstone Action, explained in an interview, strategies and tactics are "conjoined. [. . .] A strategy is a road map to build the power necessary to accomplish a purpose [. . .] and tactics are the tools/actions taken as part of a strategy" (qtd. in Adler-Kassner, *Activist* 94). Tactics, then, are where the rubber meets the road—but they must be shaped within strategy, or they just won't make any sense.

I'll return to the Common Core scenario that I've laid out above—a scenario, I might add, that many of us may encounter in the near- or middle-term future (if we haven't already)—to consider the possibilities. Let's say that one of the principles at the core of your WPA work is to build alliances. At the same time, perhaps one of your core principles is that writing instruction should cultivate writerly flexibility, the ability to analyze and move among different audiences, expectations, and genres for writing (CWPA). And let's add that a third principle is that writing should be grounded in genuine purposes, for genuine audiences, and that those purposes and audiences should be meaningful for the writer. If you read the Common Core State Standards and find that they focus on the production of domesticated genres, that might pose a conundrum.

With these principles in mind, you head to that meeting that I described earlier with the folks who have invited you—local school administrators, perhaps some teachers, others. You know that they are invested in the Common Core—because they must be, because they want to be, perhaps because of a combination of both. You, however, are not, because the Common Core (the standards themselves, the process through which they were developed, the assessments, whatever else) violates your principles. You thus bring two things: an attitude and a handout. The attitude is that the CCSS are wrong and you're going to tell people just what's wrong with them; the handout reiterates your position.

Remember that we're focusing now on principles without strategies. In this situation you might be able to explain your objections and outline your beliefs, sure. And the people in the meeting might listen and even, in some ways, agree with you. You will have outlined your principles, articulating them clearly and well. And then . . . what? Your interlocutors need to figure out a way to work within the CCSS; you've just explained that the Standards violate your principles and that you're sticking to those principles no matter what. You've effectively ended any chance for collaboration or alliance building, which might, in fact, be *another* of your principles. In a situation like this one or one of the many others that you might (will) face as a WPA, you've got to think about which principles are most important and about the always-critical relationship between what the quote on the blackboard refers to as principles and strategies. In other words, you have to decide which of your principles to privilege and which to leave (perhaps temporarily) behind. If you engage in strategies without principles, your activities might not be aligned—that is, they might reflect a number of potentially contradictory positions. On the other hand, if you act on principles without thinking strategically, you run the risk of alienating potential allies, isolating yourself and, probably, your program. Both situations are sticky.

One more thing, too, on the principles-strategies connection. For the sake of illustration, I've invoked a situation related to the Common Core State Standards where complexities are easier to see. While I'm not suggesting that the day-to-day decisions of WPA work—like scheduling, or developing new initiatives, or creating assessment projects—need to be as tricky as these discussions (or others like them) might be, I *am* suggesting that these daily decisions are as much a part of the principle-strategy continuum as more complicated situations are. As a WPA, it's critical to remember that our choices have larger implications for students, faculty, and even (sometimes) perceptions of writing and writers on our campuses. While we need to be spontaneous and go with our instincts (sometimes—and even oftentimes), we can do that more effectively when even those instincts are rooted in principle. In this sense, making the principle-strategy connection is somewhat analogous to writing itself. We start by articulating principles and consciously making connections between principles and activities; as we become more familiar with the elements of these principles and their implications for strategies, those connections become more ingrained and "second nature." At the same time, as I've tried to illustrate by sharing my thinking following Labaree's *Someone Has to*

Fail, it's also critical to continually examine these principles and their implications for practice.

Rubber Meets Road: Forming and Acting on Principles in Alliance With Others

The words "allies" and "alliances" have appeared several times here, so it probably comes as no surprise that this last section focuses on working with others from a point of principle. While the idea that acting in collaboration is an important and/or useful activity is itself a principle, I would argue that it's pretty critical—even essential—for successful WPA work. This principle extends from a number of tenets of composition and rhetoric, from the idea that writing itself is a collaborative and social act situated within and among specific communities (e.g., Bazerman) to the idea that the work of writing program administration involves, in part, building alliances with others on campus and in community (Adler-Kassner, *Activist*; Goldblatt). Your writing program won't exist in isolation from the institution where it is situated. It might also be that there are also expectations—implicit or explicit—of some relationship between the program and the broader institution. For no other reason, then, you'll want to make connections with others.

Broadly framed, principled alliances can be built proactively or reactively. Reactively, you see or respond to a situation that you find compelling or problematic and go from there. While WPAs frequently encounter efforts that put us in a reactive position, it's actually more effective to work proactively. From this stance, you as a writing program director seek conversations with others on campus in order to find areas of common interest from which to build connections. Eli Goldblatt discusses this kind of conversation in a terrific chapter called "Lunch" in *Because We Live Here: Sponsoring Literacy Beyond the College Curriculum*. As Goldblatt explains, "literacy education depends on a network of relationships that must be carefully nurtured and maintained if students are to grow and learn, if teachers are to feel supported and valued, if researchers are to dig deep into the scene they hope to understand. In fact," he goes on, "the most important job of WPAs is to build and extend the sustaining relationships that make their programs possible [. . .] caring for crucial relationships may be the necessary condition for everything else one is expected to accomplish" (146–47).

Whether reactive or proactive, precisely the approach you want to use to develop principled alliances depends, again, on your principles as a WPA. It's possible, though, to draw on approaches from community organizing to inform your choices about approach. To illustrate, I'll focus on two possible approaches and strategies. Two caveats, though: First, these approaches can definitely be blended. Second, choices about when and whether to use one or both must also be based in the principles-strategies balance.

In the first approach, you decide that your goal is to help build connections between others—others in your program, on your campus, in your community. The primary principle motivating this work is that *alliance building* is most important and that the specific agenda motivating alliances is, to some extent, secondary. Putting people into contact with each other comes first. Proceeding from this principle, you can use questions to find out where peoples' primary interests in relation to writing (and the work of writing instruction) lie. From this perspective, you'd want to start by identifying possible allies and considering why they're of interest to you. Then, you'll want to find out about those potential allies and their interests. What motivates them? Inspires them? Makes them angry? You would then have a very broad-based, "get to know you" discussion about these issues. After the conversation, you would reflect on what you learned, keeping track of those motivating/inspiring/angering elements. Then, you'd continue having these conversations with a variety of people—other faculty/instructors in the writing program and in other disciplines or departments, administrators, community members who seemed important to connect with. After a series of conversations focused on identifying interests, passions, goals, and motivations, you would then identify a defined project, activity, or other action that you and those others might undertake that represented everyone's *shared* interests, at least in relation to the immediate issues raised in discussions (though perhaps not long-term). In this way you would act on the principle of alliance building and begin to build a network of allies with whom to act based on shared principles.

The advantages of this approach to principled alliance building are many. Among them: It gives you a chance to get to know people without trying to advance a particular principle (beyond the principle that it's important to get to know people). It enables you to help put people who might (or might not) recognize their shared interests in touch with each other. And it makes it possible to identify discrete, doable projects that people from a range of positions can accomplish. On the other hand, while this is a great strategy for getting started with alliance building, connections that revolve around discrete, accomplishable projects might not always be long-sustained. Additionally, it requires you to put the principle of "alliance building" above all other principles—in other words, the project that might emerge from the shared interests of others might *not* reflect other principles that you hold. For instance, if the shared project that emerges concerns adopting a new, more efficient placement system that uses a multiple-choice grammar test, that's easy to accomplish and might represent shared interests—but might perhaps violate principles that you hold about authentic assessment. This strategy of alliance building, then, might be more useful when you're new in a position because it gives you a chance to get to know people and a place.

In the second approach to alliance building, your goal is to blend your own values and ideas with those of others. In this instance, the primary principle behind the effort is that alliances should be built on important principles shared by all partners, and that these shared principles should form the basis of short-term projects that lead to and advance longer-term goals. To engage in this kind of alliance building, the first step is to identify those principles and values that are central to you and your writing program. Then, you want to identify two to three issues that you think are critical to work on related to those principles—something like lowering class size, or decreasing teaching load, or gaining better salaries for instructors. Then, you want to articulate connections between those issues and your principles and values.

Next, you'll want to locate others—possible allies, those with an interest (aka, "stakeholders") in writing instruction and/or your program, and others. You want to think about their motivations or interests in the issues that you have in common, and then work from both of those to try to facilitate a discussion. You have a discussion with these possible allies about their interests, a conversation that might ultimately lead to shared activities. For instance, on many campuses student retention is a significant issue; because first-year writing courses are often one of the first sites where students make meaningful connections with representatives from the institution (those instructors in your program), the idea of making first-year composition courses a good experience for students *and* instructors is often a shared goal and might serve as a useful starting place for building alliances with those who are invested in this goal. Be sure to look beyond those stakeholders who might first come to mind, too, like academic deans. Student services units—deans of students, counseling centers, and other offices that are traditionally seen as focusing on the so-called "soft skills" of student life (such as time management or study habits) can be potential allies. Make contact with these folks, thinking about how you might build something together. The key, though, is to balance your principles and potential relationships, so that both are advanced simultaneously.

Conclusion: Principles and Strategies

As I hope this chapter has illustrated, principles are almost *always* at the core of what we do—whether as WPAs or as instructors. As a WPA, though, it becomes even more important to make sure that those principles are clearly articulated and then that we work from them as best we can to be consistent in our strategies. Principles with strategies; strategies underscored by principle—these are the foundational underpinnings of effective writing program administration. At the same time, though, it's critical to remember one last principle: WPA work, like all teaching and learning, is a process that involves experimentation, success, and sometimes things that aren't as successful. Just as our students benefit from encountering challenges that are unexpected, so do we—and just as they learn from occasions when things don't go quite as planned, so might we. The best we can do is keep principles in mind and work as strategically as we can to enact those in our programs, our institutions, and our communities.

Works Cited

Adler-Kassner, Linda. *The Activist WPA: Changing Stories about Writing and Writers*. Logan: Utah State UP, 2008. Print.

—. "The Companies We Keep *or* The Companies We Would Like to Try to Keep: Strategies and Tactics in Challenging Times." *WPA: Writing Program Administration* 36.1 (2012): 119–40. Print.

Bawarshi, Anis, and Mary Jo Reiff. *Genre: An Introduction*. West Lafayette, IN: Parlor Press, 2010.

Bazerman, Charles. "Speech Acts, Genres, and Activity Systems: How Texts Organize Activity and People." *What Writing Does and How It Does It*.

Ed. Charles Bazerman and Paul Prior. Mahwah, NJ: Erlbaum, 2004. 309–39. Print.

Broad, Bob. *What We Really Value: Beyond Rubrics in Teaching and Assessing Writing.* Logan: Utah State UP, 2002. Print.

Council of Writing Program Administrators (CWPA), National Council of Teachers of English (NCTE), and National Writing Project (NWP). *The Framework for Success in Postsecondary Writing.* 2011. Web. 2 January 2013.

DeCerteau, Michel. *The Practice of Everyday Life.* Minneapolis: University of Minnesota Press, 1984. Print.

Devitt, Amy. "Teaching Critical Genre Awareness." *Genre in a Changing World.* Ed. Charles Bazerman, Adair Bonin, and Deborah Figueiredo. Fort Collins, CO: WAC Clearinghouse/Parlor Press, 2009. 337–51. Print.

Downs, Doug, and Elizabeth Wardle. "Teaching About Writing, Righting Misconceptions: (Re)Envisioning 'First Year Composition' as 'Introduction to Writing Studies.'" *College Composition and Communication* 58.4 (June 2007): 552–83. Print.

George, Diana. *Kitchen Cooks, Plate Twirlers, and Troubadours.* Portsmouth, NH: Boynton/Cook, 1999. Print.

Goldblatt, Eli. *Because We Live Here: Sponsoring Literacy Beyond the College Curriculum.* Creskill, NJ: Hampton, 2007. Print.

Hesse, Doug. "Who Speaks for Writing?: Expertise, Ownership, and Stewardship." *Who Speaks for Writing: Stewardship for Writing Studies in the 21ˢᵗ Century.* Ed. Jennifer Rich and Ethna D. Lay. New York: Peter Lang, 2012. 9-22. Print.

Huot, Brian. *(Re)Articulating Writing Assessment.* Logan: Utah State UP, 2004. Print.

Labaree, David F. *Someone Has to Fail: The Zero-Sum Game of Public Schooling.* Cambridge, MA: Harvard UP, 2010.

Soliday, Mary. *Everyday Genres.* Carbondale: NCTE/CCCC and Southern Illinois UP, 2011. Print.

Whithaus, Carl. "Challenges of Using Automated Essay Evaluation (AEE) Software for Assessing Multimodal Writing." *Measuring Writing: Recent Insights Into Theory, Methodology, and Practices.* Ed. Marion Tillema, Gert Rijlaarsdam, Huub Van den Bergh, and Elke Van Steedam. London: Emerald Books, forthcoming. Print.

32 What Is a Personal Life?

Douglas Hesse

On the morning I'd set aside to begin drafting this chapter, I woke to rainwater dripping through the living room ceiling. A day imagined for writing was, instead, spent on the telephone with roofers and in an attic seeking leaks. A practical matter yet again interrupted my real work. Or that's one way of looking at it, the way I'll confess seeing most of my career. An alternative is to see the event simply as life as it is.

The very question "What is a personal life?" seems naïve in a (post) postmodern age, implying some Thoreauvian self to be created and preserved from the world's hurly-burly. Constructivist theory and daily circumstance indicate otherwise. It may be more sensible to ask, "What is an interpersonal life?" I will, in fact, ask this question below. Setting aside broad philosophical questions that have vexed folks from Plato to Montaigne to Dr. Phil, however, anyone considering WPA work should understand the relationship between the time and care one might devote to The Job versus the time and care to Life Not Working. I'll concede it's an invidious binary, easily mashed, but insisting on some distinction between the two realms is most of my point.

Despite their representation in the popular sphere, college professors work a lot. Many folks see only the nine or twelve or fifteen hours per week in the classroom, only the thirty to forty-five weeks of teaching per year, only the ample holidays and breaks, only lawns being mowed at 2:00 p.m. Tuesday or bread being bought in Safeway late mornings. They conclude we have things pretty comfy. And, to be sure, tenure-line faculty do, at least in terms of flexibility, autonomy, and self-direction. What the public doesn't see, of course, are the hours of course preparation, of responding to student writing or projects, advising, working on committees, and conducting research. When numerous surveys have shown that these efforts work out to fifty to sixty hours per week, the public tends to reject the findings as inflated self-reports. Legislators and trustees have, thus, sought to substitute "productivity" for "time" as the measure of faculty efforts: students taught, grants won, papers published, technologies and other intellectual goods transferred into the civic or commercial realm.

Now, professionals everywhere these days are working long—and longer—and longer hours. Professors should expect no sympathy from others about their workloads, not from other professionals (though pay differences might get them a nod from corporate office) and certainly not from struggling middle-class managers, laborers, adjuncts, or interns. Current economic circumstances compel everyone to work comparatively harder than thirty years ago. The particular distinction for professors, however, is that, beyond a point, their work-time is self-inflicted—and boundlessly so.

DYNAMOS THAT DRIVE WPA WORK LIFE

We can always make a class better, spend more time with students, in person or on screen, conduct another study, read another article, join another task force, attend another conference, post to another listserv, write another book or article, and so on, endlessly. The "life of the mind," however old-fashioned and embarrassing that term sounds, is autotelically seductive. Beyond the nervous engine, to some extent justified, of "Am I working hard enough?" is the reality of "I like being busy on this stuff." Although job realities batter the habits of reading, writing, thinking, and talking that seduced most of us to higher education, strong elements of our undergraduate pasts persist, including our relative autonomy and self-direction. Calls for more work and productivity, then, are catalyzed by the proclivities and desires we ourselves bring to the job. Having worked nearly a dozen summers on the back of a garbage truck, I can tell you that not every job activates the same impulse to work more.

My point, to overstay its welcome, is that for professors, "external" demands to work long hours simply magnify "internal" desires to engage in that work. The result is continuous pressure for work life to crowd out the personal.

That pressure is exacerbated for faculty in the role of department chairs or WPAs. A good deal of the nine-to-five day is spent on efforts external to a WPA's personal teaching and scholarly commitments and interests. We attend meetings, answer questions, write reports. We talk with students, talk with colleagues, interpret policies, make them. We manage budgets, plan events, change curricula. We lead faculty development, solve problems, identify opportunities. We hire colleagues, schedule them, evaluate them. We work with layers of constituents and stakeholders at levels from the program to the college to the institution and beyond. A good deal of this work is intellectually stimulating and immediately rewarding. We feel important doing it, and we are. However, like "mere" professorial work, program development and leadership is inexhaustible. Unless one assumes simply a managerial, caretaking role, there is always something to be made bigger or better.

Compounding things, if the WPA teaches or has research interests in areas beyond administration, much of that work has to happen evenings and weekends. Now, this isn't to claim that professional administrative activities consume forty hours spent in the office; realistically for me, the actual time on those tasks is probably more like twenty to thirty. The point, however, is that a certain amount of administrative time is unpredictable and disruptive; you never know when a faculty member is going to be in a car accident or a student is going to complain about her or his professor. I've found, then, that I can productively do certain kinds of things in the office during the work day, but concentrated writing isn't one of them. No doubt, many WPAs are more effective and focused than I am; I'll simply point out that the roles of administrator, teacher, and scholar each bring both external and internal drives to ever more work and that for WPAs, even more than professors, this pushes activity into weekends and evenings.

Finally impelling everything is digital life. WPAs, like people in every profession these days, are never completely out of the office (though I suggest that all of us might do a better job trying). Writing at home of an evening, I go online to check a fact, and while I'm there I check e-mail or Facebook or the WPA-L, and any of these can bring a problem or invitation. I waylay myself to put out this fire or to fan this ember into flame. Pretty soon the paragraph that might have taken thirty minutes to write has taken ninety, and the time I could have spent reading a novel or turning a chair spindle on a basement lathe or shooting baskets in the driveway has disappeared into the Internet.

Multiply this evening by three hundred days a year, and a certain dynamic of Life as Work becomes clear.

INTERLUDE: WHY SHOULD A WPA CARE ABOUT PERSONAL LIFE?

On the one hand, why should anyone tell anyone to care about having a personal life? Someone might well find being always at work, married to the job, as it were, exciting and sustaining. Ethical or social imperatives to "live a balanced life" are socially constructed, after all, and what makes one person happy might render another one miserable. Still, I suggest two main reasons for cultivating a modest to robust personal life.

The first concerns health. As someone who ran 10Ks in my twenties and played fierce basketball and tennis through my thirties, I was surprised in my forties to start getting puffy enough to make sure I was always on the "shirts" (rather than the "skins") in increasingly rare team sports. Working for tenure and promotion can be sedentary activities, with lots of time spent writing, thinking, and talking, too often with a coffee cup in hand. Success insidiously begets torpor. New curricula, committees, or speaking invitations spawn more keyboard time. For example, I'm drafting this section of the chapter on a Sunday afternoon, foregoing the hike in the mountains my wife and I usually take on Sundays. Not a little irony there. I'll leave it to Dr. Oz and the popular press to extoll the virtues of physical health and the cost of its lack. I'll just say that the press of academic work makes it easy to justify some future time when you'll get back in shape, and pretty soon your flabby self reminds you that the time is past. If you want to get even more crass about health, there's the plentiful research on the relative success of "attractive" people, "physically fit," not just desirable.

There's mental health, too. Even the best academic jobs will occasionally generate frustration and anxiety. Even when all's well, there's always more to be done. WPAs have the additional measure of fretting not only about their careers but also about their colleagues' and program's futures. If the entirety of one's identity nests in the basket of work and that basket inevitably wears a hole or gets crushed, what's the consoling alternative? Life is full of practical and existential crises, from leaky roofs to lonely Friday nights, from wondering who visits you in the hospital after surgery to who drives fifty miles when your car breaks down. A healthy personal life adds a measure of psychic resilience. Students and even colleagues pass through our lives. Timely and smart articles sediment in the archives. What remains? The midlife crisis or the rueful day after retirement are commonplaces in our culture, accompanied by homiletics like "No one on their deathbed ever wished they'd spent more of their life at the desk," and yet these homespun clichés bear truth, even for ever-so-wise intellectuals living the life of the mind.

The second reason WPAs ought to care about their personal lives is that a healthy one helps you not only deal with your job, it helps you do your job better. A lot of a WPA's stakeholders aren't professors, and they're certainly not compositionists or WPAs. It's rhetorically strategic, then, not to mention sanity-preserving, to see situations through broader lenses. When my kids were in high school, their friends would show up to watch *Lost* over pizza. Trying not to be the Creepy Dad, I nonetheless gained insights into adolescent life that complicated and complemented what I thought I knew about first-year students in my writing courses. I also learned to see students in my office as something more complex than "problems." From my friends Brian, an optometrist, and Tom, an attorney, both of whom I met in the Colorado Symphony chorus, I've gained a better understanding of smart conservative political viewpoints. Going to movies, concerts, and plays provides examples and ideas for teaching and also ice-breaking topics for talking to the provost or chancellor or meeting with community groups. Riding my bike, hiking a trail, or swimming at noon (albeit not as often as I should), clear my head in ways that make me more productive, as can the simple act of walking around campus for fifteen minutes when I realize I've been spinning my wheels.

ADVICE?

WPAs should pay attention to their personal lives, actively and intentionally so. I hope that reasons of personal wellbeing are sufficiently compelling, but if not, please take license in my assertion above that life outside work benefits life inside it.

To create personal time, first be mindful of how you're actually spending work time. The autonomous nature of WPA time, combined with the blurred boundaries of digital experience, creates invisible inefficiencies. The mere fact that I've sat at my desk for an afternoon doesn't mean that I've been highly (or even modestly) productive during that time, though I can certainly tell myself and the world that I've been busy. Now, I'm not invoking some Fordist idea of efficiency and yield; writing and other "idea work" can be fickle and resistant, but perhaps not to the degree we assume or find comfortable.

I know several WPAs who set specific boundaries. No e-mail from 6:00 p.m. to 6:00 a.m. Three nights a week and one day each weekend when no work comes home. By building even modest constraints, they force themselves to get work done in the time they have left. That always seems like a fine approach, though it's one I follow better by aspiration than by actual practice. At least, however, I check the delusion that there is no time; maybe there's less than I'd like, but there's more than I fancy.

To claim personal time, I have to schedule at least some of it, which sounds indeed perverse. But currently, I know that every Tuesday night from September through June, from 7:00 to 10:00, I'll be rehearsing with the Colorado Symphony Chorus and that, further, six to eight weekends during the year I'll be performing concerts, including four days in August at the Aspen Festival. I've made time for singing ever since high school, and while I've been a WPA, I've performed in everything from church choirs to community theater productions. I encourage WPAs, then, to make time for personal interest or passion, whether it's ceramics, Tae Kwon Do, gardening, a reading group, Bible study, working a local homeless shelter, or what have you. It pretty much doesn't matter what your interest is; the point is to have some locus beyond campus. Things that have meetings are especially valuable because they dislodge us from work, though there's the danger of overbooking ourselves as insanely as America has overscheduled its children.

Of course, your personal life circumstances frame some of your options. For example, my three children are now grown, but when they weren't, my personal life involved huge amounts of sitting in bleachers or auditoriums. I announced swimming meets. I was the parent liaison to school theater and arts activities (frequently being the only dad in a room of a dozen moms, though that's quite another story), and all of these endeavors had the decided benefit of not being among other professors and not talking about professorial things. With the nest empty and a thousand-mile move from Normal, Illinois, I realized how much

I relied on my kids' activities for social connections and opportunities. That's not a bad thing but, rather, a prod that I had to reinvent connections. At some point, I'll no longer sing well enough to perform at a high level, and I'll have to do it again.

Be attentive to both personal and interpersonal time. Because people inhabit different places on the spectrum from introversion and extraversion, the proportions of alone vs. together time they need vary. I'm not much worried about extraverts whose personal sanity will compel them out of the office. For those several of us more introverted, I fret a bit more. No doubt a healthy personal life can focus on time alone: reading, writing letters, taking photographs, watching the game no one else wants to see, attending concerts and galleries. But I think we all need some element of friendship and direct human connection in our personal lives, need to spend at least a corner of it with others. Whether that requires a partner or, even a single best friend, I won't say, but I think the number of us fitted for truly solitary lives is pretty scant. Don't let the need to finish three more e-mails keep you from joining the group for early drinks. Someone else might like that hike, too, even if it makes scheduling more complicated. If you do have a partner or spouse, it's stupidly easy to let work demands so capture your focus and time that a spring of joy and sustenance becomes a well of empty. I've told one cautionary tale elsewhere (Hesse).

Finally, there are chances to craft a semblance of personal life even within the professional, especially as a WPA. Over the years, over countless conferences, professional committees, and e-mails, I've formed friendships with several colleagues across the country. These are relationships that go beyond work. I know how the hockey season is going for one WPA's son. I know how another's church organ-building spouse fares in retirement. I know who follows college baseball (season tickets, even), who swims, who can recommend hiking trails on the California coast, how the fishing is in Canada, who is raising a daughter's daughter. I've been to the wedding of a WPA's child, though she lives two thousand miles away. When my youngest daughter moved to Los Angeles, I called a WPA friend, asking her to be the local "emergency parent," knowing she'd say yes. I've done the same in Chicago. I've been that "parent" for kids who've come to Denver. I dream my perfect neighborhood, populated by all my WPA friends.

I risk devolving into Polonius or, perhaps worse Stuart Smiley, though with Al Franken now a senator, perhaps that's not so bad. My plain message is that, as much as it seems unnecessary on your career's sunniest days—or impossible on its most harried—you'll be better off for insisting on a healthy personal life. That's triply true when the rain comes through the roof, which it certainly will.

WORK CITED

Hesse, Douglas. "The WPA as Father, Husband, Ex." *Kitchen Cooks, Plate Twirlers, and Troubadours: Writing Program Administrators Tell Their Stories.* Ed. Diana George. Portsmouth, NH: Boynton Cook/Heineman, 1999. 44 –55. Print.

Contributing Authors

Linda Adler-Kassner is Professor of Writing and Director of the Writing Program at the University of California, Santa Barbara. She is also past president of the Council of Writing Program Administrators. She is the author of seven books, including *The Activist WPA* and *Reframing Writing Instruction* (with Peggy O'Neill) and many articles and book chapters. Her recent research focuses on how disciplines (including composition) outline disciplinary identity and the implications of this outlining for broader discussions about postsecondary teaching and learning.

Paul V. Anderson is Director of Writing Across the University at Elon University. He is currently partnering with colleagues in Sweden in a study of international collaboration in globally networked learning environments. He is also co-PI in a project sponsored by the National Science Foundation that focuses on incorporating communication instruction (writing, speaking, reading, teaming) in computer science and software engineering curricula. Anderson is a Fellow of the Society for Technical Communication, Association of Teachers of Technical Writing, and Institute of Environment and Sustainability at Miami University (Ohio).

Chris M. Anson is University Distinguished Professor and Director of the Campus Writing and Speaking Program at North Carolina State University, where he helps faculty in nine colleges to use writing and speaking in the service of students' learning and improved communication. He has published fifteen books and over one hundred articles and book chapters, and has spoken widely across the United States and in twenty-six other countries. He is past president of the Council of Writing Program Administrators and currently Chair of the Conference on College Composition and Communication.

Hannah Ashley earned her PhD from Temple University in Interdisciplinary Urban Education; she has published in journals including *The Journal of Basic Writing, Pedagogy, Research in the Teaching of English,* and *Reflections on Community-Based Writing Instruction,* as well as multiple edited collections. At this writing, she serves as the Director of Composition and the Coordinator for the minor in Youth Empowerment and Urban Studies (YES) at West Chester University, and is the founder of Writing Zones 12.5, a college access writing center program. She lives in Philadelphia and is the proud parent of three children.

William P. Banks is Director of the University Writing Program and Associate Professor of Rhetoric and Writing at East Carolina University, where he teaches graduate and undergraduate courses in writing, research, and pedagogy. He has published articles on history, rhetoric, pedagogy, writing program administration, and sexuality in several recent books, as well as in *English Journal, College English, Computers and Composition, Dialogue,* and *Teaching English in the Two-Year College.* His current book project, *Queer Literacies,* explores the ways in which gay men and lesbians articulate literacies of queer(ed) identities.

Mary R. Boland is Associate Professor of English at California State University, San Bernardino, where she teaches undergraduate and graduate courses in writing, discourse studies, composition theory, literacy studies, and pedagogies for the language use classroom. Her work on the institutional politics of composition studies and academic freedom has also appeared in *College English* and in *Who Speaks For Writing? Stewardship in Writing Studies in the 21st Century.* She is a union activist, director of directed self-placement, and coordinator for the MA in English Composition.

Christiane Donahue is Director of the Institute for Writing and Rhetoric and Associate Professor of Linguistics at Dartmouth College. She has been working in particular to transform US understandings of the value of European writing research traditions and the depth and breadth of this work on higher education writing. Donahue's research interests include: cross-cultural and cross-disciplinary analysis of undergraduate student writing, longitudinal studies and studies of knowledge transfer across writing contexts, and the development of multi-method research approaches drawn from European and US traditions. She has created the Dartmouth Summer Seminar for Composition Research, a program designed to develop and support future generations of composition researchers using data-driven methods.

Doug Downs is Associate Professor and Director of Composition in the Department of English at Montana State University, where he also designed the department's broadfield writing major. He studies composition and research pedagogy through lenses of cultural and personal conceptions of writing, and his most recent research examines student reading practices in the current age of screen literacy. With Elizabeth Wardle, he authored *Writing about Writing*, an anthology of research that supports the writing-about-writing pedagogies the two first wrote about in their 2007 *College Composition and Communication* article "Teaching about Writing, Righting Misconceptions: (Re)Envisioning FYC as Intro to Writing Studies."

Lauren Fitzgerald is Associate Professor of English and Director of the Wilf Campus Writing Center at Yeshiva University, where she also directed the Yeshiva College Composition Program and coordinated YC's curriculum review. She has authored and coauthored articles and chapters on writing centers, teaching writing, and writing program administration for *Composition Studies, WPA: Writing Program Administration, The Writing Center Journal, The Writing Lab Newsletter,* and a number of edited collections. She edited *The Writing Center Journal* with Melissa Ianetta (2008–2013), co-led the CWPA Summer Workshop (2005, 2006), and was a 2007 IWCA Summer Institute leader.

Tom Fox is Professor of English at California State University, Chico and Associate Director, Site Development for the National Writing Project. He teaches rhetoric and composition at all levels of the curriculum and has been active in writing program administration at Chico. His research focuses on questions of equity and access. He is the author of three books, including *Defending Access,* and several articles and book chapters on the politics of writing instruction. He is currently working on a book-length study of networks and public argument.

Chris W. Gallagher is Professor of English and Writing Program Director at Northeastern University in Boston, where he teaches undergraduate and graduate courses in writing and rhetoric. He is author or coauthor of four books, including most recently *Our Better Judgment: Teacher Leadership for Writing Assessment* (with Eric Turley). He has also published numerous articles in writing studies and education journals. Before becoming Writing Program Director at Northeastern, he was the Composition Coordinator at the University of Nebraska.

Roger Gilles and *Dan Royer* work and teach at Grand Valley State University near Grand Rapids, Michigan, where they have each directed the composition program and served as department chair. Their 1998 article on directed self-placement, "Directed Self-Placement: An Attitude of Orientation," led to a national conversation about DSP. In 2003, they coedited *Directed Self-Placement: Principles and Practices.*

Gregory R. Glau is Director of the University Writing Program at Northern Arizona University. He is coeditor of the *Bedford Bibliography for Teachers of Basic Writing* (1st and 2nd editions with Linda Adler-Kassner; 3rd edition with Chitralekha Duttagupta). Glau is also coauthor of *Scenarios for Writing* and *The McGraw-Hill Guide: Writing for College, Writing for Life* (with Duane Roen and Barry Maid, 3rd edition in-press). He has published in *The Journal of Basic Writing, WPA: Writing Program Administration* (which he coedited from 2004 to 2007), *Rhetoric Review, English Journal, The Writing Instructor, IDEAS Plus*, and *Arizona English Bulletin*.

Eli Goldblatt is professor of English and Director of First Year Writing at Temple University. Through New City Writing, the outreach arm of the writing program, he has helped to support Open Borders Project, Tree House Books, Temple Writing Academy, and other projects in collaboration with community partners. Goldblatt was the founding director of the Community Learning Network, the office that supports community-based learning at Temple. Among other scholarly and creative publications, he is the author of *Because We Live Here: Sponsoring Literacy Beyond the College Curriculum* and *Writing Home: A Literacy Autobiography.*

Robert M. Gonyea is Associate Director of the Indiana University Center for Postsecondary Research, where he coordinates research and reporting for the National Survey of Student Engagement and associated projects. His interests include the assessment of college and university quality, writing as a form of engagement in learning, high-impact practices for undergraduate learners, and survey research methodology.

Kristine Hansen is Professor of English at Brigham Young University, where she teaches undergraduate courses in professional writing, rhetorical style, and the history of rhetoric, as well as graduate courses on rhetorical theory and research methods. She has directed the English Department's composition program; as Associate Dean of Undergraduate Education from 1998–2004, she directed the university's writing across the curriculum program. She has served on the executive board of the Council of Writing Program Administrators and on the editorial board of its journal. Her most recent book (coedited with Christine R. Farris) is *College Credit for Writing in High School: The "Taking Care of" Business*, published by NCTE in 2010.

Susanmarie Harrington is Professor of English and Director of the Writing in the Disciplines Program at the University of Vermont. Previously a department chair and first-year composition program director, she studies questions of what makes writing good and how different disciplines answer that question differently. She has explored those questions in terms of writing assessment and writing policy.

Douglas Hesse is Professor and Executive Director of Writing at the University of Denver. Previously he was Chair of the Conference on College Communication and Composition, President of Council of Writing Program Administrators, and Editor of *WPA: Writing Program Administration*. At Illinois State University, he was Director of Writing, of the Center for Teaching, and of Honors. He coordinates the NCTE/Mailer Center National Student Writing Awards. His recent books include *Creating Nonfiction* (with Becky Bradway) and *The Simon and Schuster Handbook* (with Lynn Troyka). Among the foci of his sixty-plus articles and chapters are creative nonfiction and relationships between creative writing and composition studies. He sings with the Colorado Symphony Chorus.

Melissa Ianetta is Director of Writing and Associate Professor of English at the University of Delaware, where she directs the writing center, writing program, and writing across the curriculum initiatives. Her work has appeared in *College English*, *College Composition and Communication*, *PMLA*, *Rhetoric Review*, *WPA: Writing Program Administration*, *Composition Studies*, and *The Writing Center Journal*, which she coedited with Lauren Fitzgerald from 2008–2013. With Dr. Fitzgerald, she is coauthoring *The Oxford Guide to Tutoring and Research in a Writing Center Setting*, to be published by Oxford University Press in Spring 2014.

Joseph Janangelo is past president of the Council of Writing Program Administrators and co-founded the CWPA Mentoring Project. Joe is associate professor of English at Loyola University Chicago, where he served as Director of Writing Programs for five years. His publications include *Resituating Writing: Constructing and Administering Writing Programs* (with Kristine Hansen) and *Theoretical and Critical Perspectives on Teacher Change*. His work has appeared in *College Composition and Communication*, *College English*, *Computers and Composition*, *Journal of Teaching Writing*, *Kairos*, *Rhetoric Review*, *Teaching English in the Two-Year College*, *The Writing Center Journal*, and *WPA: Writing Program Administration*.

Seth Kahn is Professor of English at West Chester University and Co-Chair of the CCCC Committee on Part-Time, Adjunct, or Contingent Labor. He serves as Grievance Chair for his local union chapter and as a delegate to the union's statewide Legislative Assembly. His publications include the coedited collection *Activism and Rhetoric* and a co-guest-edited special issue of the journal *Open Words* on "Contingent Labor and Educational Access."

Neal Lerner is Associate Professor of English and Writing Center Director at Northeastern University in Boston. His book *The Idea of a Writing Laboratory* won the 2011 NCTE David H. Russell Award for Distinguished Research in the Teaching of English. He is also the coauthor of *Learning to Communicate as a Scientist and Engineer: Case Studies from MIT*, winner of the 2012 CCCC Advancement of Knowledge Award, and of *The Longman Guide to Peer Tutoring*. He has published widely on the history, theory, administration, and practice of teaching writing in classrooms and writing centers.

Rita Malenczyk is Professor of English and Director of the Writing Program and Writing Center at Eastern Connecticut State University. Her work on writing program and center administration has appeared in numerous journals (including *WPA: Writing Program Administration*, *The Writing Lab Newsletter*, and *The Writing Center Journal*) and edited collections, including Kelly Ritter and Paul Kei Matsuda's *Exploring Composition Studies* and Shirley K Rose and Irwin Weiser's *The WPA as Theorist*. With Susanmarie Harrington, Keith Rhodes, and Ruth Overman Fischer, she coedited *The Outcomes Book*. At this writing, she is president of the Council of Writing Program Administrators.

Peggy O'Neill is Professor of Writing, and chairs the Writing Department at Loyola University Maryland, where she also served as the Director of Composition for ten years. Her scholarship focuses on writing pedagogy, assessment, and program administration. Her work appears in several journals as well as edited collections. She has coauthored two books and edited or coedited four books, including *Reframing Writing Instruction* (with Linda Adler-Kassner). She currently coedits the *Journal of Writing Assessment*.

Charles Paine is a professor at the University of New Mexico, where he directs the Rhetoric and Writing and Core Writing programs. He is an enthusiastic member of the Council of Writing Program Administrators, currently chairing the Research Grants Committee and formerly serving on the Executive Board. With Robert Gonyea, Paul V. Anderson, and Chris M. Anson, he started the Consortium for the Study of Writing in College, a collaboration between the National Survey of Student Engagement and CWPA. His most important work is teaching courses across the rhet-comp curriculum, including first-year composition, rhetorical/composition history and theory, and teaching-writing practica.

Melody Pugh is a PhD candidate in the Joint Program in English and Education at the University of Michigan. She teaches academic argumentation and professional writing and is a Teaching Consultant with the Center for Research on Learning and Teaching. She researches religious faith, literacy practices, and institutional identity.

E. Shelley Reid is Associate Professor of English and Director of Composition at George Mason University, where she teaches the composition pedagogy seminar for graduate teaching assistants as well as a range of graduate and undergraduate writing courses. Her work on teacher preparation, mentoring, program development, and writing education has appeared in *Composition Studies, College Composition and Communication, Pedagogy, WPA: Writing Program Administration, Writing Spaces*, and several edited collections.

Kelly Ritter is Professor of English and Director of the Undergraduate Rhetoric program at the University of Illinois at Urbana-Champaign. She is the author of *Before Shaughnessy: Basic Writing at Yale and Harvard, 1920–1960* (Studies in Writing and Rhetoric/Southern Illinois UP, 2009); *Who Owns School? Authority, Students, and Online Discourse* (Hampton Press, 2010); and *To Know Her Own History: Writing at the Woman's College, 1943–1963* (University of Pittsburgh Press, 2012). She is also coeditor, with Paul Kei Matsuda, of *Exploring Composition Studies: Sites, Issues, Perspectives* (Utah State UP, 2012). She is a current member of the CWPA Executive Board and is also the editor of *College English*.

Shirley K Rose is Professor and Director of Arizona State University Writing Programs in the English Department of the College of Liberal Arts and Sciences. She has published chapters on archival studies in composition and taught seminars in archival methodologies. With support of a Purdue Provost's Study in a Second Discipline Fellowship, she processed the James Berlin Papers in the Purdue Archives. She is a past president of the Council of Writing Program Administrators and regularly serves as a consultant-evaluator for college writing programs.

Dan Royer and *Roger Gilles* work and teach at Grand Valley State University near Grand Rapids, Michigan, where they have each directed the composition program and served as department chair. Their 1998 article on directed self-placement, "Directed Self-Placement: An Attitude of Orientation," led to a national conversation about DSP. In 2003, they coedited *Directed Self-Placement: Principles and Practices*.

Carol Rutz directs the writing program at Carleton College in Minnesota, where she teaches writing, works with faculty in a WAC environment, and administers a sophomore writing portfolio for a graduation requirement. In addition to coediting four collections, including *Classroom Spaces and Writing Instruction* with Ed Nagelhout, her work has been published in *Assessing Writing, College Composition and Communication, Change, Composition Studies, M/MLA, Peer Review, Rhetoric Review,* and *WPA: Writing Program Administration.* The chapter on faculty development for this volume stems directly from collaboration with Stephen Wilhoit on conference presentations over the past several years.

Eileen E. Schell is Associate Professor of Writing and Rhetoric at Syracuse University. She served as the Chair and Director of the Writing Program from 2007–2012 and as Director of the Composition and Cultural Rhetoric Doctoral Program from 2001–2004. Schell is the author of *Gypsy Academics and Mother-Teachers: Gender, Contingent Labor, and Writing Instruction* (Heinemann, 1997), the coauthor of *Rural Literacies* (SIUP, 2007) as well as the coeditor of three essay collections. She is also the cofounder and coleader of the Syracuse Veterans' Writing Group, a community writing group for military veterans.

Gail Shuck is Associate Professor of English and Coordinator of English Language Support Programs at Boise State University, where she has directed the first-year ESL writing sequence, taught courses in applied linguistics and second-language writing, and developed resources and programs for multilingual Boise State students since 2001. Her work on language ideologies, language identities, and program administration has been published in *Language in Society, Journal of Language, Identity, and Education, WPA: Writing Program Administration,* and the edited collection *Reinventing Identities in Second Language Writing.*

David E. Schwalm is Professor and Dean Emeritus at Arizona State University. He taught at UC- Berkeley, Ohio State, UT-El Paso, and ASU, serving as WPA at UT-El Paso and ASU. He is the founder of WPA-L, a listserv for writing program administrators. Subsequently he held various administrative positions at ASU focused on the development of ASU's West and Polytechnic campuses. Throughout his tenure at ASU, he was active in designing and maintaining the state-wide transfer articulation system in Arizona and consulting on transfer issues nationally. He is currently the Chair of the Board of Trustees of the Southwest College of Naturopathic Medicine and Health Sciences.

Martha A. Townsend is Associate Professor of English at the University of Missouri, former director of MU's Campus Writing Program, and author of numerous chapters and articles on WAC/WID. Her work in writing and general education has taken her to more than eighty-five universities across the US as well as to Romania, Korea, Thailand, South Africa, China, Costa Rica, Lithuania, and Turkey. Her current research project, *The Literate Lives of Athletes: How A Division I Football Program Graduated 100% of Its Senior Players*, is a literacy study of one cohort of student-athletes that managed to play highly competitive football while also maintaining a rigorous academic schedule.

Elizabeth Vander Lei is Professor of English at Calvin College in Grand Rapids, Michigan, where she directs the Written Rhetoric program and serves as co-chair of the English department. She has published articles on issues related to writing program adminis-tration in *College Composition and Communication*, *WPA: Writing Program Administration*, and The *Journal of the Assembly for Expanded Perspectives on Learning*. She has also published articles on African-American rhetoric and the intersections of religious faith and compo-sition studies. With Bonnie Kyburz she coedited *Negotiating Religious Faith in the Writing Classroom*. With Tom Amorose, Beth Daniell, and Anne Gere she is coediting *Renovating Rhetoric in Christian Tradition* (forthcoming U of Pittsburgh Press).

Elizabeth Wardle is Chair of the Department of Writing and Rhetoric at the University of Central Florida, where she also served as com-position director for five years. She previously served as composition director for five years at the University of Dayton. She is currently conducting a longitudinal study of writing-related transfer with Kevin Roozen, Angela Rounsaville, Stacey Pigg, and Mark Hall.

Irwin Weiser is Justin S. Morrill Dean of the College of Liberal Arts and Professor of English at Purdue University. His research and teach-ing concentrate on contemporary composition theory, composition research methods, and writing assessment. His recent publications include three collections of essays on writing program administration coedited with Shirley K Rose. Weiser has been a member of the Executive Committee of the Conference on College Composition and Communication and the Executive Board of the Council of Writing Program Administrators. He has led workshops for new department chairs for the Association of Departments of English and for new writing program administrators for CWPA. He is currently a member of the editorial board of *College Composition and Communication*.

Stephen Wilhoit is Professor of English at the University of Dayton and Director of the Office of Writing, Research, and New Media in the Ryan C. Harris Learning Teaching Center. He has published articles in the areas of writing pedagogy, critical thinking, creative writing, and graduate teaching assistant training. In addition, he is the author of three books with Pearson: *A Brief Guide to Writing from Readings*, *A Brief Guide to Writing Academic Argument*, and *The Longman Teaching Assistants' Handbook*.

Index

CPSIA information can be obtained at www.ICGtesting.com
Printed in the USA
LVOW11s2047300814

401647LV00006B/457/P